D0193317

Karla Zimmerman

Vancouver

The Top Five

1 Stanley Park
Cycle seafront paths fringed by beaches and urban forest (p50)

2 UBC Museum of Anthropology
Visit towering First Nations totem poles and a recreated village (p64)

3 Grouse Mountain
Skyride to night skiing, grizzly bears and chainsaw sculpture (p75)

4 Granville Island
Hop on a boat tour or wander the public market and studios (p57)

5 Canada Place
Walk and watch as seaplanes buzz, ships call and views unfurl (p43)

26879

Contents

Published by Lonely Planet Publications Pty Ltd
ABN 36 005 607 983

Australia Head Office, Locked Bag 1, Footscray,
Victoria 3011, ☎ 03 8379 8000, fax 03 8379 8111,
talk2us@lonelyplanet.com.au

USA 150 Linden St, Oakland, CA 94607,
☎ 510 893 8555, toll free 800 275 8555,
fax 510 893 8572, info@lonelyplanet.com

UK 72–82 Rosebery Ave, Clerkenwell, London,
EC1R 4RW, ☎ 020 7841 9000, fax 020 7841 9001,
go@lonelyplanet.co.uk

The Authors

KARLA ZIMMERMAN

Years ago, during Karla's first visit to Vancouver, she met a gentleman wearing a visor, a money belt – and nothing else. Yes, Karla had wandered on to the nudist Wreck Beach during a hike, and it is this incident she was referring to when she convinced Lonely Planet's editors that she knew Vancouver intimately. Subsequent visits cemented her admiration for the freewheeling City of Glass, and its unbeatable french fries, bicycle paths and lamb popsicles.

When she's not chained to her desk, Karla is a rabid traveler who might be found anywhere in the world from the misty heights of Machu Picchu to the dripping jungles of Angkor Wat, or from the cumin-colored dunes of the Sahara to that tasty doughnut shop down the road. She has written travel features for books, newspapers, magazines and radio. She lives in Chicago with her husband Eric, the ultimate trekking companion, who never says no and because of it has endured everything from bus crashes in the Vietnamese highlands to Civil War re-enactments in northern Illinois.

CONTRIBUTING AUTHOR
JOHN LEE

An expert on the British Columbia food and drink scene, John Lee is a freelance journalist and travel writer based in Vancouver. His work has appeared in the *Globe & Mail, National Post, Vancouver Sun* and international publications. He wrote the Food & Drink section of the City Life chapter, as well as boxed texts for the Eating and Excursions chapters. This is his fourth project for Lonely Planet.

PHOTOGRAPHER
LAWRENCE WORCESTER

After growing up in London through his 'pub discovery' years, Lawrence swore off dull and dreary weather forever. However, years spent living in Santa Barbara, California; Manoa Valley, Hawaii; Daytona Beach, Florida; and Yellowstone National Park – as well as years spent traveling in the tropics – grew tiresome, so Lawrence knew it was time to move to Seattle.

Lawrence feels right at home in Vancouver (but still wonders why people keep asking him to put his clothes back on and get his feet off the furniture) where the food, weather and people are familiar to anyone from Seattle, if not friendlier. Lawrence sends out a sincere thanks to everyone in Vancouver who helped out and to his wife, Gayelynn, without whom he could not have pulled it off.

Introducing Vancouver

A toy-size seaplane dives out of the clouds, whirring and purring as it makes for its watery landing strip. Sailboat masts bobble in the harbor, while freighters bellow greetings further out. A whiff of evergreen drifts over from the forest a few blocks away.

Then it happens: the sun bursts out from behind a cloud, spraying pink and yellow shards of light in all directions. To the north, they break over a range of toothy mountains. To the south, they ricochet among skyscraper windows.

While the City of Glass blazes around you at an outdoor café, you take a pull on your coffee or microbrew and shiver at your great good fortune for happening to be, at that very moment, in the most perfect place on the planet.

Others share your sentiment. Accolade after accolade has been heaped upon Vancouver for 'best quality of life' and all-round 'top foreign city.' It's the harmonic convergence of the city with nature. Here you have the skyscrapers, big business and high finance of a prosperous modern metropolis, but the urban bustle is just blocks from Stanley Park's thick rainforest. A 20-minute drive lands you amid the rugged peaks of the Coast Mountains. Want to hit the beach on your lunch break? Eleven of them fringe the city, including a couple right downtown.

It was clear from the get-go that Vancouver was going to be a winner. There is the setting, sure, but also a freewheeling, offbeat spirit that can only come from a city founded around a pub. Jack Deighton wasn't thinking about a legacy in 1867 when he rowed into Burrard Inlet with a barrel of whiskey and told the area's mill workers that if they helped him build a tavern, drinks were on him. Deighton was just thirsty. That a city happened to spring up is a testament to the relaxed attitude that prevails today.

Perhaps this laid-back mind-set is why residents aren't terribly bothered by the city's rain. With it falling 170 days per year, you might think, 'Aha! Vancouver's Achilles' heel.' But much of the rain hits during winter, which is no worry for most folks because they know that rain in the city translates into snow on nearby mountains.

Everyone wants to be outdoors, it seems, no matter what the season. Skiing is winter's top sport, but it's mild enough throughout most of the year to cycle, blade and run through Stanley Park, paddle kayaks through False Creek, sail on English Bay or golf on mountainside courses. With all this

Lowdown

Population (metro area) 2 million
Time zone Pacific (GMT -8 hours)
Nicknames City of Glass, Terminal City, Hongkouver
Three-star hotel room $125 or so nightly
Cup of coffee $1.25
Pint of microbrew beer $5
Bowl of wonton noodles $7
SkyTrain fare $2
Number of drug injections per day at Vancouver's supervised site 588

opportunity resting at the city's doorstep, is it any wonder that even the grannies are wearing fleece, looking fit and talking about hiking the Grouse Grind?

Vancouverites aren't the type to sit around on their duff – unless eating and drinking are involved. The foodie scene has exploded in recent years, with local chefs gaining international reputations for west coast cuisine, a style that combines straight-off-the-boat seafood with fresh produce from fertile farms. Stir in ethnic influences, such as Chinese, Thai, Japanese and French, and you get an idea of what all the hype is about. Local microbrews and wines complement the mix, and – here we go again with the outdoors theme – are frequently consumed on bistro patios and decks (many heated and open year-round, providing an uninterrupted fix of eye candy).

Offbeat and unexpected attractions are Vancouver's strong suit. Take log-strewn, clothing-optional Wreck Beach. Surrounded by a hulking forest, it seems incredibly remote, but is only a few kilometers from civilization. What's more, you can buy anything – a baked potato, glass of wine, haircut, West African drum, musk-ox burger – from the individuals who set up shop on the sand. Look at Dr Sun Yat-Sen Garden, a tranquil oasis where every pebble and brook gurgle has its place; it's tucked in a hidden courtyard just off Chinatown's mean streets, where people flap and squawk over bitter-melon prices. Commercial Dr has one unusual shop after the next, and visitors can have their chakras tuned, dreadlocks beaded or espresso cup filled. And downtown's Provincial Law Courts hold a secret garden on their roof.

Inevitably as you make your way around Vancouver, you'll stumble across a film crew shooting a TV series or feature film. Companies choose Vancouver not only because it's economically advantageous to shoot here versus in the USA, but because the city reflects facets of so many cultures – urban, rural, domestic, international. Granville St's Gallery Row has stood in for New York's SoHo or Chelsea. The harbor has stood in for Hong Kong. The parks have played the role of deep, dark forests. You name the place and Vancouver has served as its body double.

The cat jumps out of the bag on this place in 2010, when the Winter Olympics hits town. What are you waiting for? Grab your jacket, yoga pants, skis and in-line skates, and dive in now.

KARLA'S TOP VANCOUVER DAY

I'm a late riser, so it's 11am when I stroll into the **Roma Café** (p127) and gulp down a mini latte. I order a second. It's so good I want a third, but that would be greedy, so instead I walk down the block to **Caffé Calabria** (p127) and order an espresso.

I get on the SkyTrain and alight downtown at **Waterfront Station** (p45). Then I walk past **Canada Place** (p43) and embark on the **Coal Harbour Seawalk** (p50), which provides the quintessential sea-mountain-city views. When I reach Denman St, I rent a bicycle and start pedaling along the **Stanley Park Seawall** (p51).

Eventually I reach shimmering **Second Beach Pool** (p147) and stop for a dip. Leaving Stanley Park, I head north on Denman St to return my bike. The shop is near **True Confections** (p94), home of the divine Dark Chocolate Belgian Mousse cake, which I devour while perusing the alt-weekly *Georgia Straight* (p214).

Then I take the bus down Georgia St to **Chinatown** (p53). I need a few items – a flashing Buddha statue, Hello Kitty coin purse and jasmine tea. I buy a chestnut roll and eat it while strolling through **Dr Sun Yat-Sen Park** (p55).

I meet friends for dinner at **Vij's** (p116) – lamb popsicles! Storm beer! – then we drive over to the **Jericho Sailing Centre** (p124) for a nightcap while watching the sunset.

Essential Vancouver

Wreck Beach (p65)
Commercial Dr (p57)
Museum of Anthropology (p64)
Stanley Park (p50)
Coal Harbour Seawalk (p50)

City Life

City Life

VANCOUVER TODAY

Casual but cosmopolitan, framed by a mountain backdrop with the sea kissing its edges, Vancouver is the embodiment of a modern conundrum. People want to be here because it's so laid-back and naturally beautiful, but that carefree attitude and those natural resources come under pressure as more people want a piece of them. The Olympics will be the ultimate test of how the city handles the situation, as Vancouver prepares for the world to take a close-up during the winter of 2010.

In the meantime, eating, drinking and economic development proceed apace. Vancouver's neighborhoods are gentrifying at a bewildering rate. The city is becoming a foodie capital, and local chefs are garnering international acclaim with menus comprising regional ingredients, complemented by British Columbian wines. Vancouver continues its role as a Pacific Rim multicultural leader, attracting immigrants from Asia, Australia and even the US west coast via the film industry.

A progressive attitude prevails, be it in events like the stark naked Bun Run, the contemporary International Dance Festival or in local law enforcement response to pot smoking (it's usually overlooked). Recently the city sparked North American headlines when it introduced the continent's first safe injection site, where drug users could come in for clean needles and a safe place to shoot up – Vancouver's more conservative big neighbor to the south, the USA, was less than thrilled by the arrangement.

CITY CALENDAR

Peak season runs from Victoria Day in late May to Labour Day in early September, during which time the squeeze on accommodations and lines at ferries and major attractions can be bothersome. Everywhere stays open later during summer, and festivals fill streets on weekends. Major special events, like the Jazz Fest (p9) and Folk Fest (p10), intensify the summertime crowds.

It rarely gets sweatily hot or freezing cold in Vancouver, but it sure does rain, particularly in the winter. The fine weather from June to August is the reason many people choose these months to visit. See p212 for a list of public holidays and p210 for further information on the climate.

JANUARY & FEBRUARY

POLAR BEAR SWIM

☎ 604-665-3424; www.city.vancouver.bc.ca/parks /events/polarbear

This chilly New Year's Day affair has been taking place on English Bay Beach annually since 1920, and it might just be the ultimate cure for a hangover. At around 2:30pm, more than a thousand people charge into the ocean, the temperature of which hovers at a frosty 6.5°C.

CHINESE NEW YEAR

☎ 604-632-3808; www.vancouver-chinatown.com

The date of the lunar new year varies from late January to early February, but the fireworks crackle in Chinatown for days. The festivities take place over 15 days and, besides lots of good food, they feature the Dragon Parade, music, dancing, art exhibits and storytelling.

MARCH & APRIL

VANCOUVER INTERNATIONAL DANCE FESTIVAL

☎ 604-662-7441; www.vidf.ca; tickets $18-25

Local, national and international contemporary dance artists come together in March for this three-week-long spree of workshops and performances, most of which feature at the Roundhouse Community Centre (p49).

Top Five Quirky Events
- Bare Buns Fun Run (p10)
- Polar Bear Swim (p8)
- Cinemuerte (p133)
- Under the Volcano (p10)
- Illuminares Lantern Festival (p10)

Customers at Caffè Artigiano (p126)

VANCOUVER PLAYHOUSE INTERNATIONAL WINE FESTIVAL
☎ information 604-872-6622, tickets 604-873-3311; www.playhousewinefest.com; day pass $59

With more than 500 reds and whites to sample, from 166 international vineyards, this is one of the largest wine shows in North America. It's on at the Vancouver Convention & Exhibition Centre over the course of a week, during either March or April, and proceeds benefit the Vancouver Playhouse Theatre Company (p135).

MAY
VANCOUVER INTERNATIONAL MARATHON
☎ 604-872-2928; www.adidasvanmarathon.ca

Strap on your running shoes and race through the city's streets with athletes from around the world. The run usually happens the first weekend of May.

VANCOUVER INTERNATIONAL CHILDREN'S FESTIVAL
☎ 604-708-5655; www.vancouverchildrensfestival .com; admission $6

The red-and-white tents go up in Vanier Park on the third or fourth Monday of May and stay up for eight days. During that time, 70,000 people enjoy acts dedicated to keeping the young and young at heart entertained.

JUNE
ALCAN DRAGON BOAT FESTIVAL
☎ 604-683-4707; www.adbf.com; adult/child $10/8, 2-day pass $12

Held during the third weekend of June, about 2000 competitors from around the world take part in the Dragon Boat races on False Creek, accompanied by music, theater and food pavilions at the Plaza of Nations.

VANCOUVER INTERNATIONAL JAZZ FESTIVAL
☎ 604-872-5200; www.jazzvancouver.com; tickets up to $75

The biggest names in jazz take the stage at multiple venues, ranging from the Capilano Suspension Bridge to Maple Tree Square. A two-day New Orleans–style street festival also takes place in Gastown and Yaletown. The festivities begin on the third or fourth Friday of June and run for 10 days.

FRANCOPHONE SUMMER FESTIVAL
☎ 604-736-9806; www.lecentreculturel.com; tickets up to $25

This is a week-long celebration of Francophonic music from around the world, with performances at venues around town, plus a weekend festival at W 7th Ave and Granville St.

JULY
CANADA DAY CELEBRATIONS
☎ 604-775-8025; www.canadadayatcanadaplace.com

Canada Place is the main location for the celebrations marking the country's birthday on July 1, which include music, food and fireworks. Festivities begin at 10am and the fireworks are at 10pm.

DANCING ON THE EDGE
☎ 604-689-0691; www.dancingontheedge.org; tickets $16-25

Leading dance companies from across Canada gather at the Firehall Arts Centre (p135) for 10 days early in July to perform the genre's latest moves.

TOUR DE GASTOWN
☎ 604-836-9993; www.tourdegastown.com

In mid-July, this elite cycling race of Vancouver is on a 1.2km course through Gastown (men ride 50 laps, women ride 30 laps) for a $10,000 purse.

VANCOUVER FOLK MUSIC FESTIVAL
☎ 604-602-9798; www.thefestival.bc.ca; day pass $40-55

Jericho Beach Park is the venue for this festival, which attracts about 30,000 people and has musicians performing on seven stages during the third weekend of July.

CARIBBEAN DAYS FESTIVAL
☎ 604-515-2400; www.caribbeandaysfestival.com; admission free

Great music, dancing and food highlight these two days of fun held during the last weekend of July at Waterfront Park, Lonsdale Quay, North Vancouver.

ILLUMINARES LANTERN FESTIVAL
☎ 604-879-8611; www.publicdreams.org; admission free

On a late-July Saturday, hundreds of people gather at dusk with shimmering paper lanterns shaped like serpents, birds and other flights of fancy; participants walk around Trout Lake amid fire sculptures, music and fireworks. Lantern-making workshops take place beforehand.

MOLSON INDY VANCOUVER
☎ 604-280-4639; www.molsonindy.com/vancouver; general admission $19-50, grandstand seats $80-220

The roar of engines can be heard far and wide during the fourth weekend of July when Indy cars race around False Creek to find out who really is the hottest thing on wheels.

VANCOUVER CHAMBER MUSIC FESTIVAL
☎ 604-602-0363; www.vanrecital.com; tickets up to $25

Considered to be one of the finest music festivals of its kind, this two-week event, which starts in late July, brings together some of the best Canadian and international chamber musicians, as well as outstanding young talents.

EARLY MUSIC FESTIVAL
☎ 604-732-1610; www.earlymusic.bc.ca; tickets $26-55

This celebration of medieval to baroque music takes place from late July to early August at the UBC School of Music.

CELEBRATION OF LIGHT
☎ 604-641-1193; www.celebration-of-light.com

The world's largest musical fireworks competition takes place at English Bay over four nights in late July and early August. Three competing countries (which change each year) put on their most spectacular display of fireworks over three nights; they come together to put on a dazzling display on the fourth night.

AUGUST

GAY PRIDE DAY
☎ 604-687-0955; www.vanpride.bc.ca

Typically held on the first Sunday, watch for the outrageous parade drawing 15,000 people out along Denman St.

FESTIVAL VANCOUVER
☎ 604-688-1152; www.festivalvancouver.bc.ca; 3-concert pass from $49

More than 20,000 people come to hear national and international artists perform orchestral, choral, opera, jazz, world and chamber music. The venues vary throughout the festival's two-week span, usually held early in the month.

UNDER THE VOLCANO
☎ 604-255-0163; admission by donation ($10-20 suggested)

A day-long festival of 'art and social change,' with 50 artists and five music stages attracts the counterculture to Cates Park (where Malcolm Lowry wrote his famed novel *Under the Volcano*) in early August.

ABBOTSFORD INTERNATIONAL AIR SHOW
☎ 604-852-8511; www.abbotsfordairshow.com; adult/child 6-12 $25/10

Held on the second weekend of the month, this is known as 'Canada's national air show' and has been voted the world's best. It takes place in Abbotsford, 56km southeast of the city near the Canadian–US border.

BARE BUNS FUN RUN
www.wreckbeach.org; entry fee $25

The clothing-free Bun Run takes place – where else? – on Wreck Beach (p65), usually on a Sunday in late August. Among the prizes are those for 'best-decorated buns' and 'wackiest hat.'

PACIFIC NATIONAL EXHIBITION
☎ 604-253-2311; www.pne.bc.ca; general admission adult/child 6-13 $8/6

The PNE takes place for two weeks starting in mid-August and ending on Labour Day Monday in September. Along with the traditional

Hot Conversation Topics

- **The Winter Olympics are coming to town!** While word from the city's PR flaks is that Vancouverites are hugely excited, most are better described as cautiously optimistic. Will the Games be a financial boon and put Vancouver on the world map, like Expo '86? Or will the Games result in burdens to local taxpayers, inflated prices, horrific traffic and environmental strain? Stay tuned.
- **The real estate market is out of control.** 'Cost of average home has risen by 20% this past year, or $222 per day,' screamed a recent headline in the Province. In the mid-1990s, the real estate boom was driven by Hong Kong immigrants snapping up property; now the Olympics are fueling the market. Visitors are affected, as big old B&B houses (particularly those in Kitsilano) sell out to developers who turn the buildings into condos.
- **Who's on strike this week?** Nurses, teachers, hospital workers, ferry workers, public-transit workers – you name the profession, and people were on the picket line about it within the past year or so. The provincial government can't seem to keep its labor unions happy, and that makes for frequent service disruptions.
- **Safe injection sites are/aren't helping to solve the city's drug problem.** Vancouver has taken a progressive and controversial approach to reducing drug use (see the boxed text on p17). A survey after the first year of operation showed 46% of local businesses favored the program, 34% opposed and 20% were undecided.

agricultural exhibitions, there are concerts, car derbies, logger shows, an amusement park and all the junk food you can stomach.

SEPTEMBER

VANCOUVER INTERNATIONAL FRINGE FESTIVAL

☎ 604-257-0350; www.vancouverfringe.com; tickets $8-12

This popular theater event presents offbeat drama, musicals, comedy and dance from around the world. It takes place over 10 days from the beginning of the month, and is held in venues on and around Granville Island.

VANCOUVER INTERNATIONAL FILM FESTIVAL

☎ 604-685-0260; www.viff.org; tickets $7-9

It may not have the star-studded glamour of some other film festivals, but this is still a big one, with 500 screenings of 300 films from 50 countries. It takes place over 17 days from late September to mid-October in various city theaters. For other local film fests, see p133.

OCTOBER

VANCOUVER INTERNATIONAL WRITERS & READERS FESTIVAL

☎ 604-681-6330; www.writersfest.bc.ca; tickets from $15

Held during the third week of the month at venues on Granville Island, this event offers readings, discussion groups and book signings with popular authors, poets and playwrights.

VANCOUVER INTERNATIONAL COMEDY FESTIVAL

☎ 604-683-0883; www.comedyfest.com; tickets up to $38

Downtown's Granville St club strip is the location for this funny-bone tickler that takes place over seven days mid-month.

PARADE OF THE LOST SOULS

☎ 604-879-8611; www.publicdreams.org

A spectral Day of the Dead celebration, in which a torch-lit procession of spookily dressed performers moves through the streets around Grandview Park, near Commercial Dr; held the last Saturday of the month.

NOVEMBER & DECEMBER

NEW MUSIC WEST FESTIVAL

www.newmusicwest.com; individual concerts $10, 5-day pass $20

A slew of new and emerging pop and rock bands come to town and play live in various clubs over five days; you buy a wristband and jump from place to place. The festival's dates have been a bit erratic, but the second weekend of November seems to be the current time frame.

CHRISTMAS CAROLSHIP PARADE

☎ 604-878-8999; www.carolships.org

A Vancouver tradition, where 100 boats of all sizes are lit up like Christmas trees, and then take part in a flotilla that sails along False Creek, English Bay and beyond. On many of the boats carolers sing, while other boats play taped music. It all takes place during December.

CULTURE

IDENTITY

Vancouverites think of themselves as distinct from the rest of Canada. The feeling is based not on superiority (though you could hardly blame them, because where else is there a city that combines such knockout good looks with such a tender, tolerant heart?), but rather on geography and physiology. First, there is the distance: the city is across prairies and up and over a mountain range from the rest of the population and the country's decision-making core. Then there is Vancouver's spirit, derived from a tradition of pioneers who moved away from that core to try their luck in a new territory. And let's not forget the weather's role in forging a unique personality – Vancouverites just can't identify with the 'Great White North/Canada as a snowy hinterland' concept, because it only snows about two days per year in the city.

Vancouver is Canada's second most culturally diverse metropolis (after Toronto), and immigration continues to power its population growth and broad-minded attitude. According to the latest census 40% of Vancouver residents are foreign-born; about half of these are from China. Immigration in the mid-1990s was dominated by people arriving from Hong Kong (prompted by Britain handing over the territory to China in 1997), but today most Chinese immigrants are from the mainland. After China, other Asian countries – particularly Taiwan, the Philippines, Vietnam and Japan – are the leading source of immigrants, followed by East India (mostly from Punjab). A significant number of UK and Aussie immigrants have piled in over the years, too.

Although Vancouver has a rich indigenous heritage, the United Native Nations Society estimates there are only about 60,000 people (3% of the population) with aboriginal roots living in the Greater Vancouver area. Of these, just under 50% live on reservations, which is a drop of 14% since 1976.

Tolerance is a way of life in Vancouver. Immigrants, gays and lesbians and various religious practitioners are met with a 'You do your thing, I'll do mine, and I'll see you at the beach or ski slopes after work' mind-set. Perhaps as a result of such acceptance, Vancouver has few of the race or crime problems that plague other large urban areas. One in three residents doesn't claim a religious affiliation; among those who do, the most common are Protestant (25%), Catholic (19%), Sikh (5%) and Buddhist (4%). It seems many people prefer to worship at the church of the Great Outdoors. With mountains, forest and the sea right at the city's doorstep, there is a healthy and humble respect for the environment.

LIFESTYLE

Ask anyone why they live in Vancouver and they'll say 'the lifestyle.' The city consistently tops worldwide lists for 'most livable' and 'best quality of life.' Heck, one in every eight Toronto residents say they'd love to swap life in their megacity to start over in Vancouver. So what exactly are they putting in the local coffee here?

Top Five Books & Websites

- *City of Glass*, Douglas Coupland (2000) – Gen X author and hometown boy Coupland uses arty photographs and cheeky essays to explain the city's cultural touchstones, like British Columbian Ferries, Japanese slackers and the Grouse Grind.
- *The Greater Vancouver Book: An Urban Encyclopedia*, edited by Chuck Davis (1997) – The definitive resource book on the city. The 300-plus stories cover topics from the origins of Stanley Park to neon, prostitutes and dog pounds.
- *Vancouver: Representing the Postmodern City*, edited by Paul Delany (1994) – A look at the social and cultural milieu of a city many were saying was part of the 21st century before the 20th century had ended.
- *Canada's Cultural Gateway* (www.culture.ca) – All the facts about Canada, including what Royal Mounties actually do out there on the prairies, straight from the federal government.
- *American's Guide to Canada* (www.icomm.ca/emily) – A sassy look at the critical differences between the USA and its northern neighbor (eg which one has more doughnut shops per capita).

Let's cover a couple of basics first. People by and large are doing well in Vancouver. The economy is holding steady and job creation is keeping pace with population growth. The attainment of post-secondary education is high (Vancouver is second only to Ottawa, with 30% of those over 15 acquiring credentials). The environment is generally healthy. The air is clean.

But other cities could boast as much. The key, as ever, is Vancouver's natural bounty. The mountains. The ocean. The possibility of either just outside your door. The temperate climate. Consider what this set-up translates to in practical terms – the ability to ski in the morning, golf in afternoon and sail at sunset. Yes, tourism brochures proclaim it from every page, but it really does happen. People are drawn to Vancouver for the myriad opportunities to bike, blade, play frisbee golf and snowboard, and while they are sheepish to admit it, they are also drawn to the fact you can do it all in a single day (as most have at some point).

The environs enable an active, healthy and eco-conscious way of life for many residents, though it is carried out in a laid-back manner. The city's most like-minded US relative is probably San Francisco, which shares Vancouver's progressive political leanings.

FOOD & DRINK *John Lee*

In Vancouver, a culinary backwater for decades, a gourmet treat used to involve adding extra cheese to a hamburger that was apparently made from the same material as its packaging. To say that the last decade has delivered a seismic epicurean shift is an understatement. But it's the scale rather than the nature of this shift that's been most impressive: Vancouver's burgeoning food scene is not about better burgers – although they're available in improbably gourmet form at some high-end restaurants – but about the emergence of a vast smorgasbord of indigenous regional and imported ethnic flavors.

There are few cities in the world where visitors can eat and drink so well, and so economically. From steaming Chinatown dim sum to African hot pots on East Van's Commercial Dr to award-winning downtown French-themed taste-tripping – to say nothing of the flourishing locally produced wine and microbrew scenes – contemporary Vancouver is dripping with finger-licking options for adventurous foodies and peckish visitors.

Most arrive in the city hungry to sample what is variously known as west coast, Pacific Northwest, northwest or Pacific cuisine – the terms are interchangeable – of which Vancouver is arguably the regional epicenter. Coastal British Columbians have traditionally fed themselves from the sea and from the fertile farmlands of the interior, with Okanagan Valley peaches, apples and berries – best purchased from farmers markets throughout the city – a staple of many summer diets. But it's the local meat and seafood that entices many visitors to tuck into dishes of juicy wild salmon, Tofino swimming scallops or tender Salt Spring Island lamb, perhaps served with crisp Vancouver Island vegetables grown so close to the waterfront you can taste the sea.

Influenced by contemporary organic and slow food movements, local restaurants, such as Bishop's (p117) and Raincity Grill (p99) are showcasing these ingredients like never before. While Vancouver eateries used to brag about serving cheeses imported from exotic international locales, they now proudly serve the piquant varieties lovingly created by the province's artisan producers. This is not just idle protectionism; visitors new to the region are often surprised by the high quality of local produce, which is slowly achieving global recognition.

But there's a great deal more to Vancouver food than regional cheese and the world's best salmon dishes. In fact, it's easy to avoid west coast cuisine altogether and still scoff like a king. One of North America's largest Chinatowns – as well as its modern-day offshoot in Richmond – delivers some superb options for Asian food fans, who flock in large numbers to restaurants like Hon's Wun-Tun House (p101). Chinese flavors are not limited to Chinese restaurants either. The term 'fusion food' could have been invented here, since immigration from around the world has created a bubbling stew of cooking approaches that sees Asian, French, Mexican and African dishes influencing menus around the city. Even 'traditional' ethnic approaches have been reinvented at fusion restaurants, such as the Indian Vij's (p116), Malaysian Tropika (p100) and Chinese Wild Rice (p102), which offer some of the city's most adventurous dining experiences.

Those with a little more money to burn or looking for a special night out are also well served by a cornucopia of fine-dining options. Competing for awards, accolades and the title of best Vancouver restaurant, Lumière (p118), West (p116), C restaurant (p94) and CinCin (p98) never fail to please. Making room for sautéed halibut cheeks is also recommended at **Tojo's** (p115), the region's most justifiably celebrated sushi restaurant.

If all this talk of food is making you thirsty for an aperitif, Vancouver is also a proud showcase for some surprisingly good regional wines and beers. Not as well known internationally as they should be – even in Canada, Ontario's Niagara region claims precedence and barely acknowledges its Western brethren – BC now has more than 70 wineries. Centered on the Okanagan Valley, but also emerging on Vancouver Island and other suitable locations, the most consistently fine wines come from Mission Hill, Sumac Ridge and Gray Monk. Exciting tipples are also produced by Blasted Church, Burrowing Owl and Nk'Mip Cellars (a unique winery created by the Osoyoos Indian Band).

By the Numbers

Days of precipitation annually 170
Amount that Vancouver home prices rise per day $222
Number of Polar Bear Swim participants 1400 (in 2004)
Number of people estimated to attend the 2010 Winter Olympics 2.3 million
Estimated cost of hosting the Winter Olympics $1.92 billion
Percent of Vancouver residents who are foreign-born 40%
Number of Sikhs 99,000
Median family income $57,926
Unemployment rate 7%
Number of ladybugs released annually to protect Vancouver's trees 3 million

A night out in Vancouver should also include, preferably at the end of a decadent meal, a glass or two of ice wine, a sweet Canadian specialty that's produced in limited quantities from grapes that have frozen on the vine. If you just can't get enough, a snowy out-of-town excursion to the Okanagan Valley for the annual **Sun Peaks Icewine Festival** (☎ 250-861-6654; www.thewinefestivals.com) in January is a revelatory introduction to this increasingly popular dessert wine.

Those who prefer a cold one of a different sort will also discover a barrel of great BC beers in Vancouver. Avoid the generic Molson and Labatt brews at local bars and liquor stores, and check out some of the region's memorable craft beers instead. Brewpubs like **Steamworks** (p124) and **Yaletown Brewing Company** (p124) produce their own specialties on-site, with seasonal beers, such as rib-sticking Christmas ales and light summer lagers, that are well worth trying. Most other city bars (see p122) also sell at least one or two BC brews.

Granville Island Brewery (p59) is Vancouver's most celebrated producer and its beers – try the Maple Cream Ale – are widely available across the city. Harder to find, but perhaps even more rewarding for thrill-seeking beer connoisseurs, are the unique microbrews from Nelson Brewing, Storm Brewing and Crannög Ales – the latter claims to be the world's only certified organic brewery. Dark-beer lovers should also hunt down a bottle of rich Espresso Stout produced by Victoria's Phillips Brewing.

FASHION

You've probably heard the old joke: How do people dress up in Vancouver? Answer: They put on their new Gortex jacket instead of their old one. (You can substitute 'fleece' for 'Gortex' to the same effect.)

The fashion scene isn't really that dire, but the city's sporty, healthy lifestyle does play a significant role. Yoga-wear manufacturer **lululemon athletica** (p156) has created a sweeping trend out of sexy, comfy yoga pants, shirts and jackets, which can be seen clinging to bodies well after class time and on into the evening. Casual is probably the most apt description of local fashion. Even on weekend evenings at pricey restaurants or the theater, it's OK to wear jeans and a T-shirt. We're not talking sloppy, mind you, but most people aren't dressed to the nines either.

Vancouver designers with international reputations include **Dorothy Grant** (p166), who uses aboriginal motifs in her clothing and handbags, and **Zonda Nellis** (p163), who creates simple-styled evening wear but with luxurious materials. **Robson St** (p50) is where high-end fashion houses like Giorgio Armani, Guess and many, many others have their boutiques. A wave of newbie local designers have opened shops in the past few years, with most congregated on **Main St** (p157) in SoMa and on **Cordova St** (p154) in Gastown.

SPORTS

The sports scene is tightly intertwined with the city's culture, and if residents aren't engaging in some sort of sporting event themselves, they're likely to be watching one.

Hockey generates the most madness. Despite the fact the Vancouver Canucks have never won a Stanley Cup championship since they were formed in 1970, hope springs eternal each October when the boys take to the ice. And just remember: those pesky Toronto Maple Leafs haven't won a Cup since 1967, so Vancouver fans needn't feel too bad.

Canadian football is an odd duck, vaguely like American football, but with key differences best summed up as 'longer, wider and faster.' The BC Lions is the local team, and they've done a pretty good job in recent years. The Canadian Football League is the last remaining professional sports league made up entirely of Canadian teams, but it struggles financially to compete with its rich and powerful south-of-the-border cousin, the National Football League.

Vancouver does have a baseball team – the minor-league Canadians, which serves as the training ground for Major League Baseball's Oakland A's. However, games are more about the hot dog and beer ambience than serious sports watching. The stadium is one of the prettiest you'll ever see, by the way.

Lots of folks come to Vancouver to play golf because the mild climate permits comfortable year-round swinging. Remnants of the city's British colonial past are evident in the lawn bowling and cricket pitches scattered around town, most notably in Stanley Park.

In the winter of 2010, Vancouver heralds the arrival of the biggest sporting event of all – the Olympics.

MEDIA

Vancouver has more than 50, mostly small publishers printing everything from scholarly to aboriginal to children's to trade books. The city is also a center for TV and film production. Although newsstands aren't generally found on the street, Vancouver has an abundance of magazine shops, such as **Magpie Magazine Gallery** (p159), which fulfill residents' news needs. The city's two daily newspapers – the *Vancouver Sun* and the *Province* – are both published by Pacific Newspaper Group, so there really isn't much competition between the two.

Nitobe Memorial Garden (p64), University of British Columbia

Whatever the mainstream media lacks in diversity, the city's myriad alternative weeklies, monthly magazines, multicultural radio stations and foreign-language newspapers more than make up for. Turn to p214 for a thumbnail guide to local print media and p215 for a rundown on radio stations.

LANGUAGE

Vancouver is primarily an English-speaking city and English is the mother tongue for almost 50% of the population. Canada's other official language is French. Federal government offices in Vancouver, as well as across the country, work in English and French. However, only 1.7% of Vancouverites consider themselves to be French speakers.

Chinese is the second most common language in the city, with 26.6% of the population speaking it, followed by Punjabi, Tagalog (Filipino), Vietnamese and Spanish.

You'll notice many British terms and spellings are in common use (ie 'centre' instead of center, 'harbour' instead of harbor). As a quick glossary of Canuck (Canadian) slang, 'skidoo' means snowmobile, a 'toque' (rhymes with duke) is a winter hat and 'skookum' (from the native Chinook word for 'powerful') means 'impressive.' 'Eh' is the ubiquitous ending tacked on to most Canadian sentences.

ECONOMY & COSTS

Vancouver is the economic heart of BC, and the local and provincial economies are so closely connected that it's difficult to talk about one without mentioning the other.

The region's economic drivers have been and continue to be the resource industries of forestry and mining. The forest industry accounts for about half of BC's manufactured output, while mining contributes about $4 billion. The most important minerals are coal, copper, zinc, gold and silver, as well as gas and oil. The US snaps up much of the latter two.

Steadily increasing growth in sectors, such as tourism, advanced technology, financial services, educational services (specifically English as a Second Language Schools) and film production, are reshaping Vancouver's economic landscape. Tourism leads the pack. It is the largest industry in Greater Vancouver and is second in the province only to forestry, generating $7.4 billion in industry output and employing 89,000 people. More than eight million overnight tourists visit Vancouver each year, and about one million more pop in from cruise ships.

In addition to cruises, the Port of Vancouver is busy with cargo ships. The port is Canada's largest, and more than 66.7 million tonnes of freight worth $29 billion move through here annually, with most exports headed toward Asia. Many shipping and other Pacific Rim businesses have offices in Vancouver, as do international banks and financial institutions. The city also hosts a branch office of the Toronto Stock Exchange.

While it's one of Canada's more expensive cities (Toronto is arguably the most costly), US and European visitors should find Vancouver to be a bargain as long as

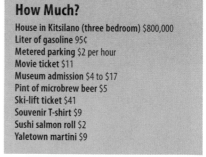

How Much?

House in Kitsilano (three bedroom) $800,000
Liter of gasoline 95¢
Metered parking $2 per hour
Movie ticket $11
Museum admission $4 to $17
Pint of microbrew beer $5
Ski-lift ticket $41
Souvenir T-shirt $9
Sushi salmon roll $2
Yaletown martini $9

the US dollar and euro remain strong against the Canadian currency. Families can take advantage of discounted admission at museums and attractions, and kids stay free at many hotels. The most expensive item in anyone's budget is likely to be their plane ticket and, after that, accommodations. Sleeping at a mid-priced hotel or B&B, eating at neighborhood restaurants and allowing yourself freedom with your entertainment dollar costs $100 or so per day each for two people traveling together.

GOVERNMENT & POLITICS

Vancouver has a mayor and 10 councilors who are elected to office for a period of three years. The mayor is the city's chief administrative official and is elected separately from the councilors. Each elected official represents the entire city; this has been the subject of ongoing debate, as many people think the city should be split into wards again, as it was until the mid-1900s.

Provincial party politics do not have a direct bearing on city government, although there are affiliations. In Vancouver, when it comes time for an election, there are civic political parties, including the Committee of Progressive Electors (COPE) and the Non-Partisan Association (NPA), that put forward candidates, although many individuals run and have been elected as independents. However, these political parties don't seem to have much bearing on the actual policy implemented by the mayor or councilors during their tenure.

For several years, Vancouver maintained a fairly conservative-leaning city council, but the new millennium has brought a more progressive group to office, including Mayor Larry Campbell, an affable former coroner who championed the safe injection sites (see the boxed text below) and environmental issues, such as reducing greenhouse gas emissions. This guy has even been known to speak at conferences on the legalization of marijuana.

Greater Vancouver consists of 20 municipalities, each with its own elected government consisting of a mayor and councilors. The Greater Vancouver Regional District (GVRD) oversees the joint interests of the municipalities in the Lower Mainland. This is a voluntary federation designed to deliver essential services more economically and equitably.

Remember that Victoria (p184), not Vancouver, is the seat of BC's provincial government.

ENVIRONMENT

THE LAND

Greater Vancouver straddles the lowlands of the Fraser River and the Coast Mountains of southwest BC. The Coast range, at only 20 million years of age, is one of North America's youngest mountain groups. The Coast's North Shore Range stretches from the Black Mountain in the west to Mt Seymour in the east. It is separated by Burrard Inlet's Indian Arm fjord from the Golden Ears mountain group, which dominates the Fraser Valley.

The Fraser River, which cuts through the center of the Lower Mainland, has its source in the Rocky Mountains and travels 1375km to its delta on the Strait of Georgia. The Fraser's tributaries include the Coquitlam, Chilcotin, Nechako, Pitt and Thompson Rivers. Not only is this Canada's third-largest river, it is also the country's fifth-largest river system and the

---

Safe Injection Sites

In September 2003 Vancouver opened North America's first safe injection site (also called a supervised injection site), a 12-seat room where users come in to inject drugs under the supervision of trained health-care staff, who issue clean needles, spoons, tourniquets and water.

The site is located on downtown's Eastside, near Main and Hastings Sts, which has one of the largest concentrations of injection drug users on the continent, a fact many say is due to the world's cheapest and purest heroin coming off the ships in Vancouver's port. As AIDS and hepatitis began to reach epidemic proportions, the city government decided something needed to be done to stop it.

The city government looked at programs in Switzerland and Germany that were based on the Four Pillars approach (harm reduction, prevention, treatment and enforcement), and were successful in reducing disease and infections, overdose deaths and drug-related crime. Amid a fair bit of controversy, the government adopted the Four Pillars approach for Vancouver.

Back at the site: after injecting, clients move to a 'chill out' room where staff can connect them with on-site services, such as medical care and counseling, or off-site services like withdrawal management. In its first year, an average of 588 injections took place daily, 107 overdose incidents were successfully prevented and two to four clients per day were referred to addiction treatment.

richest salmon river in North America. The many bays, inlets and river branches that lap the coastline are distinctive features.

GREEN VANCOUVER

Vancouver is a green city all right, both literally and figuratively. Many visitors are dazzled by all the trees and plant life that the rain and mild temperatures give life to. Cedar and fir are but a few species contributing hues like emerald and jade to the palette.

Vancouver is green in an environmental sense, too. While it's far from perfect, the city is at least trying to lessen its ecological footprint. It recently adopted a 'Green Building Strategy,' which sets standards for new construction to reduce emissions, more effectively use energy and resources, and improve the health and well-being of occupants and users. The strategy dovetails with the city's Climate Change Action Plan, which is designed to reduce greenhouse gas emissions by 20% by 2010. To achieve this 'cool' goal, the city is cutting down on energy use in civic facilities, downsizing its vehicle fleet and expanding landfill gas recovery programs, among other activities. Many public facilities, such as the library (p45) and law courts (p44), now have a 'green roof' – ie a planted roof where natural evaporation in summer and natural insulation in winter curb wasted energy.

One of Vancouver's best-known environmental activists is UBC professor David Suzuki, who has written a wealth of TV series and books, the most recent being *Tree: A Life Story* (2004). Further information on his work and ideas can be obtained from his eponymous foundation (www.davidsuzuki.org).

Finally, no mention of 'green' in Vancouver is complete without discussing Greenpeace, the global environmental organization that got its start in a Vancouver living room in 1969.

URBAN PLANNING

Much of the city's urban planning is being driven by the 2010 Winter Olympics. For instance, the city owns 19 hectares of formerly industrial land along the southeast shore of False Creek, which it plans to develop into a model sustainable residential community with a mix of housing and commercial development, and a waterfront park and seawall. The plan has been on the drawing board for a number of years, but might actually get underway now, since part of the site is slated to be an athletes' village, with apartments built for the Games and sold afterward. Hastings Park's Agrodome and Pacific Coliseum buildings are also up for renovations, thanks to the Olympics. The city may also get a new, permanent ice rink.

The oppressed downtown Eastside area around Main and Hastings Sts has long been the subject of revitalization buzz. Lo and behold, a developer was hired in late 2004 to turn the old Woodward's department store building – the area's anchor that has been desolate since 1993 – into affordable housing and small business–friendly commercial space. It's been a long time coming, so stay tuned to see how the project goes.

Shake, Rattle & Roll

Vancouver sits atop the most active earthquake zone in Canada. Every year about 300 minor quakes strike the city and the southwest region of BC; most go unnoticed. Larger quakes happen every 20 to 50 years, such as the one north of Courtenay on Vancouver Island in 1946 that measured 7.3 on the Richter scale. Every 300 to 600 years the region has been hit by a major quake measuring 8.5, and that's the one seismologists are concerned may be due, since the last one of this magnitude was in 1700. The worst-case scenario is that an 8.5+ quake would result in landslides and tsunamis along the coast, and damage up to 30% of Greater Vancouver's homes and 15% of its high-rises.

In recent years both the province and the city have taken the threat of earthquakes seriously. About $300 million is being spent to reinforce bridges, tunnels, buildings and other structures. An Emergency Operations Centre has been built at Rupert and Hastings Sts. Three saltwater pumping stations with earthquake-resistant piping have been built around town to act as a backup in case the main water supply fails or is shut down, and other waterlines are gradually being upgraded.

Arts & Architecture

Arts & Architecture

This city exerts a pull on creative types – along with everyone else who thinks that mountains, sea, mild temperatures, a liberal attitude, and good food and drink are desirable attributes in an urban experience.

You're pretty much guaranteed to stumble across a film shoot during your stay in Vancouver – maybe a Hollywood blockbuster, but more likely a low-budget flick *not* coming soon to a theater near you.

Rock, jazz and punk music shouldn't be hard to find, and classical music aficionados will be impressed by the chamber and choral music on offer. Sci-fi, Chinese immigrant and First Nations literature are well represented by local authors, and there is even a series of city-based potboilers adding spice to the fiction genre. Book lovers will hit the jackpot if their visits coincide with the city's annual Vancouver International Writers & Readers Festival.

The city put forth its own architectural style, pioneered by guru Arthur Erickson, which combines glass and concrete with the surrounding environment's natural elements; it's easy to walk around and view landmark buildings on your own or via an architectural tour. The same is true for the city's public art, placed in strategic nooks and crannies around town.

Innovative theater productions are staged everywhere, from parking lots to community swimming pools and local trains. Vancouver's melting pot of cultures continues to push contemporary dance troupes in new directions, while its Dance Centre gives them the space and support to keep growing.

CINEMA & TV

The film industry has a starring role in Vancouver's economy, and the city ranks third in North American film production only behind Los Angeles and New York. True, not many stories are set in Vancouver, and not many filmmakers are based there; nevertheless, the industry generates more than $1 billion annually. In 2003, 47 features, 79 TV movies and miniseries, 37 TV series and six animated films deposited $1.4 billion into local coffers.

Vancouver got its first real taste of Hollywood in 1970, when director Robert Altman arrived with mega-stars Warren Beatty and Julie Christie to shoot the Warner Bros feature, *McCabe & Mrs Miller*. By 1978, the industry was spending $12 million directly on production in British Columbia, which was nice, but didn't knock your socks off.

Top Five Films

Reel upon reel has been shot in Vancouver, but you have to dig deep into indie annals to find local storylines and directors.

- *On The Corner*, directed by Nathaniel Geary (2003) – A gritty look at life in Vancouver's heroin-plagued downtown Eastside follows a young man drawn into the worlds of addiction and prostitution after he comes to live with his sister.
- *Double Happiness*, directed by Mina Shum (1994) – A comedy about 20-something Jade (Sandra Oh), who is trying to keep secret her modern career choice (actress) and boyfriend (he's white) from her traditional Chinese parents in the Vancouver suburbs.
- *That Cold Day in the Park*, directed by Robert Altman (1969) – A lonely spinster (Sandy Dennis) invites a young hippie in from the Vancouver rain and then goes to drastic measures to make him stay; a bit dated, and odd, in retrospect.
- *The Delicate Art of Parking*, directed by Trent Carlson (2003) – A mockumentary about a Vancouver parking officer and the hassles he encounters as he tickets irate motorists.
- *Clerks*, directed by Kevin Smith (1994) – OK, so the connection is tenuous: Smith is from New Jersey and that's where the film takes place, but he did go to Vancouver Film School for a few months before dropping out to make this hilarious foul mouthed feature about a pair of slacker convenience store clerks left alone to run the till.

It was *The X-Files* that seemed to send local production skyward. The brooding, atmospheric TV series about the paranormal was filmed in Vancouver from 1993 to 1998, and it made the most of the city's gray misty weather. Some people say the series lost its edge when it left this climate and returned to sunny LA. It left its mark, however, and not only on the building at 1419 Pendrell St in the West End, better known as Agent Scully's Apartment (though it's actually called Pendrell Suites). More and more productions trekked north in the show's wake, boosted by the cheaper Canadian dollar and – most importantly – the array of location options.

Vancouver offers mountain, ocean, forest and urban settings, all in close proximity. It has stood in for everything from the North Pole in Will Ferrell's *Elf*, to Tibet in director Martin Scorsese's *Kundun* and back-alley New York in Jackie Chan's *Rumble in the Bronx*, as well as small-town Kansas in the TV series *Smallville*. The area's mild climate allows for year-round filming, and with a legion of local skilled film professionals, studios, post-production facilities and special effects labs in place, it's easy to see how Vancouver moved into the film hot spot. Nearly 30,000 residents work for the industry in some capacity.

Recent Hollywood titles shot in Vancouver that you may have heard of (for better or worse) include *X-Men 2, Catwoman, I Robot, Chronicles of Riddick, Scooby-Doo 2* and *Miracle on Ice*. However, big-budget movies are more the exception than the rule. What are most commonly filmed here are B flicks that go straight to DVD. And the city attracts so many TV movies-of-the-week, it's been dubbed 'MOWtown.'

TV series take a big slice of the production pie. Following *The X-Files'* lead, *Andromeda, Smallville, The L Word, Stargate* and *Da Vinci's Inquest* set up shop in Vancouver. *Da Vinci's Inquest* is a notable exception to the 'local setting' rule. Begun in 1998 and airing on the Canadian Broadcasting Corporation, *Da Vinci* is a gritty drama about a controversial coroner working in Vancouver's downtown Eastside. Sound like anyone you've heard of – say, the city's mayor Larry Campbell? Yep, he served as a forensic consultant before running for office. *Da Vinci* remains one of Canada's top-rated shows and, in fact, spawned the generation of popular American *CSI: Crime Scene Investigation* imitators. Keep an eye out from June to November, when *Da Vinci's* cast and crew film on location in the alleyways of the Eastside.

Famous actors to hail from Vancouver include Michael J Fox, Pamela Anderson (actually from Vancouver Island), Carrie-Anne Moss *(The Matrix* and *Chocolat)*, Hayden Christensen (the fifth and sixth *Star Wars* movies, and *Shattered Glass)*, Jason Priestley *(Beverly Hills 90210)*, Joshua Jackson *(Dawson's Creek)*, Bruce Greenwood *(13 Days, The Sweet Hereafter)*, James Doohan (Scotty from *Star Trek)* and Margot Kidder (of *Superman* fame).

The **BC Film Commission** (☎ 604-660-2732; www.bcfilmcommission.com) gives the weekly low-down on what's filming and who's in the cast and crew – that way you'll know who to expect to see at **CinCin** (p98) and other glamorous restaurants around town. The website also provides contact information for productions that are seeking to cast 'extras.'

MUSIC

Vancouver and its environs have given the world of music some big names – Bryan Adams, 54*40, Sarah McLachlan, Bif Naked, kd lang and Diana Krall, popster Nelly Furtado, punksters NoMeansNo and Celtic-tinged folk rockers Spirit of the West. The fact that these artists rarely perform in Vancouver is primarily because they are touring the world. Some of them call Vancouver home, but many simply used the city as a springboard to get their careers started, which in itself says something about the vitality of the music industry.

An indicator that the scene isn't exactly the world's best known is that poor Vancouver is still stuck answering the question 'Is Bryan Adams the best you have to offer?' Love him or hate him, you can't dispute he's one of the most successful in the biz, and his Gastown recording studio (at Powell and Columbia Sts, housed in the city's oldest brick building) brings in the occasional rock superstar. But can we please move on?

The New Pornographers is the indie uber-group electrifying the airwaves these days, courtesy of its guitar and keyboard power pop and the vocals of Neko Case. Since its debut in 2000, New Pornographers has struck up a following of slack-jawed devotees. Even its record company describes the need for a prescription of 'Calm the Fuck Down Pills' between albums. When in town, they're likely to turn up at the **Commodore** (p128). If you can't

Top Five CDs

- *Mass Romantic,* The New Pornographers (2000) – The band's star-making first album, which won a Juno (akin to an American Grammy award), is a perfect power-pop blast that features crafty songwriting put into play by torch-voiced Neko Case.
- *Chinatown,* Be Good Tanyas (2003) – Leave it to a group of west coast Canadians to perfect the 'American deep South back porch' sound. Mandolins, banjos, slide guitars and harmonicas set off rootsy vocals about drugs, gambling, Jesus and lost love. Sadly, the ladies broke up after this album.
- *Hardcore 81,* DOA (2002) – Re-release of the 1981 punk classic, with tunes like 'I Don't Give a Shit' and '001 Losers' Club,' all yelled by Canada's godfather of punk, Joey 'Shithead' Keithley.
- *I Bificus,* Bif Naked (1999) – The big single off the album, 'Lucky,' was part of the Buffy soundtrack, a clear indicator of the butt-kicking quality that multi-tattooed grrrl rocker Bif brings to her music.
- *Hit Parade,* Spirit of the West (1999) – Many of the rousing songs on the eight-year best-of compilation by this Celtic-influenced rock band make you want to chug beers, but there are also four rich tracks recorded with the Vancouver Symphony Orchestra.

catch the band itself, Pornographers' members have side projects that play locally on occasion: Carl Newman heads Zumpano; Neko Case solos as a Patsy Cline–like country singer; and Dan Bejar and his band Destroyer are about as close to local guitar royalty as it gets.

The side project concept is ubiquitous. Jerk With A Bomb, a popular duo performing 'folk-noir' ballads, has splintered into both Black Mountain and the Pink Mountaintops. NoMeansNo also performs as the punk Hanson Brothers. Speaking of which: punk does well in the city, hosted regularly at venues like the **Cobalt** (p128). In addition to NoMeansNo, famous names from the area include Brand New Unit, the Black Halos, the Dayglo Abortions (from Victoria) and DOA, who may be grayer since debuting in the 1970s, but they are in no way lethargic, and still honor their punk-rock mandate by performing regularly.

Vancouver has been good to its women. Sarah McLachlan has sold more than 22 million records during her career. She waited six years following her smash 1997 album *Surfacing* and the women-only Lilith Fair tours she organized before putting out the accomplished *Afterglow.* Victoria's Nelly Furtado is gearing up to match McLachlan's success by mixing pop, hip-hop and world-washed folk with big sales; they've won Grammy awards.

From Nanaimo, jazz pianist and vocalist Diana Krall can almost be considered a local. Her album post marriage to Elvis Costello took an experimental turn; time will tell whether she continues on that path. Veda Hille and Kinnie Starr represent the city's folk-jazz scene. Hille creates fierce and literate jazz with angular pop, while Starr embraces rich sounds with elements of hip-hop. They often go on the road together as part of the Scrappy Bitch Tour.

For serious jazz fans there is François Houle, a clarinetist who also likes to play classical music, and Tony Wilson, who pieces together quintets, sextets and septets and more from the reservoir of Vancouver's hottest jazz musicians. Wilson, a guitarist, tends to lean toward the post-bop and avant-garde stylings of musicians like John Coltrane or Ornette Coleman. Some of his associates to look out for include Talking Pictures, and John Korsrud and the Hard Rubber Orchestra. Also look out for Brad Turner and his quartet, Metalwood. Longtime Vancouver blues guitarist and vocalist (and sometime actor) Jim Byrnes is always worth catching in one of the clubs around the city. Violinist/mandolinist extraordinaire Jesse Zubot plays with Houle, Byrnes and others listed already, as well as with his partner, guitarist Steve Dawson.

For trivia's sake: Vancouver's '70s notables include Chilliwack, Loverboy, Terry Jacks and the Poppy Family (most notably for *Seasons in the Sun*), Bachman-Turner Overdrive and Heart (originally from Seattle). Bands of the '80s include the Payola$, Doug and the Slugs, Images in Vogue, Skinny Puppy and Grapes of Wrath, as well as guitar-sensation Colin James, who moved here from Regina, Saskatchewan.

It's little known, but true: Vancouver is a recruiting ground for the Cantonese pop industry. That fresh-faced, clean-cut Asian youth you see walking down the street here may be a multi-platinum artist who'd be mobbed walking down the street in China.

Vancouver's club scene (p129) grows and imports heavy-hitting sounds. **Sonar** (p131) is one of the premier places for experimental DJs, while **Lick** (p130) is well regarded for its female DJs. **Bar None** (p130) has drawn crowds for years to hear soul/funk/R&B band Soul Stream on Mondays and Tuesdays.

Classical music – particularly new, baroque and chamber music – has a big following in the city, perhaps because a strong base of supporters comes out of UBC's School of Music. Historically the domain of an older demographic, classical groups say their audiences have started to skew younger amid recent pop-culture crossovers.

For the skinny on the music scene and venues, see the Entertainment chapter's Live Music (p127) and Classical Music (p136) sections.

LITERATURE

It's said that British Columbians read more books per year than any other Canadians. That's believable, based on the enthusiasm the **Vancouver International Writers & Readers Festival** (p11) generates, attracting about 10,000 people to readings. The city has a number of famous writers attached to it, both those who were born here and those who moved here at some point during their careers. UBC's creative writing program brings writers in, recently graduating young talents, like Madeleine Thien, Kevin Chong and Eden Robinson, all published by major houses to critical acclaim. The spoken word scene is fair-sized and rouses the literary minded through events in local cafés and bars (p133).

Laurence Gough (1943–) is one of Vancouver's most prolific writers, best known for his Willows and Parker crime novels about a male-female detective duo on the Vancouver police force. The violent, wise-cracking series has 13 books and counting, with heaps of devoted fans. The city always plays a prominent role in the storyline: for example, a body shows up in the Vancouver Aquarium whale tank in *Killers*, a body is fished out of Coal Harbour in *Karaoke Rap*, and the list goes on.

Science-fiction author William Gibson (1948–), who was born in North Carolina but moved to Vancouver several years ago, is the godfather of 'cyberpunk.' His 1984 novel *Neuromancer* launched the genre of bleak, high-tech neo-reality, which showed up in the mainstream in popular movies like *The Matrix*. *Neuromancer* won the sci-fi Triple Crown of Hugo, Nebula and Philip K Dick awards, an unheard-of feat. Gibson's subsequent novels include *Idoru*, *Mona Lisa Overdrive* and *Virtual Light*. Speaking of Philip K Dick, how's this for a tenuous Vancouver tidbit: Dick, who wrote the story that eventually became *Blade Runner*, spent a few months in the city's downtown Eastside in 1972, including time in a heroin rehab home. Some theorize that *Blade Runner's* vision of non-stop rain and urban decay germinated there. Another well-known sci-fiction writer who now calls Vancouver home is Spider Robinson (1948–), the author of *Stardance* and *Callahan's Crosstime Saloon*.

International success is not only the domain of sci-fi writers. One of the most popular authors from Vancouver is Douglas Coupland (1961–), best known for *Generation X*, as well as *Shampoo Planet* and *City of Glass* (p12). Author and illustrator Nick Bantock (1949–) had an international hit with his 1991 novel *Griffin & Sabine*, followed by the award-winning *Sabine's Notebook* and *The Golden Mean*. William Deverell (1937–) writes bestselling thrillers, including *Needles*, *High Crime*, *Mecca*, *Platinum Blues* and *Kill All the Lawyers*.

Top Five Books

- *Stanley Park*, Timothy Taylor (2002) – Stir together a haute-cuisine chef with the park's dark secrets, and the result is a story capturing Vancouver's quirky modern ambience.
- *Karaoke Rap*, Laurence Gough (1997) – A potboiler in the Vancouver-set Willows and Parker detective series, populated by corpses, gunfire and a cigar-smoking character in a banana-yellow suit.
- *The Jade Peony*, Wayson Choy (1995) – A vivid portrayal of growing up in an immigrant family in Chinatown in the 1930s and '40s; winner of the prestigious Trillium Book Award.
- *Neuromancer*, William Gibson (1984) – This dense, spiraling book introduced the term 'cyberspace' to the masses; winner of multiple sci-fi awards and the admiration of computer geeks worldwide.
- *Legends of Vancouver*, E Pauline Johnson (1911) – A city classic that's been in print forever, it tells the legends and stories behind many prominent natural features in and around Vancouver.

Wayson Choy (1939–) is a Chinatown-born writer whose award-winning book *The Jade Peony* and its follow-up *All That Matters* focus on the Chinese immigrant experience. Evelyn Lau (1971–) shot to prominence at age 18 with *Runaway: Diary of a Street Kid*, which details her early life as a prostitute on Vancouver's streets after she left her traditional Chinese home. In 1992, Lau became the youngest poet ever to be nominated for the Governor General's Award (one of Canada's most prestigious literary prizes) for her collection *Oedipal Dreams*.

Best known for *Shoeless Joe*, which was made into the film *Field of Dreams*, WP Kinsella (1935–) lives in White Rock and has also written a number of First Nations–related stories that appear in collections, such as *The Fencepost Chronicles* and *Brother Frank's Gospel Hour*. Lee Maracle (1950–) writes about the struggles of First Nations people, particularly from a woman's perspective, in *I Am Woman, Bobbie Lee: Indian Rebel, Ravensong* and *Sundogs*.

The recipient of the Governor General's Award for both poetry and fiction, George Bowering (1936–) has more than 40 titles to his name, including the novels *Burning Water*, about Captain George Vancouver, and *Caprice*. Michael Yates (1938–) is known for his experimental writing, a combination of poetry and prose, in such works as *abstract beast*, *man in the glass octopus* and *Line Screw*, a book about his experience working as a prison guard.

Historically, E Pauline Johnson (1861–1913) is Vancouver's most famous woman of words. The daughter of a Mohawk chief and middle-class English mother, Johnson wrote poetry and recited it in public performances where she dressed in buckskin, rabbit pelts and metal jewelry, and carried a hunting knife and Huron scalp given to her by her great-grandfather. The 'Mohawk Princess' didn't come to Vancouver until later in her life, but she loved the city dearly and was quite prolific during her time here, which included the writing of *Legends of Vancouver* (see the boxed text on p23). Her ashes are in a memorial (p52) in Stanley Park.

Hard-drinking Malcolm Lowry (1909–57) wrote his masterpiece *Under the Volcano* (about a day in the life of an alcoholic consul in central Mexico) when he lived in a cheap hovel in what is now Cates Park (p76). Novelist and poet, Earle Birney (1904–95) is one of Vancouver's, indeed Canada's, better-known authors, producing experimental poetry and novels that include *Down the Long Table* and *Turvey*. The author of 150 books, George Woodcock (1912–95) was, among other things, a poet *(Tolstoy at Yasnaya Polyana* and *The Cherry Tree on Cherry Street)*, historian, literary scholar, biographer and travel writer.

Cartoonists have a stake in the city. Lynn Johnston (1947–), whose cartoon strip *For Better or For Worse* is published in 2000 newspapers worldwide, grew up and studied art in Vancouver. Local artist David Boswell's (1953–) cult classic *Reid Fleming: World's Toughest Milkman* first appeared in the *Georgia Straight* alternative weekly in 1978. A few years later comic books were published featuring Reid, a rude, short-tempered and touchy-about-his-baldness kind of guy, but one who delivers the milk better than anyone; he's surprisingly lovable, especially in his tender devotion to his favorite TV show. Check the Comicshop (p164) for copies.

For more information about Vancouver authors, read *Twigg's Directory of 1001 BC Writers* (1992) by local publisher Alan Twigg.

ARCHITECTURE

When Vancouver rose phoenix-like from the ashes of the Great Fire of 1886, Gastown was where the city's first buildings went up. Architects used stone and brick this time round, as the former wooden buildings had proved not so durable, burning to the ground in just 45 minutes.

At the turn of the century the big name in BC architecture was Francis Rattenbury, known for his 'free classical style.' He designed the Vancouver Courthouse in 1912 (now the Vancouver Art Gallery, p44), though his most famous works include the Parliament Buildings (p184) and Empress Hotel (p185) in Victoria on

Top 10 Notable & Controversial Buildings

- Provincial Law Courts & Robson Square (p44)
- Vancouver Public Library (p45)
- Marine Building (p44)
- Sam Kee Building (p55)
- Museum of Anthropology (p64)
- Vancouver Art Gallery (p44)
- Science World (p55)
- Canada Place (p43)
- BC Place Stadium (p43)
- Sikh Temple (p56)

Vancouver Island. His reputation nosedived after he began a torrid affair with a woman 30 years his junior, and he was eventually murdered by one of her other lovers.

In the early decades of 20th century, Craftsman-style bungalows and mansions sprouted up, primarily in neighborhoods such as Kitsilano, Kerrisdale and Shaughnessy. These residences were distinguished by their brick chimneys, shingle exteriors, stained glass, stone bases and interior woodwork, and they fetch a pretty penny in today's market.

Post-WWI buildings of note include the moderne City Hall on Cambie St, designed by Townley and Matheson. McCarter Nairne and Partners designed the exquisite art deco **Marine Building** (p44) in 1930, which was the British Empire's tallest building for 10 years.

Despite these few impressive structures, and the high-rise buildings that grew skyward in the West End starting in the mid-1950s, Vancouver's architecture elicited little

Science World (p55), Chinatown

Arts & Architecture – Architecture

hype. That changed in the 1960s, when the city pioneered a Modernist style called 'post and beam.' Attributes included a flat roof (considered novel at the time) and large windows to capitalize on the scenery and natural light. The premier proponent was a local architect and landscape designer, Arthur Erickson. He took it to the next level, creating a look so specific to the city that it could be recognized as 'Vancouver architecture.'

Erickson positioned his first project, Simon Fraser University, along the ridge of nearby Burnaby Mountain, using girders of Douglas fir beams and steel tie-rods to support a glazed roof. The set-up around a central mall encouraged student interaction, so much so that the design was blamed for prompting student unrest in the late 1960s. Erickson went on to design Vancouver landmarks, such as the **Museum of Anthropology** (p64), **Sikh Temple** (p56), **Robson Square** (p44) and **Provincial Law Courts** (p44). Common building features included use of concrete, partly because Erickson believed Vancouver's gray climate could not take bright colors, and glass canopies and staircases as a response to building on slopes. Erickson is still going strong today. A bit of a rascal, he got one of his biggest rises a few years back when he predicted Vancouver's population would explode to 10 million by 2020.

Expo '86 grafted several contemporary forms on to the cityscape. **Canada Place** (p43), with its five great sails of fiberglass fabric, rose on the site of an old cargo pier. Credited to designers Eberhard Zeidler (architect of Toronto's Eaton Centre), Musson Cattell Mackey Partnership and Archambault Architects, the building was intended to rival Australia's Sydney Opera House. **Science World** (p55) is renowned for its golf ball–like geodesic dome. Local boy and UBC grad Bruno Freschi designed it from 766 vinyl-covered aluminum triangles yielding a volume of 36,790 cubic meters. The best part? It lights up at night.

International architect Moshe Safdie has said there's no connection between his 1995 **Vancouver Public Library** (p45) and Rome's Coliseum, but they sure bear a striking resemblance to one another. The library drew criticism from the design community as an out-of-place eyesore, but its shop-filled piazza and bright spaces for reading, studying and hanging out are well used by Vancouverites. Safdie also designed the contemporary **Centre for Performing Arts** (p134) across the street from the library.

An influx of wealthy immigrants from Hong Kong spurred the wave of pale blue and green condominium towers that went up in the city center in the mid-1990s, lending Vancouver its nickname 'City of Glass.' Mundane on a cloudy day, it becomes an exotic glittering otherworld when the sun shines.

Meanwhile, the city has done a good job preserving some of its notable heritage buildings, such as those in Gastown. The **Sinclair Centre** (p152) is the product of four downtown historic buildings that were converted into a shopping center. Neighborhood developments, such as Yaletown and Granville Island, retain much original architecture – warehouses, loading docks and corrugated metal factory buildings – as features in their revitalized look.

The **Architectural Institute of BC** (p40) offers excellent walking tours that explore the city's unique buildings on a neighborhood-by-neighborhood basis. Our **Downtown Discovery Walk** (p82) also goes by many of the city's landmarks.

VISUAL ARTS

The natural beauty of Vancouver, with its many landscapes, colors, textures and ever-changing light, is an inspiration to artists, no matter what they've chosen as their theme or medium. The city has long had an active art scene, helped along by the **Emily Carr School of Art & Design** (p58). The Southern Gulf Islands (p198) also exert a pull over many artists. The **Vancouver Art Gallery** (p44) houses the works of most people discussed here, as do the city's private galleries (p162).

Vancouver has a cutting-edge reputation for contemporary photography and is associated with a certain brand of photo-conceptual art that has come to be called 'the Vancouver School.' Stan Douglas (1960–) and Jeff Wall (1946–) are two of the most distinguished practitioners. Douglas uses photography, film and video to explore themes of urban transformation, while Wall creates large-format transparencies with cinematic, backlit imagery.

Gathie Falk (1928–) is a painter and sculptor whose work often explores themes of female identity. Alan Storey (1960–) is a sculptor who likes to create moving machines, such as *Pendulum* (p44). Both Falk and Storey have crafted pieces for the city's Public Art Program (see boxed text below).

Famous artists from the past include Emily Carr (1871–1945), regarded as Canada's first major female artist (see boxed text opposite). Two former members of the Group of Seven, painters Frederick Horsman Varley (1881–1969) and Lawren Harris (1885–1970), are known for their landscapes and influence on the Vancouver art community.

First Nations artists have contributed mightily to Vancouver's visual arts, primarily through carving. Two carvers who preserved the past while furthering a new generation of First Nations artists were Charles Edenshaw (1839–1920), the first professional Haida artist, who worked in argillite, gold and silver, and Mungo Martin (1881–1962), a Kwakiutl master carver of totem poles. Martin passed on his skills to Bill Reid (1920–98), the outstanding Haida artist of his generation and the first Haida artist to have a retrospective exhibition at the Vancouver Art Gallery. His work is displayed at the **Museum of Anthropology** (p64).

Charles Edenshaw's great-grandson Robert Davidson (1946–) explores ways to transform Haida art, while his great-great-grandson Jim Hart (1952–) is best known for his carvings. Both were apprenticed to Bill Reid. Another family connection comes by way of Henry Hunt (1923–85) and son Tony Hunt (1942–), the son-in-law and grandson of Mungo Martin, who continued the carving tradition at the **Royal British Columbia Museum** (p184).

Top Five Public Art

The city's Public Art Program requires developers of large construction projects to spend 95¢ per construction foot on public art, which contributes to the generous number of sculptures, murals and fountains in public spaces. A city-run website – www.city.vancouver.bc.ca/publicart – provides an online registry of works (there are more than 80 in the downtown peninsula alone) and a downloadable booklet for a walking tour of shoreline-based artworks; the print booklet is also available at the TouristInfo Centre (p216).

- **Inukshuk** (West End, on the beach beyond foot of Bidwell St) – Blocks of granite stacked in an Inuit symbol of welcome.
- **Joe Fortes Drinking Fountain** (West End, Alexandra Park near foot of Bidwell St) – Dedicated to the famous lifeguard of English Bay Beach.
- **Footnotes** (Yaletown, 1300 block Pacific Blvd) – Words are inset in the sidewalk, creating a poem.
- **Street Light** (Yaletown, foot of Davie St) – These are 14m-high bronze girders from which hang city images either stamped in metal or etched in glass.
- **Collection** (Yaletown, 1300 block Homer St) – Six wedge-shaped sculptures: three time-capsules interspersed between three garbage bins.

The Life & Work of Emily Carr

Through her evocative and impressionistic paintings of west coast forests and First Nations people, Emily Carr produced a rich body of work unlike that of any other Canadian artist and is regarded as Canada's first major female artist. Her story, however, is an all-too-familiar one of an artist who struggled for recognition in her own lifetime only to be lionized in the years following her death.

Carr was born to prosperous parents in Victoria in 1871. At age 16 she wanted to attend art school in San Francisco, but her family felt it was 'unladylike' and she was forced to make a living from teaching instead. In 1899 she experienced a career-defining event. She accompanied a churchman to his mission at Ucluelet on the west coast of Vancouver Island, and, inspired by what she saw, Carr began using both the landscape and First Nations people as her subject matter.

In 1906, after traveling to Europe, Toronto and the Cariboo region of BC and studying landscape painting, Carr moved to Vancouver, where she taught art classes and rented a studio at 570 Granville St. Still not satisfied that she had the skills needed to produce the sort of painting she wanted to create, she went to Paris in 1910 at the age of 39, where she absorbed some of the more modern painting techniques and styles, like Cubism and Fauvism. It was during this time that Carr developed her unique approach that combined the use of dark colors and strong brush strokes.

Returning to Vancouver in 1912, Carr rented a studio at 1465 W Broadway to exhibit her French paintings, and held another exhibit of 200 paintings in 1913. Her work, however, wasn't taken seriously. Some of her paintings were even found to be offensive, resulting in the removal of students from her art classes. A social outcast at 42, and with no means of support, she returned to Victoria to live on family property and to work as a landlady.

It wasn't until the late 1920s that her scorned paintings were shown in eastern Canada and in a sense 'discovered.' She then met the members of the influential school of painters known as the Group of Seven – an all-male group who traipsed around the Canadian wilderness painting vibrant, light-filled landscapes – and with renewed energy and confidence Carr filled canvas after canvas during the ensuing 10 years. She revisited many of her cherished First Nations locales and painted some of her best-known works.

As her health failed and she became bedridden, she took to writing. Her book *Klee Wyck*, meaning 'laughing one,' the name given to her by the Kwakiutl people, is a collection of stories recalling her life among the First Nations people. *The Book of Small* chronicles her childhood in Victoria and *The House of All Sorts* describes her years as a landlady.

Her house in Victoria, **Emily Carr House** (p188), is open to the public, and her paintings can be viewed at **Vancouver Art Gallery** (p44) and the **Art Gallery of Greater Victoria** (p188), as well as at major galleries across Canada.

Lawrence Paul Yuxweluptun (1957–) is a modern, well-known First Nations artist. He graduated from Emily Carr with a painting degree, and uses Coast Salish mythological images to comment on political, environmental and aboriginal issues. Look out also for Roy Henry Vickers (1946–) of Tofino, who expresses traditional themes through wildlife paintings, and Susan Point (1952–), a Coast Salish artist whose traditional themes show up in a variety of media. For further details on First Nations art and where to buy it, see p155.

THEATER & COMEDY

Vancouver has one of Canada's most energetic independent theater scenes, with more than 30 professional theater groups and 21 venues contributing to the entertainment. The **Arts Club** (p135) and **Vancouver Playhouse** (p135) theatre companies are the big players on the block, and have certainly earned their stripes. Both were formed in the 1960s, making them the city's oldest, and both stage classics and new works by Canadian playwrights, often starring a recognizable name or two.

The real excitement lies in the emerging companies and their creation of new works. Vancouver is known for 'site-specific' theater, for which troupes find a venue and then create a show that fits the space. **Electric Company** (p135) is the master of the concept. The troupe staged a recent production around a community center's pool and another at an abandoned factory building; a third was staged at the **Vancouver East Cultural Centre** (p135), taking advantage of its location beside a bar by moving the audience to the bar during the play. **Mortal Coil** (p136) stages annual productions in October and December that revolve around Stanley Park's Miniature Railway (p51). **Radix Theatre** (p136) produced a show that takes place in a parking lot, with audience members seated inside their cars; the troupe provided sound via a special station to which the audience tuned their car radios.

A shortage of mid-size venues (those in the 100- to 250-seat range) means groups have to be creative. The aforementioned Cultural Centre is a renovated church, the **Firehall Arts Centre** (p135) is in an old fire station. The **Performance Works** (p135) theater is in an old machine shop. Smaller companies without a permanent home often use these spaces.

The **Vancouver Fringe Festival** (p11) attracts more than 100 smaller companies to the city each fall, many performing site-specific works everywhere from garages to dance clubs to a moving mini ferry. This event is Canada's third-largest fringe fest, after Edmonton and Winnipeg.

Outdoor theater also is a hit in Vancouver, which is no wonder given the environs. **Bard on the Beach** (p135) is Shakespeare performed beside Kitsilano Beach against a backdrop of mountains and ocean. The group recently started Bard in the Vineyard, with plays taking place outdoors at a winery in the Okanagan Valley. The outdoor Malkin Bowl in Stanley Park has been around since 1940 and is home to the current **Theatre Under the Stars** (p135).

Vancouver may not offer an overwhelming selection of comedy, but it does have the **Vancouver TheatreSports League** (p134), one of the largest non-profit improv-based companies in the world. The TheatreSports concept, which was started by an acting teacher in Calgary and subsequently has been adopted by troupes across the globe, fuses the dramatic elements of comedy and tragedy with the excitement of sports. Vancouver's troupe gathered international interest in the concept after it held an improv tournament at Expo '86. The group earns its laughs four nights a week, 52 weeks a year, at Granville Island's New Revue Stage.

Amateur community theater groups, which come under the umbrella organization **Theatre BC** (☎ 250-714-0203; www.theatrebc.org), staging three or four productions a year. The **Playwrights Theatre Centre** (☎ 604-685-6228; www.playwrightstheatre.com) chooses from about 250 scripts submitted by aspiring playwrights, and eight productions are staged annually.

The city's original theater was put on by First Nations people. In the late 19th century they staged ceremonies featuring spectacular singing, dancing, masks and stagecraft until these sorts of celebrations, called potlatches, were banned by European settlers. The ceremonies weren't legalized again until the 1950s.

For more information on Vancouver's theaters, see p134.

DANCE

Vancouver, along with the Pacific Northwest in general, has a growing reputation in contemporary dance. Vancouver's scene is anchored by the impressive **Scotiabank Dance Centre** (☎ 604-606-6400; www.thedancecentre.ca), a former bank transformed into its modern, glass-enclosed incarnation by local hero Arthur Erickson (p25). Opened in 2001, the seven-story venue – purpose-built for dance – is one of the few of its kind in North America. It supports more than 30 diverse dance companies with studio and rehearsal space.

Dance in Vancouver, at least before the second half of the 20th century, was represented more by those who were trained in the city and went on to greater things elsewhere than it was by local companies. The creation of Pacific Ballet Theatre by Maria Lewis in 1969 saw the first permanent ballet company take hold in Vancouver and, now renamed **Ballet British Columbia** (p137), it has become one of the country's top ballet companies.

One of the first modern dance companies to emerge was the Western Dance Theatre in 1970. It inspired a generation of Vancouver dancers to form companies, including **Karen Jamieson** (p137), Terry Hunter (of Vancouver Moving Theatre), Paula Ross and Anna Wyman.

Experimental Dance and Music (EDAM; p137), founded in 1982, is an internationally respected company taking a multimedia meets improvisational approach. It inspired companies such as Mascall Dance and Lola Dance, plus a host of choreographers and dancers.

Vancouver's cultural diversity has resulted in creative fusions of world and contemporary dance. Choreographers and companies crossing bridges in this manner include Rosario Ancer and Centro Flamenco, Jai Govinda and the Mandala Arts and Culture Society (Indian classical dance), and Kokoro Dance (butoh modern Japanese dance). The Lorita Leung Dance Association preserves Chinese dance forms. All are members of the Scotiabank Dance Centre.

Many of the companies listed converge at Vancouver's annual dance festivals, which help foster the city's reputation as a dance stronghold. The three-week **Vancouver International Dance Festival** (p8) is held during spring, and the 10-day **Dancing on the Edge Festival** (p9) is in July. For more information on Vancouver's dance companies and venues, see p137.

History

History

THE RECENT PAST

The 1990s were good to the city, and it began receiving the first of its many honors as one of the globe's 'most livable' and 'best' places during that decade. Vancouver stepped brightly into the 21st century wearing a mantle of economic and cultural dazzle, almost – but not quite – obscuring the skeletons in its closet.

A MULTICULTURAL MECCA

In the years just prior to the reversion of Hong Kong to China in 1997, tens of thousands of wealthy Hong Kong Chinese migrated to Vancouver's Lower Mainland area, boosting the area's permanent Asian population by about 85%, and creating the largest Asian population in any North American city. Real estate prices rose, with Vancouver's cost-of-living figures suddenly rivaling those of London, Paris and Tokyo. Many of the new arrivals shunned the city proper in favor of the suburbs, especially Richmond, but the influx also resulted in plenty of glassy new skyscrapers popping up downtown. By 1998, immigration had tapered off by about a third, but the city's transformation into a modern, multicultural mecca was already complete. By then, about 40% of Vancouver residents were foreign-born, and an ethnic smorgasbord of restaurants, stores and cultural activities catered to the crowds, solidifying the worldly reputation Vancouver earned when it hosted the Expo '86 world's fair (p36).

In the late 1990s problems with Asian economies slowed down the meteoric economic development seen earlier in the decade. But globalization and technological growth, especially among high-tech and biotech industries, buffered Greater Vancouver's fortunes. Film production in particular became a city staple. Films and TV series had been shot here sporadically for years, but the brooding *X-Files* series, taped in Vancouver from 1993 to 1998,

Murder at the Piggy Palace

In February 2002 Vancouver police arrested 53-year-old Robert William 'Willie' Pickton on charges of murder, touching off the largest serial killer investigation in Canadian history.

A 21-month search of Pickton's 14-acre pig farm and nearby private party venue known as 'Piggy Palace' – located in Port Coquitlam, about an hour's drive from Vancouver – turned up the remains of 30 women. All were prostitutes living in Vancouver's drug-infested downtown Eastside neighborhood.

The killings had been going on since 1983, but police didn't see a pattern at first, due in part to the transient nature of the Eastside population. Many of the women weren't even reported missing for up to six years after their disappearance. A total of 69 women are now listed as missing.

While the case has put a spotlight on the disproportionate and largely ignored violence against prostitutes and drug addicts, it has also brought criticism to the local police force for taking so long to apprehend Pickton. He had been arrested initially in 1997 for trying to murder a prostitute, but went free after the charges were dropped. A year later, a worker on the pig farm went to police and reported his suspicions about Pickton, but nothing came of it.

The story turned even more sordid recently with reports that Pickton – described as a loner who lived in a trailer – may have mixed human remains with pork he distributed to friends and neighbors. Pickton's trial is scheduled to begin in 2005. Because Canada does not have a death penalty, he faces a number of consecutive life sentences if convicted.

TIMELINE	AD 500	1774	1791
	Communities encountered by the first Europeans to arrive in BC take up residence.	Spanish send first of three expeditions to discover the fabled Northwest Passage.	Strait of Georgia explored by Spanish navigator José María Narváez.

Haunted by the Past

Vancouver may be hurtling toward the future, but the city's ghosts like to remain in the past. As you wander about town, you're likely to visit more than a few of the city's haunted sites, including:

Vogue Theatre (p127) – Staff have reported unexplained footsteps, a 'cold presence' and apparitions of a tall man in a white tuxedo, who was even seen in the aisle from the stage by a well-known performer.

Vancouver Art Gallery (p44) – The late-19th-century building used to be to be the courthouse; rumor has it a ghost roams underground where the holding cells were located.

Hotel Vancouver (p170) – The hotel's elevator has been known to stop unaccountably on the 14th floor, and, as the door opens on its own, a woman in red is seen gliding through the hallway.

UBC (p63) – An old woman in a white dress has been seen swooping through the main library.

seemed to unleash a flurry of Hollywood-esque activity, including the appearance of more and more swanky hotels and restaurants. Tourism was becoming an economic powerhouse, too, as the number of cruise ships calling on the port increased.

THE 21ST CENTURY

Urban development continues at an extraordinary pace in the city's core. Yaletown, Coal Harbour and SoMa have all brought young, moneyed residents to once bleak neighborhoods fringing downtown.

One area – just steps from the aforementioned successes – has proved resistant to such change. Downtown's Eastside, centered on Main and Hastings (or 'Pain and Wastings') Sts, is the heart of Vancouver's drug scene. Estimates of its junkie population range from 5000 to 10,000 at any given moment. Heroin and crack cocaine are the drugs of choice, reputedly supplied by motorcycle gangs or Asian cartels. Attendant problems include prostitution (how most female addicts support their habit) and HIV (the neighborhood has the highest HIV infection rate in North America).

When Mayor Larry Campbell took office in 2002, he vowed to improve the downtown Eastside. Many had said it before him, but Campbell was the city's coroner for 20 years prior, and he had seen firsthand thousands of drug overdoses and people suffering from drug-related harm. He has championed some rather unorthodox methods, such as safe injection sites that offer clean needles and a place to shoot up for users, and legalizing marijuana so it can be taxed to fund health care and drug treatment. The injection sites went into effect in 2003; the pot issue is still being debated, though it has a fair number of supporters given that the current trade is estimated at $4 billion annually.

Vancouver is showing that a city can maintain its conscience amid rapid-paced development. The progressive city council has passed a number of green mandates, such as reducing greenhouse gas emissions and setting energy-efficient construction codes. Its biggest challenge will come in 2010, when it hosts the Winter Olympics. The city teamed with Whistler on a bid, and won in 2003. Now the hard work of coughing up the cash and preparing the venues is underway. The overall cost of hosting the Games is estimated at nearly $2 billion.

In the same way the city used Expo '86 as a springboard to beef up its international reputation, residents hope the Olympics will keep Vancouver's momentum going far into the 21st century. Some worry that the commercial and physical onslaught may stun the city, but Vancouver – which has grown up in less time than perhaps any other city in modern times – is poised, as ever, to take it all in stride.

1792	1827	1858	1859
Captain George Vancouver sails into Burrard Inlet; stays 24 hours, then departs.	Hudson's Bay Company builds Fort Langley, the first European settlement in the region.	Prospectors discover gold on the Fraser River; 25,000 people rush in with picks and pans.	Richard Moody builds a trail (North Rd) from New Westminster to Burrard Inlet.

FROM THE BEGINNING

LIVING OFF THE LAND

While people had been living along this part of the west coast for more than 10,000 years, the communities encountered by the first Europeans took shape around AD 500. The people lived in villages consisting of large rough-hewn plank houses arranged in rows, often surrounded by a stockade; totem poles were set up nearby as an emblem of family or clan. No wonder groups were attracted to the area – the beaches teamed with seafood, the forests teamed with wildlife, and fat silvery salmon seemed to be everywhere.

Several distinct communities formed. The Musqueam populated Burrard Inlet, English Bay and the mouth of the Fraser River, although they shared some of this area with the Squamish, who were largely based at the head of Howe Sound, but also had villages in North and West Vancouver, Kitsilano Point, Stanley Park and Jericho Beach. The area around New Westminster was controlled by the Kwantlen, while Delta and Richmond were home to the Tsawwassen. The Tsleil-Waututh occupied much of North Vancouver, while Coast Salish tribes, such as the Cowichan, Nanaimo and Saanich, set up seasonal camps along the Fraser River when the salmon were running.

CAPTAIN VANCOUVER'S LUCKY DAY

By the late 1700s Europeans had penetrated the local waters. The race was on, and the Spanish, English and French began jockeying to grab land.

The Spanish sent over three expeditions between 1774 and 1779 to discover the fabled Northwest Passage (the water route across North America from the Pacific Ocean to the Atlantic Ocean) and gain control of the region north of San Francisco. They ended up by the entrance to Nootka Sound on Vancouver Island and never ventured into the Strait of Georgia (but that didn't stop their influence from seeping into Vancouver, evidenced by today's street names, such as Cordova, Cardero and Valdez, and places like Spanish Banks Beach).

British explorer Captain James Cook arrived from the South Pacific in 1779 with a similar motive – finding the Northwest Passage – and a similar result: he hit the west coast of Vancouver Island and believed it to be the mainland coast.

It wasn't until 1791 that the Strait of Georgia was explored. Spanish navigator José María Narváez did the honors and sailed all the way into Burrard Inlet. Alas, he stopped short of the inner harbor, concluding that Point Grey was actually a group of islands, which he named Islas de Langara.

Enter Captain George Vancouver, a British navigator who had sailed with Cook the previous year. In 1792 he glided into the inner harbor and spent one day here – a lucky day, as it turned out, though it didn't seem that way at first. When he arrived, he discovered that the Spanish, in ships under the command of captains Valdez and Galiano, had already claimed the place. The men met at what is today Spanish Banks Beach, and shared information and charted the coastline. Vancouver made a note of the deep natural port, which he named Burrard after one of his crew. Then he sailed away, not spilling much sweat for a place that would be named for him 100 years later.

As Spanish influence in the area waned in favor of the British, explorers, such as Simon Fraser, Alexander Mackenzie and

Top Five Historic Sites

- Roedde House & Barclay Heritage Square (p50)
- Maple Tree Square (p47)
- Chinese Cultural Centre Museum & Archives (p54)
- Hastings Mill Store Museum (p62)
- Gulf of Georgia Cannery (p80)

1867	1886	1887	1901
Talkative 'Gassy' Jack Deighton opens a saloon by a sawmill; Gastown springs up around it.	City of Vancouver incorporates; the Great Fire burns new town to the ground in 45 minutes.	First transcontinental train pulls into Vancouver; 11,000 Chinese immigrate to help build railway.	Aboriginal settlements in Vanier Park displaced to Capilano Reserve and Squamish.

David Thompson, mapped the interior of the province, opening it up for overland travelers and the arrival of the famed Hudson's Bay Company.

GOLD, FUR & TIMBER

The area's natural resources spurred Vancouver's development throughout the first half of the 19th century. In 1824, the Hudson's Bay Company, under the leadership of James McMillan, began setting up a network of fur trading posts. McMillan noted a particularly good location along the Fraser River, about 50km from its mouth, and he built Fort Langley there in 1827. It was the region's first permanent European settlement, sustained by fur trading – the fort shipped out more than 2000 beaver pelts in 1832 – and later by salmon fishing and farming. Remarkably, the Hudson's Bay Company still makes a living trading wares in the region. Today it's called The Bay department store, and the buying and selling take place at Georgia and Granville Sts downtown, just one of more than a hundred such stores spread across Canada.

In 1858 an interesting tidbit of news began making the rounds: gold had been discovered on the banks of the Fraser River. More than 25,000 American prospectors flocked to the region with picks, pans and dreams of getting rich quick. Concerned that the influx of prospectors might inspire the USA to think about expanding north, the mainland followed the lead of Vancouver Island, which had been a crown colony since 1849, and declared itself a British colony. James Douglas, already the governor of Vancouver Island, was sworn in as governor of the new colony of British Columbia (though BC and the island remained separate protectorates). The proclamation was made at Fort Langley on November 19, 1858.

Douglas asked the British government for support, so the Royal Engineers, under the command of Colonel Richard Moody, arrived at the end of 1858 to build roads and a military reserve. Alarmed by the poor strategic location of Fort Langley, Moody selected another site on the Fraser River – closer to its mouth – and built New Westminster, which was declared the first capital of BC. In 1859, he built a trail (known today as North Rd) from New Westminster to Burrard Inlet to provide the colony with an ice-free harbor in winter. In 1860 he built a trail, more or less where Kingsway Rd is, linking New Westminster to False Creek. The foundation was in place for the settlement to shift to present-day downtown, though at this point the area was still a thick, virgin rainforest of cedar, fir and hemlock.

The sawmills sent the wheels of change spinning. The first mills were set up along the Fraser River in 1860, and their logging operations provided cleared land for farms in areas like Surrey and south Vancouver. It wasn't long before the companies moved north toward the bulging forests that fringed Burrard Inlet. In 1867, Edward Stamp's British-financed Hastings Mill, on the south shore of the inlet, established the starting point of a town that would become Vancouver.

In 1866 the colonies of Vancouver Island and BC merged and both were known by the name British Columbia. With the creation of a new country called Canada in 1867 on the continent's eastern side, BC became concerned about its future and feared it could be swallowed up by the USA. So with the promise of access to a national railway, BC joined the Canadian Confederation in 1871, although it would be another 15 years before the railway actually reached the West Coast.

THE PUB THAT LAUNCHED A CITY

True, Hastings Mill was there first, but it was the pub that really launched Vancouver. In 1867 an Englishman named 'Gassy' Jack Deighton – a character and windbag of a storyteller – rowed into Burrard Inlet with his First Nations wife, a yellow dog and a barrel of whiskey. He knew the nearest drink for the thirsty mill workers was a 5km row through the inlet to the North Rd, followed by a 15km walk through the bear-filled forest to New

1920	1938	1949	1956
First Polar Bear swim event; 10 people plunge into English Bay on New Year's Day.	Lions Gate Bridge built, connecting the North Shore and downtown.	Chinese, Japanese and aboriginal people given the provincial right to vote.	West End rezoned to allow greater population density; high-rise boom begins.

Vancouver's first passenger train, housed at the Roundhouse Community Centre (p49)

Westminster. So he announced to mill workers that if they helped him build a tavern, drinks were on him. Within 24 hours the Globe Saloon was in business, and when a village sprang up around the establishment it was called Gastown. In 1869 it was incorporated into the town of Granville.

Another town thriving around a sawmill was Port Moody, at the eastern end of Burrard Inlet. In 1882 this was where the first electric lights north of San Francisco were switched on, and the town was chosen to be the western terminus of the Canadian Pacific Railway (CPR). However, a CPR official, who also happened to be an influential businessman and landowner in Granville, 'discovered' that the eastern end of Burrard Inlet wasn't a practical harbor for large ships and – much to the outrage of Port Moody citizens – Granville was selected to be the terminus instead.

The CPR negotiated with the provincial government for 2400 hectares in the area, making it Granville's largest private property holder. The story goes that in 1884, while workers rowed CPR's general manager William Van Horne around what would later become Stanley Park, he commented that the new city needed a name that would live up to its future stature as a great metropolis. Van Horne reasoned that, since Granville was an unknown name, the new city should be called Vancouver after the man whom everyone knew was responsible for literally putting the area on the map. CPR's directors approved the new name and in April 1886 the town of Granville – population 1000 – was incorporated as the City of Vancouver.

The first piece of business by the new city council was to lease a 400-hectare military reserve from the federal government and establish it as the city's first park, eventually opened as Stanley Park. The young city faced its first hurdle at the tender age of two months. On June 13, 1886, CPR workers lit a fire to clear brush, and it spread out of control – fast. The 'Great Fire,' as it came to be known, took less than 45 minutes to destroy Vancouver's 1000 wooden structures, kill as many as 28 people (the number remains disputed) and leave 3000 people homeless.

1969	1970	1979	1980
The organization that later became Greenpeace is founded in a local living room.	National Hockey League's Vancouver Canucks take to the ice.	Granville Island developed from industrial wasteland; public market opens.	Terry Fox runs Marathon of Hope across Canada to raise money for cancer research.

Within hours the rebuilding had got underway, but this time the buildings were constructed with stone and brick. By 1887 – when the first CPR passenger train pulled into Vancouver – the city was back in business. Within four years of the railway arriving, the city grew to a population of 13,000, and between 1891 and 1901 the population skyrocketed to more than twice that again.

GROWING PAINS

The CPR was responsible for shaping much of the city as it exists today. The rail company built Granville St from Burrard Inlet to False Creek, cleared and paved Pender and Hastings Sts, and developed the land around False Creek for railway yards and housing. Other areas developed by the CPR for housing included the West End (originally designed to be an upper-income neighborhood), Kitsilano and Shaughnessy Heights in south Vancouver. Shaughnessy Heights, once known as 'CPR Heaven,' was created to be the home of Vancouver's new upper classes, just so long as the residents weren't Jewish or Asian – the deeds of sale contained a clause forbidding the resale of property to people from either of these groups.

Anti-Asian feeling was not new to Vancouver. Between 1881 and 1885 more than 11,000 Chinese arrived by ship to work on the construction of the railroad. In many respects they were treated as second-class citizens. They were paid $1 a day, half of what white workers were paid (but almost 20 times what they were paid at home). Government legislation denied all Asians the right to vote in federal elections, and did not allow Chinese women to immigrate unless they were married to a white man. In 1887 a white mob destroyed a Chinese camp in False Creek, and in 1907 an anti-Asian riot ripped through Chinatown and Japantown.

It was an issue the city would have to remedy, because by 1911 the census showed that Vancouver was a city of immigrants, with most people born outside of Canada. Aboriginal rights were also taking a beating during this time. In 1901 the local government displaced a First Nations community from Vanier Park, sending some families to the Capilano Indian Reserve on the North Shore and others to Squamish.

The city benefited enormously from the opening of the Panama Canal in 1914, which allowed quicker access to markets in Europe and North America's east coast. That same year, BC Rail began life as Pacific Great Eastern Railway, the beginning of the push into the province's center.

During the first 30 years of the 20th century all the suburbs around the city grew substantially. By 1928 the population outside the city was about 150,000 people. When Point Grey and South Vancouver amalgamated with the city in 1929, bringing in a combined population of more than 80,000 people, Vancouver became Canada's third-largest city – the ranking it retains today.

While the Great Depression of the 1930s saw the construction of several public works – the Marine Building, Vancouver City Hall, the third and present Hotel Vancouver, and Lions Gate Bridge, to name a few – many people were unemployed, as was the case throughout Canada. This marked a time of large demonstrations, the occupation of public buildings, riots and public discontent.

WWII helped to pull Vancouver out of the Depression by creating instant jobs at shipyards, aircraft-parts factories and canneries, and in construction with the building of rental units for the increased workforce. Japanese Canadians, however, didn't fare so well. In 1942, following the bombing of Pearl Harbor, Japanese Canadians were shipped to internment camps in the province's interior, and had to endure the confiscation of all their land and property, much of which was never returned to its rightful owners. Chinese, Japanese and aboriginal people were finally given the provincial vote in 1949.

1982	1986	1993	1996
Canada's first brewpub – the Troller – opens in Horseshoe Bay.	Expo '86 puts Vancouver on the map as a city of international prominence.	*The X-Files* TV series begins shooting in Vancouver, sparks film-industry boom.	Asian immigration peaks in lead-up to China's takeover of Hong Kong.

REACHING FOR THE SKY

By the start of the 1950s the city's population was 345,000 and Vancouver was thriving. The high-rise craze hit in the middle of the decade, mostly in the West End. During the next 13 years, 220 apartment buildings went up – and up – but the ensuing congestion was not always to residents' liking. Part two of the modern urban plan was to be a freeway racing through downtown, but public outcry put an end to the idea, and Vancouver's cityscape remains unique because of this quirk.

In the 1960s and '70s Vancouver was known for its counter-cultural community centered in Kitsilano. Many draft dodgers came from the USA, seeking to escape service in the Vietnam War. Canada's gay rights movement began in Vancouver in 1964 when a group of feminists and academics started the Association for Social Knowledge, the country's first gay and lesbian discussion group. In 1969 the Don't Make a Wave Committee formed to stop US nuclear testing in Alaska; a few years later, the group morphed into the environmental organization Greenpeace.

Nothing was more important to Vancouver in the 1980s than Expo '86, the world's fair that many people believe helped the city to come of age and transform into a place of international eminence. The six-month event, which coincided with the city's 100th birthday, brought more than 21 million visitors. Many of the city's landmarks – Science World, Canada Place, the Millennium Gate, among others – were built for the Expo. During the '80s the SkyTrain hit the tracks, Pacific Spirit Regional Park was created and 60,000-seat BC Place Stadium was inflated (via an air-supported roof). For perspective on the city's growth, consider this: if the stadium had been built 97 years earlier when Vancouver was first incorporated, and you put all of the residents at that time into it, 59,000 seats would remain empty.

The brewing issue of Aboriginal land rights spilled over by the late 1980s with a growing number of rallies, road blockades and court actions. Aside from a few treaties covering a tiny portion of the province, land-claim agreements had not been signed and no clear definition of the scope and nature of Aboriginal rights existed. Until 1990, the provincial government refused to participate in treaty negotiations. That changed in December, when the BC Claims Task Force was formed among the governments of Canada, BC and the First Nations Summit with a mission to figure out how the three parties could solve land-rights matters. It's a slow-moving, ongoing process that in Vancouver's case involves the Tsawwassen, Tsleil-Waututh, Katzie, Squamish and Musqueam nations.

The 1993 summit meeting between Bill Clinton and Boris Yeltsin thrust the city back into the international eye, building on the reputation it garnered during Expo '86.

2001	2002	2002	2003
BC Marijuana Party receives 3.5% of the vote in provincial elections.	Mayor Larry Campbell takes office and vows to improve the downtown Eastside.	Arrest of Willie Pickton, starts largest serial killer investigation in Canadian history.	Vancouver and Whistler win Olympic bid for 2010 Winter Games.

Neighborhoods

Neighborhoods

Stunning mountain and ocean views present themselves from one side of the city to the other, and they're yours to gawk at whether you're on a bus, bike, foot or ferry. Most people start their visit in the downtown's business-and-retail district, looking out over the cruise ships and floatplanes in Burrard Inlet backed by the Coast Mountains' commanding peaks. A few steps east is historic Gastown, the original heart of the city that sprouted up around a loquacious Englishman's pub. Dip south and you're in Yaletown where city planners converted crumbling industrial docklands into showy town homes, and restaurants are filled with rich and beautiful urbanites.

West of downtown is the sensibly named West End, densely packed with people and glass high-rises. Abutting it still further west is the city's sweet garland: Stanley Park, a hulking cedar, hemlock and fir forest that serves as Vancouverites' favorite playground.

Southeast of Gastown sits North America's third-largest Chinatown, whose steamy-windowed restaurants and bakeries lure with aromas both sweet and savory. Granville Island floats in False Creek just south of downtown. Many visitors take the bathtub boat-like mini ferries over to browse the abundant artisans' studios and public market.

Hip SoMa is the city's upstart, and the place to come for bold restaurants and fashion designers' shops. East Vancouver is, yes, east of the city center; of primary interest to visitors is Commercial Dr, the old Italian corridor still laced with espresso houses, turned multicultural mecca for skateboarders, palm readers and dreadlocked shopkeepers. The West Side, south of downtown and across False Creek and English Bay, encompasses (from east to west) outdoorsy Fairview, art gallery–laden South Granville, the old hippie enclave Kitsilano and rugged University of British Columbia.

And the city sprawls on throughout Greater Vancouver (often called the Lower Mainland). Notable suburbs are mountain-and-park-filled North Vancouver, moneyed West Vancouver, the 'new Chinatown' of Richmond and the historic fishing village of Steveston.

A word regarding street savvy: generally, the avenues in Vancouver run east to west and the streets go north to south. The downtown east–west streets begin numbering at Carrall St, near Chinatown; on the West Side they start with Ontario St. North–south streets begin numbering at Waterfront Rd, on Burrard Inlet.

Walking about Vancouver certainly won't wear out your shoes, but if your tootsies do tire, you can always rent a bike, hop on a ferry, or board a bus or SkyTrain. Each of the following sections contains transport details, and there's more information on p204.

Peak summer season runs from Victoria Day in late May to Labour Day in early September. Note that most attractions and services reduce their hours out of season.

ITINERARIES

One Day

Start at white-sailed **Canada Place** (p43) for excellent mountain, sea and city views. Take the **Coal Harbour Seawalk** (p50) to **Stanley Park** (p50). Rent a bike (p142) before entering, then spend the better part of the day pedaling through the remarkable forest, swimming the beaches and visiting the sights, such as the

Top Ten Things to Do When It Rains

- Ogle the **Museum of Anthropology's** totem poles (p64)
- Caffeinate in a **Commercial Dr** coffee shop (p126)
- Take a calligraphy class at the **Chinese Cultural Centre** (p54)
- Duck in and out of **Granville Island's** market, galleries and shops (p59)
- Bowl or shoot pool at **Commodore Lanes** (p131)
- Sample wasabi, kimchi and the 200-plus other flavors at **La Casa Gelato** (p94)
- Sample the wares on the **Granville Island Brewery** tour (p59)
- Visit **Richmond's** Asian malls (p78)
- Chill out at the **Planetarium Star Theatre's** Pink Floyd laser show (p62)
- Be like a Vancouverite: put on your Gortex and do all the usual fair-weather activities (p139)

Vancouver Aquarium (p53). Afterward, reward such strenuous activity with a robust meal in the **West End** (p98). Denman and Robson Sts are rich restaurant veins, serving everything from hot garlic fries to steaming Japanese noodles, and West Coast oysters to alder-grilled salmon. Finish with a drink atop the commanding Empire Landmark Hotel's **Cloud Nine Lounge** (p125).

Three Days

Start your second day in **Chinatown** (p101) with a dim sum feast. Meditate upon the stone-laid paths at **Dr Sun Yat-Sen Classical Chinese Garden** (p55), then switch gears and visit the **Vancouver Police Museum** (p47), where an autopsy room and weaponry case are among the not-so-serene displays. Head over to Granville Island in the late afternoon for snacks at the **public market** (p59), then browse among the prints, ceramics and glassware studios, or have drinks on one of the neighborhood's view-friendly patios (p122). Afterward, you can see a **play** (p134) or move on to **Yaletown** (p97) to indulge in dinner and martinis. Day three is for the **West Side** (p59). Begin with the totem pole and wood carvings at the **UBC Museum of Anthropology** (p64). Visit undeveloped – and clothing-optional – **Wreck Beach** (p65). Have dinner in **Kitsilano** (p117) at one of its upscale or casual, vegetarian or meat-abiding eateries. Swing by the **Cellar** (p129) for live jazz.

One Week

With one week you can broaden your Vancouver horizons. Take a day to have your chakras opened or buy a poetry chapbook on **Commercial Dr** (p57), ski or hike **Grouse Mountain** (p75), kayak in **Deep Cove** (p76) or take a ferry over to **Bowen Island** (p198). You can travel further afield with a couple of days to spare: **Victoria** (p184), with its English tea-and-gardens ambience, is a 3½-hour car-and-ferry ride away. **Whistler** (p193), a 2½-hour drive north on the jaw-dropping Sea to Sky Hwy, is one of the world's most famous resorts, skiable well into the summer. During evenings in Vancouver, try to score tickets to a Canucks **hockey game** (p141) in winter or drop by Nat Bailey Stadium for a **baseball game** (p140) in summer.

What's Free?

Here's a quick rundown of things to do when your wallet is running on empty. See the City Calendar (p8) for free-for-all festivals and celebrations. Most architectural sights, cathedrals, parks and beaches are also free, as are private art galleries (p162).

Tuesday

Museum of Anthropology (p64; ☽ 5-9pm)

Chinese Cultural Centre (p54)

Thursday

Vancouver Art Gallery (p44; admission by donation; ☽ 5-9pm)

Every Day

Lynn Canyon Suspension Bridge (p76)

Dr Sun Yat-Sen Park (p55)

Nitobe Garden (p64; ☽ mid-Oct–mid-Mar only)

UBC Garden (p65; ☽ mid-Oct–mid-Mar only)

Historic Gastown Walking Tour (p46)

Gordon MacMillan Southam Observatory (p62)

Capilano Salmon Hatchery (p66)

ORGANIZED TOURS

Air Tours

If you're short on time and long on money, air tours are a good way to get a city overview (literally). All the seaplane companies – Baxter Aviation, Harbour Air and West Coast Air – that provide regular transport from Vancouver to the islands also offer 20-minute panoramic city tours (per person $95), 1¼-hour wilderness excursions to secluded mountain lakes (per person $225) and other longer tours. See p204 for contact details.

Boat Tours

Most of the tours listed below stay close to Vancouver's skyline. For something more aquatically adventurous, see p41.

ACCENT CRUISES Map pp236-7

☎ 604-688-6625; www.dinnercruises.com; 1676 Duranleau St; 2½hr cruise $25, with dinner $60; ☽ 5:45pm May-Oct; bus 50

Accent's yachts provide an optional all-you-can-eat buffet dinner during its cruise along English Bay, Stanley Park beaches and Ambleside Beach in West Vancouver. Departures are from Granville Island.

HARBOUR CRUISES Map pp230-3
☎ 604-688-7246; www.boatcruises.com; north foot of Denman St; adult/child 5-11/senior & student $19/7/16; ☺ 11:30am, 1pm & 2:30pm mid-May–mid-Sep, 2:30pm Apr & Oct; bus 19

Harbour Cruises' narrated, 75-minute paddlewheel boat tour of the inner harbor churns past Stanley Park, Lion's Gate Bridge, cruise-ship terminals and North Shore mountains. It also offers a 2½-hour sunset dinner cruise (adult/child aged two to 11 $65/55) with West Coast cuisine and live music. The cruise departs at 7pm and 9:30pm from June to September; in May and October this same tour is known as the 'Starlight Cruise' because the sun sets before departure.

MINI FERRIES
Depart from Granville Island near the public market; adult/child $6/3; ☺ roughly 9am-6:30pm, every 15 min; bus 50

Both Aquabus and False Creek Ferries (p206) zip around False Creek for amusing, narrated 25-minute tours. Basically, you just stay on board while the ferry makes its regular loop to Yaletown, picking up and dropping off passengers.

Bus Tours
Bus tours are convenient, particularly for accessing the North Shore's sights in a short time frame. Each of the companies listed here (except the Vancouver Trolley Company) offer day trips to Victoria and Whistler from Vancouver, but be prepared for a long (ie nine- to 13-hour) day; see p184 and p193 for details. For bus tours further afield, such as into BC's interior or beyond to the Rockies, try Bigfoot Adventure Tours (p206).

GRAY LINE TOURS
☎ 604-879-3363; www.grayline.ca/vancouver; ☺ departure times vary

Reliable Gray Line offers a wide array of traditional bus sightseeing tours, including the 3½-hour deluxe grand city tour (adult/child $49/32), five-hour 'Mountains and Sea' tour (adult/child $79/55, reduced fees in winter) that includes Grouse Mountain and Capilano Suspension Bridge, and the double-decker hop-on, hop-off attractions loop tour (adult/child $30/17, good for 2 consecutive days). Buy tickets at the Empire Landmark Hotel (p174) or call for other departure locations.

LANDSEA TOURS
☎ 604-662-7591, 877-669-2277; www.vancouvertours.com

Landsea offers tours in smaller, 24-passenger buses, including a four-hour city highlights tour (adult/senior/child $49/46/30), departing 9am and 2pm late-February to mid-November and at 10:30am December to early February; a five-hour North Shore and Grouse Mountain tour (adult/child/senior incl admission $78/46/74), at 2pm late February to mid-November; and tours to accommodate passengers before and after cruise-ship voyages. Tour departure points and schedules vary.

VANCOUVER TROLLEY COMPANY
☎ 604-801-5515; www.vancouvertrolley.com; adult/child $28/14; ☺ every half hr, 9am-6pm, to 4:30pm in winter

This company operates wheeled replicas of the famous San Francisco trolleys, which loop from Gastown to Chinatown, downtown and Stanley Park; you can get on or off at 23 attractions, including Canada Place, the Vancouver Aquarium, English Bay and Vanier Park. The circuit takes two hours. Buy tickets from the driver.

WEST COAST CITY & NATURE SIGHTSEEING
☎ 604-451-1600; www.vancouversightseeing.com, www.vancouverspecialtours.com

In addition to the five-hour city and Capilano Suspension Bridge tour (adult/senior & student/child 4-12 $58/55/34) at noon from April to October, this company offers niche tours that explore First Nations culture (including the Stanley Park totem poles and UBC's Anthropology Museum), local gardens and the city's art galleries. Prices fluctuate and departure times vary.

Cycling & Walking Tours
The TouristInfo Centre (p216) has brochures for self-guided tours. Neighborhood-specific tours, such as the Historic Gastown Walking Tour (p46), are covered under individual neighborhood headings throughout the rest of this chapter.

ARCHITECTURAL INSTITUTE OF BRITISH COLUMBIA Map p234
☎ 604-683-8588; www.aibc.bc.ca; departure points vary; tours $5; ☺ 1pm Tue-Sat mid-Jun–Aug

Local architectural students conduct excellent tours (1½ to two hours) through Gastown, the West End, Chinatown, downtown and other city neighborhoods. Different tours are featured on different days, so call for the schedule.

SPOKES BICYCLE RENTALS Map pp230-3
☎ 604-688-5141; www.vancouverbikerental.com; 1798 W Georgia St; ☾ mid-May–mid-Sep; bus 19
Those who rent from Spokes can sign up for the 9am 1½-hour guided cycling tour of the Stanley Park Seawall ($30) or the 11am 3½-hour cycling tour of Granville Island ($60). Tour prices include bicycle rental.

WALKABOUT HISTORIC VANCOUVER
☎ 604-720-0006; www.walkabouthistoricvancouver .com; departure points vary; tours $25; ☾ 10am & 2pm
Informative and lively guides in period dress lead two-hour tours exploring the architecture and history of downtown and Gastown; Chinatown and Gastown; or Granville Island. Call for reservations.

Specialty Tours
Be it by kayak, First Nations canoe or horse-drawn carriage, visitors can commune with nature on a variety of entertaining specialty tours. A few additional excursions and rental outfitters are listed in the Sports, Health & Fitness chapter (p139).

LOTUS LAND TOURS
☎ 604-684-4922, 800-528-3531; www.lotuslandtours .com
This group offers 'wilderness trips for softies' – ie experience and fitness are not required. The five-hour kayaking tour ($145) includes a guided paddle in Indian Arm off Deep Cove, a barbecued salmon lunch on Twin Island, and a chance to explore forest and beach; departs at 9am April to October. It also offers six-hour orca-watching tours ($145), departing at 7:15am May to October; snowshoeing ($99), departing at 9am December to March; and hiking trips. Pick-ups are available from hotels or residences.

SEWELL'S SEA SAFARI Map pp228-9
☎ 604-921-3474; www.sewellsmarina.com; 6409 Bay St, Horseshoe Bay, West Vancouver; adult/child under 12 $55/25; ☾ 10am, 1pm & 4pm; bus 250
Sewell's offers a rollicking two-hour adventure in a high-speed, 26ft inflatable boat. Harbor seals are among the featured wildlife, but you will likely see eagles, too, plus you get a chance to check out the steep cliffs of Howe Sound and some of West Van's outrageously pricey seafront homes. It can be a cold and bouncy ride, but visitors are suited up in cushiony red coveralls to absorb some of the bite. A shuttle bus may be available for pick-ups from downtown.

STANLEY PARK HORSE-DRAWN
CARRIAGES Map pp240

☎ 604-681-5115; www.stanleyparktours.com;
departures near information booth, just off Georgia
St entrance to Stanley Park; adult/child 3-12/senior
& student 13-19 $22/14/20; ⏱ every 20-30 min,
9:40am-4pm mid-Mar–Jun & Sep-Oct, 9:40am-5:30pm
Jul-Aug; bus 19

These narrated, one-hour tours are a leisurely
and informative way to see the park. Clydesdale
and Grey Shire horses pull the 20-passenger carriages by all the park highlights. A free shuttle
bus runs from select downtown and West End
hotels to the departure point six times a day.

TAKAYA TOURS

☎ 604-904-7410; www.takayatours.com; most departures from Deep Cove, North Vancouver; tours $25-135;
⏱ May–early Oct; bus 212

Takaya Tours is owned by the Tsleil-Waututh
Nation of North Vancouver and offers eco-
tours highlighting the history and culture of
the Coast Salish peoples. One of the most
popular tours is the two-hour trip ($55) in a
traditional canoe through gorgeous Indian
Arm fjord. Takaya also offers traditional dance
performances, a nature walk, a full-moon
paddle, kayaking lessons and overnight kayaking trips.

DOWNTOWN

*Walking & Cycling Tours pp82–3; Eating pp94–6; Shopping pp152–4;
Sleeping pp169–72*

What sets Vancouver apart from the world's other great cities is best
demonstrated downtown. You have the skyscrapers, big business,
and high finance of a prosperous modern metropolis. Suit-clad
men and women scurry around generating the money that makes
Vancouver the economic engine behind all of western Canada.

But turn a couple of downtown corners and look up to see spectacular views of the Pacific Ocean and rugged peaks of the Coast
Mountains. And they're not far in the offing – excellent beaches are
a 10-minute walk from the city center, and those mountains are but a 20-minute drive away. It's
amazing, and a bit baffling, how such a contemporary city rests amid such splendid nature.

Most visitors will spend a fair bit of time downtown. It's a major transport center, with cruise
ships sailing into **Canada Place** and the SkyTrain and SeaBus chugging into **Waterfront Station**. The
sports stadiums and major theaters are here, as are most clubs and the infamous red-eyed 'Little
Amsterdam' quarter. Walking tours with the **Architectural Institute of British Columbia** (p40) help you
get acquainted with notable buildings, such as the library, law courts and art gallery.

Orientation

Downtown radiates from the intersection of W Georgia and Granville Sts, where the business, financial and shopping areas meld into one. The two principal east–west streets are W
Georgia St and, one block south, Robson St. The main north–south streets are, from west to

---

Transportation

SkyTrain Downtown's northern half is well served by Waterfront, Burrard, Granville and Stadium stations.

Bus No 1 travels along Pacific St at the southern edge of downtown near False Creek; bus 2 goes along Burrard St; bus 4
goes along Granville en route to UBC; bus 10 runs along Hastings and Granville Sts; bus 15 goes from Granville Station
along Hornby and Smithe Sts to Cambie St; bus 20 runs along Seymour St and E Hastings en route to Commercial Dr;
and bus 240 travels along Georgia St.

SeaBus The SeaBus travels between Waterfront Station and Lonsdale Quay in North Vancouver.

Mini Ferry Boats to Granville Island dock at the foot of Hornby St.

Car Downtown street parking is a chore. Meters are everywhere, cost $1 to $2 per hour and are in effect daily. Parkades
make life easier, if more expensive; convenient ones include 900 W Cordova St (per half hour $2, daily maximum $10,
evening/weekend flat rate $4) by Canada Place; 777 Dunsmuir St (per half hour $1.50, daily maximum $12, evening/
weekend flat rate $4) at Pacific Centre; and 688 Cambie St (per hour for the first two hours $1, per additional hour $2,
daily maximum $6, evening/weekend flat rate $8) near the stadiums.

east: Burrard, Howe, Granville and Seymour. Two bodies of water sandwich downtown – False Creek to the south, and Burrard Inlet to the north.

North of W Georgia St, bordered by Howe and Burrard Sts, is the office, banking and financial district. At the water's edge at the foot of Howe St is impressive Canada Place, with its five jagged white 'sails.' Much of Granville St, from Nelson St north to W Hastings St, is closed to cars (though it's not a true pedestrian mall, as buses and service and emergency vehicles are permitted). South on Granville St, between Drake and Robson Sts, is the slightly seedy club strip peppered with pawn shops, peep shows, and hip club-clothes stores. The stadiums and playhouses are east near Beatty and Georgia Sts, while the pot (marijuana) cafés are sequestered near the corner of Hastings and Cambie Sts.

Top Five Downtown, Gastown & West End

- **Canada Place** (p43)
- **Coal Harbour Seawalk** (p50)
- **English Bay Beach** (p50)
- **Robson Street** (p50)
- **Vancouver Police Museum** (p47)

BC PLACE STADIUM Map pp230-3

☎ 604-669-2300; 777 Pacific Blvd South; SkyTrain Stadium

Opened in 1983, BC Place was once the toast of the town, but now some want to tear it down. Personal opinions aside, there's no denying that the marshmallow of its translucent dome-shaped roof is unique. The quilted appearance is due to crisscrossing steel wires holding down the air-supported Teflon roof. The 60,000-seat venue is home to the BC Lions (p140) of the Canadian Football League. It also hosts concerts, trade shows and other sporting events. Swell **tours** (☎ 604-661-7362; adult/child/concession $6/5/4) take you into the locker rooms and celebrity suites; they depart from Gate H at 11am and 1pm Tuesday and Friday from mid-June to early September.

In front of the stadium is the **Terry Fox Memorial** – a postmodern-style arch made of steel, tile and brick, and topped by four fiberglass lions. It's a tribute to Fox, whose one-legged run across Canada to raise money for cancer research was cut short by his own fight with the disease, which ended when he was 22.

BC SPORTS HALL OF FAME & MUSEUM Map pp230-3

☎ 604-687-5520; Gate A, BC Place Stadium; adult/child 6-17/family $6/4/15; ☼ 10am-5pm, closed Mon Labour Day–Victoria Day; SkyTrain Stadium

Located inside BC Place Stadium, the small but excellent Sports Hall of Fame showcases top BC athletes, both amateur and professional, with special galleries devoted to each decade in sports, as well as to Terry Fox and his 'Marathon of Hope' across Canada, and Rick Hanson's 'Man-in-Motion' worldwide wheelchair journey.

CANADA PLACE Map pp230-3

☎ 604-647-7390; north foot of Howe St; SkyTrain Waterfront

This leviathan is a major city landmark with its distinctive five white 'sails' jutting into the harbor. The promenade circling the complex has wonderful views of the mountains, Stanley Park, and floatplanes splashing up and down; information plaques point out Vancouver's major historical moments. Built for Expo '86, the building now houses a cruise ship terminal, the **CN IMAX Theatre** (p132), **Vancouver Convention & Exhibition Centre** (p217), **World Trade Centre**, **Pan Pacific Hotel** (p171) and retail shops. A new **interpretive center** describes the activities of Vancouver's port, Canada's largest, where more than 66.7 million tons of cargo worth $29 billion passes through annually.

CHRIST CHURCH CATHEDRAL

Map pp230-3

☎ 604-682-3848; 690 Burrard St; ☼ 10am-4pm, opening hr vary depending on services & events; SkyTrain Burrard

Completed in 1895, Christ Church Cathedral is the biggest and best Gothic-style church in the city, nestled amid the glass towers of the business district. Originally an Anglican parish church for what was then a residential neighborhood, it became a cathedral in 1929. Fresh from a $9.6 million restoration, it's worth a visit to see the stained-glass windows (check out the William Morris beauty in the basement).

GM PLACE Map pp230-3

☎ 604-899-7889; 800 Griffiths Way; SkyTrain Stadium

Also known as 'the Garage,' this 20,000-seat venue is adjacent to BC Place. It is swankier and has better acoustics than its neighbor. This is where the Vancouver Canucks (p141) of the National Hockey League play home games, and it hosts concerts. **Tours** (☎ 604-899-7440; adult/child 4-12/senior & student $9/4/6) go into the locker rooms (sans players) at 10:30am, noon and 1:30pm Wednesday and Friday.

LITTLE AMSTERDAM Map pp230-3
north side of W Hastings St btwn Richards & Cambie Sts; SkyTrain Waterfront
Vancouver's 'Little Amsterdam' is packed into W Hastings St at the seamy edge of Gastown. The **BC Marijuana Party** (☎ 604-684-7076; www .bcmarijuanaparty.ca; 307 W Hastings St), a legitimate provincial governmental party that garnered 3.5% of the vote recently, is head-quartered here. A gaggle of stores sell grow guides, mushroom kits and hemp clothes, as well as the to-be-expected array of pipes, pa-pers and bongs.

There are also a couple of cafés where you can smoke 'em if you got 'em (just do so in the designated room). Note that you can't buy drugs at these places. It's still illegal to sell pot in Canada and illegal to possess it. The laws are slowly being bent and, for whatever reason, the police overlook what goes on in this area.

Since Blunt Brothers burned down (a 're-spectable joint' that acted as the area's an-chor), the munchie options have slimmed. Cafés like the **New Amsterdam** (☎ 604-682-8955; 301 W Hastings St) don't offer much beyond a Snickers bar or pack of M&Ms, though it may have picked up the slack by the time you read this.

MARINE BUILDING Map pp230-3
355 Burrard St; ⏱ 8am-6pm Mon-Fri; SkyTrain Burrard
The Marine Building is a fantastic, 22-story, art deco tribute to Vancouver's maritime history. Sea horses, waves and marine fauna are de-picted on a frieze around the building's front, while a ship's prow sails over the Burrard St en-trance. Step into the ornate lobby to see more creatures on the walls and doors. For 10 years, it was the tallest building in the British Empire.

PENDULUM GALLERY Map pp230-3
☎ 604-879-7714; HSBC Bank Bldg, 885 W Georgia St; ⏱ 9am-6pm Mon-Wed, 9am-9pm Thu-Fri, 9am-5pm Sat; SkyTrain Granville
Located in the sunny atrium of the HSBC Bank Building, the gallery's namesake centerpiece is a funky work of kinetic art called *Pendulum*. The 27m-long buffed aluminum sculpture,

designed by Alan Storey, is hollow from top to bottom, weighs 1600kg and moves about 6m (the swing is assisted by a hydraulic me-chanical system at its top). The public exhibits around the piece change regularly.

PROVINCIAL LAW COURTS Map pp230-3
219 Smithe St; ⏱ 8:30am-4:30pm Mon-Fri; bus 5
The series of waterfalls on the outside wall of Arthur Erickson's law courts is only a glimpse of the tranquility that lies within. It may not be your usual sight but the architecture that went into creating this sloped glass–roofed work of art is truly incredible. You don't have to stay long, and you should be quiet since these are real law courts (35 courtrooms are in here, to be exact), but it's remarkably relax-ing walking through the atrium up to the 7th floor with nothing but natural light showing the way.

ROBSON SQUARE Map pp230-3
btwn Hornby, Howe, Smithe & Robson Sts; bus 5
Between the law courts and the art gallery is Robson Square, an outdoor concrete plaza with waterfalls, fountains and steps staggered in all directions. It's a great place to just sit, think and watch Vancouver. The development goes under Robson St and houses a few cafés, as well as UBC's downtown campus. Rob-son Square merges into the law courts and, like them, was designed by Arthur Erickson (p20).

VANCOUVER ART GALLERY Map pp230-3
☎ 604-662-4700; www.vanartgallery.bc.ca; 750 Hornby St; adult/student 13 & over/senior $15/10/11, admission by donation 5-9pm Thu; ⏱ 10am-5:30pm, to 9pm Thu, closed Mon in winter; SkyTrain Granville or bus 5
Modernist Emily Carr's swirling, bold-stroked paintings of mountain, forest and aboriginal scenes are the main attraction of Vancouver Art Gallery and her work takes up the en-tire 4th floor; Carr is BC's best-known artist (see the boxed text on p27), and the museum owns the largest collection of her work in the world. The other floors shuffle temporary exhibits among a permanent collection that focuses on regional landscape artists and contemporary photo-based works. The hand-some, late-19th-century building used to be the courthouse, and rumor has it that a ghost still roams underground where the holding cells were. The Gallery Café, which over-looks the Sculpture Garden, is a great place to stop for coffee and a snack. The Gallery

Shop is also worth a look, with especially good gifts and local crafts.

VANCOUVER LOOKOUT! Map pp230-3

☎ 604-689-0421; www.vancouverlookout.com; Harbour Centre Tower, 555 W Hastings St; adult/child 5-10/student/senior $10/4/7/9; ☼ 8:30am-10:30pm May-Sep, 9am-9pm Oct-Apr; SkyTrain Waterfront

A glass elevator whisks visitors 169m up to the space needle–like viewing area, from where awesome 360° panoramas unfurl. Educational plaques and hourly tours reveal nuggets of information that help you get your bearings before heading out to see the sights. Tickets are pricey, but they're valid all day and coming back at night is fun; check the website for coupons. Vancouver Lookout! is free if you're dining at the restaurant on top, but better eateries are nearby. Another view option is the Empire Landmark's **Cloud Nine Lounge** (p125), with great vistas for the price of a drink.

VANCOUVER PUBLIC LIBRARY

Map pp230-3

☎ 604-331-3600; www.vpl.ca; 350 W Georgia St; ☼ 10am-9pm Mon-Thu, 10am-6pm Fri & Sat, 1-5pm Sun; SkyTrain Stadium

This terracotta-colored, Roman Colosseum–like building is one hell of a library. Oddly enough, Moshe Safdie, the architect, insists there's no connection between his $100 million design and the Italian original. Built in 1995, it houses 1.2 million books and other items spread out on seven levels, plus a 21-story office building. Overarching it all is an enviro-friendly, plant-covered 'green' roof. The awesome glass atrium is filled with tables and cafés perfect for whiling away time reading newspapers, writing letters or just general slacking, or join the throngs basking on the outdoor steps.

WATERFRONT STATION/ SEABUS TERMINAL Map pp230-3

Cordova St btwn Granville & Seymour Sts; SkyTrain Waterfront

Opened in 1915, this heritage building was originally the old Canadian Pacific Railway (CPR) station as well as being the western terminus for transcontinental passenger trains. These days it houses an array of offices, cafés and retail shops, and acts as a hub for Sky-Train and SeaBus. Be sure and hop aboard the latter for the 12-minute crossing to Lonsdale Quay (p75); while it's no thrill ride, SeaBus does provide a cool duck's-eye view of harbor life as you toodle by cruise ships, barges and freighters.

GASTOWN

Walking & Cycling Tours pp86–7; Eating p96; Shopping pp154–6; Sleeping p172

Gastown's major attraction is Gastown itself – cobblestone streets, old-fashioned lampposts and Victorian heritage buildings are some of its open-air exhibits.

The area is Vancouver's birthplace, and 'Gastown' was Vancouver's first official name. Where did the moniker come from? The most believed theory revolves around an Englishman named 'Gassy' Jack Deighton, a character and windbag of a storyteller. The story goes that in 1867 Deighton rowed into Burrard Inlet with his First Nations wife, a yellow dog and a barrel of whiskey, and told the area's mill workers that if they helped him build a tavern, drinks were on him. Within 24 hours the Globe Saloon was in business. When a village sprang up around the establishment, it was called Gastown.

The Great Fire of 1886 wiped out most of the settlement. By 1887 it was back in business, thanks to the arrival of the transcontinental Canadian Pacific Railway. Eventually the center of Vancouver moved westward, and Gastown hit hard times, returning to the dirty, muddy place it started as.

For many years it was an unsavory skid row. Just as the city was about to bulldoze it, a group of preservationists in the 1970s got the provincial government to declare the neighborhood a heritage site (it's one of two in the city, Chinatown being the other one). Thus began a concerted effort to restore the district, which pushed Vancouver's seedier characters further east toward Main and Hastings Sts.

Locals will tell you they don't come to Gastown much, and it's mostly a place where cruise-ship tourists come to buy fudge, T-shirts and First Nations trinkets. That's true to an extent, but the old Victorian buildings – now housing restaurants, bars, boutiques and galleries – have a certain charm, and the area's role as Vancouver's progenitor is undeniable. It's not a good place to be at night, but during the day it's safe enough.

Gastown's draws include the beers at **Steamworks Brewing Company** (p124) and the grisly but fascinating **Police Museum** (p47). To learn more about the area's rich history, take a free, 90-minute **Historic Gastown Walking Tour** (☎ 604-683-5650). Tours begin at Maple Tree Square at 2pm from mid-June to August.

Orientation

Water St, north of W Hastings St between Richards and Columbia Sts, is the main thoroughfare where most of the attractions are found. However, Gastown does branch off to a couple of side streets – Cambie and Abbott Sts – and continues a block or so off streets that intersect at Maple Tree Square: Alexander, Powell and Carrall Sts. Go east a few blocks beyond this and you'll enter the squalid Main and Hastings St zone. Both Hastings and Cordova Sts east of Abbott St heading toward Chinatown are lined with shelters, Salvation Army facilities, cheap hotels and thin, haunted-looking residents.

Transportation

SkyTrain/SeaBus Both modes of transportation come into Waterfront Station, near Gastown's western edge. It's an easy walk to Water St from there.

Bus No 7 serves the area as it loops around Cordova, Powell and Pender Sts. Buses that travel along Hastings St (bus 10 or 20) are handy.

Car As in neighboring downtown and Yaletown, street parking in Gastown can be brutal. Look for lots at 160 Water St/155 E Cordova St (per half hour $1, daily maximum $12, evening/weekend maximum $4) and 107 E Cordova St (per hour $1.25, daily maximum $6, evening/weekend flat rate $3).

GASTOWN STEAM CLOCK Map p234
cnr Water & Cambie Sts; SkyTrain Waterfront

The much ballyhooed steam clock is a silly little landmark, though its charm is that it's the only one of its kind in the world. Misleadingly historic looking, it was built in 1977. Join the hordes waiting for it to belch steam and sound the quarter-hour like a train whistle, but keep this secret to yourself: the 'steam clock' is actually powered by electricity. Check out its interior workings through the side glass panels.

MAPLE TREE SQUARE Map p234

cnr Alexander, Powell & Carrall Sts; bus 7

Several sights are situated near the square, which is the original heart of Gastown. The **statue of Gassy Jack**, perched atop a whiskey barrel, rests in about the same place where the Globe Saloon stood. The **Byrnes Block** (2 Water St) was built shortly after the 1886 fire; it was one of the city's first brick buildings and stands on the site of Gassy Jack's second saloon, a two-story hotel and billiard parlor called Deighton House. In the 1960s it was also the first building in Gastown to be renovated. Behind the Byrnes Block is **Gaolers Mews** (12 Water St), the location of the city's first jail, customs house and home to Gastown's first constable, Jonathan Miller, who also held the posts of custom collector and postmaster. Today it houses an architect's office and the **Irish Heather** (p96) bistro. Also here is the **Mews**, a small square containing restaurants and shops.

STORYEUM Map p234

☎ 604-687-8142; www.storyeum.com; 142 Water St; adult/child 6-12/senior & student $22/16/19 May-Oct, $20/15/18 Nov-Apr; ☺ 9am-7pm May-Oct, 10am-6pm Nov-Apr; SkyTrain Waterfront

Gastown's newest attraction (opened in June 2004) relays BC's history through storytelling. An antidote to the stuffy display cases of most museums, visitors here move through a series of live-action theatres where they find out how the First Nations lived, what the gold rush was all about and how Canada became a nation. Some of the vignettes are pretty cheesy, but Storyeum's heart is in the right place, and you'll definitely leave with a richer understanding of local history. The 70-minute show takes place underground in an impressive venue the

Neon Capital

In the 1950s, Vancouver was home to the largest neon company in the world and was second only to Shanghai in neon per capita. The city was lit up with 18,000 neon signs, or one for every 19 residents. At the time, it was considered by pilots to be the best illuminated city in North America. Most of the signs that remain are in Chinatown and Gastown, including the fabulous glowing pig at **Save On Meats** (43 W Hastings St) and the colorful **Ovaltine Café** (251 E Hastings St) marker.

size of six hockey rinks; visitors are lowered down on a giant circular elevator.

VANCOUVER POLICE CENTENNIAL MUSEUM Map p234

☎ 604-665-3346; 240 E Cordova St; adult/senior & child 7-13 $6/4; ☺ 9am-3pm Mon-Fri, also 10am-3pm Sat May-Aug; bus 7

The Police Museum is a distinctive Vancouver highlight, provided you have a strong stomach. Housed in the city's former morgue and coroner's court, the macabre displays include an autopsy room with pieces of damaged body parts posted on the wall (note the brain with a .22 caliber bullet in it) and an exhibit describing how to determine a corpse's age via insects (blowflies appear in 15 days, cheese-skippers in 40 days). Visitors can also see what a 1oz lump of heroin looks like, sit behind the wheel of a real police cruiser, or examine the bad-ass case of weaponry that includes a braided nylon flail with U-nails and gangster-era Thompson submachine gun. The museum is located at Gastown's far eastern edge, en route to Chinatown.

YALETOWN

Walking & Cycling Tours pp89–90; Eating pp97–8; Shopping p156; Sleeping pp172–3

Yaletown, with its new young money, is often compared to New York City's SoHo. This is Vancouver's trendiest neighborhood (why else would the Mini Cooper car showroom be here?), a former rail yard whose warehouses have been converted to brick lofts and whose loading docks now serve as popular restaurant patios. Hummers, BMWs and shiny convertibles sparkle in front of the many oyster and martini bars. Cigar shops, day spas, designer furniture stores and upscale grocery stores selling $100 baguettes from Paris feed the needs of the urban professionals living here.

Yaletown's come a long way, baby. The area was originally populated by Canadian Pacific Railway workers who settled there in the late 19th century to be close to the rail yards that amalgamated near False Creek. Many of these men had worked at the CPR yards in Yale, about 180km northeast of Vancouver, hence the neighborhood name. Yaletown thrived as Vancouver's industrial core until the 1940s, when highways replaced rail for goods transport. By the 1970s, Yaletown was known for its rough bars and derelict warehouses, where getting beaten up was a distinct possibility for visitors.

Expo '86 helped the city rediscover the neighborhood. City planners designated it a historic district. First came the artists seeking studio space, then the bohemian coffee shops and galleries, and then those who prospered in the 1990s economic boom, primarily tech types riding the dot.com wave. A lot of the latter not only live here, but have their offices in the minimalist, high-ceilinged warehouses, too.

Today Yaletown is the see-and-be-seen place to eat, drink, window-shop and revel in all the luxe, especially if you have lots of disposable income. No real attractions exist here besides the Roundhouse Community Centre. **Urban Fare** (p93) is fun to wander through and sniff the pricey bread, while Yaletown Landing is a good place to jump into a mini ferry (assuming you don't possess your own yacht) and make a beeline for Granville Island.

Transportation
Bus No 1 proceeds from the West End to Yaletown along Pacific Blvd and Davie St; bus 15 stops at the intersection of Nelson and Cambie Sts.
Mini Ferry Ferries dock at Yaletown Landing at the foot of Davie St.
Car So many hipsters with gleaming wheels, yet so little street parking. Head for the lots at 1180 Mainland St (per half hour for first two hours $1, per additional half hour $1.50, daily maximum $10, evening/weekend flat rate $4), 1321 Richards St (per hour $1, daily maximum $7, evening/weekend flat rate $3) or at the Roundhouse Community Centre (per hour $1, daily maximum $6, evening flat rate $2).

Orientation

Trim Yaletown consists of about seven blocks, roughly bound by Nelson, Homer and Drake Sts and Pacific Blvd. Hamilton and Homer Sts contain most of the posh restaurants and martini bars.

Neon signs like this one in SoMa are a feature of Vancouver (see the boxed text on p47)

ROUNDHOUSE COMMUNITY CENTRE

Map pp230-3

☎ 604-713-1800; www.roundhouse.ca; 181 Roundhouse Mews, cnr Davie St & Pacific Blvd; ⏰ hr vary; bus 1

Those interested in the Canadian Pacific Railway's history should visit the Roundhouse, formerly a CPR repair shed. It now houses Engine No 374, which brought the first passenger train into the city in 1887. The center also provides a variety of arts (p210) and fitness classes.

Top Five Places to Escape the Crowds

- **Provincial Law Courts** (p44)
- **Roedde House** (p50)
- **Dr Sun Yat-Sen Park** (p55)
- **Spanish Banks Beach** (p64)
- **Nitobe Memorial Garden** (p64)

WEST END

Eating pp98–100; Shopping pp156–7; Sleeping pp173–6

The West End – not to be confused with the West Side (p59) across False Creek and English Bay, or with West Vancouver (p76) on the North Shore – ranks as one of Vancouver's most appealing neighborhoods, harboring sandy beaches, shaded walkways, sidewalk cafés, and plentiful trails for biking, running and rollerblading. No wonder more people live here than anywhere else in the city, packed into the myriad glassy high-rises that burst up from the landscape. The West End is also the heart of the city's gay community, and its buff residents are, on average, younger than the rest of the city (50% are between 20 and 40 years old).

In 1862 the only people who lived in this area were a small group of Musqueam and Squamish Indians, who had lived here for about 3000 years, and three settlers from England. 'The three greenhorns,' as they came to be known, paid $550 for a parcel of land that covered pretty much the same area as today's West End. When the Canadian Pacific Railroad came to town in 1885, it purchased much of this property and slowly developed it for high-priced homes. English Bay became the preferred area for the wealthy to build their mansions.

The high-rise craze hit in the mid-1950s. Until then, the eight-story **Sylvia Hotel** (p175), built in 1912, reigned as the area's tallest building, surrounded by houses and three-story apartment blocks. The city decided it wanted to attract more people to the downtown shopping and business district, and that high-rises would be the best way to do it. During a 13-year period 220 apartment buildings went up, and in so doing took away many of the fine old buildings that had made the West End such a gracious place to live. Fortunately, a few of these properties survived and have since been designated as heritage homes, mostly around Barclay Heritage Square.

For the visitor, the West End is a lively place to spend time. The Coal Harbour Seawalk and English Bay Beach provide ample opportunities to get out and soak up the glorious scenery. If food, drink and shopping are your thing, the neighborhood runneth over with restaurants, bars, cafés and retail outlets, especially on Robson St. It all stays open from morning to late at night, especially during summertime.

Orientation

The West End is generally defined as the area west of Burrard St, bordered to the

Transportation

SkyTrain Burrard Station is convenient for Robson St.

Bus No 1 runs from Burrard Station along Burrard and Davie Sts and Beach Ave; bus 5 travels primarily along Robson and Denman Sts; buses 2 and 22 run along Burrard St; and bus 240 proceeds along Georgia St.

Mini Ferry Ferries go from Sunset Beach's Aquatic Centre to Vanier Park and Granville Island.

Car The neighborhood's dense population makes parking a nightmare. Residential streets are either metered or restricted. Try the lots at 490 Broughton St (per hour $2, daily maximum $8, evening/weekend flat rate $4) or 900 Denman St (per hour $1, daily maximum $2, evening/weekend flat rate $3).

Walking, Bicycle & Skates The seawall fringes Coal Harbour, English Bay Beach and Sunset Beach.

north by Coal Harbour, to the west by Stanley Park, to the south by English Bay and to the east by downtown.

Three major streets run through the area, each about seven blocks long: north–south Denman St, a strip dominated by a vast range of mid-priced restaurants, gelato parlors, and bicycle and in-line skate rental shops; east–west Davie St, lined with flower shops, bohemian coffee bars, greengrocers, and gay art and erotica stores; and east–west Robson St, with innumerable eateries, trendy designer shops and boutique chain stores.

COAL HARBOUR SEAWALK Map p240
north foot of Thurlow St; SkyTrain Waterfront
Pick up this path a few blocks west of Canada Place, near the floatplane terminals. It winds along the water for 1km or so before hooking up Stanley Park's seawall near Denman St. It's a lovely walk with high-rises glinting in the background, the sea twinkling in the foreground and sailboats bobbing under buzzing, toy-like seaplanes. The path runs right by the **Coal Harbour Community Centre** (p210) and a lively dog park; plenty of benches and bistros provide command posts from where you can watch it all.

ENGLISH BAY BEACH Map pp230-3
west foot of Davie St; bus 1
Whether it's a hot, still day in August with families and sunbathers mobbing the beach, or a blustery day in November with just you and a dog-walker watching the waves pound the shore, English Bay is magnificent. It's a premier place to picnic, gaze at the freighters moored offshore and view golden sunsets.

Facing out to the bay at the foot of Bidwell St is *Inukshuk*, a 6m, 31,500kg figure of an ancient Inuit symbol traditionally used as a hunting aid and navigational landmark, as well as an emblem of welcome. It was moved here in 1987 after being a part of the Northwest Territories' pavilion at Expo '86.

ROBSON STREET Map pp230-3
btwn Burrard & Denman Sts; bus 5
Locals, international tourists and recent immigrants all throng to the hotels, eateries and shops along Robson St. It's a mix of high- and not-so-high-class places, ie a hole-in-the-wall

noodle shop filled with homesick Japanese students may reside next to a pricey bistro filled with Hollywood power brokers. The eclectic shops are fun to browse – you can find everything from Giorgio Armani suits to hologram portraits of Elvis, to fancy condom shops and the mammoth **Virgin Megastore** (p157).

ROEDDE HOUSE & BARCLAY HERITAGE SQUARE Map pp230-3
☎ 604-684-7040; www.roeddehouse.org; 1415 Barclay St; adult/senior & child $4/3; ☽ 10am-4pm Mon-Sat mid-Jun–Aug, 2-4pm Wed-Fri & Sun Sep–mid-Jun; bus 5
The 1893 Queen Anne–style Roedde House is a superb re-creation of how well-heeled Vancouverites lived back when the city was a pioneer town nestled among virgin rain forests. Designed by famed and shamed architect Francis Rattenbury (see p184), the house is packed with period antiques and the surrounding gardens planted in period style. Entry on Sunday costs $1 more and includes tea. The abode is the showpiece of **Barclay Heritage Square**, a one-block site containing nine historic West End houses dating from 1890 to 1908. The houses give a sense of what the area was like before the high-rises took over.

SUNSET BEACH Map pp230-3
along Beach Ave, west of Burrard Bridge; bus 1
This is actually a strip of sandy beaches running along False Creek, sprinkled with colossal driftwood logs that serve as windbreaks and privacy providers. As the name implies, it's a good place to watch the sun drop. Swimmers will enjoy the **Aquatic Centre** (p147).

STANLEY PARK
Walking & Cycling Tours pp84–5; Eating pp100–1
Resting atop the city like a crown jewel, **Stanley Park** (☎ 604-257-8400; www.city.vancouver.bc.ca/parks; admission free; ☽ 24hr) is a 404-hectare forest of cedar, hemlock and fir, mingled with meadows, lakes, beaches and cricket pitches. On a sunny day, it seems all of Vancouver is here hiking, cycling and jogging through the woods. As the refuge is one of North America's largest urban parks, there's room for everyone.

Canada's Governor General Lord Stanley (the same man who lent his name to the National Hockey League's prestigious Stanley Cup trophy) opened the park in 1889 with these words: 'To the use and enjoyment of people of all colors, creeds and customs for all time.' Today it's estimated that eight million visitors come to the park annually, making it Vancouver's most popular attraction.

It's a must-visit place, one of those rare draws that outshines its hype. It's probably best viewed while pedaling a bicycle (p84) along the Seawall Promenade, which brings you by totem poles, Siwash Rock, Second and Third Beaches, and several other points of interest. The Vancouver Aquarium is the other big attraction.

The visitor **Information Centre** (☎ 604-681-6728; ⊙ 10am-4pm, later in summer) by the park's main entrance east of Georgia St provides good maps and has bathrooms. The horse-drawn carriages (p42) depart from there.

Transportation

Bus No 19 stops near the park's entrance and by the Children's Farmyard; catch it downtown as it routes along Pender St to Nicola St, then moves over to Georgia St. Once inside the park, the **Stanley Park Shuttle** (☎ 604-257-8400; admission free) makes 14 stops at points of interest throughout the park; departs every 15 minutes from 10am to 6:30pm from mid-June to late September.

Car Several pay lots speckle the park (hour/day Apr-Sep $2/5, Oct-Mar $1/3), with plenty of spaces available.

Walking, Bicycle & Skates The 9km Seawall Promenade skirts the park's perimeter.

Tours See p42 for details of hour-long horse-drawn carriage tours.

Orientation

The park sits northwest of downtown. Entering the park, W Georgia St becomes Stanley Park Causeway, which cuts through the park's center and goes over the Lions Gate Bridge. The causeway is not to be confused with Stanley Park Dr, the road that travels around the park's perimeter. The Seawall Promenade parallels Stanley Park Dr through most of the park.

North of the information center you'll find Painters Circle (where artists work and sell their paintings), the outdoor summer theater **Malkin Bowl** (p135), the Rose Garden, aquarium, and Children's Farmyard and Miniature Railway.

CHILDREN'S FARMYARD & MINIATURE RAILWAY Map p240

☎ 604-257-8531 railway, farmyard 604-257-8530; adult/child 2-12/senior/youth 13-18 $5/2.50/3.50/3.75; ⊙ 11am-4pm Sat & Sun Mar-May, 11am-4pm daily Jun–early Sep; park shuttle bus

Near the aquarium is the Children's Farmyard & Miniature Railway, where youngsters can interact with llamas, sheep, goats, cows, hens and other small animals, and everyone, no matter what their age, will enjoy the 15-minute train ride. The engines are replicas of actual locomotives, one being engine No 374 that pulled the first passenger train into Vancouver (see the real deal at Yaletown's **Roundhouse**, p49). Note that this little railway carries more passengers annually than all Vancouver's cruise ships combined.

SEAWALL PROMENADE Map p240

The 9km Seawall Promenade – ideal for cycling, walking, jogging and in-line skating – hugs the park's shoreline. Keep in mind that cyclists and skaters, like vehicles, must travel counterclockwise around the park, and it can get crowded on weekends. Points of interest on the route, in order of appearance, include:

Deadman's Island Today used as a naval reserve, though its history is more illustrious: it has been a First Nations burial site; a quarantine station during the smallpox epidemic of 1888–90; a logging camp; a squatters' village; the site of numerous jurisdictional battles; and, since 1943, a military installation (called HMCS *Discovery*).

Top Five Stanley Park, Chinatown & Granville Island

- Seawall Promenade (p51)
- Granville Island Public Market (p59)
- Dr Sun Yat-Sen Classical Chinese Garden (p55)
- Vancouver Aquarium Marine Science Centre (p53)
- Science World (p55)

Bridging the Gap Across First Narrows

Among the many bridges that cross the Lower Mainland's waterways, it is the Lions Gate Bridge that stands out as a Vancouver icon.

The Guinness family led the charge to build it. Its British Pacific Syndicate had paid $50 a hectare for 1600 hectares on Hollyburn Ridge in West Vancouver, and they were keen to sell the lots on what had come to be known as British Properties. However, it took several years for the development to be approved, as the plan to build a 2.4km causeway through the center of Stanley Park was a contentious issue. Construction finally began in 1936, and the project was completed in 1938 at a cost of $6 million. The Guinness family came back into the picture in 1986, when they donated the bridge's lights.

As the years passed, residents increasingly criticized Lions Gate Bridge as inadequate for handling traffic needs. In the early 1990s, the provincial government examined a variety of plans to solve the issue: build a tunnel under the inlet, build a new, larger bridge or widen the current bridge's span. In total, more than 90 technical reports were evaluated.

In July 1999, the government began a $99.8 million rehabilitation project of the existing structure, a plan deemed 'clearly superior' to other options for reasons of cost effectiveness and compatibility with existing roads. Improvements included a seismic upgrade and widened traffic lanes. Many residents complain it's still not enough, especially when they're sitting in snarled 'bridge traffic' during rush hour.

Brockton Point The name refers to the eastern end of the park as well as the eastern tip of the peninsula. The area contains **Brockton Oval** playing field and cricket pitch, a good collection of **totem poles** from several different First Nations people (the adjacent information center explains their origins), and the **Nine O'Clock Gun** on Hallelujah Point – an electrically fired cannon that sounds at 9pm nightly and was originally used by ships' captains to set their chronometers. The **Brockton Point Lighthouse** was completed in 1915. Around the point, the **Chehalis Monument** commemorates the loss of a tugboat that was struck by the CPR ship *Princess of Victoria* in 1906, killing nine of the 15 people aboard.

Lumberman's Arch Once a Coast Salish village, the area received its modern name from an arch donated by the Lumberman's and Shingleman's Society. The **Variety Kids Water Park** is beside the structure. Just east of the arch are *Girl in a Wetsuit*, a bronze **statue** by Elek Imredy, and the **ship's figurehead** of the SS *Empress of Japan* that commemorates Vancouver's early trade with Asia.

Prospect Point It's one of Vancouver's most glorious lookouts, off the park's northern tip. Until 1939 there was a beacon on the bluffs, but this was removed, leaving only the terraces and steps, which provide great views of the **Lions Gate Bridge** (see boxed text above), First Narrows and passing ships. The cairn here commemorates the 1888 wreck of the SS *Beaver*, a Hudson's Bay Company steamship that was the first to travel the entire west coast of North America. **Prospect Point Café** (p101) offers refreshments.

Siwash Rock As First Nations legend has it, this 15.2m monolith soaring just offshore is a Squamish warrior named Skalsh whom the god Q'uas the Transformer turned into a rock as a reward for being unselfish. Inland from Siwash is famous **Hollow Tree**, whose burnt-out remains once measured 18.3m in diameter.

Third Beach A popular place to swim or to enjoy the views, and maybe see a seal or bald eagle.

Ferguson Point Site of the **Pauline Johnson memorial fountain** and **cairn** that marks the grave of the First Nations poet (1861–1913), and the **Sequoia Grill** (p101).

Second Beach Rather more developed than Third Beach, and with a heated outdoor **swimming pool** (p147), a snack bar, a playground, a pitch-and-putt golf course, a lawn-bowling green, tennis courts and the **Fish House** (p101) restaurant.

Lost Lagoon At one time this was an extension of Coal Harbour, but by 1916 the bridge was replaced with a causeway, and in 1922 the body of water was given its name from a poem, *The Lost Lagoon*, written by Pauline Johnson. By 1929 it was a true freshwater lake. Today it's a wild-bird sanctuary and the path around it makes for a wonderful walk. The **Jubilee Fountain**, originally a feature at the Chicago World's Fair, was installed in 1936 to commemorate Vancouver's 50th anniversary. The **Lost Lagoon Nature House** (☎ 604-257-8544; foot of Alberni St; admission free; ☺ 10am-6pm Tue-Sun) provides exhibits on the park's history and attractions, and information on the shoreline, forest, wildlife and birds. Guided walks through the park leave at 1pm every Sunday, rain or shine; call for prices and for other scheduled events.

VANCOUVER AQUARIUM MARINE SCIENCE CENTRE Map p240

☎ 604-659-3474; www.vanaqua.org; adult/child 4-12/senior & youth 13-18 $16.50/9.50/12.50; ☟ 9:30am-7pm Jul & Aug, 10am-5:30pm Sep-Jun; shuttle bus

The aquarium, Canada's largest, swims with frisky dolphins, black-tip reef sharks, lazy sea lions, hypnotic jellyfish and – the most popular residents – beluga whales. It is one of the city's premier destinations, where there's just a sheet of glass between you and 60,000 creatures representing 300 species. Other exhibits include octopuses, eels, otters, and a wide variety of local sea life and freshwater fish. A standout exhibit is the Amazon Gallery, a re-creation of a tropical rain forest, complete with sloths, crocodiles, toucans, piranhas, tree frogs and hourly rainstorms. The aquarium is also Canada's largest marine mammal rescue-and-rehabilitation center. Inquire about the 45-minute behind-the-scenes tours with the animal training staff ($20 to $35) or all-night sleepovers ($83). Plan on spending at least half a day here.

CHINATOWN

Walking & Cycling Tours pp86–7; Eating pp101–2; Shopping p157

Exotic sights and sounds pervade Canada's largest Chinatown (and North America's third largest). You'll find families bargaining over a pineapple in a flurry of Cantonese, shops wafting the smell of sweet spice and sour fish; street vendors selling silk, jade and Hello Kitty footstools. At first glance, the steamy-windowed won-ton restaurants, gruesome butchers with pig snouts and flayed frogs, and ubiquitous firecracker-red awnings (red symbolizes good luck) make you believe you're in Hong Kong.

Chinatown has been around since before the City of Vancouver was incorporated in 1886. At that time, Shanghai Alley (close to what is now the intersection of Carrall and Pender Sts) housed a small Chinese settlement. Ironically, it was the Great Fire in 1886 that helped Chinatown develop further. In an attempt to rebuild the city, 60 hectares of forested land were leased to Chinese immigrants, who were given a 10-year rent-free agreement on the condition they clear and farm the land. By the end of 1886 almost 90 Chinese lived on Dupont St (now Pender St) west of Westminster Ave (now Main St) on farms yielding pigs or other produce.

It wasn't long before two-story wooden buildings sprang up along Pender and Carrall Sts, which became a gathering place for banking (to wire money home) and socializing, as well as providing shelter for new arrivals. The Chinese were enticed by the opportunity to make money working in sawmills, lumber camps, fish canneries, mines and on railroad construction gangs. In 1883 alone, of the nearly 2000 gold miners in BC, 1500 were Chinese, and during the period from 1881 to 1885 more than 11,000 Chinese arrived by ship to work on the construction of the CPR and were paid $1 a day; half what white workers were paid, but 95¢ more than they were paid at home.

Many locals will tell you that Chinatown isn't what it used to be, and that the 'real' Chinatown is now located in Richmond (p78), where most of Vancouver's Asian immigrants have landed in the last 10 years. What's more, Chinatown, along with Gastown, has contended for years with spillover from the blighted, high-crime Main and Hastings Sts area, which has sent many

Transportation

SkyTrain Two stations flank Chinatown: Stadium is about four blocks west, while Main St/Science World is about four blocks south (the latter is convenient for Science World, though not so good if you're trying to reach Chinatown's center, as you have to walk from the station along busy Main St).

Bus Take bus 19 or 22, both of which travel along Pender St (bus 19 continues on Main St), or any of the buses that travel along Hastings St, such as bus 10 or 20, and get off at Main St.

Mini Ferry Ferries sail to/from Science World.

Car Street parking poses a challenge. There are parkades at 801 Quebec St (per hour $1, daily maximum $3, evening/weekend flat rate $3), near Dr Sun Yat-Sen Garden; and 1500 Quebec St (per hour for first two hours $1, per additional hour $1.50, daily maximum $5, evening/weekend flat rate $3), near Science World.

Millenium Gate (below), Chinatown

shopkeepers packing and heading for the quiet of the suburbs. There's a definite hard edge to today's Chinatown, but still plenty of vitality to make it well worth a visit.

The dazzling, dragon-covered **Millennium Gate** at Taylor and Pender Sts heralds your arrival; it was originally used for the China pavilion at Expo '86. Just east on Pender St is the world's narrowest office building; you'll soon be wider than the building after stuffing your face at the surrounding restaurants and bakeries. The Dr Sun Yat-Sen Classical Chinese Garden & Park offers a calming study in yin and yang. The Night Market bustles on summer evenings (p157). And don't forget **Chinese New Year** (p8) celebrations if you visit during the lunar new year. Science buffs will appreciate the exhibits under Science World's futuristic dome, just south of Chinatown proper.

Orientation

Compact Chinatown is great for gazing and grazing. Most restaurants, tea shops, bakeries, butchers and herbalists reside along the section of Pender St from Abbott to Gore Sts, and on the part of Keefer St from Main to Gore Sts. Chinatown backs up against decaying Main and Hastings Sts to the north (see p46). Science World is four blocks south of central Chinatown, just west of Main St and nestled against False Creek. This area, near the intersection of Main St and Terminal Ave where Pacific Central Station (p206) is located, is rough at night.

CHINESE CULTURAL CENTRE
MUSEUM & ARCHIVES Map p234

☎ general 604-658-8850, tours 604-658-8883; www
.cccvan.com; 555 Columbia St; adult/senior, student &
child 6-12 $4/2.50, admission free Tue; ⏱ 11am-5pm
Tue-Sun; SkyTrain Stadium

It's worth visiting this museum to get a good understanding of Chinese history in Vancouver. Changing exhibits are on the main floor, while the 2nd floor's permanent collection high-lights Gold Rush history and Chinatown settlement. It also houses the Military Museum showcasing Chinese-Canadian soldiers' role in WWI and WWII. The museum is linked to the **Cultural Centre** (50 E Pender St), where visitors can sign up for short workshops (adult/senior and student $6/4) in calligraphy, t'ai chi and Chinese music (call for times), and/or Chinatown walking tours (adult/senior and student $10/7) at 10:30am and 1pm from June to September (call for other times).

DR SUN YAT-SEN CLASSICAL CHINESE GARDEN & PARK Map p234

☎ 604-662-3207; www.vancouverchinesegarden
.com; 578 Carrall St; garden adult/senior/student
$8.75/6.75/5.75, park free; ☺ 9:30am-7pm mid-Jun–
Aug, 10am-6pm May–mid-Jun & Sep, 10am-4:30pm
Oct-Apr; SkyTrain Stadium

This unassuming garden is a soothing sanctuary amid Chinatown's hubbub. Its jade-colored pools, stone paths, shaded pavilions and trees take you into a Zen-like state. To appreciate its subtle beauty (flowers play only a minor role), take the 45-minute tour (included with admission; running hourly in summer, reduced schedules in winter). Knowledgeable docents will offer you a cup of tea, then show you how the Taoist principles of yin and yang are incorporated throughout the grounds, ie how rugged and hard are offset by soft and flowing, dark is tempered by light, and large is tempered by small. Everything in the garden reflects balance and harmony, and every item – including the placement of each plant – has a specific purpose.

The garden is named after Dr Sun Yat-Sen, 'the father of modern China,' who overthrew the Qing dynasty in 1911 and was the Republic's first president. It's modeled after the classical gardens of the Ming dynasty (1368–1644) in Suzhou.

Adjacent to the garden is Dr Sun Yat-Sen Park. It's a bit more dowdy than its neighbor, but still a pleasant oasis of whispering grasses, a large fish pond, small pagoda and bridge. The entrance is behind the Dr Sun Yat-Sen bust in the Cultural Centre courtyard; there's another entrance on Columbia St near E Keefer St.

SAM KEE BUILDING Map p234

8 W Pender St; SkyTrain Stadium

This structure near the corner of Carrall St has made it into *The Guinness Book of Records* as the world's narrowest office building. It's easy to miss not only because of its thinness but because it looks like the front of the larger building behind, to which it is attached. It's currently used as an insurance company office, so there isn't much to see inside, but it's still nifty.

A businessman's vendetta against city hall led to the building's anorexic shape. Chang Toy, the Sam Kee Co's owner, bought land at this site in 1906, but in 1926 all but a 1.8m-wide strip was expropriated by the city as it widened Pender St. Toy's way of thumbing his nose at city officials was to build anyway, and up sprang the 'Slender on Pender' dwelling.

SCIENCE WORLD & ALCAN OMNIMAX THEATRE Map p234

☎ 604-443-7443; www.scienceworld.bc.ca; 1455
Quebec St; adult/senior, student & child 4-18/family
$12.75/8.50/42.50, IMAX show adult/child $17.75/13.50;
☺ 10am-5pm Mon-Fri, 10am-6pm Sat & Sun; SkyTrain
Main St-Science World or mini ferry; Ⓟ per 2hr $3

Inside the gleaming geodesic dome (or 'golf ball' as it's sometimes called, another remnant of Expo '86) are two levels of science, technology and natural-history exhibits filled with beeping and buzzing interactive displays. It's geared toward kids, though the gallery exploring sustainability issues is good, and the giant hamburger where you can learn how fast food is made is a hoot. Level 3 holds the 400-seat **Omnimax Theatre** (adult/senior, student & child $11.25/9), with one of the world's largest domed screens at five stories high and 27m in diameter.

SOUTH MAIN (SOMA)

Eating pp102–4; Shopping pp157–8

Call it what you will – SoMa (short for South Main), Mt Pleasant or the Main St Corridor – but this is Vancouver's newest contender for up-and-coming neighborhood. On a strip of Main St, its vintage stores are side by side with boutiques of on-the-rise local designers, making it one of the city's hottest shopping districts.

SoMa is another 'old' community that's been 'rediscovered,' akin to Yaletown or Commercial Dr (not as moneyed as the former or eccentric as the latter). It was a desolate place with an abundance of empty condom wrappers littering the ground, but it has been gentrifying gradually since the 1980s. The pace has picked up considerably in the last few years. The hookers and crack dens have retreated, lofts and condos have popped up, young creative professionals are moving in, and city planners are working to introduce a new library, community center and gardens.

SoMa's attractions are mostly what you can buy at the boutiques (where else can you get a $25 pair of hand-painted boxer shorts?) or shove into your gullet at the slew of restaurants (see p102). Further south is the Punjabi Market (below), where chai and dal flow freely.

Orientation

SoMa is on Main St from about 6th to 29th Aves. Hip restaurants and shops cluster between 6th and 10th, taper off between 11th and 19th Aves (mostly doctors' offices and second-hand stores), then pick up again at 20th. The designers' boutiques are bunched between 20th and 23rd Aves. A series of stores known as Antique Row are grouped between King Edward Rd and 29th Ave. Punjabi Market lies a fair way south on Main St between 48th and 51st Aves.

Transportation

Bus No 3 travels the length of Main St and can be caught downtown along Seymour St.
Car Street parking should be easy, but there's a lot at 199 E 7th Ave (per hour $1, daily maximum $4) if need be.

PUNJABI MARKET Map pp228-9
Main St btwn 48th & 51st Aves; bus 3

You won't find cows wandering the streets, or bicycle rickshaws weaving between the traffic, but many of the sounds, smells and colors of the subcontinent are condensed into this vibrant area, often referred to as 'Little India.' The commercial strip is lined with street signs in Punjabi, as well as food markets, sari and fabric shops, music stores, jewelers and, of course, restaurants (p104). Incidentally, there are more than 130,000 Indo-Canadians living throughout Greater Vancouver, of which about 99,000 are Sikhs.

Not in the market, but close enough to be worth the extra trip, is the **Sikh Temple** (Map pp228-9; ☎ 604-324-2010; 8000 Ross St; 8am-8pm; bus No 22), off SE Marine Dr near Knight St. Designed by Arthur Erickson, the building has the hallmarks of traditional Indian architecture. Visitors are welcome to look inside as long as they follow the prescribed customs. Women need to bring a scarf to cover their head; and you'll be asked to leave your shoes at the entrance.

EAST VANCOUVER

Walking & Cycling Tours pp87–8; Eating pp104–6; Shopping pp158–60; Sleeping p176

East Vancouver encompasses a large swathe of the city, literally and figuratively. It includes the Commercial Dr area, often referred to as Vancouver's 'mini UN' because it melds Italian, Portuguese, Latin American, Caribbean and Southeast Asian communities. Stir the pot some more by adding the artist, student and lesbian communities, who also live there and you've got the city's most culturally diverse quarter – a definite highlight. East Van also takes in Vancouver Harbour to the north and the blighted, junkie-laden area east of Main and Hastings Sts (see Gastown, p46, for further details).

The East End was historically where the working class lived. The region developed from the houses and businesses built for the people who worked in the mills and factories or along the waterfront. Throughout the 1900s, waves of immigrants arrived – Japanese, Russians, Ukrainians, Scandinavians – laying the foundation for the neighborhood's diversity.

Commercial Dr has its own unique past. It got its name in the early 1900s when it was the first road built along the interurban rail line from New Westminster to Vancouver (constructed in 1891), and it developed into a main shopping thoroughfare. From the 1950s to the 1970s the Italian community settled around Commercial Dr, and it was dubbed 'Little Italy.' You'll still find many family-owned cafés here serving traditional cappuccino and *panini*, and spot boccie tournaments in nearby parks.

Transportation

SkyTrain The Expo Line's Broadway Station and Millennium Line's Commercial Station are both near the intersection of E Broadway and Commercial Dr.
Bus No 20 travels along Commercial Dr to/from downtown (via Seymour St).
Car Street parking is widely available on Commercial Dr.

Neighborhoods – East Vancouver

Vancouver for Kids

Vancouver will keep the wee ones every bit as occupied as the adults in the crowd. For free publications and other resources on entertaining children, see p209.

King of the kid pleasers is **Vancouver Aquarium** (p53), drenched with whales, sharks and weird-looking fish. Kick it up a notch by staying overnight at one of the sleepovers in front of the beluga viewing tanks. You won't go wrong at the **Children's Farmyard & Miniature Railway** (p51), also in Stanley Park, where youngsters can pet llamas and ride a replica of a locomotive. If the tots aren't worn out yet, splash it up in the **Variety Kids Water Park** (p52) or Second Beach's family-friendly outdoor **swimming pool** (p147).

Granville Island's **Kids Market** (p59) reels 'em in with clowns, magicians, face painters and stores featuring everything from fun wet-weather gear to toys and puppets. The free **Water Park** (p59) nearby helps kids cool down after the market's excitement. Train enthusiasts will want to see the toy engines chugging through the mountainside at the **Model Train Museum** (p59).

In Vanier Park, the **HR MacMillan Space Centre** (p62) lets kids touch a real moon rock and blast off to Mars in the Virtual Voyages Simulator. They can climb aboard ships and wear pirate hats at the Vancouver Maritime Museum's **Children's Maritime Discovery Centre** (p63). In May the **Vancouver International Children's Festival** (p9), a family-oriented performing arts event, takes over the park.

Speaking of ships, why not take a **mini ferry** (p40) around False Creek or the **SeaBus** (p45) from Waterfront Station to Lonsdale Quay? Or get your aquatics fix at **VanDusen Botanical Garden** (p60), which provides a map and informative leaflet for a two-hour pond tour for little ones.

Kidsbooks (p164) has story readings and other events, in addition to mammoth stacks of children's books. See p118 for recommended restaurants.

Orientation

East Vancouver stretches a long way east from the boundary of Chinatown, all the way over to the suburb of Burnaby. The majority of the area is residential, with the attention focused on Commercial Dr; the main of Commercial Dr's action happens in the 17 blocks between E Broadway and Venables St.

COMMERCIAL DRIVE Map p235
btwn Broadway Ave & Venables St; bus 20

The Drive, like Wreck Beach (p65), is one of those special Vancouver places where anything goes. Old-world bakery aromas mingle with the smell of patchouli and pot wafting down the street. Shops advertise mediums who will read your palm or communicate with your spirit animal. Leather pants-wearing skateboarders glide down the sidewalk by dainty girls with monstrous tattoos. And this is undoubtedly the only place in the city where you can shop for a talisman, soy wax candles, belly-dancing supplies and a Che Guevara backpack in one fell swoop. The Drive's eclectic ethnic restaurants (p104) – many with patios – are a good perch from which to watch the madness.

GRANVILLE ISLAND

Walking & Cycling Tours pp88–9; Eating pp106 & 115; Shopping pp160–1; Sleeping p176

Fifteen hectares brimming with artisan studios, theaters, bars with eye-popping views, and a bountiful public market – it may have taken 100 years or so, but you've got to admit Granville Island has finally hit upon the right mix.

In the beginning Granville Island was not an island but rather two sandbars, favored by the Squamish people as a winter fishing ground. In 1916, after industrialization hit town, city planners transformed the sandbars into an island where factories could set up business and service the sawmills and rail yards that surrounded False Creek, as well as having easy access to shipping lanes.

Industrial Island, as it was called, was administered by the government of Canada and underwent a number of ups and downs in the ensuing years, including a couple of spectacular fires. During the area's third incarnation, the city dumped dredging fill between the island and False Creek's south shore, and the island became a peninsula. This was part of an overall plan to completely fill in False Creek, but due to cost overruns the plan was abandoned.

Interest in redeveloping the island as a people-friendly area then took hold, and after a large financial commitment from the federal government the public market opened for business in 1979. Voila! Granville Island was lauded as one of the largest urban redevelopment projects in North America, and a successful one at that. The neighborhood is more of an attraction than a place where people live, though some folks do reside in floating houses moored on the island's eastern side.

It's not hard to spend the better part of a day here. You can paddle around False Creek with a kayak from **Ecomarine Ocean Kayak Centre** (p146), roam the boardwalk that circles the island, or hop on a mini ferry for a tour (p40). See artists carving, weaving or throwing clay in their studios, and buy their wares in local craft shops (p160). At night, the focus shifts from shopping to the performing arts when three theaters – **Waterfront** (p135), **Arts Club** (p135) and the **New Revue Stage** (Map pp236-7; Vancouver Theatresports League; 1585 Johnston St) – open their doors. **Bridges** (p106) and the **Backstage Lounge** (p125) are good places to have a drink or a bite to eat, no matter what the time of day.

The **Granville Island Information Centre** (☎ 604-666-3619; www.granvilleisland.com; 1398 Cartwright St; ☺ 9am-5pm, to 6pm in summer; bus No 50) provides good free maps and other island resources. You'll find a **currency-exchange booth** (☺ 9am-1:30pm & 2:30-5pm Mon-Fri, 10am-4pm Sat & Sun) plus ATMs outside the BC Wood Co-op at 1592 Johnston St.

Transportation

Bus No 50 runs along Granville St (including pick-ups at both Waterfront and Granville stations downtown), and drops off on the southeast side of W 2nd Ave at Granville Island's southern foot. There are no buses on the island proper, but it's compact enough to get around by foot.

Mini Ferry Docks for Aquabus and False Creek Ferries flank the Public Market.

Car Free parking (for up to three hours) is available in designated areas; your odds of finding a spot drop considerably in summer. There's a parking lot at 1100 The Castings (cnr Lamey's Mill Rd; per hour $1, daily maximum $4). All island streets are one way.

Streetcar See below for details.

Orientation

Despite its name, Granville Island is in reality a peninsula, connected to Fairview to the south. The massive Granville Bridge passes overhead near the island's center. Johnson St is the main artery, cutting northwest–southeast. Most shops are located on north–south Duranleau St and east–west Cartwright St.

The **Mound** is a green space with good views at the island's southeast tip.

DOWNTOWN HISTORIC RAILWAY

Map pp236-7

cnr 2nd Ave & Anderson St below Granville Bridge; adult/senior & child $2/1; ☺ every half hr, 1-5pm Sat & Sun mid-May–mid-Oct; bus 50

Beautifully restored streetcars roll from Granville Island to **Science World** (Quebec St & Terminal Ave) during a smile-inducing 15-minute journey. The railway used to be part of the Vancouver tramcar system, and today it's still operated by the city's Engineering Services department. If you want to take the reverse journey (from Science World to Granville Island), you can park free at the 1st Ave railcar barn.

EMILY CARR INSTITUTE OF ART & DESIGN Map pp236-7

☎ 604-844-3800; www.eciad.ca; 1399 Johnston St; ☺ 10am-6pm; bus 50

Named after BC's most famous painter (see p27), the institute is well regarded for visual and media arts programs. Housed in a corrugated metal factory building by a cement plant, it has a gritty, angst-worthy vibe that matches that of its young students. The school presents a range of exhibits in its three galleries; the **Charles H Scott Gallery** (☺ noon-5pm Mon-Fri, 10am-5pm Sat & Sun) is the main one open to the public.

GRANVILLE ISLAND BREWERY

Map pp236-7

☎ 604-687-2739; 1441 Cartwright St; adult/senior & student $9.75/8.75; bus 50

Canada's oldest microbrewery offers half-hour tours at noon, 2pm and 4pm where you'll imbibe samples and take home a souvenir glass. The company is famed for its locally named beers (see p124) sold in stores and bars; it also brews concoctions that are only available on site. Join the crowd propped up in the tasting room after the tour and find out what's in those taps.

GRANVILLE ISLAND MUSEUMS

Map pp236-7

☎ 604-683-1939; 1502 Duranleau St; adult/child 4-12/senior & student/family $7.50/4/6/20; ⏰ 10:30am-5:30pm; bus 50

Of the three museums that are contained here under the one roof, the train museum is the winner of the bunch. It features the world's largest collection of toy trains available on public display. And what a display it is, with a large variety of railcars zipping through a scale model of a BC mountain scene. The train museum sprawls all the way across the 2nd floor. On the 1st floor, the ship museum exhibits include model freighters, frigates and tugboats housed in glass cases. Also on the 1st floor is the sport fishing museum but, unless fishing is your passion, how many reels, rods, flies, outboard motors and stuffed fish do you want to see?

GRANVILLE ISLAND PUBLIC MARKET

Map pp236-7

☎ 604-666-6477; cnr Johnston & Duranleau Sts; ⏰ 9am-6pm, closed Mon in Jan; bus 50

This lively market is a wonderful place to experience the bounty of the Lower Mainland. Stalls overflow with fish, vegetables, fruits, meat, cheese and everything else you might need to put together an afternoon picnic or the evening's home-cooked meal. Coffee shops and take-out counters make it easy to graze on-site; favorites include **Terra Breads**, **Origins** coffee and à la mode pies. For cooks, **South China Seas Trading Co** stocks Asian specialty ingredients, and the **Stock Market** churns out flavorful soups and stocks.

The market fronts on to False Creek, and unless it's pouring rain the waterfront plaza behind the market is filled with shoppers, children, tourists, buskers, and swarms of pigeons and gulls. It's estimated that about 250,000 people visit the market monthly. On a sunny day, finding an empty table can be tricky, as can protecting your food from the birds.

KIDS MARKET Map pp236-7

☎ 604-689-8447; 1496 Cartwright St; ⏰ 10am-6pm; bus 50

Children will love all the pint-sized things to do and buy at the two-story Kids Market. The Beanstalk Bistro serves hot dogs, ice cream and other foods on youngsters' Top Five list. Stores proffer puppets, kites and wooden toys. Behind the market is the **Granville Island Waterpark** (admission free; ⏰ 10am-6pm Victoria Day–Labour Day), where wee ones can splash it up.

WEST SIDE

You've already read about the West End (p49), and soon you'll read about West Vancouver (p76). It's time now to discuss the West Side, the long-established residential neighborhoods and bustling commercial centers south of downtown and across False Creek and English Bay. From east to west these neighborhoods – sprawled across a large peninsula – are **Fairview**, **South Granville**, **Kitsilano** and the **University of British Columbia**. The three main access points to the West Side are the Cambie, Granville and art-deco Burrard Bridges.

FAIRVIEW

Eating pp115–16; Shopping p161;
Sleeping pp177

Fairview lies just to the south of False Creek, roughly between Granville and Main Sts, and is the place where all the brawny outfitter shops, like **Mountain Equipment Co-op**

Transportation

Bus No 15 travels Cambie St; bus 17 runs along Oak St; and bus 9 runs along Broadway Ave.
Car Parking can be difficult on both Broadway and Cambie St; be prepared for a search.

(p161), cluster. Just taking a look around these places can make you feel as though you've recently climbed a mountain or paddled through rapids, and incite hunger. Luckily, your nosh needs can be met at a plethora of restaurants cooking everything from Jamaican to Fijian cuisine to the world's best sushi (see **Tojo's** p115).

If nature beckons, the trees and flowers of Queen Elizabeth Park and VanDusen Botanical Garden bloom south of King Edward Ave.

Orientation

North–south Cambie St (to about 19th Ave) and east–west Broadway carry the most restaurants and shops. The gardens and parks are south, around W 33rd Ave, in an area often referred to as Cambie (W 16th Ave serves as the dividing line: north is Fairview, south is Cambie).

Top Five West Side

- Museum of Anthropology (p64)
- Wreck Beach (p65)
- Kitsilano Beach (p62)
- Camosun Bog (p65)
- Queen Elizabeth Park (left)

QUEEN ELIZABETH PARK Map pp236-7

☎ 604-257-8584; cnr W 33rd Ave & Cambie St; admission free; ⏰ 24hr; bus 15; P per hr $1

It is said that in this park, the city's third largest at 52 hectares, you can find a specimen of every tree native to Canada, including the white-flowered dogwood, the province's floral emblem. The space probably is best known for being the highest point in Vancouver, and at 167m above sea level there are great views of the city from every direction. Sports fields, manicured lawns, formal botanical gardens (a *very* popular spot to have wedding photos taken), tennis courts, a pitch-and-putt golf course, lawn-bowling greens, a Frisbee golf course and **Seasons in the Park restaurant** (p115) comprise the gorgeous mix. On the east side is the **Nat Bailey baseball stadium** (p140) – 'the prettiest in the world.'

Crowning the hill at the park is **Bloedel Conservatory** (☎ 604-257-8584; adult/child 6-12/youth 13-18 $4.10/2/3.10; ⏰ 9am-8pm Mon-Fri, 10am-9pm Sat & Sun Apr-Sep, 10am-5pm daily Oct-Mar). This Buckminster Fuller–inspired 'garden under Plexiglas' has three climate zones with 400 plant species and 150 free-flying tropical birds. It's a good place to pretend you're somewhere balmy when the weather blusters. Free brochures help identify the flora and fauna.

Queen Elizabeth Park was named in honor of the royal, who visited Vancouver with hubby King George VI in 1939.

VANDUSEN BOTANICAL GARDEN

Map pp236-7

☎ 604-878-9274; www.vandusengarden.org; 5251 Oak St; adult/child 6-12/senior/youth 13-18/family $7.50/3.90/5.20/5.70/17, reduced in winter; ⏰ 10am-dusk; bus 17

About four blocks west of Queen Elizabeth Park, this 22-hectare space is a web of paths wandering through 40 theme gardens and stands of bamboo and giant redwoods, among others. Find your way through the spooky Elizabethan Hedge Maze, walled in by 3000 pyramidal cedars. Intriguing marble sculptures are also scattered throughout the grounds. The **Flower & Garden Show** takes place the first week of June, and in December a section of the garden is illuminated with 19,000 Christmas lights for the popular **Festival of Lights**. The **Botanical Library** (☎ 604-257-8668) is an excellent resource for information about Vancouver's flora and the city's garden clubs.

SOUTH GRANVILLE

Eating p116; Shopping pp162–3

This chic neighborhood, basically a 10-block strip of Granville St, is known as 'Gallery Row' and often stands in for New York's SoHo or Chelsea when film crews come to town. A staggering number of dealers sell fine arts, like contemporary photography and paintings (see the boxed text on p162), while artsy boutiques sell designer jewelry, housewares and clothes. It's all a natural extension of the arts scene on Granville Island, which is just a few blocks north.

Of course, chic creative people need chic creative food, and the local restaurants – including several of Vancouver's premiere ones – serve it up. Try **West** (p116), where the walls are lined with wine to complement the regional cuisine, or **Vij's** (p116), where the legendary lamb popsicles provoke tears of joy.

Orientation

The name doesn't lie: South Granville centers on Granville St south of downtown and Granville Island. The vast majority of galleries, eateries and boutiques are on this dominant road, though a few are within a one-block range east or west. All are squeezed between W 5th Ave to the north and W 15th Ave to the south.

Transportation

Bus No 10 plies to/from downtown via Granville St, stopping every few blocks between W 5th and W 15th Aves.

Car Street parking can be tough to find. There's a public lot at The Castings (see the boxed text on p58).

KITSILANO

Eating pp117–19; Shopping pp163–5; Sleeping pp177–8

Kitsilano (or 'Kits') is Vancouver's old hippie neighborhood. While you can still find incense-burning bookstores and raw-food cafés, chances are they will be sitting beside a European clothing boutique or an upscale French bistro. Yes, Kits has grown up. It's now more yuppie than hippie – who else besides doctors or lawyers can afford the outrageously priced real estate? However, these professionals are yoga-loving, healthy-lifestyle advocates. It's easy to see why they want to live here: Kits is leafy, laid-back and genteel, and the beach is at your doorstep.

The area was named after Chief Khahtsahlanough, leader of the aboriginal village Sun'ahk, which stood on the land that today is Vanier Park. In 1901 the local government displaced the community, sending some families to the Capilano Indian Reserve on the North Shore and others to Squamish.

The first streetcar service in 1905 prompted the construction of a mixture of housing in Kits, from the 'Vancouver Box' (two- or 2½-story homes) to small apartment buildings and full-fledged estates. During the 1950s and '60s many of these properties were converted into rooming houses popular with university students, thus creating the underpinning for the countercultural community that Kits became in the '60s and '70s.

Kits today is a fun fusion of groovy patchouli and slick retail therapy, particularly along W 4th Ave and Broadway, the primary commercial streets that are lined with unusual shops, bookstores, and ethnic and vegetarian restaurants. The neighborhood's beaches (Kits and

Burrard Inlet, from Stanley Park (p50)

Neighborhoods – West Side

Transportation

Bus Nos 2 and 22 run from Burrard St downtown, then along Cornwall Ave by Kits Beach before heading south on MacDonald St. Bus 4 runs from downtown via Granville St, and then west along 4th Ave. Bus 9 runs the entire length of Broadway from Boundary Rd to UBC. Bus 99 B-Line runs an express route along Broadway from Commercial Dr to UBC.

Mini Ferry Mini ferries sail to Vanier Park from Sunset Beach's Aquatic Centre.

Car Street parking usually is findable. There are also lots at the parks: Kits Beach (per hour $1, daily maximum $5 May–September, reduced in winter), Jericho Beach (same fees as Kits, but open May–September only) and Vanier (per two hours $1, daily maximum $3, evening flat rate $1).

Jericho) and museums (maritime, history and space) rank among the city's finest. And if you find yourself jonesing for a soy smoothie or dandelion coffee at 3am, the **Naam** (p118) accommodates; it's the city's oldest natural foods eatery, open 24/7.

Even Kits' panhandlers retain the vibe. As one man's cardboard sign reads beside his change-filled plastic cup: 'Please, spare a little karma.'

Orientation

Kitsilano takes up the south shore of English Bay, extending west roughly from Burrard to Alma Sts, and south as far as about W 16th Ave. The area west from Alma St to UBC is Point Grey, a mostly affluent residential neighborhood. In this book we refer to a portion of Point Grey as being part of Kitsilano. The main commercial thoroughfares are W 4th Ave and Broadway, both running east–west (though note that Broadway peters out at Alma St, and 10th Ave takes over as the primary road).

JERICHO BEACH Map pp238-9
north foot of Alma St; bus 4

Jericho Beach is a fashionable place to strut your stuff, though it's more subdued than Kits Beach. The **Jericho youth hostel** (p146) and **Sailing Centre** (p146) are here, so travelers and windsurfers spill on to the beach. Birds and ducklings also favor the grounds – for nesting, not windsurfing!

While in the area, you can visit the **Hastings Mill Store Museum** (☎ 604-734-1212; 1575 Alma St; admission by donation; ⊙ 11am-4pm Jun–mid-Sep, 1-4pm Sat & Sun only mid-Sep–May), the city's oldest building and its first store (also post office, church and meeting house). Built in 1865 and originally located at the foot of what is now Dunlevy Ave near Gastown, it was one of the few buildings to survive the Great Fire of 1886. It was floated here in 1930.

KITSILANO BEACH Map pp238-9
cnr Cornwall Ave & Arbutus St; bus 2 or 22

Mega-popular Kits Beach, bordered by Cornwall Ave west from Arbutus to Trafalgar Sts, faces English Bay with views to the Coast Mountains. The long, sandy strand that flanks the water attracts nubile young sun worshippers, volleyball players and others who like to preen. The beach is fine for a dip, though serious swimmers go to the heated 137m **Kitsilano Pool** (p147), the

world's largest outdoor saltwater pool. For refreshments, check out the cafés and restaurants along Cornwall Ave or south up Yew St.

HR MACMILLAN SPACE CENTRE
Map pp238-9

☎ 604-738-7827; www.hrmacmillanspacecentre .com; 1100 Chestnut St; adult/child 5-10/senior & youth 11-18 $13.50/9.50/10.50; ⊙ 10am-5pm, closed Mon Sep-Jun; bus 2 or 22

The Space Centre, which shares with the Vancouver Museum, has two main highlights. The first is the Virtual Voyages Simulator, a flight simulator that takes 30 people on a 'mission' to Mars or to divert a comet's collision with Earth. It's a fun, noisy and jerky ride (participants must wear seatbelts throughout its 15-minute duration), and it's included in the admission price.

The second highlight is the laser show in the Planetarium Star Theatre (admission $10). The shows are presented Thursday to Saturday at 9:30pm, with additional shows Friday and Saturday at 10:45pm. The later shows are popular, so get there early or make reservations.

Part of the Space Centre complex is the **Gordon MacMillan Southam Observatory** (☎ 604-738-2855; admission free; ⊙ 7-11pm Fri & Sat). It features a 0.5m telescope available for public viewings if volunteers are available.

VANCOUVER MARITIME MUSEUM
Map pp238-9
☎ 604-257-8300; www.vmm.bc.ca; 1905 Ogden Ave; adult/senior & youth 6-19/family $8/5.50/18; ☾ 10am-5pm Victoria Day–Labour Day, 10am-5pm Tue-Sat & noon-5pm Sun rest of year; bus 2 or 22

This museum is probably of most interest to boat buffs and children, although it will seem tame if you have come here from the HR MacMillan Space Centre. The main attraction is the *St Roch*, the 1928 RCMP Arctic patrol sailing ship that was the first vessel to navigate the legendary Northwest Passage in both directions. The museum was actually built around the ship; guided tours of the vessel are every half-hour or so.

The rest of the museum displays wooden models, old rowboats, First Nations kayaks, and exhibits on shipwrecks and pirates. The reconstruction of the bridge of an actual tugboat working in Burrard Inlet is interesting. The Children's Maritime Discovery Centre has lots of hands-on displays where kids can pretend to be pirates (complete with hats). The museum is near the foot of Cypress St, a five-minute walk west from the Vancouver Museum.

VANCOUVER MUSEUM Map pp238-9
☎ 604-736-4431; www.vanmuseum.bc.ca; 1100 Chestnut St; adult/youth 5-19/senior/family $10/6/8/35; ☾ 10am-5pm, to 9pm Thu, closed Mon Sep-Jun; bus 2 or 22

The Vancouver Museum recounts both distant and recent city history. Permanent exhibits include a look at the everyday life of First Nations people; passenger quarters on a groaning life-size immigrant ship; and a full-scale sawmill wheel. The changing exhibits are usually excellent, too; one recently focused on skateboarding's colorful history in Vancouver.

VANIER PARK Map pp238-9
west of Burrard Bridge on English Bay; bus 2 or 22

Vanier Park, which winds along around Kitsilano Point and eventually connects with Kitsilano Beach Park to the west, is actually more a host site than a destination in itself. It's best known as the home of the MacMillan Space Centre and Observatory, Vancouver Maritime Museum and Vancouver Museum. The well-used park also provides the grounds for the **Vancouver International Children's Festival** (p9) in mid-May and the tented **Bard on the Beach** (p135) in summer.

UNIVERSITY OF BRITISH COLUMBIA
Sleeping pp178–9

The **University of British Columbia** (UBC; ☎ 604-822-4636; www.ubc.ca) is more than just your average campus. Its 402-hectare grounds are part of an area called the University Endowment Lands, and are amid rugged forest. Three of the city's most treasured and wild beaches – Locarno, Spanish Banks and Wreck – are located there. The tranquil Nitobe Garden and sweeping UBC Botanical Garden flourish nearby. And one of the world's foremost museums rests among the trees: the Museum of Anthropology, with its fantastical totem poles.

Although UBC is often referred to locally as being in Point Grey, technically it's not a part of the city of Vancouver. The provincial government's ministry of municipal affairs administers the area, which harks back to the 1908 University Loan Act, when the government set up the site for the province's first university.

Even though the area was heavily logged from 1861 to 1891, it wasn't clear-cut, mainly because many of the trees in the area were too difficult to reach. This allowed the remaining trees to generate substantial regrowth, hence the remarkable forests standing today. With the creation of the 763-hectare Pacific Spirit Regional Park in 1988 (administered by the Greater Vancouver Regional District), an area almost twice the size of Stanley Park has been preserved for future generations to use and enjoy.

Neighborhoods – West Side

Transportation
Bus The UBC bus loop is at the campus' center on the corner of University Blvd and East Mall. Catch bus 4 or 17 from downtown along Granville St; both take about 30 minutes to reach the loop. Bus 99 B-Line travels along Broadway/10th Aves from Broadway Station.

Car Parking in the area isn't bad, with the exception of near Wreck Beach. Try to get a spot on Marine Dr.

On campus If you are on the campus at night and would like to be accompanied back to your accommodations or car, call ☎ 604-822-5353 from 6pm onward.

Orientation

UBC is at the most westerly point of Vancouver, on the peninsula jutting out into the Strait of Georgia. The main roads going into UBC include W 4th Ave, which becomes Chancellor Blvd at Blanca St; W 10th Ave, becoming University Blvd at Blanca St; and W 16th Ave. Marine Dr is the main route that loops around the peninsula.

LOCARNO & SPANISH BANKS BEACHES Map p241

cnr NW Marine Dr & Trimble St; admission free; bus 4
There are some stunning views from these beaches, looking back at the city and across to West Vancouver; the ships in Burrard Inlet look almost close enough to touch. Locarno has a reputation as the most laid-back of Vancouver's beaches, while Spanish Banks is the most striking (and also the place for skim-boarding, see p147). Locarno eventually melds into Spanish Banks, located to the west.

MUSEUM OF ANTHROPOLOGY Map p241

☎ 604-822-3825; www.moa.ubc.ca; 6393 NW Marine Dr; adult/senior & student $9/7, admission free 5-9pm Tue; 🕑 10am-5pm Wed-Mon, 10am-9pm Tue Victoria Day-Labour Day, 11am-9pm Tue, 11am-5pm Wed-Sun rest of year; bus 4
This museum is the best Vancouver has to offer, with a collection of totem poles and wood carvings unsurpassed anywhere in the world. The focus, technically speaking, is on arts and artifacts from global cultures, and, while Asia, Africa and the Pacific are all well represented, the real show belongs to BC's coastal First Nations people and their work.

Arthur Erickson (see p25) conceived the museum's architecture, and its design is almost as exhilarating as the exhibits it houses. It was inspired by the post-and-beam long-houses favored by many coastal groups, and the Great Hall with its fabulous use of glass allows the huge totem poles and other artifacts inside to be set off against a backdrop of mountains and sea.

The museum has the world's largest collection of works by Haida artist Bill Reid, including the famous sculpture *The Raven and the First Men*, carved from a 4½-ton block of yellow cedar that had to be lowered in through the ceiling. Also of interest is the Koerner Ceramics Gallery, displaying a collection of European ceramics unique to North America.

This is the largest teaching museum in Canada, and you likewise can learn a thing or two from the museum's open storage galleries that allow more than 50% of its collection to be displayed. A database provides detailed information on the exhibits, and free guided tours will take you through the various galleries (call for times). Also be sure to step outside to see the **Haida village**, a re-creation of a traditional village, with a longhouse, a smaller mortuary house and 10 totem poles.

There is a fabulous, albeit pricey, gift shop featuring First Nations jewelry, carvings, prints, and an extensive collection of books on First Nations history and culture.

If driving, there is metered parking in front. If you're coming from the bus loop, walk west on University Blvd, turn right (north) on West Mall and follow it to the end; it's about a 1km walk.

NITOBE MEMORIAL GARDEN Map p241

☎ 604-822-6038; www.nitobe.org; 1903 West Mall; adult/student/senior mid-Mar–mid-Oct $3/1.50/2, rest of year free ; 🕑 10am-5pm mid-Mar–mid-May & mid-Sep–mid-Oct, 10am-6pm mid-May–mid-Sep, 10am-2:30pm Mon-Fri rest of year; bus 4
This beautiful Japanese-style garden, near Gate 4 at the foot of Memorial Rd off West Mall, isn't far from the anthropology museum and, aside from the sound of cars zipping along Marine Dr behind it, is a tranquil retreat perfect for quiet meditation.

Nitobe is considered by some to be the most authentic Japanese garden outside Japan. It has two parts: the Tea Garden, with its ceremonial teahouse, is designed for peaceful contemplation; and the Stroll Garden, the layout of which conforms to the map of the Milky Way, is a symbolic journey through life following the principles of yin and yang. It's enclosed within high walls that help to create the feeling that you are in another world, as do the gently curving paths and soothing sounds of waterfalls and tiny streams.

The garden is named for Dr Inazo Nitobe, a Japanese scholar whose mug appears on Japan's ¥5000 note. If you also plan on visiting the UBC Botanical Garden, ask about the combination pass, which saves $2.

PACIFIC SPIRIT REGIONAL PARK

Map p241
☎ 604-224-5739; cnr Blanca St & W 16th Ave; 🕑 8am-4pm Mon-Fri; bus 4

This 763-hectare park – the city's largest – is essentially a long, wide strip stretching northwest from Burrard Inlet on one side of the peninsula to the North Arm of the Fraser River on the other, and acts as a green zone between the campus and the city. It is a fantastic area to explore, with 54km of walking, jogging, cycling, and even equestrian trails making their way through forests of giant cedar and fir that aren't much different from the forests the first Europeans found when they arrived.

Inside you'll also find the 12,000-year-old **Camosun Bog** (accessed by a boardwalk at 19th Ave & Camosun St), a unique wetland that is the home of many native bird and plant species. The Park Centre has information and maps on the park and bog. From downtown, either take bus No 4 to Blanca St and 10th Ave and then walk south six blocks, or (and this is a longer route) take the SkyTrain to Nanaimo Station and from there take bus No 25 to UBC, which will drop you off right next to the center.

UBC BOTANICAL GARDEN Map p241

☎ 604-822-9666; www.ubcbotanicalgarden.org; 6804 SW Marine Dr; adult/student/senior mid-Mar–mid-Oct $5/2/3, rest of year free, combination pass with Nitobe Garden $6; ☯ 10am-6pm mid-Mar–mid-Oct, 10am-3pm late Oct–early May; bus 41

A real gem, this 44.5-hectare garden near the corner of West 16th Ave is actually made up of about eight separate gardens, which contain 10,000 different trees, shrubs and flowers. There are several thematic plantings, including gardens with plants that are specific to regions of the world and to particular environments: the Alpine Garden and the Asian Garden, which has the largest rhododendron collection in Canada and rare blue Himalayan poppies; the BC Native Garden, which has around 3500 specimens from dunes, bogs and more; the Food Garden, containing seasonal vegetables, berries and fruit; and the Physick Garden, an enclosed 16th-century apothecary herb garden. Even 'out of season,' the Winter Garden features plants that bloom during the cooler months.

If driving, there is free parking beside the garden entrance. From the bus loop, walk west on University Blvd, turn left (south) on West Mall and follow it to the end; it's about 1.5km total. You also can switch to bus No 41 at the loop, which stops at 16th Ave and Marine Dr, about 500m away.

UNIVERSITY TOWN Map p241

www.ubc.ca

The developed portion of the UBC campus resembles a small town. For information about services or to grab something to eat, make your way to the **Student Union Building (SUB)**, which is just north of the bus loop. Free 1½-hour **walking tours** (☎ 604-822-8687) leave from SUB at 10am and 1pm Monday to Friday from May to early September. If you fancy a swim, the nearby **UBC Aquatic Centre** (p147) is also open to the public.

WRECK BEACH Map p241

Trail 6 from the foot of University Blvd; admission free; bus 4

Wreck Beach is a microcosm of what makes Vancouver great. Here you'll find an undeveloped, log-strewn beach surrounded by a hulking forest that makes you feel worlds away from the city, yet downtown is only 20 minutes away. What's more, Wreck Beach is one of those liberal, anything goes kind of Vancouver places. In this case, what goes are your clothes, as it is the city's only nude beach (though as long as you're respectful, you don't have to be in the buff).

'Undeveloped' doesn't mean you'll want for creature comforts. You can get a baked potato, hash cookie, glass of wine, haircut, massage, musk-ox burger or just about anything else from the enterprising individuals who set up shop on the sand. Further information on nudist events is online (www.vantan.ca).

At low tide the beach gives way to mudflats that extend to the Strait of Georgia and the mouth of the North Arm of the Fraser River. People do swim here, but the thought of all that industrial waste emptying into the Strait of Georgia from the river can be off-putting.

Beach regulars are currently up in arms as the university is planning to build student residential towers near the shore. They are lobbying to stop construction, which is slated for completion in 2006. Check with the Wreck Beach Preservation Society (www.wreckbeach.org) for the plan's progress.

Access to Wreck Beach is via SW Marine Dr not far from Gate 6 at the foot of University Blvd; follow Trail 6 down the steps. On a warm day, parking along Marine Dr is next to impossible unless you're early. From the bus, walk west about 750m along University Blvd to Marine Dr where, on the west side of the road to the right (north), you'll find signs to Wreck Beach.

GREATER VANCOUVER

Eating p120; Shopping pp165–6; Sleeping pp179–80

Greater Vancouver – sometimes referred to as the Lower Mainland – is chock full of fat mountains, coastal parks, wildlife sanctuaries and fishing villages, all within a 45-minute drive of central Vancouver.

North Vancouver and West Vancouver together make up the North Shore, across Burrard Inlet from Vancouver proper. There are three ways to get there: the Lions Gate Bridge, accessed via the causeway (Hwy 99) through Stanley Park; Iron Workers Memorial Second Narrows Bridge, a continuation of the Trans-Canada Hwy (Hwy 1), which goes through East Vancouver; and the SeaBus from Waterfront Station (p45).

Richmond lies directly south of Vancouver via Hwy 99. Steveston is located in Richmond's southwest corner.

NORTH VANCOUVER

North Vancouver, or 'North Van' in localese, is the place to hike or night ski (Grouse Mountain and Mt Seymour); visit a fish farm (Capilano Salmon Hatchery); teeter across a suspension bridge (Capilano or Lynn Canyon); or kayak a fjord (Deep Cove). The neighborhood is easily accessed – it's just a quick zip from downtown via bridge or boat across Burrard Inlet.

> ### Top Five Greater Vancouver
> - Grouse Mountain (p75)
> - Lynn Canyon (p76)
> - Deep Cove (p76)
> - Horseshoe Bay (p77)
> - Lighthouse Park (p77)

Like so much of the Lower Mainland, North Van had industrial beginnings as a logging and sawmilling center (of which there are remnants in places like Cates Park). Transportation across the inlet started in 1866 when Navvy Jack Thomas, a gravel merchant, fired up his rowboat and charged a small fee to get mill workers over to Gassy Jack's Globe Saloon (p46) and home again. In 1873 Thomas eventually moved to the area that is now West Vancouver with his wife, Row'i'a (the granddaughter of Chief Ki'ep'i'lan'o, after whom the Capilano River is named), becoming the first white resident on the North Shore.

Life in the area remained quiet until the Lions Gate Bridge opened in 1938, which sparked a residential influx. The area boomed further after the opening of the Iron Workers Memorial Second Narrows Bridge, supporting both cars and trains, in 1958 (replacing an earlier version that was built in 1925) and cut the total travel time to Vancouver to about 20 minutes.

Orientation

North Vancouver extends east of the Capilano River to Indian Arm fjord. Capilano Rd (which eventually becomes Nancy Greene Way) runs north–south, more or less parallel to the Capilano River, up toward Grouse Mountain. The Dollarton Hwy holds close to Burrard Inlet's shoreline en route from the Second Narrows Bridge to Deep Cove.

CAPILANO SALMON HATCHERY

Map pp228–9

☎ 604-666-1790; 4500 Capilano Park Rd; admission free; ⊗ 8am-4pm, later during spawning months; bus 236 from Lonsdale Quay

Located in Capilano River Regional Park, about 2km north of the suspension bridge (see below), the hatchery is a fish farm run by the Federal Department of Fisheries and Oceans to help stop the depletion of valuable salmon stocks. From July to November is the best time to visit, when you can see adult salmon swim through fish ladders past the Capilano River rapids to reach spawning grounds upstream. Eye-level tanks display the creatures and enlightening exhibits help explain the whole process.

(Continued on page 75)

1 The 'golf ball' that is Science World (p55), Chinatown 2 The exterior of the 22-story art deco Marine Building (p44), downtown 3 Lions Gate Bridge at night (p52), Stanley Park 4 A glass tower at BC Place (p43), downtown

1 *Music on the steps of Vancouver Art Gallery (p44), downtown* 2 *BC Place has the world's largest air-supported dome arena (p43), downtown* 3 *Commuter trains and Canada Place (p43), downtown*

1 Gastown Steam Clock (p46)
2 The glass atrium of the
Vancouver Public Library (p45),
downtown 3 Ultra-posh Urban
Fare (p93), Yaletown 4 Sculpture
at the waterfront (p47), Yaletown

1 *Totem Poles at Stanley Park (p50)* 2 *Stanley Park during the fall (p50)* 3 *Sam Kee Building (p55), Chinatown* 4 *Dr Sun Yat-Sen Classical Chinese Garden & Park (p55), Chinatown*

1 Nitobe Memorial Garden (p64), UBC *2* Buddhist Temple (p79), Richmond *3* Maze at VanDusen Botanical Garden (p60), Fairview

1 Queen Elizabeth Park (p60), Fairview *2* Temperate rainforest, North Vancouver (p66) *3* Striding out near Kitsilano Beach (p62), Kitsilano

1 *A rollerblader by Burrard Inlet, Stanley Park (p50)*
2 *Salmon fishing, Capilano Salmon Hatchery (p66), North Vancouver* 3 *Cyclists on English Bay beach (p50), West End*

1 *Broken Column sculpture in the Pendulum Gallery (p44), downtown* 2 *Tiled Chinese zodiac in the courtyard of the Chinese Cultural Centre (p54), Chinatown* 3 *Masks on display in a Granville Island gallery (p57)* 4 *Inukshuk Inuit sculpture, English Bay beach (p50), West End*

(Continued from page 66)

CAPILANO SUSPENSION BRIDGE
Map pp228-9

☎ 604-985-7474; www.capbridge.com; 3735 Capilano Rd; adult/child 6-12/youth 13-16/student 17+/BC resident $21.95/5.50/10.95/16.50/19.95; ☽ 8:30am-8pm Victoria Day–Labour Day, 9am-dusk rest of year; bus 236 from Lonsdale Quay; ℗ $3

As you walk out on to the world's longest (140m) and highest (70m) suspension bridge swaying gently over the Capilano River, consider that the original was made of nothing but hemp rope and cedar (compared to the current wire cables and concrete) and you'll feel more steady. The bridge's capacity is 1333 people, and at times it seems as though that many tourists are traipsing across at once. Capilano can get oppressively busy – and expensive – especially when you consider the less-carnival-like, free Lynn Canyon Park bridge (p76) is just a few kilometers away. Then again, Capilano's admission includes extras like the Treetops Adventure (which enables visitors to walk from giant fir to giant fir via a series of small, elevated suspension bridges some 24m above the forest floor), a totem-pole and nature park, and a First Nations Carving Centre.

GROUSE MOUNTAIN Map pp228-9

☎ 604-980-9311; www.grousemountain.com; 6400 Nancy Greene Way; Skyride adult/child 5-12/youth 13-18/senior $26.95/9.95/14.95/24.95; bus 236 from Lonsdale Quay; ℗ free gravel lot, paved lot $5 per car

With the Lower Mainland sprawling below it, Grouse Mountain is a Vancouver must-see. Not only is this the city's most convenient ski area (a mere 12km from downtown), several runs are even lit for night skiing, but in summer it's great for hiking and mountain biking. Stellar views, orphan grizzly bears at the Refuge for Endangered Wildlife, live lumberjack shows (summer only), an ice rink (winter only), 32 giant chainsaw sculptures and the Hiwus Feasthouse (a cedar longhouse with First Nations storytelling, music, dancing and cuisine) round out the offerings.

The 125-passenger Skyride, the largest aerial tramway in North America, whisks you from the mountain's base to 1100m above sea level in eight minutes; it departs every 15 minutes from 9am to 10pm. At the top is a stone-and-wood chalet that holds shops, eateries and a

Transportation

Bus Catch buses from two main transfer points: Lonsdale Quay (reached from downtown Vancouver by SeaBus or buses traveling west on Georgia St) or Phibbs Exchange near the north end of the Iron Workers Memorial Second Narrows Bridge (reached from downtown by buses traveling east on Pender St). Buses 212, 229 and 236 swing by most of North Van's major sights.

SeaBus The SeaBus chugs between Waterfront Station in downtown Vancouver and Lonsdale Quay.

Car Parking in the area is not a problem.

theater showing the high-tech video *Born to Fly* (price included with the Skyride).

You can also hoof it to the top via the **Grouse Grind**, probably the most popular hike in the metro area. More of an outdoor gym than a wilderness trail (some refer to it as a 'Stairmaster in the woods' and there are no real views until you reach the top), the 3km route has a steep elevation gain of 853m. In the early evening it's fun to watch the lululemon-clad (see p156) hordes streaming out of the woods, puffing and checking their wristwatches for performance times. Fit people make it in an hour, lesser mortals in 1½ hours. The trailhead is in front of the chalet. Wear boots and insect repellent, and bring water. It's free to hike up; if your knees are shaking, you can catch the Skyride down for $5.

If you are going up just for the views and there is the slightest hint of cloud around the mountain, wait until it clears because you won't see a thing. Consider going up in the late afternoon so you can see the city's lights come on. For further information on skiing, hiking or mountain biking on Grouse, see p145, p143 and p142, respectively.

LONSDALE QUAY Map pp228-9

☎ 604-985-6261; 123 Carrie Cates Court; ☽ market 9:30am-6:30pm Sat-Thu, 9:30am-9pm Fri; SeaBus from Waterfront Station

In addition to serving as a transportation hub, Lonsdale Quay (pronounced 'key') contains a market with more than 90 stores and services. The 1st floor is devoted to fresh and cooked food, the 2nd floor has specialty shops and restaurants with views, and the top floor holds the Lonsdale Quay Hotel (p179). A booth in the SeaBus terminal offers info on the North Shore.

Deep Cove/Indian Arm

The small village of Deep Cove makes an idyllic getaway, with sailboats bobbing in the bay surrounded by forested hills and little islands. A strip of galleries, gift shops, and pizza and gelato cafés lead down to the rocky beach. It's well worth renting a kayak (p146) to explore stunning Indian Arm fjord.

Cates Park (nearby on the Dollarton Hwy) provides another vantage point from which to see Indian Arm. It's best known as the place where author Malcolm Lowry, who wrote *Under the Volcano*, lived with his wife from 1940 to 1954; a walk dedicated to him meanders past where his squatter's shack once stood. The park also shelters the remains of the Dollar Lumber Mill (in operation from 1916 to 1942), a 15m First Nations war canoe, forest walks and a sandy beach.

To get yourself there, take bus No 212 from Phibbs Exchange.

LOWER SEYMOUR CONSERVATION RESERVE Map pp228-9

☎ 604-987-1273; north end of Lillooet Rd; ⏰ 7am-dusk

Seemingly part of Mt Seymour Provincial Park but actually administered by the regional government, this 5668-hectare reserve has alpine meadows, forested slopes and floodplains, plus 40km of trails (many are paved) that can be used by walkers, hikers, cyclists and in-line skaters. There's no public transportation. Take the Trans-Canada Hwy (Hwy 1) to the Lillooet Rd exit and head north into the park.

LYNN CANYON PARK Map pp228-9

☎ 604-981-3103; 3663 Park Rd; admission free; ⏰ 7am-dusk; bus 229 from Lonsdale Quay

Set amid thick woods, the main feature of this provincial park is its suspension bridge. It's not as long or high as the Capilano bridge (p75), but it gives the same impression – swaying over a river 50m below – plus it's free and less commercialized. The park also has hiking trails, picnic areas and swimming spots. Near the bridge, the **Ecology Centre** (⏰ 10am-5pm Jun-Sep, 10am-5pm Mon-Fri, noon-4pm Sat & Sun Oct-May) educates about the area's temperate rainforest through dioramas, films and slide shows.

MT SEYMOUR PROVINCIAL PARK

Map pp228-9

☎ 604-986-2261; www.mountseymour.com; 1700 Mt Seymour Rd; ⏰ 24hr, skiing 9:30am-10pm Mon-Fri, 8:30am-10pm Sat & Sun

Less visited than Grouse Mountain (p75) but also a 15km escape from downtown, Mt Seymour (1000m) is well regarded for hiking, with 14 trails varying in difficulty and length that wind past lakes and 800-year-old Douglas firs (the easiest path is the 2km Goldie Lake Trail). A downhill ski area operates in winter (see p145) and doesn't get as congested as the other local mountains. No public transportation goes into the park; however, in winter there is a resort-operated shuttle bus (p145) from Lonsdale Quay. If driving, take the Trans-Canada Hwy (Hwy 1) to the Mt Seymour Pkwy (near the Second Narrows Bridge) and follow it east to Mt Seymour Rd, which then heads north to the parking lot.

WEST VANCOUVER

West Van, the kissing cousin of North Van, is one of the region's poshest neighborhoods, a place where sprawling waterfront homes snuggle into the cliffs above Burrard Inlet, and rocky beaches and small coves lie hidden away from the road. Residents of West Vancouver earn a higher per capita income (and read more library books) than any other group of Canadians. They're also the proud developers of Canada's first shopping mall, the Park Royal.

While West Van's attractions aren't the biggest must-sees in town, the neighborhood does accommodate some truly lovely parks, like Lighthouse and Whytecliff, as well as Cypress Provincial Park, Greater Van's best skiing mountain, which is to host many Winter Olympic events in 2010.

Marine Dr itself is an attraction, as it winds its way past multimillion-dollar

Transportation

Bus West Vancouver's buses are part of the TransLink system, but are distinguished by their blue color. Park Royal, just west of the Lion's Gate Bridge, is the area's main bus exchange. Bus 250 travels between downtown Vancouver (catch it along W Georgia St) and Horseshoe Bay, making frequent stops along Marine Dr. Bus 257 goes express to Horseshoe Bay via Hwy 1. Bus 239 travels between Phibbs Exchange, Lonsdale Quay and Park Royal.

Car Parking around Dundarave Pier, the coastal parks and Horseshoe Bay can be challenging. Horseshoe Bay has a pay lot (per hour $2, daily maximum $12).

homes en route to Horseshoe Bay. Bus No 250 offers an inexpensive way to 'tour' it all. Once at Horseshoe Bay, you can either spend time wandering around the marina, or jump on the ferry to Bowen Island (p198) or the Sunshine Coast (p201).

Orientation

West Van stretches west from the Capilano River to Horseshoe Bay. Marine Dr is the main east–west thoroughfare of the neighborhood. It hugs the shore while passing through **Ambleside** and **Dundarave**, collectively known as 'the Village' – the commercial center of West Vancouver, where you'll find designer shops, cafés and restaurants. Upper Levels Hwy (Hwy 1) runs almost parallel to Marine Dr to the north.

Park Royal mall sits just west of the Lion's Gate Bridge, straddling Marine Dr. Behind it, extending west from the mouth of the Capilano River to 13th St, is **Ambleside Park**, with its sandy beach, playing fields, pitch-and-putt golf course, duck pond, dog park and historic ferry building. **Dundarave Pier**, where outdoor enthusiasts can hook up with the popular **Centennial Seawalk**, is at 25th St.

CYPRESS PROVINCIAL PARK Map pp228-9

☎ 604-419-7669; www.cypressmountain.com; Cypress Bowl Rd; ☼ 24hr, skiing 9am-10pm Mon-Fri, 8:30am-10pm Sat & Sun

Cypress competes with **Grouse** (p75) for activity popularity, and it has even more terrain to play on. Locals say it's tops for downhill and cross-country skiing in winter (see p145) and hiking in summer. The eight hiking trails, including the Baden-Powell, Yew Lake and Howe Sound Crest trails, cut through forests of huge Douglas fir, yellow cypress and cedar, past little lakes and alpine meadows. No public transportation goes to the park during summer, although a resort-operated shuttle bus (p145) from Lonsdale Quay runs during the ski season. If driving, take Cypress Bowl Rd off the Upper Levels Hwy; on the way up the mountain you'll get great views all the way to Vancouver Island. As mentioned, Cypress will be one of the venues for the 2010 Winter Olympics.

LIGHTHOUSE PARK Map pp228-9

☎ 604-925-7200; cnr Beacon Lane & Marine Dr; admission free; ☼ dawn-dusk; bus 250

This 75-hectare park is probably the easiest access to virgin forest you'll find in the Lower Mainland. Some of the 500-year-old Douglas firs stand as tall as 60m – these were big trees even in 1792 when Captain Vancouver mapped this coast. You'll also see the unusual arbutus, a wide-leaf evergreen with orange peeling bark.

And yes – there is a lighthouse. Point Atkinson Lighthouse, to be exact, which guards the entrance to Burrard Inlet from its rocky perch. Built in 1912 to replace the 1875 original, it's one of the few staffed lighthouses left on the coast, but it's not open to visitors. Still, it's a great spot

Horseshoe Bay

The small coastal community of Horseshoe Bay marks the end of West Vancouver. It's a pretty spot, with great views across the bay and up Howe Sound to distant glacial peaks. Cutesy places to eat and shop line the waterfront on Bay St, near the marina. Of course, what Horseshoe Bay is really all about is the BC Ferries terminal (p206), where ferries travel between Nanaimo on Vancouver Island, Langdale on the Sunshine Coast and Bowen Island.

To get yourself there, take bus No 250 (local) or 257 (express).

to hike to; out of the park's 13km of gentle trails, the most popular path leads to the lighthouse. Maps are available in the parking lot.

Don't be surprised if you stumble over a film crew while walking around, or trip over electrical cables stretched across the forest trails, or see helicopters hovering overhead while you try to enjoy the views across to Point Grey. The park has become a popular location for TV series and films shot in Vancouver, to many local residents' chagrin.

WHYTECLIFF PARK Map pp228-9

☎ 604-925-7200; admission free; 7100 block Marine Dr; ☼ dawn-dusk; bus 250

Just west of Horseshoe Bay, this is an exceptional little park right on the water. Trails lead to vistas and a gazebo, from where you can watch the boat traffic in Burrard Inlet. The rocky beach is a great place to play, go for a swim or scamper over the large rock protruding from the beach. And as the park contains an underwater reserve, it's a favorite place with divers.

RICHMOND

'Chinatown?' Many locals raise a quizzical eyebrow when asked about the location of this Vancouver neighborhood (p53). 'It moved to Richmond.'

Indeed, what started as an agricultural and fishing community at the turn of the 20th century has become a mini Hong Kong, as immigrants flocked to Richmond in the mid-1990s prior to Britain's territorial handover to China in 1997. Perhaps Richmond's geography reminded the immigrants of home, for, like Hong Kong, Richmond is an island city.

Today Richmond is a bit of a dichotomy. It's a place for nature lovers, who can get their fill at the Reifel Bird Sanctuary and Richmond Nature Park. But it's also a mecca for urban shoppers. Strung along No 3 Rd south from Bridgeport Rd to Granville Ave are malls and more malls – two large ones (Lansdowne Shopping Centre and Richmond Centre) plus the smaller, Asian-influenced Yaohan Centre, Aberdeen Centre, President Plaza and Parker Place. The Asian shopping centers, in particular, are worth exploring; they're filled almost exclusively with Chinese stores, Chinese products and Chinese shoppers, and most of the signs are in Chinese. See p165 for details. You'll also find excellent Chinese food at very reasonable prices here.

Transportation

Bus The No 98 B-Line runs from Burrard Station in downtown Vancouver to Richmond Centre, the area's main transfer point. Buses to the local area are numbered in the 400s and according to what road they service, ie No 404 goes along No 4 Rd. For buses to the airport, see p205.
Car Street parking is manageable.

Orientation

Richmond is made up of a group of islands that are sandwiched between the North Arm of the Fraser River on one side and its main channel on the other. Most of the municipality is situated on two islands: Lulu Island (named after Lulu Sweet, who was a popular San Francisco entertainer of the mid-1800s) and Sea Island, which is the home of Vancouver's international airport. Essentially, No 3 Rd is the main north–south thoroughfare, while Westminster Hwy (which indeed goes all the way to New Westminster) is the main east–west road.

Neighborhoods – Greater Vancouver

An Array of Airport Art

Vancouver International Airport (YVR), on Sea Island in Richmond, receives frequent accolades as the world's nicest airport, thanks in no small part to its stunning art and architecture. With floor-to-ceiling glass walls stretching upwards to skylights and large open spaces, it's the perfect venue to reflect BC's natural and artistic splendor.

As you make your way to the top of the escalator that goes down to Canada Customs and the arrival halls, look for the *Spindle Whorl*, a 4m-high Musqueam cedar carving. At the bottom of the escalator you'll be greeted by *Welcome Figures*, a 5.2m-high red-cedar carving of a First Nations man and woman displaying a traditional Coast Salish welcome.

On level 3 in the main departures area you'll find the magnificent large bronze sculpture *The Spirit of Haida Gwaii (The Jade Canoe)* by Bill Reid, and behind it, acting as a backdrop, is *The Great Wave Wall* by Lutz Hauschild. This wall of glass panels captures light in such a way that the effect is that of a shimmering ocean.

Worth hunting out in the US flight check-in area is a small grove of trees, the back of which houses a projection screen and a photo mural showing the eagles in the winter trees at their sanctuary in Brackendale, near Squamish. Two other exhibits tell the story of eagles' habitat and their life cycle.

Finally, when you get outside the main entrance to the international terminal, be sure to take a look at the three totem poles, carved by Ksan artists Walter Harris and Earl Muldoe, set among reflective pools of water and a miniature forest.

BUDDHIST TEMPLE Map pp228-9
☎ 604-274-2822; 9160 Steveston Hwy, near south end of No 3 Rd; admission free; ☽ 9:30am-5pm; bus 98 B-Line from Burrard Station downtown, transfer to bus 403 at Richmond Centre

This two-tiered building – with flaring eaves, flying dragons and a golden roof – is a beautiful example of traditional Chinese architecture surrounded by landscaped gardens, complete with bonsai plants. It's open to the public for viewing, meditation classes and tea ceremonies.

GEORGE C REIFEL BIRD SANCTUARY
Map pp228-9
☎ 604-946-6980; www.reifelbirdsanctuary.com; 5191 Robertson Rd, Westham Island; adult/senior & child 2-14 $4/2; ☽ 9am-4pm

Bald eagles, Siberian swans, peregrine falcons, blue herons and 264 other species roost in the sanctuary. The most spectacular sight is the 50,000 snow geese that stop off in the fall and early spring on their journey from and to Wrangel Island off Siberia's eastern coast. The **Snow Goose Festival** heralds their arrival on the first weekend of November. In springtime millions of Western Sandpipers pass through; spring is also good for viewing hawks, eagles, seals, cormorants, ospreys and other fish-eating wildlife that follow migratory salmon to the Fraser River's mouth. The sanctuary has an observation tower, 3km of paths, and picnic tables. Keep in mind that there is very little activity here in summer. October to April is the best time to visit, but dress warmly. It's accessible by car only; call for directions.

RICHMOND NATURE PARK Map pp228-9
☎ 604-718-6188; 11851 Westminster Hwy; admission by donation; ☽ 9am-5pm; bus 98 B-Line from Burrard Station downtown, at Richmond Centre walk across street to Bay 2A & transfer to bus 405

This 80-hectare park is dedicated to the preservation of a 3000-year-old peat bog. Boardwalks wind through various ecosystems (a marsh, a forest and a pond), accompanied by educational displays. The Nature House Centre continues the theme with interactive exhibits designed with children in mind.

Finn Slough

Settled by Finnish pioneers in the 1890s, Finn Slough has been a working fishing community for more than 100 years. It's a motley collection of houses on stilts and old wooden boardwalks at the south end of No 4 Rd. The community now attracts painters, photographers and others drawn to the serene, misty atmosphere of the tidal inlet and surrounding wetlands. No public transportation serves the area; it's probably best visited in conjunction with Steveston (below). Its website is www.finnslough.com.

STEVESTON

It's all about fish in the village of Steveston, from the barnacle-covered boats that chug in and out of port selling fresh catches, to the historic Gulf of Georgia Cannery, to the pubs and shops frying up hot battered fish and chips.

In the late 1800s Steveston was one of the largest fishing ports in the world, with 15 canneries packing 195,000 cases of salmon yearly. Hard work meant hard play, and bordellos, gambling dens and opium dens sprang up to cater to the rough crowd of 10,000 who lived here during fishing season.

Japanese immigrants settled in Steveston in the early 20th century. However, like other minorities at that time, they were often treated as second-class citizens and it wasn't until 1949 that Japanese Canadians were granted the right to vote. During WWII, nearly all of the Japanese Canadians in the province, and specifically from Steveston, were sent to the interior of BC to live in internment camps, and their boats and homes were sold at auction without a penny from the sales going to the owners. Financial compensation was finally made by the government in 1988.

Orientation

Steveston is located in the southwest corner of Richmond. Moncton St runs through the center of the old village that fronts on to the South Arm of the Fraser River, and is bordered by Chatham St to the north, No 1 Rd to the east and 4th Ave to the west.

GULF OF GEORGIA CANNERY NATIONAL HISTORIC SITE Map pp228-9

☎ 604-664-9009; www.gulfofgeorgiacannery.com; 12138 4th Ave; adult/child 6-16/senior & student/family $6.50/3.25/5/16.25; ⏱ 10am-5pm Thu-Mon Apr, May, Sep & Oct, 10am-5pm Jun, 10am-6pm Jul & Aug; bus 98 B-Line, transfer to bus 402 or 410 at Richmond Centre

For those who've always wanted to see the machinery used in herring reduction, this is the place. The building formerly housed the largest cannery on the Fraser River, which operated from 1894 to 1979. You can also see how a canning line worked, chill in the Ice House and watch a film on the BC's fishing history.

STEVESTON MUSEUM Map pp228-9

☎ 604-271-6868; 3811 Moncton St; admission by donation; ⏱ 9:30am-1pm & 1:30-5pm Mon-Sat; bus 98 B-Line, transfer to bus 402 or 410 at Richmond Centre

This humble museum – which is also an active post office – tells the story of the town's fishing past and the internment of the Japanese. Pick up a walking tour guide here to help navigate the village.

Walking & Cycling Tours

Walking & Cycling Tours

The best way to explore such an active, outdoor-oriented city is on foot or by bicycle. (That way you're active and outdoors yourself, don't you know?) We've included all sorts of options here to cover various aspects of Vancouver's personality.

So what are you waiting for? Stroll by downtown's architectural treats. Cycle Stanley Park's famed seawall through forests, past totem poles and along beaches. See what all the fuss is about at Gastown's Steam Clock, Chinatown's gardens and the other popular attractions in these two neighborhoods. Caffeinate in Commercial Dr's Old World espresso houses. Browse Granville Island's artisan galleries. Or party in Yaletown's entertainment district and downtown's club strip. Each tour also includes eating and drinking choices en route to keep up your energy level.

If you're feeling ambitious, you can link various tours together, ie the Chinatown to Gastown Walk can hook into the Commercial Dr Coffee Jag, and the Granville Gallery Hop can link to Yaletown & Downtown After Dark. For more information about organized group tours, see p39.

DOWNTOWN DISCOVERY WALK

Begin at Robson and Beatty Sts, in front of the giant puffed pillow that is **BC Place Stadium 1** (p43). The roof of the 60,000-capacity venue – home of the BC Lions football team – is 'air-supported,' which means inflated by huge fans (no, not meaty sports aficionados, but rather wind-blowing machinery), hence its cushiony appearance. Sports enthusiasts can pop into the **BC Sports Hall of Fame & Museum 2** (p43). The postmodern lion-topped arch in front is the Terry Fox Memorial, a tribute to the young cancer patient whose run across Canada raised $24 million for research before he lost his fight with the disease.

Walk west on Robson St past parking lots and burger-smelling sports bars to the **Vancouver Public Library 3** (p45). No gladiators dwell inside the Roman Colosseum-like building, but you will find 24km of shelves propping up 1.25 million books, as well as coffee, pizza and ice cream shops under the stunning glass atrium. Like many buildings in eco-conscious Vancouver, the library is topped by a 'green roof,' ie a planted roof that helps conserve energy.

Continue northwest to Howe St and **Robson Square 4** (p44), a multitiered public space designed by architect Arthur Erickson, which connects the Law Courts to the south and Vancouver Art Gallery to the north (both covered later in the tour). Begin your exploration at the northwest corner of Robson and Howe Sts, where a pagoda shelters a stairway. Head down to behold a hidden underground layer of the city that includes an extension of the University of British Columbia's campus.

Walk Facts

Best Time Any weekday morning or afternoon.

Start BC Place Stadium (SkyTrain Stadium)

End Mill Marine Bistro (bus 19)

Distance 3km

Time 1¾ hours

Fuel Stop Vancouver Public Library (p45), Caffé Artigiano (p126)

Return to street level by walking south and up the stairs toward the fountain. Thus begins a series of stairway by fountain climbs; keep jogging through gardened terraces with great views. After the third rise, you'll come to the **Provincial Law Courts 5** (p44), whose sloped-glass atrium measures well over an acre. Walk through to Nelson St.

Turn northeast on tree-lined Hornby St and proceed to the **Vancouver Art Gallery 6** (p44), best known for its boldly colored Emily Carr paintings. Coffee art takes place across the street at **Caffé Artigiano 7** (p126), where baristas draw leafy designs in latte foam.

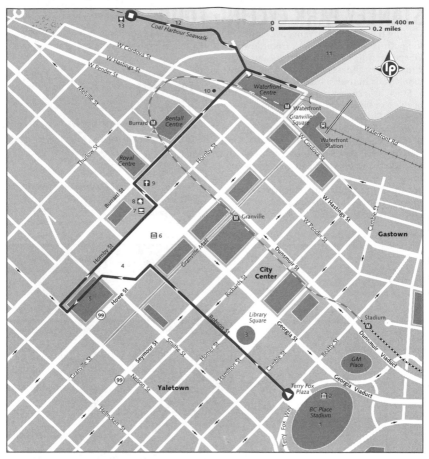

Fueled for further discoveries? The **Fairmont Hotel Vancouver 8** (p170) awaits you, a fine example of the chateau style hotels built across the country in the early 1900s by the Canadian National Railway. Cross to Georgia St's north side for the best view of the Renaissance detail and creepy gargoyles.

Nearby at Georgia and Burrard Sts stands **Christ Church Cathedral 9** (p43), Vancouver's oldest church dating from 1895, and worth a peek inside to see its timber framework and stained-glass windows.

Cross Burrard St and travel northeast past several tall, glassy towers to Hastings St. The **Marine Building 10** (p44) dominates the northwest corner – a spectacular, 22-story art deco tribute to Vancouver's maritime history.

Continue on Burrard St until it dead-ends into the road fronting the water. Turn southeast toward **Canada Place 11** (p43), recognized by its five white-fabric sails and the cruise ships docked alongside. There are great harbor views from here, including North Vancouver's neon-yellow sulphur piles.

Backtrack along the waterfront and follow the road in the other direction as it slopes down to the path known as the **Coal Harbour Seawalk 12** (p50). **Mill Marine Bistro 13** (p124) is about 400m west, and is an excellent place to have a fuel stop and discover your favorite microbrew.

STANLEY PARK CYCLING TOUR

Cycling the seawall is a Vancouver must. Not only is the ride gorgeous, but it's easy to do – the path is just a few blocks from downtown, it's flat, paved, well marked and well used.

Of special note to couch potatoes and exercise slackers: fitness not required. So get up, plonk your butt on a bike and go.

Start by renting a two-wheeler at one of the **bike shops** 1 (p142) on Denman near Georgia St. Ride northeast on Denman St a few blocks to the waterfront. Pick up the seawall trail heading northwest (left). The trail hugs the park's perimeter; throughout the ride the water will be to your right and towering cedars and firs to your left. There are three main rules to remember: traffic moves counter-clockwise around the park; bikes stay on the path's left side, while foot

Tour Facts

Best Time Any day, daytime

Start Denman & Georgia Sts (bus 19)

End True Confections (bus 5)

Distance 10.5km

Time 2 hours

Fuel Stop Refreshment stands at children's water park and Second Beach

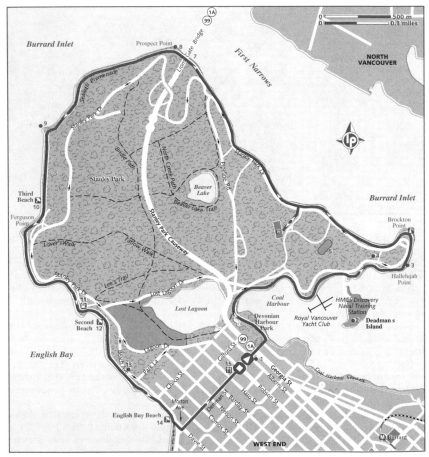

traffic stays right; and sometimes the path splits, with bikes routed away from the footpath – keep an eye on the posted signs.

Almost immediately, as you pedal around the inlet past the Rowing Club, you'll have your first eye-popping view, with sailboat masts in the foreground, glass buildings glinting in the middle ground and swooping white Canada Place in the background.

After 1km, you'll come to **Deadman's Island 2** (p51), once a First Nations burial ground, now a naval reserve. At 1.5km is the **Nine O'Clock Gun 3** (p52), a historic cannon that lets loose at 9pm nightly, formerly so ships' captains were able to set their chronometers. Go around Brockton Point and soon you'll see a colorful **totem pole collection 4** (p52), followed by **Brockton Oval 5** (p52), where white-clad athletes play cricket.

At the children's water park (3.25km), dismount from your bike as the sign instructs and walk your way left (away from the water), past the refreshment stand and up the slight rise. You can then re-mount, and ride past the Japanese Canadian WWI monument to where a huge tree stands. Across from here is the **Vancouver Aquarium 6** (p53) entrance – not the main one, but a back door you can enter for free to take a gander at the belugas and seals.

If you want to go in for a more thorough visit, cycle about 200m further along to the roundabout outlined with benches. Go left (east), and you're at the main doorway. There's a bike rack by the bathrooms near the killer-whale sculpture by renowned Haida artist Bill Reid.

Retrace your steps to the children's water park and turn left (northwest) on the seawall trail. Pedal 1.5km to **Lion's Gate Bridge 7** (p52). The ride underneath it and around **Prospect Point 8** (p52) is jaw-dropping. The mountains are seemingly an arm's length away, and as you round the bend the view breaks wide open across a shimmering expanse of water. Cruise ships bellow in and out of here, and there are bound to be guys fishing off the point.

Dr Sun Yat-Sen Classical Chinese Garden & Park (p55),

Keep cycling – you've just passed the halfway point. Trees spill down the cliffs, and sometimes the path narrows considerably as rocky outcrops lean over it. Such is the case 1km later, near **Siwash Rock 9** (p52); this is a lone protrusion just offshore which, according to legend, is a Squamish warrior the gods turned to stone as a reward for his unselfish behavior.

Third Beach 10 (p52) appears 750m further along, where you might observe a seal or bald eagle. Often there's an artist here who stacks sea stones into precariously balanced, obelisk-like sculptures.

About 1km onward you reach the freshwater aquamarine **Second Beach Pool 11** (p147), followed by busy **Second Beach 12** (p52) itself, where snacks and bathrooms are also to be found.

Cycle another 1km, and you'll see folks in crisp whites pitch 'bowls' next to 'jacks' at the **lawn bowling green 13** (p144). Soon after, the trail begins to hug Beach Ave above **English Bay Beach 14** (p50).

Go another 250m to where Beach Ave intersects Morton Ave; the latter empties immediately on to Denman St. Turn left (northeast). You can return to the rental shop and then indulge in a sugar hit at **True Confections 15** (p94), or stop anywhere that looks inviting along restaurant-rich Denman St.

CHINATOWN TO GASTOWN WALK

Start at W Pender and Taylor Sts at the brightly painted three-story **Millennium Gate 1** (p54), Chinatown's entry point. Walk east on Pender to Carrall St. On the corner is the **Sam Kee Building 2** (p55), the world's narrowest building.

Turn right (south) on Carrall St. Midway between Pender and Keefer Sts you'll come to a courtyard. Enter it. The first doorway is for the **Dr Sun Yat-Sen Classical Chinese Garden 3** (p55), a tranquil oasis and a good place for an introduction to the Taoist principles of yin and yang. If you don't want to pay, you can walk to the next entrance for the free Dr Sun Yat-Sen Park, which is not quite as impressive as the garden but still lovely.

Exit the gardens on to Columbia St and go right (south). At Keefer St turn left (east). Keefer, along with Pender, are Chinatown's main streets, lined with herbalists, grocers, almond cookie–stacked bakeries, and vendors selling Buddha statues and Hello Kitty footstools. **Hon's Wun-Tun House 4** (p101) is on Keefer St, proffering pot stickers to the peckish, or any of the other dishes on its menu of 300-plus items.

Turn left on Gore Ave and left again on E Pender St for more fun and footstools. At Carrall St turn right. The next few blocks headed east are pretty shabby, with abandoned buildings and bony, haunted-looking people wandering the streets. It's part of the overflow from the drug-riddled, 'poorest postal code in Canada' crux at Main and Hastings Sts (though a redevelopment plan

Walk Facts

Best Time Any day, late morning or early afternoon

Start Millennium Gate (SkyTrain Stadium)

End Steamworks Brewing Company (SkyTrain Waterfront)

Distance 2km

Time 1¼ hours

Fuel Stop Hon's Wun-Tun House (p101)

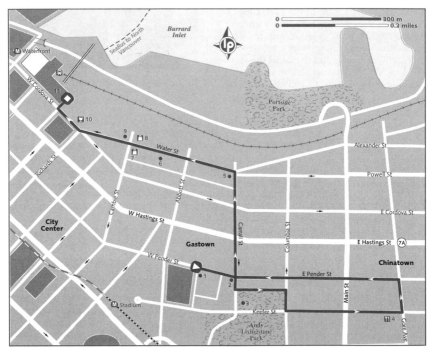

for the area is in the works). Take Carrall St to Water St, Gastown's main thoroughfare. The corner here is **Maple Tree Square 5** (p47), home of the Gassy Jack Statue, which stands on the site of Jack's original saloon that launched Gastown in 1867; Gaolers Mew, the city's first jail; and Byrnes Block, Vancouver's oldest building in its original lot.

Walking west on Water St puts you in the thick of touristy shops selling T-shirts, fudge and moccasins. The **Storyeum 6** (p47), just west of Abbott St, recounts BC's history. **Hill's Native Art 7** (p155) and the **Inuit Gallery 8** (p155) display Aboriginal crafts.

The **Steam Clock 9** (p46) blows its whistle every quarter of an hour on the corner of Water and Cambie Sts. Why this is such a thrill remains a mystery – it's not even steam, for crying out loud, but powered by electricity.

Finish with a frosty pint of homemade beer at **Steamworks Brewing Company 10** (p124), and mull over your next move: You've got two options since you're conveniently located by **Waterfront Station 11** (p45). From here you can hop on the SeaBus and chug through the freighters for the ride over to Lonsdale Quay, or you can hop on the SkyTrain and take it to the Broadway or Commercial Dr station and begin the Commercial Drive Coffee Jag following (see below).

COMMERCIAL DRIVE COFFEE JAG

If 'coffee promotes confidence,' as the old saying goes, you'll walk away from this tour positively swaggering. The path is basically a straight shot north on Commercial Dr, past all the old Italian espresso houses now interspersed with funky shops and restaurants. The caffeinated new you may finish the afternoon with a fresh set of dreadlocks, a 'family jewels harness' or some other special purchase. Take the SkyTrain to either the Commercial Dr or Broadway station (the Millennium Line goes to the former, the Expo line to the latter). Walk to Commercial Dr and head north.

In the same way you fill a car with gas before embarking on a journey, you'll stop at three coffee shops to begin: **Continental Coffee 1** (p127), followed by **Caffé Calabria 2** (p127) and a few blocks later by **Roma Café 3** (p127). Continental and Roma are populated by natty, cap-wearing old timers hunkered down beside young bo-ho types, all yelling at the soccer matches being screened on satellite TV. Roma is the best on the strip for sports watching. Calabria works best for kitschy atmosphere (does that fresco really show God passing Adam a cappuccino?) or if you're looking for a fat deli sandwich.

Now that we've got the blood flowing and heart pounding, it's time to zip onward. **Knotty Boy 4** (p149), a salon specializing in dreadlocks, is across Grant St from Roma. The next block north, between Kitchener and Charles Sts, is home to four unique stores: **People's Co-op Bookstore 5** (p159), with leftist tomes and 'zines; jam-stacked **Magpie Magazine Gallery 6** (p159), sporting the city's largest periodical selection; **Highlife World Music 7**

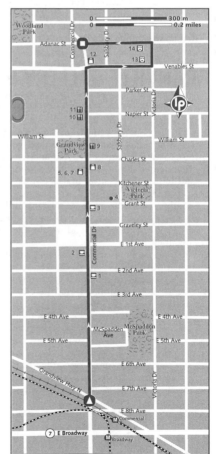

(p159) for global beats; and **Dr Vigari Gallery 8** (p159), displaying groovy teapots and rocking chairs among its eclectic wares.

Havana 9 (p105) is on the next block. Grab a front patio seat and watch life on the Drive – mohawked skateboarders, men in capes, little old ladies shopping for tomatoes – wheel by. The restaurant also hosts a theater and art gallery, so don't forget to check out what's showing.

A bit further north, **Drive Organics 10** (p93) and **Sweet Cherubim 11** (p93) are organic stores/cafés where you can dig into some brown rice porridge or find yeast-free gifts.

Womyns' Ware 12 (p160) is at the end of the strip, across Venables St, and has one of North America's largest sex toy selections. The cool staff can enlighten you on items like the Hellraiser. (C'mon, who isn't curious about something with a name like that?)

If you're looking for evening entertainment, turn east on Venables St and walk a block to the **Vancouver East Cultural Centre 13** (p135). This rehabbed church now serves as an out-of-the-ordinary theater, often for new music performances. Around the corner on Adanac St is **Wise Hall 14** (p129), a noted folk music venue.

Return west along Adanac St to Commercial Dr, and catch bus 20 back downtown.

GRANVILLE GALLERY HOP

Start at Granville Island's entrance, marked by a sign under the Granville Bridge overpass at the intersection of W 2nd Ave and Anderson St. As you walk toward the sign, you soon come to Cartwright St – turn right (southeast). The **Granville Island Brewery 1** (p59) is on your left. Step into the Taproom for a Kitsilano Maple Cream Ale or take the tour and see how it's made.

Get your wallet ready, because next you will pass in rapid succession the **Crafthouse 2** (p160), **Gallery of BC Ceramics 3** (p160) and **Forge & Form 4** (p160). Like just about everywhere on the island, these galleries sell one of a kind, BC–artisan made objects; in this case it may be a hand-blown goblet, silver bracelet or carved wooden box that catches your eye.

Keep walking southeast down Cartwright St past all the corrugated metal warehouses (remember, Granville was once a factory-filled place nicknamed Industrial Island). Follow the train tracks through the parking lot to the left of the **Performance Works building 5**. Keep heading toward the water, and within a few steps you'll come to a waterfront boardwalk. Follow it left (east).

You'll notice the boardwalk skirts a big hill – aka the **Mound 6**. At some point, scramble up it. The top has excellent views of False Creek's harbor, especially east toward the Science Center's geodesic dome. You'll even find a nice bench atop the Mound from where you can admire it all.

Head down to the boardwalk and continue left until you come to the **Dockside Brewing Company 7** (p123). If it's nice weather, enjoy the view from Dockside's patio; if it's cold or rainy, wander inside for a seat by the fire.

Pick up where you left off, following the boardwalk round the point; note that you're moving northwest now. Keep an eye to the right, as you pass a floating 'village' of waterborne homes bobbing alongside.

Soon after the floathouses, the boardwalk abruptly tapers off into private property.

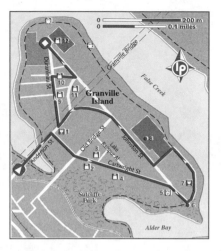

Turn left at the green wooden poles, and go through the corrugated metal tunnel. Voila – you've come out on to Johnston St. Turn right, and you're in front of the **Charles Scott Gallery** 8, part of the expansive **Emily Carr Institute of Art & Design** (p58), which you'll walk past. Just after crossing Old Bridge St (about 100m), take a soft left on to the unmarked street, which will lead you to Duranleau St.

Turn right (north) on Duranleau St and look for **Malaspina Printmakers Gallery** 9 (p161), where you can take a lithograph-making workshop or peruse the wall hangings. **Net Loft** 10 (p160) is a big warehouse filled with shops and studios, such as **Maiwa Handprints**, specializing in global fabrics and textiles. Walk through the Net Loft and you'll reach **BC Wood Co-op** 11 (p160), a good place to shop for carvings or handcrafted furniture.

Turn left (northwest) on Johnston St and you're at the **Granville Island Public Market** 12 (p59). Here you can feast on sweet or savory, or both: alternate between red snapper soup and warm currant scones, or oysters and chips and lemon meringue pie. If the weather cooperates, take your goodies to the outdoor benches; buskers often perform here, but don't get too distracted lest the seagulls swipe your food.

From the market, you can either take a mini ferry to Hornby St downtown or to Yaletown (where you can hook into the Yaletown & Downtown After Dark walk following).

YALETOWN & DOWNTOWN AFTER DARK

This tour will take you through Yaletown and downtown's entertainment strip. Live blues bands, bouncy-floored rock clubs, bowling, handcrafted brews, juicy martinis and shake-your-groove-thing clubs are all part of the package. Make sure you have money in your pocket, as drinks can be expensive and the clubs often have cover charges. Even if you decide not to go inside, it's fun to pass by and crowd gaze.

Start at Granville and Drake Sts at the **Yale** 1 (p129). This is Vancouver's long-standing blues joint, a dark place that certainly would be smoky if smoking was allowed. Walk southeast three blocks on Drake St to Homer St, passing a variety of swanky condos and lofts. If it's a nice night at least three sparkly convertibles will whiz by. **Automotive Billiards** 2 (p131) is on Homer St near its intersection with Drake and is a fashionable place to shoot stick.

Walk one block further southeast to Hamilton St and you're in the heart of Yaletown, an area often compared to New York City's SoHo. Three drinking establishments appear in rapid succession. **Elixir** 3 (p125), the house bar of the Opus Hotel, is perhaps the most mod and has the widest-ranging drink list. **Yaletown Brewing Company** 4 (p124) crafts its own, and you can sip while relaxing on the expansive outdoor patio. **AFTERglow** 5 (p125) is the place to go if you're craving a martini, which you can choose from a list of James Bond–worthy names, like the Pink Pussycat.

Turn left (northwest) on Nelson St and walk four blocks; you'll notice the ambience gets trashier – literally – the further away from Yaletown you go. Turn right on Granville St and you're smack in the thick of Vancouver's club strip.

Walk Facts

Best Time Wednesday to Saturday evening

Start The Yale (bus 4)

End Railway Club (SkyTrain Granville)

Distance 2.25km

Time 1½ hours

Fuel Stop Each and every place listed

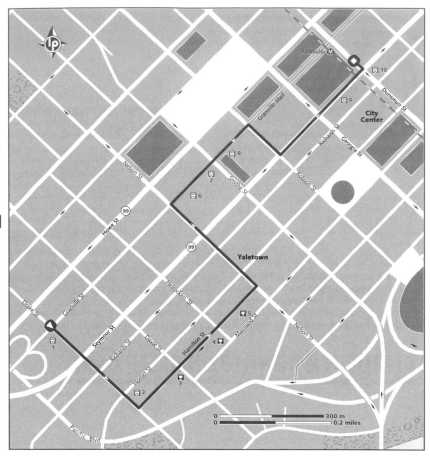

First up is the **Roxy 6** (p131), a fun, silly place that may have a hockey-related comedy show or 'Vancouver Idol' singing contest on stage. Around the corner on Smithe St is **Skybar 7** (p137), a seriously upscale club ballyhooed for its retractable roof. The **Commodore 8** (p128) is more earthy, with a springy dance floor buoyed by under-the-surface tires. There's live music several nights a week, including international touring groups, but if perchance the house is dark, the venue also houses a rock 'n' roll bowling alley/pool hall next door.

Turn right (southeast) on Robson St, then immediately left (northeast) on Seymour St. After a block and a half you'll come to **AuBar 9** (p130), which pulls crowds who dance to Top 40, hip-hop and house music. The best venue in town – the old-time **Railway Club 10** (p128) – is around the corner on Dunsmuir St. Live music crackles from the speakers nightly in the main room, but there is also a quieter back nook where patrons can quaff from dimpled pint glasses amid more hushed tones.

The Granville SkyTrain station is nearby, but it stops running in the wee hours, in which case it's time to catch a Night Bus (p208).

Eating

Eating

Eating well in Vancouver is guaranteed, and the city's varied restaurant scene is one of its crowning glories. Powerhouse chefs flex their muscles at top dining rooms throughout town, while nestled next to them are bare-bones but cozy Japanese noodle shops, European cafés and hippie vegetarian havens.

West coast cuisine dominates the tables, combining straight-off-the-boat seafood with fresh produce from the Fraser Valley's fertile farms. Stir in ethnic influences, like Chinese, Thai, Japanese and French, complement the mix with local microbrews and Okanagan Valley wines, and you can see why Vancouver has become a foodie favorite. See Food & Drink (p13) for more on local cuisine, and p210 for cooking courses.

Vancouverites love to eat outdoors amid their stunning environs, so patios and decks are widespread. Many are heated and stay open throughout the year. Most restaurants are licensed to serve alcohol, even if it is just wine and beer, but a city bylaw against smoking is strictly enforced. Dress is casual, even at the priciest places.

Publications (p214) that keep up with food trends and chef gossip, as well as archive restaurant reviews, include *Vancouver Magazine*, *City Food* and the *Georgia Straight*.

Opening Hours

Restaurants in Vancouver are usually open for lunch on weekdays from 11:30am to 2:30pm and most serve dinner daily from 5pm to 9pm, sometimes later on weekends. Many also serve weekend brunch, usually from 11am to 3pm. For those that serve breakfast, the time is around 7:30am to 10am. If restaurants take a day off, it's Monday or Tuesday. Some restaurants may close early or on additional days in winter, and stay open later during summer.

How Much?

Prices are low compared to what most US and European visitors are used to, so eating out can be a Vancouver highlight. Stretch your budget even further by eating well at lunch, when most restaurants charge about half as much for a meal as at dinner – often for exactly the same menu. At dinner expect to pay between $10 and $20 (before taxes and tip) for an entrée (main course) at a mid-range establishment, and $35 or more at a top-end restaurant. The 'Cheap Eats' reviews at the end of each neighborhood section list places where you are likely to be fed well for less than $10. The *Georgia Straight* often has coupons for restaurants tucked within its pages. In late January many top-tier restaurants join forces for the Dine Out promotion, where they offer three-course prix-fixe menus for just $15 to $25 (call ☎ 604-682-2222 for details).

Making Reservations

As a general rule of thumb, the higher the prices on the menu, the more strongly reservations are advised. Without a reservation, try to show up for an early or late seating, say, before 5:30pm or just after 9pm. Downtown, Yaletown and the West End are probably the most difficult neighborhoods to score a table. A few restaurants still refuse to bother with reservations despite raging crowds; such holdouts include Vij's (p116), Bin 941 (p94) and Bin 942 (p116).

Taxes & Tipping

Taxes are the only unpleasant taste on the dining scene. Food gets hit at 7% (the federal goods and service tax – GST), and any alcohol on your bill gets whacked with an additional

10%. Then you need to add a tip – 15% of the pre-tax bill is the standard, 20% for exemplary service. Thus, if you order a burger ($7) and beer ($3), you'll end up paying a total bill of $12.50 (70¢ GST plus 30¢ alcohol tax plus $1.50 tip). Either leave the tip discreetly on the table or hand it directly to the server. At cafés where you order at the counter, the tipping etiquette is less clear. A tip jar will often be displayed prominently, where you can drop in whatever you feel is appropriate.

Groceries

The indoor **Granville Island Public Market** (p59) is as much of a sightseeing experience as a destination for take-out meals, snacks and picnic goodies. For vegetarian and health-food eats, local chain **Capers** (Map pp230-3; ☎ 604-687-5288; 1675 Robson St; ⏰8am-10pm Mon-Sat, 8am-9pm Sun; bus 5) stocks all-natural and organic foods, and runs healthful on-site cafés. Small greengrocers thrive along Commercial Dr and throughout the West End. If your recipe calls for more obscure ingredients – say frogs or a giant splayed pig – head to Chinatown's butchers and grocers. And, hmm, where to go for that $100 loaf of bread flown in fresh from Paris each morning? In Yaletown, of course, to uber-upscale **Urban Fare** (☎ 604-975-7550; 177 Davie St; ⏰6am-midnight; bus 1). For bread that's more in the $2 range, supermarket chain giant **Safeway** has outlets throughout Vancouver, usually open 8am to midnight daily.

Also try:

Drive Organics (Map p235; ☎ 604-255-2326; 1045 Commercial Dr; bus 20)

Robson Public Market (Map pp230-3; ☎ 604-682-2733; 1610 Robson St; bus 5)

Sweet Cherubim (Map p235; ☎ 604-253-0969; 1105 Commercial Dr; bus 20)

Excellent **farmers markets** (☎ 604-879-3276) take place at local parks and community centers such as **Trout Lake Community Centre** (Map pp228-9; E 15th & Victoria Dr; ⏰9am-2pm Sat mid-May–early Oct), at **Nat Bailey Stadium** (Map pp236-7; 30th & Ontario Sts; ⏰1-6:30pm Wed mid-Jun–late Oct) and also at **Nelson Park** (Map pp230-3; Comox St btwn Bute & Thurlow Sts; ⏰9:30am-2pm Sat mid-Jun–early Oct).

Top Five Chefs to Dine For *John Lee*

No matter how friendly and laid-back Vancouverites might seem, the city's top chefs are highly competitive. But while street fights between gangs of flour-smeared, white-hatted culinary rogues are rare, the air of high-end kitchen-based combat has created an ideal climate for visiting gourmands. Among the city's leading culinary creators are:

- **Rob Feenie** Not content with the success of his award-winning French-inspired **Lumière** (p118), the city's most celebrated chef recently opened **Feenie's** (p117), a gourmet faster-food joint next door. You have to be confident about yourself to name your high-end hot dog 'Feenie's Weenie.' It's still the delicate innovations at Lumière's tasting bar that draw the most plaudits.
- **Hidekazu Tojo** Expect to drop quite a few dollars more than at your last sushi meal over at **Tojo's** (p115), where diners flock to sample a complex haiku of supreme dishes prepared by the multi award–winning Hidekazu Tojo. This colorful character has been sharpening his knives in Vancouver for 30 years and has developed an unrivaled encyclopedic mastery of 2000 traditional Japanese recipes.
- **Robert Clark** Those who worship at the altar of seafood will not want to miss Clark's dedication to the subtleties of the region's great fishy flavors at **C** (p94) restaurant. He encourages diners to experiment with flavors and textures with which they are unfamiliar, and his innovative salmon tasting menu is highly recommended.
- **Vikram Vij** A unique take on Indian cuisine – who else would have thought of lamb popsicles? – is de rigueur for this Asian expat whose **Vij's** (p116) fusion restaurant routinely wins 'best Indian' in local dining awards. Unlike many chefs, he is happy to wander out from his kitchen to meet diners, offering adventurous and original menu recommendations to the undecided.
- **Romy Prasad** Far more modest than most of the city's loud and proud celebrity chefs, Prasad continues to deliver the goods at the Tuscan-themed **CinCin** (p98), where he regularly caters to the comfort food requests of homesick Hollywood glitterati. Another slice of alder-smoked wild salmon pizza, Halle?

DOWNTOWN

Downtown has it all, from cheap restaurants strung along Granville St that cater to clubbers to fancy five-star hotel restaurants. Bountiful Robson St hosts a mix of eateries that extends on through the West End.

BIN 941 Map pp230-3 *Fusion Tapas*
☎ 604-683-1246; 941 Davie St; dishes $6-14;
☽ 5pm-2am Mon-Sat, 5pm-midnight Sun; bus 1
Specializing in 'hedonistic nocturnal feasting,' this small, orange candelabra-lit tapas bar dreams up big bouquets of 'tapatisers' like venison with broken truffle vinaigrette or portobello mushroom cutlets. Pair your own choices with something from the wine list or 'hip hops' beer menu. Reservations are not accepted. Sister restaurant Bin 942 is in South Granville (p116).

C Map pp230-3 *Seafood*
☎ 604-681-1164; 1600 Howe St; lunch $17-20, dinner mains $28-39, 8-course tasting menu $90;
☽ 11:30am-2:30pm Mon-Fri, 5:30-10:30pm Mon-Sun; bus 1
Nowhere is seafood prepared more adventurously than at C. Smoked salmon with cucumber jelly and octopus bacon-wrapped scallops are just a few of the sumptuous items from the awe-inspiring menu. The lunchtime Taster Box ($29), with tuna tartare, side-striped shrimp, smoked sockeye and beef carpaccio, is a good way to sample the goods. The waterfront patio is tops in the city.

CARLOS 'N BUD'S TEX-MEX SALOON
Map pp230-3 *Mexican*
☎ 604-684-5335; 555 Pacific St; snacks $6-11, mains $10-17; ☽ 11:30am-midnight; bus 4
This family-style joint rustles up Cancun enchiladas, buzzard wings and BBQ ribs courtesy of the only original Texas smoker in western Canada. Kamikaze shooters are $2.50, to top it off. It closes early or stays open later, depending on the crowd.

DIVA AT THE MET Map pp230-3 *West Coast*
☎ 604-602-7788; 645 Howe St; breakfast $10-16, lunch $15-25, dinner mains $30-40; ☽ 6:30am-2:30pm Mon-Fri, 7am-2:30pm Sat & Sun, 5:30-10pm Mon-Sun; SkyTrain Granville
This is the Metropolitan Hotel's premier dining space. From breakfasts of steel-cut oatmeal with

Top Sweet Treats

You've skied, you've cycled, you've kayaked, you've earned it – indulge.

Along with the tapas and fusion fads is Vancouver's gelato craze. A visit to **La Casa Gelato** (Map p235; ☎ 604-251-3211; East Vancouver, 1033 Venables St; ☽ 10am-11pm) is a must to sample its 200-plus flavors, including the ridiculous wasabi, kimchi and balsamic vinegar. Winter brings out the curry flavors, and summer begets the beer flavor. Many locals also wax rhapsodic about more traditional **Mum's Gelato** (Map pp238-9; ☎ 604-738-6867; Kitsilano, 2028 Vine St; ☽ 11:30am-10:30pm).

Nanaimo Bars are a regional specialty, with three layers of richness – chocolate/cream/chocolate – stacked in brownie-like form. **Benny's Bagels** (p119) serves a sweet one.

sen5es (Map pp230-3; ☎ 604-633-0138; downtown, 801 W Georgia St; ☽ 7am-6pm Mon-Thu, 7am-7pm Fri, 8am-7pm Sat, 10am-6pm Sun) gourmet bakery makes 'the world's best cookie' – the Chocolate Sparkle. It's laden with dark Valrhona chocolate and tastes like a truffle.

Savary Island Pie Company (Map pp228-9; ☎ 604-926-4021; West Vancouver, 1533 Marine Dr; ☽ 6am-8pm Mon-Sat, 6am-7pm Sun) has replenished many a weary skier returning from the north slopes with flaky-crusted fruit pies, such as its strawberry rhubarb, while **Honey's Doughnuts & Goodies** (Map pp228-9; ☎ 604-929-4988; North Vancouver, 4373 Gallant Ave; ☽ 6am-11pm, reduced in winter) proffers glazed treats to hikers and kayakers in Deep Cove. Other places to ramp up your caloric intake:

Death by Chocolate (Map pp230-3; ☎ 604-688-8234; downtown, 818 Burrard St; ☽ 7am-midnight Mon-Thu, 7am-1am Fri, 9am-1am Sat, 9am-midnight Sun) Try the 'Multitude of Sins.'

True Confections (Map pp230-3; ☎ 604-682-1292; West End, 866 Denman St; ☽ 1pm-midnight Sun-Thu, 1pm-1am Fri & Sat) Gigantic slices of 40 different cheesecakes, layer cakes and pies.

Miriam's (Map pp230-3; ☎ 604-683-7624; West End, 1184 Denman St; ☽ 9am-1am, reduced in winter) Homemade pie and ice cream.

steamed nutmeg milk to dinners of cinnamon-smoked duck breast with morel mushroom risotto, Diva never misses a step. The vintage wine bar delights, and desserts include symphonies of chocolate, homemade ice cream or fresh berries. Head for the patio in summertime.

DV8 Map pp230-3 *Eclectic/Vegetarian*
☎ 604-682-4388; 515 Davie St; dishes $8-13; ⏰ 5pm-3am Mon-Thu, 5pm-4am Fri & Sat, 5pm-2am Sun; bus 1

This grungy, late-night haunt provides swell bites, like Cajun potatoes, sushi rolls and burgers, along with a mixed bag of entrées that include a vegan hot pot, mango chili cream penne, garlic yogurt chicken and mustard-seed curried jackfruit. The space also houses a club (p130) and a gallery.

ELBOW ROOM Map pp230-3 *Comfort Food*
☎ 604-685-3628; 560 Davie St; mains $5-11; ⏰ 8am-4pm; bus 20

At this Vancouver mainstay for breakfast and lunch, the servers are abusive by design, so have fun with it. When they ask 'Are you ready to order or what?' answer that you'll be ready when you're bloody ready. Breakfast runs until closing. The menu highlights the mood of the joint, as evidenced by the 'You've Got to be F--king Kidding' burger (two 8oz beef patties with mushrooms and bacon).

FIDDLEHEAD JOE'S
Map pp230-3 *Seafood/Café*
☎ 604-688-1969; 1012 Beach Ave; tapas $7-10, mains $15-19; ⏰ 11am-10pm Mon-Fri, 9am-10pm Sat & Sun; bus 1

This energetic seafood café mixes good food with superb people-watching opportunities from its False Creek/seawall vantage point. Dine on tapas of blue crab and salmon cakes, or mains that include curried cream mussels and tomato-braised lamb shank.

FIVE SAILS Map pp230-3 *West Coast*
☎ 604-891-2892; 3rd fl, 999 Canada Place; mains $30-40, prix-fixe dinner $68-80; ⏰ 6-10pm; SkyTrain Waterfront

The Pan Pacific Hotel's five-diamond restaurant has views to match the bill you'll get at the end of the evening. Extensive surf-and-turf options come with creative twists, like the seared swordfish with tomato fondue, or hazelnut-crusted halibut topped with honey and port wine–glazed horseradish. Window-side tables

are best. The weekly 'fresh sheet' offers whatever is in season, likely hauled in earlier that day.

GOTHAM Map pp230-3 *Steakhouse*
☎ 604-605-8282; 615 Seymour St; mains $26-50; ⏰ dinner from 5pm; SkyTrain Granville

Gotham is dark, sultry and intimate, setting the mood with leopard-print stuffed chairs, stage lighting and Vegas table lamps. Rooms on various levels provide different dining experiences. Order the steaks or seafood that have made this place justifiably famous, particularly with the Hollywood North crowd.

KETTLE OF FISH Map pp230-3 *Seafood*
☎ 604-682-6661; 900 Pacific St; mains $16-25; ⏰ 11:30am-2pm Mon-Fri, 5-9:30pm Sun-Thu, 5-10pm Fri & Sat; bus 1

'Eat lotsa fish' is its motto, and staff will do what they can to help you fulfill it. Oddly and overly decorated with land-based vegetation, Kettle makes phenomenal dishes with ingredients from under the sea. Daily fresh sheets might include Szechuan spearfish or cornmeal-encrusted oysters.

LA BODEGA Map pp230-3 *Tapas*
☎ 604-684-8814; 1277 Howe St; tapas $4-7, mains $12-19; ⏰ 4:30pm-midnight Mon-Thu, noon-midnight Fri, 5pm-midnight Sat, 5-11pm Sun; bus 4

This may be the most authentic Spanish restaurant in Vancouver, which is why you'll find a lot of Spanish expats enjoying the tapas and sangria or outstanding paella from a small menu of entrées.

LE CROCODILE Map pp230-3 *French*
☎ 604-669-4298; 909 Burrard St; lunch $16-25, dinner mains $22-34; ⏰ 11:30am-2pm Mon-Fri, 5:30-10pm Mon-Thu, 5:30-10:30pm Fri & Sat; bus 2

Set in a sumptuous Parisian-style dining room, Le Crocodile specializes in satisfying modern French dishes, like lobster bisque, tomato-and-gin soup, veal and sweetbreads, plus a few Alsace specialties like tart à l'ognion.

SUBEEZ CAFÉ Map pp230-3 *Eclectic*
☎ 604-687-6107; 891 Homer St; sandwiches $8-11, mains $13-17; ⏰ 11:30am-1am Mon-Sat, 11:30am-midnight Sun; bus 15

Subeez counts gallery artists and nearby Yaletown lofters among its regulars, who come for the industrial warehouse decor, DJs, extensive drinks list and eclectic menu (similar to sister WaaZuBee Café, p105). Good choices include

Eating – Downtown

the butternut squash tortellini, eggplant tajine and miso-marinated ahi tuna. All-day breakfasts help cure hangovers.

GASTOWN

Gastown incubates a lot of tourist traps, but if you look hard, you'll find a few gems hidden away.

ALIBI ROOM Map pp234 *Comfort Food*
☎ 604-623-3383; 157 Alexander St; dishes $7-18; ⏲ 5pm-midnight Mon-Wed, 5pm-1am Thu-Sat, 5-11pm Sun, brunch 10am-3pm Sat & Sun; bus 7
Such stylish comfort food creations as the vegetarian meatloaf with sweet potato mash and macaroni and cheese tossed in crab-and-shrimp cream win this film industry hangout rave reviews. There's a great bar (p125), too.

BORGO ANTICO AL PORTO
Map p234 *Italian*
☎ 604-683-8376; 321 Water St; pasta $12-15, mains $20-26; ⏲ 11:30am-10:30pm Mon-Fri, 5:30-10:30pm Sat & Sun; SkyTrain Waterfront
Borgo is a lovely trattoria serving hearty staples, like grilled calamari salad, and a wide range of pizza and pasta dishes, all accompanied by a solid wine list.

A window table at Eatery (p117), Kitsilano

INCENDIO Map p234 *Italian*
☎ 604-688-8694; 103 Columbia St; dishes $10-14; ⏲ 11:30am-3pm Sun-Fri, 5-10pm Sun-Thu, 5-11pm Fri, 5-11pm Sat; bus 7
A refuge from the mean streets outside, this boldly painted Italian café makes its own wood-fired pizza, calzone, gorgeous salads and pasta.

IRISH HEATHER Map p234 *Irish Pub*
☎ 604-688-9779; 217 Carrall St; dishes $7-15; ⏲ noon-11pm Mon-Thu, 11am-midnight Fri-Sun; bus 7
Authentic Irish country fare, like Jamieson-cured smoked salmon, hearty beef stew and bangers and mash, help absorb the pints of Guinness. The lack of smoke is the only thing that prevents the belief that you're in the Emerald Isle.

THAI PALACE Map p234 *Thai*
☎ 604-331-1660; 100 Water St; lunch specials from $8, mains $11-15; ⏲ 11am-10pm; SkyTrain Waterfront
Guarded by shimmering Thai temple figures, this justifiably popular restaurant specializes in savory Thai salads, and authentic bowls of curry infused with salmon, chicken or ostrich.

WATER STREET CAFÉ
Map p234 *West Coast*
☎ 604-689-2832; 300 Water St; pasta $13-16, mains $19-25; ⏲ 11:30am-9pm Mon & Tue, 11:30am-10pm Wed-Sun; SkyTrain Waterfront
Housed in one of the buildings that escaped the Great Fire of 1886, this elegant café serves warm, homemade focaccia with fresh pasta and seafood at streetside tables across from the Steam Clock. For starters, try the Dungeness crab, sweet potato and rock shrimp chowder.

CHEAP EATS
COOK STUDIO CAFÉ
Map p234 *Comfort Food*
☎ 604-696-9096; 374 Powell St; dishes $5-7; ⏲ 8am-2pm Mon-Fri; bus 7
This cheerful, sea-green and berry-blue room is a sweet oasis amid the Main and Hastings Sts decay. The café's mission is to train at-risk youth as cooks and food-industry workers. The soup, salad and sandwich-based menu changes each week, but includes a few standbys, like sweet potato–crusted salmon and a veggie burger with garlic mushrooms. Everything, even the bread, is made from scratch. Eat well, and know your money is going to a good cause.

YALETOWN

Posh, stylish restaurants and martini bars line Hamilton and Homer Sts. Most places are located in former warehouses whose loading docks now serve as popular outdoor patios.

BLUE WATER CAFÉ Map pp230-3 *Seafood*

☎ 604-688-8078; 1095 Hamilton St; lunch $16-20, dinner mains $20-33; ⏰ 11:30am-3pm, 5-11pm; bus 1

This high-concept seafood restaurant is the pinnacle of Yaletown dining. House music gently throbs throughout the cobalt-blue interior, while seafood towers grace the outdoor patio tables. There's an ice bar for chilled sake and vodka, and an Asian-style raw seafood bar for nouveau sushi. Fresh fish entrées often come straight from Granville Island, while more than a dozen kinds of oysters are flown in from the Gulf Islands, Atlantic Canada and France.

BRIX Map pp230-3 *Contemporary European*

☎ 604-915-9463; 1138 Homer St; tapas $9-12, mains $20-29; ⏰ 5-10pm Mon-Thu, 5-10:30pm Fri & Sat; bus 1

As if this were the back streets of Paris, Brix bistro offers lamp-lit courtyard tables and imaginative food. Tapas include mussels with yellow curry, while entrées could be applewood-smoked chicken or bison strip loin. Fashionably Yaletown all the way, Brix is decorated in violet and burgundy to complement the hardwood floors and polished aluminum trim. A late-night fondue menu is served until 2am.

CIOPPINO'S MEDITERRANEAN GRILL

Map pp230-3 *Italian/Mediterranean*

☎ 604-688-7466; 1133 Hamilton St; pasta $15-30, mains $30-45; ⏰ 12-3pm Mon-Fri, 5:30-11pm Mon-Sat; bus 1

Chef Pino Posteraro concentrates on 'cucina naturale' at this wood-interior restaurant, which minimizes animal fats, and uses olive oil to bring out ingredients' natural taste. Dishes are made with seasonal fish, game, fruit and vegetables, and can include west coast salmon, Fraser Valley pork tenderloin and Canadian angus beef. Pasta dishes like lobster tortelli with sweet pepper sauce are lighter than expected. **Enoteca** (mains $19-23) is its tasting room.

GLOWBAL Map pp230-3 *Eclectic*

☎ 604-602-0835; 1079 Mainland St; mains $17-26; ⏰ 11am-midnight; bus 1

This place has cast a wide net that catches the power-lunch, after-work, dinnertime, late-night and weekend brunch crowds. Glowbal is the sleek 'grill and satay bar' whose inventive menu features items like black tiger prawns in saffron cream and lobster Benedict. **AFTERglow** (p125) is its lounge side, serving tapas and martinis on the granite bar or out on the patio.

RODNEY'S OYSTER HOUSE

Map pp230-3 *Seafood*

☎ 604-609-0080; 1228 Hamilton St; entrées $8-13; ⏰ 11am-midnight Mon-Sat, 3-9:30pm Sun; bus 1

Rodney's offers up to 20 oyster varieties from the east and west coast of Canada, plus clams, garlic-butter steamed mussels, Haida Indian candy (hot smoked salmon) and sockeye tart. The ambience is laid-back for Yaletown, with service that is, ahem, informal (for instance, when a customer asked if tables were available, the waiter replied, 'Looks like you're shit out of luck.'). Happy hour is 4pm to 6pm, when most items are half-price.

YOPO CAFÉ Map pp230-3 *Chinese*
☎ 604-609-9676; 1122 Homer St; dishes $6-12;
🕑 11:30am-10:30pm Mon-Fri, noon-10:30pm Sat; bus 1
YoPo may be rather tiny, but like most Chinese restaurants it has a mondo selection of fried

noodle, rice, seafood, pork, chicken and vegetable items. We recommend you try hot-pot items like 'Sizzling and Singing Chicken', which does as advertised.

CHEAP EATS
SOUP ETC Map pp230-3 *Eclectic*
☎ 604-689-4505; 1091 Hamilton St; dishes $4-6;
🕑 8am-6pm Mon-Fri, 10am-5pm Sat & Sun; bus 1
This sparkling-clean joint serves bowls of stew and soup from around the globe. Try the 'Afrikaan Safari,' 'Cauliflower Power' or ginger-and-carrot puree, along with sandwiches, wraps and breakfast *panini*.

WEST END
People and high-rise buildings aren't the only things packed into the West End – restaurants are equally densely packed. More than 50 eateries are sardined into seven blocks along Denman St. Robson St between Denman and Burrard Sts is a mish-mash of 30-plus restaurants ranging from chic, power-Hollywood places to hole-in-the-wall Japanese noodle houses. Davie St is also chockablock with eateries.

BANANA LEAF Map pp230-3 *Malaysian*
☎ 604-683-3333; 1096 Denman St; dishes $8-15;
🕑 11:30am-10:30pm Sun-Wed, 11:30am-11:30pm Thu-Sat; bus 5
The bright, primary color–jumble interior hints at this local darling's vividly spiced dishes. Seafood is a specialty, kissed by sauces like spicy tomato, assam curry (tamarind juice, curry spice and coconut cream) and sambal (chili and garlic blended with lemon grass and dry shrimp paste).

BOATHOUSE Map pp230-3 *Seafood*
☎ 604-669-2225; 1795 Beach Ave; lunch $8-18, dinner mains $16-33; 🕑 11am-11pm; bus 5
This casual, popular bistro serves halibut fish and chips, while the beachside deck and upstairs dining room have fresh fish available nightly. Cedar-plank maple salmon and Dungeness crab and shrimp cakes are specialties, and are accompanied by an impressive BC wine list.

BRASS MONKEY Map pp230-3 *Eclectic*
☎ 604-685-7626; 1072 Denman St; mains $13-20;
🕑 5pm-2am; bus 5
Adorned with an array of hanging lamps, tables and chairs that have been cobbled from various spare parts, and a large fireplace, this retro bistro offers a small menu of pasta and seafood entrées (rock-crab ravioli, mushroom risotto), plus inventive and tasty dishes like

yam fries with spicy yogurt. Wash it down with a martini or highball. Food is 30% off from 5pm to 7pm.

CINCIN
Map pp230-3 *West Coast/Mediterranean*
☎ 604-688-7338; 1154 Robson St; mains $16-39, tasting menu with/without wine pairings $69/125;
🕑 11:30am-2:30pm Mon-Fri, 5-11pm Mon-Sun; bus 5
A favorite haunt of Hollywood types, casual-yet-elegant CinCin was voted 'best place to be seen by a movie executive.' The pasta and entrées change based on the seasonal availability of produce, but have included items like buffalo striploin, Salt Spring Island mussels and Fraser Valley duck. Pizza is another specialty, produced by the wood-fired brick oven flickering in back, and topped with smoked salmon, black cod or artichokes. Factor in the 800-label wine list, beautiful circular stairway and outdoor patio, and it makes CinCin the city's top splurge.

Top Five Eat Streets
- **Commercial Dr** (p104)
- **Robson St** (above)
- **Main St** (p102)
- **Denman St** (above)
- **Broadway** (p115)

Eating – West End

DA PASTA BAR Map pp230-3 _Italian_

☎ 604-688-1288; 1232 Robson St; dishes $11-17;
🕑 11:30am-10pm Sun-Thu, 11:30am-11pm Fri & Sat;
bus 5

This relaxed bistro puts a few dozen mouth-watering pasta creations on the menu: Try the house pasta (prawns, caramelized shallots and pink peppercorns in a lobster-based broth) or curried chicken sauce.

DELILAH'S Map pp230-3 _Eclectic_

☎ 604-687-3424; 1789 Comox St; 2-/4-course dinner $26.50/38; 🕑 5:30-11pm; bus 5

The kitsch factor will leave you speechless while you watch people odder and more famous than yourself downing martinis from the city's original snazzy cocktail list. Check off what you want to eat from preprinted menu cards, which favor whimsical dishes, like port-glazed bison shortribs and seafood bouilla-baisse with lavender.

HERMITAGE Map pp230-3 _French_

☎ 604-689-3237; 1025 Robson St; lunch $13-20, dinner mains $27-32; 🕑 11:30am-2:30pm Mon-Fri, from 5:30pm daily; bus 5

The French antique–filled Hermitage serves classic French and Quebecois cuisine, with sumptuous dishes of escargot, duck pâté, foie gras and asparagus-and-mushroom pastry in champagne cream sauce. The acclaimed wine list boasts one of the city's top Burgundy selections. Located in an alcove off Robson St, with a secluded patio.

JOE FORTES Map pp230-3 _Seafood_

☎ 604-669-1940; 777 Thurlow St; lunch $11-20, dinner mains $23-35; 🕑 11am-11pm; SkyTrain Burrard

Joe's is a Vancouver classic, with its gold rush–era dark wood and brass grand room and rooftop garden patio. Named after the city's first lifeguard, it is an excellent place to go for oysters, grilled fish and other stalwarts of traditional northwest cooking.

KAM'S PLACE Map pp230-3 _Singaporean_

☎ 604-669-3389; 1043 Davie St; dishes $8-13;
🕑 11am-3pm Mon-Fri, noon-3pm Sat & Sun,
5-10:30pm Mon-Sun; bus 1

Vancouver has no shortage of Singaporean restaurants, but few match the tranquility and quality of cooking at Kam's. Lots of chilies go into dishes like the pink shell scallops, red and green curries and hot-and-sour soup. Vegetarians will rejoice at the tofu cornucopia.

LE GAVROCHE Map pp230-3 _French_

☎ 604-685-3924; 1616 Alberni St; lunch $14-19, dinner mains $25-40, 3-course meal with/without wines $50/75;
🕑 12-2:30pm Mon-Fri, 6-10:30pm Mon-Sun; bus 19

Classic La Gavroche bridges the northwest larder and French haute cuisine, emphasizing _les fruits de mer_ with unexpected flair, like Alaska black cod with burnt orange and anise sauce. It's an excellent choice for a romantic dinner, and the wine list alone wins accolades.

O'DOUL'S Map pp230-3 _West Coast_

☎ 604-661-1400; 1300 Robson St; breakfast $4-10, lunch $12-16, dinner mains $22-35; 🕑 6:30am-11pm Mon-Fri, 7am-11pm Sat & Sun; bus 5

The Listel Hotel's bright, skylighted lounge has a sweeping 65ft-long mahogany bar and a menu that fuses west coast cuisine with the American deep south in dishes like chicken-prawn-salmon jambalaya with saffron risotto. While you listen to live jazz, look up at the 17th-century world map sprawled across the ceiling (staff say 'Where's Waldo' is hidden in there). A bar menu nourishes until 1am.

RAINCITY GRILL Map pp230-3 _West Coast_

☎ 604-685-7337; 1193 Denman St; lunch $12-16, dinner mains $21-32; 🕑 5-10pm; bus 5

Set enticingly close to the English Bay, Raincity has time and again been voted the best place for west coast cuisine in Vancouver. The service bubbles over with friendliness. An organic menu changes with the seasons, but might include fresh crab and apple salad, and Nicola Valley venison with roasted yams or new ideas for vegetarians. Each item is paired with wines from the stellar list. The take-away window sells gourmet boxed lunches to beach-goers.

ROMANO'S MACARONI GRILL

Map pp230-3 _Italian_

☎ 604-689-4334; 1523 Davie St; mains $11-21;
🕑 11am-10pm Mon-Fri, noon-11pm Sat & Sun; bus 1

Set in a beautiful Queen Anne stone mansion, this Italian restaurant's bag of tricks includes opera singers, cooking exhibitions, pay-what-you-drink jugs of wine, and a lasagna and pizza–filled children's menu.

ROOSTER'S QUARTERS

Map pp230-3 _Rotisserie_

☎ 604-689-8023; 836 Denman St; mains $10-14;
🕑 noon-10pm; bus 5

Table manners be damned: most folks here use their fingers to rip apart the 'Montreal-style' (ie barbecued) chicken and ribs, with mutterings of 'Pardon my French' following the frequent belching. Great spicy wings and maple sugar pie are on the menu.

TAPASTREE Map pp230-3 *Tapas/West Coast*
☎ 604-606-4680; 1829 Robson St; dishes $5-9;
⏰ dinner from 5:30pm; bus 5

One of the city's first tapas restaurants, and one that still commands a loyal following for its 60-plus dishes tinged with west coast seafood influences. The airy, white linen–tablecloth atmosphere and fine wine list encourage patrons to linger over a post-dinner glass or two.

TROPIKA Map pp230-3 *Malaysian*
☎ 604-737-6002; 1128 Robson St; dishes $8-15;
⏰ 11am-10:30pm; bus 5

Tropika's extensive selection of Malay, Thai and Singaporean dishes taste like they're from a Kuala Lumpur night market. Jumbo prawns and fresh coconut flown in from the motherlands enhance authenticity. The roti canai (pan-fried Malay bread with curry sauce) and pulut hitam (black sticky rice cooked with sugar and coconut milk) are but two of the addictive delicacies awaiting you.

TSUNAMI SUSHI Map pp230-3 *Japanese*
☎ 604-687-8744; 1025 Robson St; dishes $8-13;
⏰ 11:30am-11pm; bus 5

Catch the wave up to this 2nd-floor 'floating' sushi bar, where little boats drift in a watery conveyor belt around the bar. The grand windows overlook Robson Street.

ZIN Map pp230-3 *Global Fusion*
☎ 604-408-1700; 1277 Robson St; lunch $10-15, dinner mains $16-25; ⏰ 7am-11pm Tue-Fri, 8am-11pm Sat & Sun; bus 5

At the Pacific Palisades Hotel, artful Zin looks good enough to eat itself. Berry colors are lavished on the mod furniture with a sexy cherry of a wine bar at the room's center. Diners can go 'taste-tripping' around the world, from sake-cured salmon to the mysterious 'global soup,' butter curry scallops or mole tuna with sweet corn tamale.

CHEAP EATS

Two exceptional Japanese noodle houses are in the 'hood, both tiny places where legions of homesick students hunch over steaming bowls of ramen: **Ezogiku Noodle Café** (Map pp230-3; ☎ 604-685-8606; 1329 Robson St;

Top Five Cheap Eats
- **Belgian Fries** (p106)
- **Hawkers Delight** (p104)
- **Copper Onion** (below)
- **Café Crepe** (below)
- **Flying Wedge** (p119)

dishes $5-8.50; ⏰ 11am-11pm; bus 5) and **Kintaro** (Map pp230-3; ☎ 604-682-7568; 788 Denman St; dishes $6-9; ⏰ noon-11pm Tue-Sun; bus 5).

CAFÉ CREPE Map pp230-3 *Italian Café*
☎ 604-488-0045; 1032 Robson St; crepes $4-7;
⏰ 8am-11pm Sun-Thu, 8am-midnight Fri & Sat; bus 5

The menu at this bustling, Euro-style café is loaded with quick and delicious, sweet and savory crepes. For sweet, indulge in the dark chocolate or Nutella versions; for savory, the egg and cheese satisfies. You can dine in or order take-away from the window.

COPPER ONION Map pp230-3 *Japanese*
☎ 604-642-0755; 1313 Robson St; dishes $6-8;
⏰ 11am-10pm Mon, Wed, Thu & Sat, 11am-10:30pm Fri, noon-10pm Sun; bus 5

It's a great-value Japanese curry bar where mountainous plates of thick meat or vegetable curry come with sticky rice and a tangy pickled radish garnish. Red adzuki bean or green tea–flavored milkshakes help wash it down.

HAMBURGER MARY'S Map pp230-3 *Diner*
☎ 604-687-1293; 1202 Davie St; items $7-10;
⏰ 8am-3am Mon-Thu, 8am-4am Fri & Sat, 8am-2am Sun; bus 1

Mary's is a throwback to the days of black-and-white checkered floors, chrome trim, and juke box–playing diners. Burgers and mondo milkshakes are the specialties of the house, and the all-day breakfasts and weekend brunches are suitably gluttonous. Sitting on the patio watching the life on Davie St is a West End pleasure.

STANLEY PARK

The park doesn't have a lot of restaurants to offer, but those that are located within its confines provide great views (and pretty good food).

FISH HOUSE IN STANLEY PARK

Map p240 *Seafood*

☎ 604-681-7275, 877-681-7275; 8901 Stanley Park Dr; lunch $13-17, dinner mains $20-39; ☺ 11:30am-9pm Mon-Sat, 11am-9pm Sun; bus 19

Possessing old-fashioned charm, the Fish House emphasizes seasonal Pacific northwest fish. There's also an oyster bar, and a seafood cornucopia of lobster tail, king crab and more, available at market price. During the early-bird dinner special (5pm to 6pm Sunday to Thursday), buy one entrée and get $15 off the second one. Tea is served from 2pm to 4pm.

PROSPECT POINT CAFÉ Map p240 *Café*

☎ 604-669-2737; Stanley Park Dr; burgers $9-15, mains $11-20; ☺ 11am-11pm, reduced in winter; bus 19

This semi-casual restaurant surrounded by totem poles and perched on a 300ft cliff beneath Lions Gate Bridge offers breathtaking views. The burgers and sandwiches are fine. Salmon, be it ginger garlic, pine nut pesto or other combinations, is the house specialty.

SEQUOIA GRILL Map p240 *West Coast*

☎ 604-669-3281, 800-280-9893; Ferguson Point; lunch $9-18, dinner mains $16-26; ☺ 11:30am-9:45pm Mon-Sat, 10:30am-9:45pm Sun; bus 19

Formerly the Teahouse, it's now cheery-chic Sequoia, but the food remains contemporary west coast with seafood draped in creative sauces and dishes like quail with polenta. It's the kind of place Vancouverites save for special occasions, especially since the terrace affords sunset views over the ships moored in English Bay.

CHINATOWN

Most Chinese restaurants reside along Pender and Keefer Sts between Columbia and Gore Aves. If you still have stomach capacity after your meal, head into one of the myriad bakeries for an almond cookie or creamy chestnut roll. A few blocks east you'll find dirt-cheap diners on rough E Hastings St – not really where you want to go for a meal.

BRICKHOUSE LATE NIGHT BAR & BISTRO Map p234 *Comfort Food*

☎ 604-689-8645; 730 Main St; mains $8-15; ☺ 6pm-3am Tue-Sat; bus 3

Located a bit south of Chinatown in a dodgy-after-dark neighborhood, the Brickhouse is a bohemian favorite. The cooking is divine, especially the burgers and nachos, which are complemented by beers and pool tables. It's bicycle friendly and the preferred drinking spot after the monthly Critical Mass event, in which cyclists ride en masse on Vancouver's main streets to reclaim public space from car traffic.

BUDDHIST VEGETARIAN RESTAURANT

Map p234 *Chinese/Vegetarian*

☎ 604-683-8816; 137 E Pender St; dishes $8-15; ☺ 11am-9pm; SkyTrain Stadium

Where else can vegetarians sample sweet-and-sour tripe, curried fish belly and diced duck's gizzard (all made with gluten)? Chili black bean sauce makes several appearances on the menu, and vegetables star in the chow meins and hot pots. Dim sum is served all day at diner-esque booths and tables.

FOO'S HO HO RESTAURANT

Map p234 *Chinese*

☎ 604-609-2889; 102 E Pender St; dishes $7-13; ☺ 11:30am-9:30pm; SkyTrain Stadium

Pierre Trudeau liked to come to this old-style restaurant, hunker down in a booth and dig into the large portions of retro-Chinese food, such as chow mein and whole de-boned chicken stuffed with sticky rice. You'll like it, too.

HON'S WUN-TUN HOUSE

Map p234 *Chinese*

☎ 604-688-0871; 268 E Keefer St; dishes $5-12; ☺ 8:30am-10:30pm; bus 19

It's got the predictable tiled floors, black vinyl and chrome chairs, constant din and mouth-watering smells you'd expect from a restaurant in the heart of Chinatown. Huge bowls of soup

---

Top Five Asian Eateries

Vancouver's Asian influence reveals itself in a variety of unbeatable cuisines. Some say the city's Chinese food is the best outside Hong Kong, and its sushi is on par with that of Tokyo. Thai and Malaysian restaurants are cooking up innovative dishes, too. For a taste of the East try:

- Montri's (p118)
- Banana Leaf (p98)
- Tojo's (p115)
- Hon's Wun-Tun House (above)
- Sushiyama (p104)

A chef working at Lumiére (p118), Kitsilano

and pie plates full of noodles are served steaming. A whopping 334 dishes are on the menu, and the pot stickers have achieved mythical status. The branch on **Robson St** (☎ 604-685-0871; 1339 Robson St) has a separate vegetarian menu and serves dim sum, including the vegetarian variety.

PHNOM PENH

Map p234   *Cambodian/Vietnamese*
☎ 604-682-5777; 244 E Georgia St; dishes $6-15;
⊙ 10am-9pm Sun-Thu, 10am-10pm Fri & Sat; bus 19
Don't think that just because you're in Chinatown you have to eat Chinese food. The menu here is split between Cambodian and Vietnamese dishes, such as spicy garlic crab, steamed rice cakes with pork, shrimp, coconut and scallions, and bank xeo (a prawn- and sprout-filled pancake).

ONLY SEAFOOD RESTAURANT

Map p234   *Seafood*
☎ 604-681-6546; 20 E Hastings St; dishes $7-12;
⊙ 11am-8pm; SkyTrain Stadium
In the same location since 1912 (look for the vintage seahorse neon) and looking very much like a dive, this restaurant serves great fresh seafood at reasonable prices. There are just 17 counter stools and two booths. Daily specials, perhaps three fried oysters, a cup of clam chowder and coffee, cost $8.50.

WILD RICE Map p234   *Asian Fusion*
☎ 604-642-2882; 117 W Pender St; mains $10-15;
⊙ 11:30am-midnight Mon-Wed, 11:30-1am Thu & Fri, 5pm-1am Sat, 5pm-midnight Sun; SkyTrain Stadium
The concept here is East meets West in an ultramodern space with an illuminated bar. Chinese cuisine is fused with local BC ingredients resulting in tapas-size appetizers, like tuna tataki lettuce wraps, and main dishes along the lines of wild boar with jasmine rice and plantain chips. The martini list helps wash it all down.

SOMA

South Main St is the city's hip strip for adventurous new restaurants, with most clustered at Broadway Ave and further south around King Edward Ave. Well beyond that, along Main St from E 48th to E 51st Aves, is the Indian neighborhood known as Punjabi Market.

AURORA Map pp236-7   *West Coast*
☎ 604-873-9944; 2420 Main St; dishes $10-20;
⊙ 5:30-10pm Tue-Sun, 10am-2pm Sun; bus 3
The chef here was formerly the sous chef at Bishop's (p117). The concept at Aurora is similar – seasonal, regional, organic ingredients dictate the changing menu (perhaps buffalo marinated in root beer or potato-wrapped smoked sablefish), accompanied by BC wines

and beers – but you'll experience top-quality cuisine for less stress on your wallet.

LOCUS Map pp236-7 _Eclectic_
☎ 604-708-4121; 4121 Main St; mains $10-16;
☷ 11am-2am Mon-Fri, 10am-3pm & 4pm-2am Sat & Sun; bus 3

Locus attracts an artsy crowd with its crimson gothic interior of spooky lacquered trees and massive candles. Join the friendly folks scarfing down seafood fettuccini with coconut curry sauce or fish. Many a Benny goes down the hatch during the popular brunch timeslot.

MONSOON Map pp236-7 _Pan Asian_
☎ 604-879-4001; 2526 Main St; mains $13-19;
☷ dinner from 5pm; bus 3

Hip Monsoon's pan-Asian menu draws heavily on the subcontinent: try the Indian-spiced fries with hot banana chutney, vegetable subji or chai brulee. The aquamarine walls and rustle of bamboo will calm you, as will the extensive wine, martini, scotch, rum and champagne list.

REEF Map pp236-7 _Caribbean_
☎ 604-874-5375; 4172 Main St; mains $8-13;
☷ 11am-midnight Sun-Wed, 11am-1am Thu-Sat; bus 3

Potent Caribbean mojo works overtime in this island-y restaurant, where the only thing fast-paced is the service. Dip your chips into three kinds of chutney, then savor the coconutty flavors, seasoned rice and marinated meat in

dishes, like calypso oxtail, jerk chicken, and curried mango and sweet potato soup. Umbrella-laden cocktails and brunch add to the fun.

SEB'S MARKET CAFÉ Map pp236-7 _Eclectic_
☎ 604-298-4403; 592 E Broadway Ave; mains $10-19;
☷ 7:30am-5pm Mon & Tue, 7:30am-10pm Wed-Sun; bus 9

Unassuming Seb's offers coffee, take-out sandwiches, groceries and an 11-table restaurant. It's a neighborhood favorite for breakfasts, serving omelettes with bacon and caramelized apple or strawberries and Camembert. Dinners might include organic chicken coated in sweet barbecue sauce atop spiced fries, or pork tenderloin roulade with spinach and onion. Wine, beer and weekend live music complement the food.

SLICKITY JIM'S CHAT 'N CHEW
Map pp236-7 _Comfort Food_
☎ 604-873-6760; 2513 Main St; mains $6-9;
☷ 8:30am-4:30pm Mon-Fri, 8:30am-5:30pm Sat & Sun; bus 3

Slickity soothes the soul with sassy breakfast, lunch and dinner dishes, like the 'Mean Teen Queen' (sourdough French toast with Belgian chocolate and Kentucky bourbon sauce), 'Vagrant Elements of the Human Soul' (grilled and chilled vegetable and avocado sandwich) and 'Abstract Notion' (slinging together whatever is at hand). The hodge-podge, thrift-store tables are topped by random items like typewriters.

Eating – SoMa

Brunch Hunt

If Vancouverites aren't zipping off to the ski hills first thing Sunday morning, or hoisting the sails on their boats for a day on the water, they're probably heading to their favorite restaurant for brunch. People argue and froth about which place is best, but the fact is the city is loaded with restaurants serving scrumptious versions of eggs Benedict ('Eggs Benny' in local parlance), fruity waffles and more. Most places serve brunch on weekends from 11am to 3pm. Luckily, standard plates rarely exceed $10 to $15 no matter where you go, making it the one time of the week when regular joes can splash out and dine with the big boys. Try:

- **Locus** (above) Many a Benny from which to choose.
- **Reef** (above) French toast stuffed with cream cheese and fried bananas, or ackee and saltfish top the Caribbean menu.
- **Tangerine** (p119) Wholegrain banana pancakes or jack cheese and scallion scramblettes soak up last night's pain.
- **Alibi Room** (p96) A fusion brunch menu accompanies jazzy and soulful Sunday DJs.
- **Sophie's Cosmic Café** (p119) Twenty cases of BC eggs and 2000lbs of potatoes go into hangover-curing dishes weekly.

Dim sum is a sort of Chinese version of brunch, served during similar hours and also inexpensive. Waitstaff wheel carts from table to table, each piled with little bamboo baskets of hot food. Just point to what you want. Portions are small, like tapas, so you can sample many of the 100-plus types of dim sum; popular dishes include steamed pork buns, turnip cakes and shrimp dumplings. **Pink Pearl** (p105) is the king of dim sum.

SUSHIYAMA Map pp236-7 *Japanese*

☎ 604-872-0053; 371 E Broadway; dishes $6-10;
🕑 11:30am-10:30pm Mon-Thu, 11:30am-11pm
Fri,12:30-10:30pm Sat; bus 3

Nothing fancy at this sunny restaurant, just really good, affordable sushi. Sit at one of the eight tables and, within a few minutes of drinking your free tea and miso soup, a spread of succulent California, tuna, rainbow and other rolls arrives. Try the bento box specials at lunchtime.

WHIP Map pp236-7 *Eclectic*

☎ 604-874-4687; 209 E 6th Ave; mains $8-14;
🕑 noon-midnight Mon-Thu, noon-1:30am Fri, 10-1:30am Sat, 10am-midnight Sun, reduced in winter;
bus 3

Whip is an all-ages hipster hangout with a compact but decent menu of items, like vegan risotto, jerk chicken, braised lamb shanks and vegan stroganoff. The front patio is excellent for relaxing over a cocktail (draft beers are only $3.50), but if the weather or crowd dictates an indoor seat, you can always enjoy the changing art exhibits, like the giant penis sculpture.

CHEAP EATS
HAWKERS DELIGHT

Map pp236-7 *Singaporean*

☎ 604-709-8188; 4127 Main St; dishes $4-5;
🕑 11am-9pm Mon-Sat; bus 3

This Singaporean fast-food hole in the wall doesn't look like much, but the dishes are flavorful and very filling. Head straight to the counter to order after taking a gander at the menu's photos of yellow noodles with tofu and spicy sweet potato sauce, deep-fried tofu and green beans with peanut sauce, and various satays.

SOLLY'S BAGELRY

Map pp236-7 *Bagels/Sandwiches*

☎ 604-872-1821; 189 E 28th Ave; sandwiches $5-7;
🕑 7am-6pm Tue-Thu & Sat, 7am-7pm Fri, 8am-6pm
Sun; bus 3

The map on the wall shows where in the world Solly's has sent its famous cinnamon buns – brick-sized blocks of delicious goo that leave hands sticky for hours afterward. It also serves knishes, kugel, soups and bagel sandwiches.

If you like Indian food, there are numerous delights awaiting you in the Punjabi Market, which runs south along Main St from E 48th to E 51st Ave. Good choices with buffets and an abundance of vegetarian options include:

All India Sweets & Restaurant (Map pp228-9; ☎ 604-327-0891; 6505 Main St; buffet $7; 🕑 11am-9pm; bus 3) This place sets out a 45-item all-you-can-eat vegetarian buffet with endless trays of sweets.

Pabla's Himalaya Restaurant (Map pp228-9; ☎ 604-324-6514; 6587 Main St; dishes $4-6; 🕑 10:30am-9pm; bus 3) Pabla's has a fabulous selection of specialty dishes, samosas and sweets.

EAST VANCOUVER

East Vancouver's restaurants concentrate on Commercial Dr, from Venables St to E 8th Ave. Known simply as 'the Drive,' this bohemian neighborhood springs from Italian roots, which explains the trail of Old World delis and coffee shops amid the contemporary eateries. Many of these older places, like Tony's Neighbourhood Deli & Café (Map p235; ☎ 604-253-7422; 1046 Commercial Dr; items $6-8; 🕑 7am-6pm Mon-Fri, 8am-6pm Sat; bus 20), make awesome *panini* and focaccias. See p127 for additional low-cost eating options. Healthy-minded folk should look into organic grocery store Sweet Cherubim (p93), which also operates a vegetarian restaurant.

BUKOWSKI'S Map p235 *Eclectic*

☎ 604-253-2777; 1447 Commercial Dr; mains $8-15;
🕑 5pm-1am Mon-Thu, 3pm-1am Fri, 11am-1am Sat,
11am-midnight Sun; bus 20

The burgers, crepes and chicken dishes are pretty tame for a restaurant named after a boozy Beatnik, but the original barfly would be pleased by Bukowski's beer and wine selection, and lineup of jazz musicians and performance poets who play here regularly. The shady willow tree makes the patio a perfect place to spend a hot afternoon or chill with the evening lounge crowd.

CANNERY SEAFOOD HOUSE

Map p235 *Seafood*

☎ 604-254-9606; 2205 Commissioner St; lunch $16-25, dinner mains $23-29; 🕑 11am-2:30pm & 5:30-9:30pm Mon-Fri, 5-10pm Sat, 5-9:30pm Sun; bus 4

Down near the docks off Victoria Dr, this rustic place offers fireplaces inside and some great views looking back at the city. Don't miss the whale's rib, Jacob's ladder and suspended lifeboats that are hanging around. A daily menu of fresh fish always includes west coast bouillabaisse. It may take you most of the evening just to read through the wine list.

CLOVE CAFÉ & RECORD BAR

Map p235   *Indian*

☎ 604-255-5550; 2054 Commercial Dr; dishes $3-10; ⏰ 5-10pm Mon-Thu, 5-10:30pm Fri &Sat, 5-9:30pm Sun; bus 20

Definitely one of Vancouver's most eclectic Indian restaurants, the Clove Café offers seafood and vegetarian fare. The chairs are an ode to grade school, and you can peruse or buy vintage vinyl while awaiting your phenomenal calamari salad, mango naan roll-ups or other dishes.

EL COCAL Map p235   *Brazilian/Mexican*

☎ 604-255-7920; 1037 Commercial Dr; dishes $10; ⏰ dinner from 5:30pm; bus 20

El Cocal specializes in Salvadoran and Brazilian food, with more familiar Mexican fare thrown in for good measure. So you'll see tacos alongside stewed beef rolled in egg batter alongside cheese and chutney pastels. The venue also hosts open-mic, comedy and poetry nights, with live rock, Latin or folk music on weekends.

HAVANA Map p235   *Eclectic/Latin*

☎ 604-253-9119; 1212 Commercial Dr; tapas $7-10, mains $13-19; ⏰ 11am-11pm Sun-Thu, 11am-midnight Sat & Sun; bus 20

Havana defies easy categorization, so we'll just call it Cuban fusion. There are burgers, portabella mushroom *panini*, Caribbean fried chicken with buttermilk mashed potatoes, and salmon with lime-cumin dressing tapas. Port, brandy and single malts lead the drink list, enjoyed outdoors on the front porch or indoors on the red velvet cushioned seats by graffitied walls. There's also an art gallery and 60-seat theater on site, and Cuban cigars are sold.

LATIN QUARTER Map p235   *Tapas*

☎ 604-251-1144; 1305 Commercial Dr; tapas $6-12, mains $15; ⏰ 5pm-midnight Sun-Thu, 5pm-1am Sat & Sun; bus 20

This brightly colored Mediterranean tapas bar doubles as a venue for gypsy, jazz and flamenco music in the evening. Entrées include fajitas, paella (the house specialty) and grilled salmon.

Top Five Vegetarian & Vegan

As you'd expect from a progressive city, most restaurants in Vancouver provide meat-free menu options. Hippie-dippie Kitsilano and Commercial Dr are the most concentrated areas for vegetarian eateries.

One local nonprofit that promotes vegetarianism for optimal health and sustainability is EarthSave Canada (☎ 604-731-5885; www.earthsave.bc.ca), which also organizes monthly restaurant 'dine-outs' ($15-20), bi-monthly potlucks (free if you bring a dish, $12 otherwise), weekly Toastmasters public speaking sessions and sporadic speed-dating events for vegetarians.

For good eats, try:
- Naam (p118)
- Buddhist Vegetarian Restaurant (p101)
- Planet Veg (p119)
- Deserts (p106)
- Yogi's (p106)

MARCELLO'S Map p235   *Italian*

☎ 604-215-7760; 1404 Commercial Dr; dishes $11-15; ⏰ 11am-11pm Sun-Wed, 11am-midnight Thu-Sat; bus 20

With wrought-iron candelabra and marble tabletops, Marcello's looks more expensive than it actually is. The ambience is as heartwarming as the Italian comfort food: pizzas, pastas, gnocchi and calzones.

PINK PEARL Map p235   *Chinese*

☎ 604-253-4316; 1132 E Hastings St; dishes $10-18; ⏰ 9am-10pm; bus 10

This giant banquet hall is beyond the boundaries of Chinatown, but it is Vancouver's best-known place for a dim-sum feast (show up well before 3pm) with astonishing seafood dishes on the regular menu. Crying babies and wedding parties are all part of the happy hubbub.

WAAZUBEE CAFÉ Map p235   *Eclectic*

☎ 604-253-5299; 1622 Commercial Dr; dishes $8-16; ⏰ 11:30am-midnight; bus 20

One of the Drive's most popular spots, WaaZuBee outfits itself with huge painted murals, velvet curtains and recycled metal sculptures, like the spoon chandelier. An equally stimulating menu runs the gamut from vegetarian samosas to lamb focaccia to roasted pumpkin-seed vegetable curry. There's an excellent selection of local beers, plus a few sinfully rich desserts.

YOGI'S Map p235   *Indian/Vegetarian*
☎ 604-251-9644; 1408 Commercial Dr; mains $9-13;
🕙 11:30am-2:30pm, 5-10pm Mon-Fri, noon-11pm Sat
& Sun; bus 20

No yoga contortions are required to seat yourself inside this relaxed café where painted Buddhas smile down upon the vegetarian bounty. Chew on smokin' samosas, nutty naan or Tofu Taj Makani while your lassi is spiked with Indian rum.

CHEAP EATS

BELGIAN FRIES Map p235   *Comfort Food*
☎ 604-253-4220; 1885 Commercial Dr; items $3-6;
🕙 11am-10pm; bus 20

The concept is pure genius: take fresh cut spuds, fry them, fry them *again*, toss, salt and serve in a paper funnel. You then dip the beauties into one of a dozen hot or cold mayo-based sauces, including wasabi, hot garlic, Jamaican heat and curry/chutney. What could be better? Beer, which you choose from the Storm brews on tap or bottled Belgian lambics. Sure, you get a few smoked-meat sandwiches on the menu so the whole thing doesn't look so indulgent, but let's be honest – it's the spuds and suds we're after.

DESERTS Map p235   *Middle Eastern*
☎ 604-251-4171; 905 Commercial Dr; dishes $4-6;
🕙 noon-midnight; bus 20

This Middle Eastern vegetarian restaurant makes its own spinach pies, falafel pita sandwiches and racks of honeyed sweets to eat in or take away. The falafel is the best this side of Amman. There's another outlet under different management in **Kitsilano** (Map pp238-9; ☎ 604-731-2393; 1925 Cornwall Ave; 🕙 8am-11:30pm).

JUICY LUCY'S GOOD EATS
Map p235   *Vegetarian*
☎ 604-254-6101; 1420 Commercial Dr; dishes $4-7;
🕙 7am-8pm Mon-Sat, 8am-8pm Sun; bus 20

Lucy's offers healthy veggie and fruit juices, plus a small vegan-friendly menu of soups, wraps and all-day breakfasts. Diehard health nuts will revel in drinks like the wheatgrass shooter.

GRANVILLE ISLAND

If you haven't completely stuffed yourself at the public market (p59), the island has several seafood-oriented restaurants to choose from, most with aquatic views.

> **Top Five Patios**
> - **Bridges** (below)
> - **Joe Fortes** (p99)
> - **Sandbar** (below)
> - **C** (p94)
> - **Fish House in Stanley Park** (p101)

BRIDGES Map pp236-7   *West Coast*
☎ 604-687-4400; 1696 Duranleau St; bistro $12-19,
dinner entrées $18-34; 🕙 bistro 11am-midnight, pub
11am-1am, dining room 9:30am-2pm Sun & 5:30-10pm
daily; bus 50

On a warm summer evening, there is no place better than Bridges in a position overlooking False Creek. There's a setting for everyone: the casual bistro downstairs, which offers small seafood dishes and more than two-dozen wines by the glass, the high-ceilinged formal dining room upstairs tempts with more serious northwest cuisine, the pub offers typical grub, and the outdoor dock is a long-time favorite for drinkers.

PACIFIC INSTITUTE OF CULINARY
ARTS Map pp236-7   *West Coast*
PICA; ☎ 604-734-4488; 1505 W 2nd Ave; 3-course
lunch/dinner $22/34; 🕙 restaurant 11:30am-2pm
Mon-Fri, 6-9pm Mon-Sat, bake shop 8am-7pm Mon-
Sat; bus 50

For gourmet dining on a budget, try this cooking school, which is to be found at the entrance to Granville Island. Chefs in training prepare delicious surprises and the Institute's signature dessert, Chocolate Pasuwa. The bake shop serves breads, decadent pastries and cakes.

SANDBAR Map pp236-7   *Seafood*
☎ 604-669-9030; 1535 Johnston St; mains $13-27;
🕙 lunch 11:30am-4pm Mon-Fri, 11:30am-3pm Sat
& Sun, dinner 4:30-11pm Mon-Sat, 4:30-10pm Sun;
bus 50

Stone bridges lead into the impressive Sandbar's foyer, which is graced with a waterfall. From there a soaring wooden staircase rises to the main dining room and excellent rooftop patio. More than 1800 wines are cellared below, ready to complement the seafood tapas and west coast cuisine prepared in the busy open kitchen.

(Continued on page 115)

Eating – Granville Island

1 A neighborhood mural on Commercial Dr (p56), East Vancouver 2 Silk Road walking route, Chinatown (p53) 3 Sari shopping, Punjabi Market (p56), SoMa

1 *The dining room at CinCin (p98), West End* 2 *Coffee art at Caffè Artigiano (p126), downtown* 3 *Chef Tojo at work at Tojo's (p115), Fairview* 4 *Local wines are served at Aurora (p102), SoMa*

1 French fusion on offer at Lumiére (p118), Kitsilano 2 Classic Indian with a modern twist at Vij's (p116), South Granville 3 Seats overlooking False Creek at Bridges (p106), Granville Island 4 Beachy bamboo at Octopus' Garden (p118), Kitsilano

1 *Brood over a martini at the Alibi Room (p125), Gastown* 2 *Prop up the bar at Rob Feenie's swish Lumiére (p118), Kitsilano* 3 *A neon sign adorns the 19th-century Yale hotel (p129), downtown*

1 *German beer meisters inspire the brew at Dockside Brewing Company (p123), Granville Island* 2 *Enjoy a pint in the traditional atmosphere of Irish Heather (p124), Gastown* 3 *Ron Hayward and guests perform at Railway Club (p128), downtown*

1 *Browse the shops in Chinatown (p157)* 2 *Products for sale at Hill's Native Art (p155), Gastown* 3 *Local designers' clothing and accessories at Twigg & Hottie (p158), SoMa* 4 *Hempy designs in Kitsilano Hemp Company (p164)*

1 Ginseng shop, Chinatown (p157) 2 Produce on display at Urban Fare (p93), Yaletown 3 Sari shopping in Punjabi Market (p56), SoMa 4 Hand-blown glass pipes at BC Marijuana Party Bookstore (p153), downtown

1 Whistler Mountain becomes a mountain biker's paradise in summer (p193) *2 The lovely Ross Fountain in Butchart Gardens (p188), Victoria* *3 A good dump of snow on Whistler Mountain (p193)*

(Continued from page 106)

TONY'S FISH & OYSTER CAFÉ

Map pp236-7   *Seafood*
☎ 604-683-7127; 1511 Anderson St; items $7-16;
⊙ 11:30am-8pm, to 7pm Sun; bus 50

Tony's is a small, prim seafood joint dishing up fish and chips, oysters on the half shell, pan-fried tiger prawns and unique burgers (fish, oyster and cajun salmon). Oyster pepper stew is a nice way to start a meal, while bananas Foster with vanilla-bean ice cream is a fine way to end it.

WEST SIDE
FAIRVIEW

Cuisines from around the world appear in restaurants along both Cambie St and W Broadway (particularly between Cambie and Granville Sts).

MAJOR CHUTNEY

Map pp236-7   *Indian/Fijian*
☎ 604-875-9533; 3432 Cambie St; veg/meat mains $9.50/11.50; ⊙ 6-9:45pm Tue-Sun; bus 15

This 26-seat bistro with red walls and white linen tablecloths focuses on dishes with a Fijian influence. Kasba chicken (with a tangy cream sauce, tomatoes, caraway, ginger and garlic) is a house specialty, as is tomato lamb curry. Of course there are chutneys – a rainbow of them – served with delicately fashioned appetizers.

NICE 'N SPICY REGGAE CAFÉ

Map pp236-7   *Caribbean*
☎ 604-877-0189; 382 W Broadway; dishes $6-13;
⊙ 11am-2pm Mon, 11am-9pm Tue-Sat; bus 9

The Rasta folk here make outstanding Jamaican coco bun sandwiches, Caribbean stews and West Indian roti, with five different vegetarian platters and imported chili sauces. Gorge on the all-you-can-eat jerk chicken on Tuesday and Saturday.

RASPUTIN Map pp236-7   *Russian*
☎ 604-879-6675; 457 W Broadway; mains $14-25;
⊙ 5-11pm, to midnight Fri & Sat; bus 9

Rasputin brings fine Russian dining to Vancouver. If you're feeling wealthy, start off with fresh Caspian Sea caviar, then feast on blinis, cabbage rolls, borscht and perhaps a little chicken Kiev.

SEASONS IN THE PARK

Map pp236-7   *West Coast*
☎ 604-874-8008, 800-632-9422; Cambie St at W 33rd Ave; lunch $12-19, dinner mains $18-27; ⊙ 11:30am-2:30pm Mon-Sat, 10:30am-2:30pm Sun, 5:30-9:30pm Mon-Sun; bus 15

Amid the gardens of Bloedel Conservatory in Queen Elizabeth Park with the north shore mountains as a backdrop, world leaders have dined here at the highest point within the city limits. Lucky diners with reservations (to get past the busloads of tourists) feast on the views and zesty Pacific northwest cuisine, such as sea bass with gingered potatoes and soy butter sauce or baked green lentils in phyllo.

SHAO LIN NOODLE RESTAURANT

Map pp236-7   *Chinese*
☎ 604-873-1816; 548 W Broadway; dishes $5-9;
⊙ 11:30am-3:30pm Wed-Mon, 5-9:30pm Mon-Sun; bus 9

Look behind the glass enclosure and watch the chefs at this northern Chinese restaurant toss the handmade noodles that are the base of the menu's meat and vegetable dishes. Adding to the fun is special tea served from a pot with a three-foot long spout (the remnant of a long-ago tradition to ensure servants kept a polite distance from their royal masters). Cash only.

TOJO'S Map pp236-7   *Japanese*
☎ 604-872-8050; Ste 202, 777 W Broadway; sushi $8-15, mains $17-29; ⊙ 5-10pm Mon-Sat; bus 9

Tojo's is peerless when it comes to sushi or views of downtown Vancouver after dark. Expect to spend about $85 for a seat at the sushi bar, where you simply surrender to Chef Tojo's mastery of seasonal ingredients and fresh seafood. Everyone from visiting celebrities to local DJs raves about the house-smoked salmon. Otherwise, there's a changing menu of raw items and cooked Japanese specialties.

TOMATO FRESH FOOD CAFÉ

Map pp236-7   *West Coast*
☎ 604-874-6020; 3305 Cambie St; lunch $6-11, dinner mains $12-20; ⊙ 9am-10pm; bus 15

Lip-smacking breakfast, lunch and dinner offerings and modern-chic diner ambience make this a neighborhood pet. The Westcoaster Salad (greens topped with Indian candy smoked salmon, peppers, goat's cheese and warm maple syrup balsamic vinaigrette) provokes ecstasy; the cornbread provokes swooning. Menus are built around the offerings of local BC farmers.

Eating – West Side

Cheap Eats

THAI AWAY HOME Map pp236-7 *Thai*
☎ 604-873-8424; 3315 Cambie St; dishes $7-9;
🕙 11:30am-9:30pm Mon-Sat, noon-9:30pm Sun; bus 15
Locals go crazy for this place, which offers a standard yet scrumptiously prepared arsenal of curries (green with eggplant, red with pumpkin), noodles (pad thai, pad nar, pad si ew), soups (tom yum, tom ka gai) and mains (cashew chicken). It's served counter-and-stool or take-away. Another branch is in **East Vancouver** (Map p235; ☎ 604-253-8424; 1736 Commercial Dr).

SOUTH GRANVILLE

Plenty of creative upstarts and proven favorites hover around the area where Granville St meets W Broadway.

BIN 942 Map pp236-7 *Fusion Tapas*
☎ 604-734-9421; 1521 W Broadway; dishes $6-14;
🕙 5pm-2am Mon-Sat, 5pm-midnight Sun; bus 10
To prove it hasn't exhausted its creative juices, revered Bin 941 (p94) operates this sister restaurant that serves equally great food and keeps the same late-night hours.

OUISI Map pp236-7 *Cajun*
☎ 604-732-7550; 3014 S Granville St; lunch $8-13, dinner mains $13-22; 🕙 11am-10pm Mon-Fri, 9am-10pm Sat & Sun (bar open later every night); bus 10
This New Orleans–style bistro has live jazz several times a week, and spices up its menu with dishes like habanero coconut chicken, oyster loaf, marinated alligator and vegetarian etouffee. A large selection of single malts and bourbons rounds out the southern fare.

SALADE DE FRUITS CAFÉ
Map pp236-7 *French*
☎ 604-714-5987; 1551 W 7th Ave; lunch $6-10, dinner mains $10-20; 🕙 10am-2:30pm, 5:30-9pm Tue-Sat; bus 10
The French Cultural Centre hosts this sunny yellow café, where the menu is whatever it

rustles up that day – maybe a steamy pan of mussels with fries and mayo, or a quiche or lamb dish. You may not know what the French-speaking waitstaff is saying, but you know the food will be mouthwatering. The unfussed atmosphere means they don't bother with credit cards.

VIJ'S Map pp236-7 *Indian*
☎ 604-736-6664; 1480 W 11th Ave; mains $18-26;
🕙 5:30-10pm; bus 10
Sleek, modern Vij's stirs up Indian food unlike any you've tasted before. It's hard to explain exactly what Vij does with the spices, but the effects of dishes like lamb popsicles in cream curry have made many customers weep with gratitude. Vij doesn't take reservations, but that's OK – just buy a drink and sit by the lotus ponds out front; hostesses will swing by with free papadums, nan and other snacks while you wait.

WEST Map pp236-7 *West Coast*
☎ 604-738-8938; 2881 Granville St; lunch $10-20, dinner mains $33-43, tasting menus $59-94;
🕙 11:30am-3pm Mon-Fri, 5:30-11pm Mon-Sun; bus 10
With an awards list longer than the waiter's apron, well-chiseled West looks as sophisticated as it tastes. Changing menu selections focus on contemporary regional cuisine, so there are lots of salmon, halibut and crab dishes. Over 3000 wine bottles line the walls; waitstaff use sliding ladders to fetch your desire.

ZIZANIE Map pp236-7 *French*
☎ 604-738-7387; 1607 W 7th Ave; dishes $8-10;
🕙 5pm-1am; bus 10
Modest, folksy Zizanie serves Quebecois home cooking like poutine (french fries with curd cheese and gravy), tortiere (meat pie with fruit ketchup and salad) and croque monsieur (open-faced ham and cheese baguette) in heaping portions, along with potent Quebec beers and wine. Live music (usually folk) happens on Wednesday and weekends.

Cheap Eats

PAUL'S PLACE Map pp236-7 *Comfort Food*
☎ 604-737-2857; 2211 Granville St; dishes $6-10;
🕙 7am-3pm; bus 10
This perfect breakfast place has a short but sweet menu of hotcakes and omelettes, including 'the Conundrum,' which has both the chicken *and* the egg. Club sandwiches are on the lunch menu.

Top Five for West Coast Cuisine

- **Bishop's** (opposite)
- **West** (right)
- **Raincity Grill** (p99)
- **CinCin** (p98)
- **Lumiére** (p118)

KITSILANO

Kitsilano's main arteries – W 4th Ave and W Broadway – have a healthy mix of eateries, many of which are the best of their kind in the city. It's well worth the trek out here to sup near the beach, and Cornwall Ave's breezy take-away joints enable you to do just that. The neighborhood's hippie past has left a rich legacy of vegetarian restaurants, while its Greek immigrant past is evident in the 3000 block of Broadway, known as 'Little Greece.' Several restaurants also cluster near W 10th Ave and Sasamat St.

Roosts for Night Owls

These places serve well into the night; Naam and Calhoun's serve 24/7.

- **Naam** (p118)
- **Benny's** (p119)
- **DV8** (p95)
- **Calhoun's** (right)
- **Hamburger Mary's** (p100)

ACROPOL Map pp238-9 *Greek*
☎ 604-733-2412; 2946 W Broadway; mains $14-19;
🕒 11:30am-10:30pm Mon-Sat, 4-10pm Sun; bus 9
Watch everyone relax with decanters of wine as breezes blow by the outdoor tables at this elegant little taverna. Exohiko (slow-roasted lamb shoulder) is a house specialty. Unusual appetizers include the unpronounceable *kolokethokeftedes* (zucchini and feta cakes).

BISHOP'S Map pp238-9 *West Coast*
☎ 604-738-2025; 2183 W 4th Ave; mains $30-38;
🕒 5:30-11pm Mon-Sat, 5:30-10pm Sun; bus 4
John Bishop has cooked for a host of celebrities and visiting diplomats, as well as loyal Vancouver epicureans who have a fondness for this intimate space where table lamps glow and Canadian artwork fills the walls. Main courses are too eclectic to categorize easily – mingling Thai, Chinese, French and Italian – but absolutely fresh ingredients, strong complementary flavors and ingenious presentation are Bishop's hallmarks. The service is flawless, and the man himself often ushers guests in at the door.

BISTRO PASTIS Map pp238-9 *French*
☎ 604-731-5020; 2153 W 4th Ave; lunch $10-16, dinner mains $20-29, 3-course prix-fixe menu $45-52;
🕒 11:30am-2pm Tue-Fri, 11am-2pm Sat & Sun, 5:30-10pm Tue-Sun; bus 4
Crisp Pastis focuses on classic French bistro fare (coq au vin or steak frites, for instance), but enhances its menu with fresh northwest seafood and market produce. It's a real slice of Paris, with a slate of by-the-glass wines.

BURGOO BISTRO
Map pp238-9 *Comfort Food*
☎ 604-221-7839; 4434 W 10th Ave; dishes $10-13;
🕒 11:30am-3pm & 5-10pm Mon-Thu, 11am-10pm Fri-Sun; bus 17
Stews are the concept here, with soups and curries. Seasonal bowls include Kentucky burgoo (chicken, lamb, pork, beef, okra and corn on mashed potatoes) or Irish stew (lamb in Guinness, vegetables and dumplings atop mashed potatoes). The rustic ambience is perfect for the food, packages of which you can buy to take home and cook. House beers are on tap.

CALHOUN'S Map pp238-9 *Sandwiches*
☎ 604-731-7062; 3035 W Broadway; items $4-9;
🕒 24hr; bus 9
A 24-hour refueling spot for insomniacs and students, Calhoun's looks like a log cabin inside. Take a number and head to the counter to choose from the baked goods and sandwiches. Live music acts are sprinkled through the week.

EATERY Map pp238-9 *Japanese*
☎ 604-738-5298; 3431 W Broadway; items $7-18;
🕒 4:45-11pm; bus 9
Wooden booths, lava lamps, a wall of photos and a neon 'miso horny' sign are all part of the experience. Admittedly, the atmosphere is better than the food, but the salty Japanese bar fare goes well with the many microbrews on tap, and the daily sushi specials are filling and cheap.

FEENIE'S Map pp238-9 *West Coast*
☎ 604-739-7115; 2563 W Broadway; dishes $8-19; 3-course price-fixe dinner $35; 🕒 11:30am-2:30pm Mon-Fri, 10am-2pm Sat & Sun, 5:30-11:30pm Mon-Sun; bus 9
Celebrated chef Rob Feenie recently opened this bistro as a more casual and affordable alternative to **Lumiére** (p118). The focus is on Canadian ingredients, and dishes include pork chops in ice wine and mustard sauce, shepherd's pie with duck confit and truffled mashed potatoes, and Feenie's Weenie (a cheese smokie with sauerkraut).

Eating – West Side

GREENS & GOURMET

Map pp238-9   *Vegetarian*

☎ 604-737-7373; 2582 W Broadway; buffet dishes $1.69 per 100g; ☽ 11am-9:30pm Sun-Thu, 11am-10pm Fri & Sat; bus 9

Grab a tray and load up with curries, casseroles, non-dairy desserts and other dishes from the all-vegetarian buffet. It's a quintessential hippie kind of place, attached to a yoga studio and with new-age music playing, but it's commendable for its wide, flavorful selection. Note it won't be cheap by the time you pile your plate, though.

LUMIÉRE Map pp238-9   *French*

☎ 604-739-8185; 2551 W Broadway; wine pairings $50-65, tasting menus $90-100; ☽ 5:30-10:30pm Tue-Sun; bus 9

One of Canada's most esteemed restaurants, Lumiére embraces a kind of French-fusion cooking that takes the best of world cuisine and drapes it in wonderful sauces. Diners order one of the tasting menus (either seafood, vegetarian or chef's choice), then sit back while chef/owner Rob Feenie's masterpieces come out one by one. Menus vary seasonally, but might include offerings like rhubarb and vanilla soup, seafood mousse ravioli or scallop ceviche with watermelon tartare. You can order à la carte in the attached Tasting Bar if you can't commit to the full-course meal.

MONTRI'S Map pp238-9   *Thai*

☎ 604-738-9888; 3629 W Broadway; mains $10-15; ☽ 5-10pm Tue-Sun; bus 9

Widely considered the city's best Thai restaurant, Montri's reserves dishes with a spiciness rating of five chilis for 'masochists and Thai nationals only.' Superb pad thai and a deft range of curries will impress culinary purists and vegetarians alike.

NAAM Map pp238-9   *Vegetarian*

☎ 604-738-7151; 2724 W 4th Ave; dishes $6-11; ☽ 24 hr; bus 4

A relic of Kitsilano's hippie past, this vegetarian restaurant has the charm of a comfy farmhouse. A nearly endless menu covers stir-fries, Mexican platters and all kinds of veggie burgers. Don't miss the sesame-fried potatoes with miso gravy. Organic beers are on tap and live music is on nightly, which will keep you entertained during the long line-ups and unhurried service. The fireplace burns in winter, the garden patio shades in summer, and it seems everyone might burst into a group hug at any moment.

Top Five for Kids

- Sophie's Cosmic Café (opposite)
- Café Deux Soleil (p126)
- Sunshine Diner (below)
- Romano's Macaroni Grill (p99)
- Naam (left)

NYALA RESTAURANT

Map pp238-9   *Ethiopian*

☎ 604-731-7899; 2930 W 4th Ave; dishes $9-15; ☽ dinner from 5pm; bus 4

This Ethiopian restaurant offers hands-on (ie without utensils) eating. Foamy pieces of flat, sour *injera* bread serve as knife, fork and spoon to scoop up richly spiced stews; finish off with the traditional coffee ceremony. There's a vegetarian buffet a couple of days each week (currently Wednesday and Sunday).

OCTOPUS'S GARDEN

Map pp238-9   *Japanese*

☎ 604-734-8971; 1955 Cornwall Ave; mains $8-10; ☽ 5-10:30pm Tue-Sat, 5-9:30pm Sun; bus 2

Sushi gets sliced up with impish delight at this beachy, bamboo hut–like restaurant. Meanwhile seasonal noodle dishes, like 'Pavarotti Udon,' need an entire poster of explanation.

PROVENCE MEDITERRANEAN GRILL

Map pp238-9   *French/Italian*

☎ 604-222-1980; 4473 W 10th Ave; lunch $10-17, dinner mains $22-27; ☽ 11:30am-10pm Sun-Thu, 11:30am-11pm Fri & Sat; bus 17

It's like dining on the Riviera. Lunch brings baguettes with combinations of salmon, chicken, cheese and vegetables. Dinner brings baked, grilled, stewed or marinated antipasti, appetizers like *merguez* (spicy lamb sausage with fennel) and mains like porcini-dusted ostrich. Tea is served from 2:30pm to 4:30pm (except Sunday), or you can buy a gourmet picnic.

SUNSHINE DINER

Map pp238-9   *Comfort Food*

☎ 604-733-7717; 2756 W Broadway; dishes $7-10; ☽ 7:30am-5pm Mon-Sat, 8:30am-4pm Sun; bus 9

Slide into this rock 'n' roll diner's shiny red booths and order up a milkshake with an omelette or burger. All ages of neighborhood folk linger under the Elvis, Sinatra and Monroe posters: adults read their newspapers while children play with stuff from the tub of house toys.

TANGERINE Map pp238-9 *Asian Fusion*
☎ 604-739-4677; 1685 Yew St; dishes $9-17;
🕒 dinner 5-11pm Mon-Thu, 5pm-late Fri & Sat,
brunch 9am-2:30pm Sat & Sun; bus 2

Tangerine's daring menu and unbeatable proximity to Kits Beach render it a local favorite, especially for brunch. The changing fusion tapas menu might include tamarind chicken satay with ginger noodles or red spinach curry with scallion pancakes. After-dinner martinis like the chocolate cosmo go well with the rich desserts.

WILD GARLIC Map pp238-9 *Asian Fusion*
☎ 604-730-0880; 2120 W Broadway; tapas $6-10,
dinner mains $15-27, prix-fixe menu $31-34;
🕒 11am-2pm Wed-Fri, 5-10pm Wed-Mon; bus 9

Vampires beware: garlic makes its way into most dishes at this adventurous, Asian-inspired bistro, including the chef's signature dish of roasted candied garlic. Other pleasures include zippy Szechuan asparagus in black bean sauce, roasted duck breast with orange cranberry sauce, and the vodka scallop martini.

Cheap Eats
BENNY'S BAGELS
Map pp238-9 *Bagels/Sandwiches*
☎ 604-731-9730; 2503 W Broadway; sandwiches
$4-7; 🕒 7-1am Sun-Thu, 24hr Fri & Sat; bus 9

Benny's rises above the usual bagel joint with its cool metallic walls, cushy couches by the fireplace, beer list, and menu of scrumptious, bagel-encased sandwiches and melts. It's a great place to remedy late-night weekend munchies.

PLANET VEG Map pp238-9 *Indian/Vegetarian*
☎ 604-734-1001; 1941 Cornwall Ave; dishes $2-6;
🕒 11am-9:30pm, reduced in winter; bus 2

Healthy eaters swear a deep allegiance to this friendly vegetarian take-out place. The Indian owners bake rather than fry the samosas, and fill them with ingredients like spinach and tofu. The roti rules; try the Katmandu Roll, filled with cabbage and mixed veggies and lined with fried noodles and jalapeno cilantro chutney. Vegetable burgers and *subjis* are on the menu, too.

RAW Map pp238-9 *Vegetarian*
☎ 604-737-0420; 1849 W 1st Ave; dishes $4-7;
🕒 10am-6pm Mon-Sat; bus 2

The café's feng shui–friendly layout entices passersby to take their pick of salads, soups and sandwiches, or the chef's totally new creations.

Dining at bistro-style Feenie's (p117), Kitsilano

The emphasis is on organic, uncooked and unrefined foods, resulting in items like mock salmon roll, mango tango burrito and chickpea pesto salad. Organic coffees, herbal teas and yogi soy shakes round out the experience.

SOPHIE'S COSMIC CAFÉ
Map pp238-9 *Diner*
☎ 604-732-6810; 2095 W 4th Ave; dishes $5-12;
🕒 8am-9:30pm; bus 4

Sophie's is a museum of garage sale–item kitsch. The menu is mostly standard diner, with burgers, club sandwiches and big-ass milkshakes, but there are a few offbeat dishes like BC oyster burgers, too. Bits of broken crayon are scattered on the floor and small children run wild, but that's the organized chaos of Sophie's. Brunches are popular and a good opportunity to use the smokin' homemade hot sauce.

Two pizza joints in Kits produce pies that are lip-smacking (a slice costs $2.50 to $4):

Flying Wedge Pizza (Map pp238-9; ☎ 604-732-8840; 1937 Cornwall Ave; 🕒 10:30am-10:30pm; bus 2)
Thick-crust slices may come up with anything from vegetarian pesto to honey-curried chicken.

Nat's New York Pizzeria (Map pp238-9; ☎ 604-737-0707; 2684 W Broadway; 🕒 11am-10pm Mon-Sat, noon-9pm Sun; bus 9) Thin-crust lovers, rejoice! Nat's does the real thing, and also makes 1ft-long Italian subs.

GREATER VANCOUVER

The burbs offer a couple of first-rate dining options, and you don't have to travel all that far to reach them.

HART HOUSE Map pp228-9 *West Coast*

☎ 604-298-4278; Burnaby, 6664 Deer Lake Ave; lunch $11-15, dinner mains $15-23; ⏱ lunch 11:30am-2:30pm Tue-Fri, 11am-2pm Sun, dinner 5:30-9pm Tue-Sun; bus 144

This romantic Tudor revival-style mansion looks on to the shores of Deer Lake. The creative menu has updated northwest cuisine classics and weekend brunches are especially worthwhile. Afternoon tea is served by the fireplace, and lobster festivals are held outside in the heritage Rosedale Gardens during summer.

PEAR TREE Map pp228-9 *West Coast*

☎ 604-299-2772; Burnaby, 4120 E Hastings St; mains $17-23; ⏱ dinner from 5pm Tue-Sat; bus 135

This modest storefront garners big applause from downtown foodies, who say it's worth the trek out to the 'burbs for refreshingly bright west coast inventions, like salmon with star-anise butter sauce and crushed sour-cream potatoes.

SALMON HOUSE ON THE HILL

Map pp228-9 *West Coast/Seafood*

☎ 604-926-3212; West Vancouver, 2229 Folkestone Way; lunch $13-17, dinner mains $24-30; ⏱ lunch 11:30am-2pm Mon-Sat, 11am-2pm Sun, dinner 5-10pm Sun-Thu, 5-11pm Fri & Sat; bus 251

The Salmon House ranks among Vancouver's finest culinary experiences, especially with the entire city lying at your feet view-wise. First Nations art sets off the Pacific northwest cuisine beautifully. As you'd expect, salmon dominates the menu. Chef Dan Atkinson grills the fish and other meats over green alderwood, which imparts a sweet, smoky flavor. The House Sampler provides a fine way to get acquainted with local fortes, like candied salmon, smoked wild Sockeye salmon, smoked salmon spinach roulade and alder-grilled salmon.

TOMAHAWK Map pp228-9 *Comfort Food*

☎ 604-988-2612; North Vancouver, 1550 Philip Ave; meals $10-12; ⏱ 8am-9pm Sun-Thu, 8am-10pm Fri & Sat; bus 240

For more than 70 years, breakfasts, burgers and homemade desserts have been served in this old-fashioned wooden cabin. The food is greasy (not necessarily in a good way), but the collection of First Nations art and the cartoon menu make it worth while.

Entertainment

Entertainment

Vancouverites do like to go out and play. The city's worldliness and progressive attitude, combined with the film industry and local university ensures that there's a great entertainment scene. Choose from indie flicks (p132), butoh dance performances (p137) or Shakespeare on the beach (p134). If the evening calls for something with a bit more mass appeal, try one of the rock clubs or quaff a microbrew on an outdoor patio (many of which are heated and open year-round). The city's 'no smoking' ordinance prevails in bars, clubs and restaurants, though some places have 'smoking rooms' or patios where puffing is permitted.

The city's entertainment bible is the free alternative weekly *Georgia Straight*. The *Vancouver Sun*'s Thursday 'Queue' section also lists local happenings. Turn to p214 for details. For professional theater, dance, classical music, literary and visual arts information, stop by the all-knowing **Alliance for Arts & Culture** (Map pp230-3; ☎ 604-681-3535; www.allianceforarts.com; downtown, 938 Howe St; 9am-5pm Mon-Fri; bus 4).

Tickets

For an added booking fee, **Ticketmaster** (☎ 604-280-4444; www.ticketmaster.ca) sells tickets for major concerts, sports games, theater and performing arts events. Buy tickets either online or at various city outlets, including **GM Place** (p43), **Pacific Centre Mall** (p152) and **Tickets Tonight** (Map pp230-3; ☎ 604-684-2787; www.ticketstonight.ca; downtown, TouristInfo Centre, plaza level, 200 Burrard St; 10am-5pm Tue-Sat, to 6pm in summer). For premier seats and tickets to sold-out events, scalpers circle the entrances to major venues like vultures waiting to pounce. You'll pay a big premium for their 'service,' but if you wait until the event has just started, you might strike a deal as scalpers will be anxious to recoup their losses.

For half-price, day-of tickets to theater, comedy and dance performances, stop by the Tickets Tonight booth at the TouristInfo Centre. Tickets are sold in person only on a first-come, first-served basis, but you can get the scoop on what's available by calling or looking online first. Last-minute tickets may also be available at theater box offices.

DRINKING

Pubs listed here include the more traditional drinking establishments and microbrew joints, whereas bars give off a trendy, lounge-y air and there's often a DJ controlling the tunes. Pubs usually open earlier than bars, around 11am versus 5pm. Most drinkeries close at 2am, although they are allowed to stay open until 3am and will do so if they're busy enough, particularly on weekends. Some have a special license to stay open until 4am or 5am.

Only recently have British Columbia's draconian liquor laws begun to loosen. Entertainment wasn't allowed in bars until the mid-1970s. In those days it was also technically illegal to walk around a bar with a beer (if you wanted to change tables, you had to ask the waiter to move your drink). Today, strict licensing laws often prohibit patrons from drinking outside without ordering food, but in practice keeping a menu on your table may be enough.

For off-premises sales, you'll have to visit a government-run liquor store operated by **BC's Liquor Distribution Branch** (BCLDB; ☎ 604-252-3000; www.bcliquorstores.com). Outlets are scattered throughout the city; the largest is at 5555 Cambie St (Map pp228-9; ☎ 604-660-9463; 9:30am-11pm Mon-Sat, 11am-6pm Sun; bus 15). A handful of private stores are attached to neighborhood pubs and hotels, but like consumers they must buy from BCLDB.

Drinking Strips & Neighborhoods

Pubs and bars are spread all over the city. Downtown has its share, particularly near the stadiums where boisterous sports bars are within brisk walking distance. Yaletown is regaining its chock-a-block reputation: in the late 19th century it packed in a greater number of

Small Labels, Big Taste

Little microbreweries are big business in Vancouver. They produce an astonishing array of ales, bitters, lagers, pilsners, bocks, porters, stouts and Belgian-style fruit beers. Canada's first brewpub, at least in recent times, was Horseshoe Bay's Troller Pub, started by legendary brewmaster John Mitchell in 1982. The Troller has stopped making beer, but Mitchell went on to establish **Spinnakers Brew Pub & Restaurant** (p191) in Victoria, which is now the oldest licensed brewpub in Canada, and helped set up **Howe Sound Inn & Brewing Company** (p192) in Squamish.

Here's the skinny on Vancouver's top five reigning brewpubs:

- **Granville Island Brewery** (p59) – Great tour.
- **Dix BBQ & Brewery** (below) – Tasty pitchers at reasonable prices.
- **Dockside Brewing Company** (below) – Sparkling, waterside views of False Creek.
- **Steamworks Brewing Company** (p124) – Great beer, plain and simple.
- **Yaletown Brewing Company** (p124) – The place to sip suds among the beautiful people.

Micro Labels

For small, flavorful brewers whose products you'll find in local bars and restaurants, keep an eye on the taps for:

- **Backwoods Brewing Company** – Stinger Ale, Nut Brown Ale and Dam Lager are easy on the taste buds.
- **Okanagan Spring Brewery** – A small enterprise started by German immigrants, known for its pale ales and Bavarian lager.
- **R&B Brewing Company** – Wicked Red Devil and dark, mystical Raven Cream ales flow from distinctive tap handles.
- **Storm Brewing Company** – Often considered the best in town, with brews like Black Plague Stout and Black Cherry Fruit Lambic. Sadly, they're hard to find; try **Vij's** (p116) or places on **Commercial Dr** (p104) near the brewery.

saloons per hectare than anywhere else in the world. Remember, too, that you can get a drink at many of the places in the Eating chapter (pp91–120), especially those with vista-friendly patios, such as **Bridges** (p106) and the **SandBar** (p106).

PUBS

Vancouver's plethora of microbrews make drinking here a beautiful thing; see above for details.

CAMBIE Map p234

☎ 604-684-6466; Gastown, 300 Cambie St; bus 3

At the seamy edge of Gastown, the outdoor picnic tables at the **Cambie International Hostel** (p172) overflow with folks from all walks of life, brought together by their mutual love of cheap beer, cheap burgers and colorful tattoos.

CARDERO'S MARINE PUB Map pp230-3

☎ 604-669-7666; West End, 1583 Coal Harbour Quay; bus 19

Cardero's is a stellar waterfront pub, jutting out between the yachts and near where the sea-planes land. Drink in the sights of Stanley Park, Coal Harbour and the North Shore mountains while drinking down tasty tap brews, wine or scotch on the heated patio or leather couches inside.

DIX BBQ & BREWERY Map pp230-3

☎ 604-682-2739; downtown, 871 Beatty St; SkyTrain Stadium

Dix welcomes sports fans from nearby BC Place, southern BBQ-lovers and other normal folk who are drawn by the lack of pretension and the fine, house-crafted lagers. Pitchers are so reasonably priced you can chivalrously offer to buy a round without sweating. The menu includes huge burgers and sandwiches, and you can smell the burning applewood under the grill from the street.

DOCKSIDE BREWING COMPANY

Map pp236-7

☎ 604-685-7070; Granville Island, Granville Island Hotel, 1253 Johnston St; bus 50

Dockside's German beer meister has been brewing treats like Old Bridge Dark Lager and fruity, hibiscus-toned Jamaican Lager for more than 30 years. Take your drinks outside to the patio for awe-inspiring views of False Creek's boat traffic and the mountain-backed downtown skyline. Or stay indoors by the fireplace.

Tuesday is popular for $3 pints and $6.50 wood-oven pizza; Wednesday offers $10 pitchers.

ELWOOD'S JOINT Map pp238-9

☎ 604-736-4301; Kitsilano, 3145 W Broadway; bus 9
A laid-back, low-cost place to quaff a tap beer or three, especially out front on the well-worn wooden patio. Elwood's owners operate the Metropolitan Bartending School, so they certainly know how to pull a good pint and mix a mean martini.

GRANVILLE ISLAND BREWERY

Map pp236-7
☎ 604-687-2739; Granville Island, 1441 Cartwright St; ☽ closes 7pm Sun-Thu, 8pm Fri & Sat; bus 50
Granville has the distinction of being Canada's oldest microbrewery. While its main beers – all donning local monikers like Robson St Hefeweizen, Kitsilano Maple Cream Ale and English Bay Pale Ale – are widely available in bottles, Granville also makes limited-release beers that are only available in its taproom. See p59 for tour information.

IRISH HEATHER Map p234

☎ 604-688-9779; Gastown, 217 Carrall St; bus 7
Not only does this popular pub pour the best Guinness in town, it also shows genuine Irish hospitality by offering excellent country fare (see p96), live music most weekdays and a glassed-in back patio among its labyrinth of rooms. Seek out the Shebeen Whisky Bar in back, where 140 varieties lie in wait.

JERICHO SAILING CENTRE Map pp238-9

☎ 604-222-1331; Kitsilano, 1300 Discovery St; closed Mon-Fri, Nov-Apr; bus 4
This is a terrific, unfussed perch at sunset, with a view out over English Bay toward downtown and the mountains. Plop down in one of the outdoor deck chairs, if you can find an empty one, and watch all the sailboats try to steer to shore. Their navigators will be joining you shortly.

LENNOX PUB Map pp230-3

☎ 604-408-0881; downtown, 800 Granville St; bus 4
Poised at a coveted intersection, this sleek brass-and-wood pub caters to those who find waiting hours to get into the dance clubs too tedious. The Lennox keeps a few Belgian beers among its tap stash, as well as several single-malt scotches.

MILL MARINE BISTRO Map pp230-3

☎ 604-687-6455; West End, 1199 W Cordova St; bus 19
The location is similar to Cardero's (see above), but with even better panoramas. Seaplanes buzz overhead almost within touching distance, the mountains beckon across Burrard Inlet and the city's best dog park is adjacent. Canines are welcome on the outdoor patio, where they inevitably drag their owners for a post-run drink. Boat owners can pull right up to the front dock.

RAVEN PUBLIC HOUSE Map pp228-9

☎ 604-929-3834; North Vancouver, 1052 Deep Cove Rd; bus 212
If you've just been for a stroll along Malcolm Lowry's Walk in Cates Park (p76), come and pay your respects to the great man, who was known to enjoy a drink or two himself. There are 26 beers on tap, excellent food and a toasty fireplace.

SAILOR HAGAR'S BREWPUB Map pp228-9

☎ 604-984-7669; North Vancouver, 86 Semisch Ave; SeaBus
A short walk uphill from Lonsdale Quay, this popular brewpub offers good views of the city skyline, over a half-dozen European-style beers on tap and plenty of good pub grub. There's a bottle shop on the premises.

STEAMWORKS BREWING COMPANY

Map p234
☎ 604-689-2739; Gastown, 375 Water St; SkyTrain Waterfront
Admire the tall wooden timbers inside Vancouver's original brewpub, where you can play pool or lounge by the fireplace while swilling exceptional beer. Meanwhile outside on the patio the scent of hops mixes with the inlet breezes.

YALETOWN BREWING COMPANY

Map pp230-3
☎ 604-681-2739; Yaletown, 1111 Mainland St; bus 1
The crowd here is more casual than one might expect for Yaletown. The enormous patio makes a nice roost to watch the moneyed and well-dressed loft owners sashay by.

Other recommended pubs:

Fogg 'n Suds (Map pp230-3; ☎ 604-683-2337; West End, 1323 Robson St; bus 5) Restaurant chain with 24 beers on tap and 120 bottled brands.

Fringe Café (Map pp238-9; ☎ 604-738-6977; Kitsilano, 3124 W Broadway; bus 9) Casual pub with daily beer specials.

Morrissey's (Map pp230-3; ☎ 604-682-0909; downtown, 1227 Granville St; bus 4) Jovial Irish pub with fireplace.

BARS
The lounge trend has hit hard in VanCity.

ALIBI ROOM Map p234
☎ 604-623-3383; Gastown, 157 Alexander St; bus 7
Alibi's low-ceilinged basement lounge creates an ideal setting for Vancouver's film and design crowd to brood over their martinis. The moping ends upstairs, where a menu of ridiculously good comfort food awaits you (see p96).

AFTERGLOW Map pp230-3
☎ 604-602-0835; Yaletown, 1082 Hamilton St; bus 1
It's the lounge side of Glowbal satay bar (p97), with a frosty pink interior, silhouettes of naked women à la James Bond and coy cocktails, like the Pink Pussycat (vodka, raspberry, white grape juice and lemon) and the Bombshell (gin, ice wine and lemon).

BACCHUS Map pp230-3
☎ 604-608-5319; downtown, 845 Hornby St; bus 5
This decadent lounge has a heady air of sophistication. The carved limestone fireplace, cherry-

wood paneling, leather chairs and gold silk accents make it the premier place to warm up when the weather won't cooperate. Choose from a wide selection of martinis, whiskey and scotch, while a piano man jangles the keys.

BACKSTAGE LOUNGE Map pp236-7
☎ 604-687-1354; Granville Island, 1585 Johnston St; bus 50
After fighting your way through the crowds at the market, escape to this breezy deck overlooking False Creek. There's live music almost nightly (with a focus on BC artists), buskers during the day and a variety of local beers on tap – some from Granville Island Brewery. All profits benefit the Arts Club Theatre, so bottoms up.

CLOUD NINE LOUNGE Map pp230-3
☎ 604-687-0511; West End, 1400 Robson St; bus 5
Patrons at the 42nd-story Cloud Nine, atop the Empire Landmark Hotel (p174), are treated to Vancouver's most gasp-worthy view. The city – that's the *whole* city – spreads out before you as the glassy bar rotates six degrees every 60 seconds. It's brilliant just before sundown.

ELIXIR Map pp230-3
☎ 604-642-0557; Yaletown, 350 Davie St; bus 1
In the Opus Hotel (p173), and in keeping with its modder-than-thou ambience, Elixir is a mélange

The bar at Railway Club (p128), downtown

of swanky tables and chairs (like the green cushions atop a gold claw-foot base) surrounded by sparkly wall tiles. The crowd, skewing 30-plus, downs tempting tipples from an extensive list.

MALONE'S SPORTS BAR Map pp238-9
☎ 604-737-7777; Kitsilano, 2202 Cornwall Ave; bus 2
Malone's, overlooking Kits Beach, is packed with outdoorsy young singles seeking refreshment after a hard day of playing volleyball. Though it's still all the rage, developers want to raze Malone's for a mall. The beach-clad are fighting hard to prevent it and preserve rituals like 'Toonie Tuesdays,' when most drinks are $2.

SECTION (3) Map pp230-3
☎ 604-684-2777; Yaletown, 1039 Mainland; bus 1
A neon 'NERD' sign hangs over the bar, but the pretty people sipping cocktails here are anything but. The room radiates a pink-orange glow, and provides high-backed booths for those weary after DJ-fueled dancing to plop down in, as well as private, curtained-off rooms.

SHARK CLUB BAR & GRILL Map pp230-3
☎ 604-687-4275; downtown, 180 W Georgia St; SkyTrain Stadium

Top Five Pubs & Bars

- Irish Heather (p124)
- Cambie (p123)
- Alibi Room (p125)
- Backstage Lounge (p125)
- AFTERglow (p125)

This anything-goes sports bar boasts big-screen TVs and weekend DJs; it's especially popular before or after a hockey game and for bachelor/bachelorette parties.

Other recommended bars:

Aqua 1066 (Map pp230-3; ☎ 604-683-5843; West End, 1066 W Hastings St; SkyTrain Burrard) Swanky film-industry types enjoy the appetizers and boutique wine list.

Bimini's Tap House (Map pp238-9; ☎ 604-732-9232; Kitsilano, 2010 W 4th Ave; bus 4) A classy, young Kits crowd takes advantage of streetfront pool tables and martini drink specials.

Urban Well (Map pp238-9; ☎ 604-737-7770; Kitsilano, 1516 Yew St; bus 2) Popular bar-resto-club hybrid with glowing decor, energetic DJs and comedy nights (Monday and Tuesday).

COFFEEHOUSES

No matter whether you call it espresso, cappuccino or plain ol' Joe, Vancouver is awash with good coffee. Big-name chains like Vancouver's own local-roasters-made-good Blenz dominate the market. Seattle coffee-magnate Starbucks even has two stores facing each other kitty-corner at Robson and Thurlow Sts.

Independent neighborhood coffee shops offer stronger perks, including homemade baked goods, free reading material, notice boards and local color. Most places open around 7am on weekdays and an hour or two later on weekends, and close about 6pm (an hour or so earlier on weekends).

Commercial Dr is tops for characterful coffee shops. Old-timers from the Old Country share space with pierced artists, skateboarders and lesbians, all sipping attitude-adjusting roasts. Main St in SoMa also has several hipster cafés.

For those who scorn the java gods, or travelers who miss out on high tea in Victoria on Vancouver Island (see p190), look to **Secret Garden Tea Company** (Map pp228-9; ☎ 604-261-3070; Kerrisdale, 5559 West Blvd; bus 16). A charming assortment of chinaware hangs on the walls at this tearoom, and classical musicians often play during afternoon tea; reservations are required.

CAFÉ DEUX SOLEIL Map p235
☎ 604-254-1195; East Vancouver, 2096 Commercial Dr; ☉ to midnight; bus 20
This overgrown coffee house is a hip, healthy and child-friendly eatery. On sunny days folks relax outside with a beer, and acoustic musicians, performance poets and DJs take the stage several nights a week. Veggie burgers

and dishes like black bean roll ups cost $6 to $10.

CAFFÈ ARTIGIANO Map pp230-3
☎ 604-696-9222; downtown, 763 Hornby St; SkyTrain Granville
Artigiano is home to Canada's barista champion and three latte art champions. Drinks ap-

pear with a maple leaf, clover or other design adorning the foam – no wonder this place is located by the Vancouver Art Gallery. The café is packed with downtown workers at lunchtime, who file in for salami, prosciutto, mozzarella, pinenuts and other *panini* staples served in inventive breads like rosemary-potato and fig-anise (sandwiches cost $7 to $10).

CAFFÉ CALABRIA Map p235
☎ 604-253-7017; East Vancouver, 1745 Commercial Dr; ✹ to midnight; bus 20
Soak up kitsch along with cappuccino in Calabria's colorful atmosphere. Plaster statues of nymphs and a nude David are scattered about, chandeliers and boxes of cake hang from the ceiling, and there's a Sistine Chapel–like mural that depicts God passing Adam a cup of coffee. The deli case showcases scrumptious sandwiches. Unlike most of its peers, Calabria has no sports-tuned TVs.

GRIND Map pp236-7
☎ 604-874-1588; SoMa, 4124 Main St; ✹ 24hr; bus 3
The Grind's claim to fame is that it's open for business 24/7, fueling starving students, artists and writers through the dark night. The large, open space hosts an art gallery, concerts and spoken word performances, as well as the philosophical and political discussions of patrons.

ROMA CAFÉ Map p235
☎ 604-215-8801; East Vancouver, 1510 Commercial Dr; bus 20
While it's a favorite subject of debate among locals, many think Roma serves the Drive's best espresso and lattes. It's the best place to watch soccer and is crammed cup-to-cup during big games. It takes other sports seri-

ously, too: witness the logos of Vancouver's teams painted alongside the Virgin Mary over the entrance.

Also recommended:

Bean Around the World (Map pp238-9; ☎ 604-739-1069; Kitsilano, 1945 Cornwall Ave; ✹ to 10pm; bus 2) Mellow local hangout by the beach.

Big News Coffee (Map pp236-7; ☎ 604-739-7320; South Granville, 2447 Granville St; bus 10) Flip through old magazines, Japanese comics and today's newspapers.

Café Luna (Map p234; ☎ 604-687-5862; Gastown, 113 Water St; ✹ closed Sun in winter; SkyTrain Waterfront) A rare, non-touristy place to find solace in Gastown.

Continental Coffee (Map p235; ☎ 604-255-0712; East Vancouver, 1800 Commercial Dr; bus 20) Slightly scruffy but good coffee; why else would all the Vespas be lined up outside?

Darryl's Coffee Café (Map pp230-3; ☎ 604-689-5354; downtown, 945 Davie St; ✹ closed Sun in winter; bus 1) Aboriginal owned; also sells bannock (First Nations bread) and First Nations artwork.

JJ Bean (Map p235; ☎ 604-254-3723; East Vancouver, 2206 Commercial Dr; bus 20) Competition-winning baristas, but in a non–hoity toity atmosphere.

Joe's (Map p235; ☎ 604-255-1046; East Vancouver, 1150 Commercial Dr; ✹ to 1am; bus 20) Enjoy the pool tables and sports-tuned TVs, but be sure to heed the 'no kissing' policy (long story – ask a local for details).

Lugz (Map pp236-7; ☎ 604-873-6766; SoMa, 2525 Main St; ✹ to 11pm; bus 3) Bike messengers congregate outside, while neighborhood artists dream away on the leather couches inside.

Melriche's (Map pp230-3; ☎ 604-689-5282; West End, 1244 Davie St; ✹ to 11pm; bus 1) A favorite pit stop after Little Sister's bookstore (p156).

SoMa (Map pp236-7; ☎ 604-873-1750; SoMa, 2528 Main St; ✹ to 11pm; bus 3) Peaceful place to swill and chill.

LIVE MUSIC
It's difficult to categorize the types of music any given venue might present. Some clubs offer just straight rock, jazz or blues, but most present a mixed bag over the course of a week.

Musical superstars perform at the sports stadiums and downtown theaters, like the **Queen Elizabeth** (p134), the **Orpheum** (p136) and the **Vogue Theatre** (Map pp230-3; ☎ 604-331-7909; www .voguetheatre.com; downtown, 918 Granville St; bus 4). In addition, some of the big dance clubs, like **Richards on Richards** (p131) and **Sonar** (p131), to name just a few, double as live-music venues for a wide array of touring acts.

Opening hours for venues vary, depending on the bookings. Cover charges range from about $5 to $20, but can go well above that for bigger acts. Tickets can be purchased at the door or ahead of time at record stores like **Zulu** (p165), **Highlife** (p159) or **Scratch** (p154).

Several places (often those with the word 'club' in their title) offer 'memberships' for $5 to $25 annually, which provides discounts to shows, member-night parties and other perks.

Some venues may claim you need to be a member to enter, but usually you just need to sign in at the door or explain that you're thinking about becoming a member, and you'll get in without a problem.

ROCK & ALTERNATIVE

Places known for attracting a young, rough-and-ready crowd include the **Cobalt** (Map p234; ☎ 604-764-7865; Chinatown, 917 Main St; SkyTrain Main St-Science World), a breeding ground for punk, hard-core metal and the extreme alternative scene, located in the tough area around Pacific Central Station; and the **Marine Club** (Map pp230-3; ☎ 604-683-1720; downtown, 537 Homer St; SkyTrain Granville), a wood-paneled live hotspot with 'Rockabilly Saturdays' among its line-up.

ANZA CLUB Map pp236-7
☎ 604-876-7128; www.anzaclub.org; Fairview, 3 E 8th Ave; bus 9
Local alt-music acts favor this rental hall, stripped to its bare essentials, but here really anything goes. There are weekly bluegrass, drumming circle and dart-team nights, as well as meetings of Celluloid Social Club. The stage is upstairs, while downstairs houses a tiki lounge.

COMMODORE Map pp230-3
☎ 604-739-4550; www.commodoreballroom.com; downtown, 868 Granville St; bus 4
Up-and-coming local bands know they've finally made it when they play the old Commodore Ballroom, now managed by the House of Blues entertainment group. The club also books international touring acts, and on disco nights its big bouncy dance floor (buoyed by tires) gets packed.

MEDIA CLUB Map pp230-3
☎ 604-608-2871; www.themediaclub.ca; downtown, 695 Cambie St; SkyTrain Stadium
This intimate space, which is located underneath the Queen Elizabeth Theatre complex is prone to booking inventive acts that mix and match the genres, so you may have the chance to see electro-symphonic or acoustic metal groups alongside power pop and hip-hop bands.

PIC (PICCADILLY PUB) Map pp230-3
☎ 604-682-3221; downtown, 622 W Pender St; SkyTrain Granville
The laid-back Pic has been around a while, and can be counted on for local rock and blues bands on weekends, with a bit of open-mic, acoustic or retro midweek. Sometimes it even plays classic movies like *A Clockwork Orange* with free admission.

RAILWAY CLUB Map pp230-3
☎ 604-681-1625; www.therailwayclub.com; downtown, 579 Dunsmuir St; SkyTrain Granville
The old-fashioned Railway is one of the city's best clubs. The nightly (and weekend afternoon) live music could be anything by local songwriters and musicians: rootsy rockabilly, jazz or boozy campfire-type sing-alongs. For those who need a break from the tunes, there's another room that's just for drinking and conversing.

JAZZ, BLUES, FOLK & WORLD

Contact the **Coastal Jazz & Blues Society** (CJBS; ☎ 604-872-5200; www.jazzvancouver.com) for club links and a citywide calendar of gigs, concerts and festivals, including the **Vancouver International Jazz Festival** (p9), which CJBS produces. **O'Doul's** (p99) hosts nightly jazz, and the attached Listel hotel is where many touring jazz musicians stay when they come through town. On Commercial Dr, **Café Deux Soleil** (p126) and **Bukowski's** (p104) attract local acoustic, jazz and blues musicians.

The **Rogue Folk Club** (☎ 604-736-3022; www.roguefolk.bc.ca) presents folk music shows around town and can provide updates on the **Vancouver Folk Festival** (p10). The **Jericho Sailing Centre** (p124) hosts the **Jericho Folk Club** (☎ 604-222-4113) on Tuesday night.

Keep an eye out for the **Caravan World Rhythms Society** (☎ 604-886-0895; www.caravanbc.org), which organizes live music performances by artists from a diverse range of cultures and backgrounds; events take place at venues citywide.

CELLAR JAZZ CAFÉ Map pp238-9

☎ 604-738-1959; www.cellarjazz.com; Kitsilano, 3611 W Broadway; ⊗ closed Tue; bus 9

People actually stop talking and eating long enough to listen to the music at this underground 70-seat club/restaurant, that's known for showcasing truly great local jazz, as well as some touring acts. There's a $10 minimum charge on Thursday, which rises to $15 on Friday and Saturday, in addition to the ticket price.

HOT JAZZ SOCIETY Map pp236-7

☎ 604-873-4131; www.hotjazzsocietybc.com; SoMa, 2120 Main St; bus 3

This good-time dance hall has jazz, swing, Dixieland, salsa and big-band music, and if you come early, you can probably catch a free dance lesson as well. The cover charge is usually $10 to $15, except on 'Toonie Tuesdays' when it's $2.

Top Five Spots for Local Live Music

- **Railway Club** (opposite)
- **Cellar Jazz Café** (above)
- **Commodore** (opposite)
- **Hot Jazz Society** (above)
- **ANZA Club** (opposite)

KINO CAFÉ Map pp236-7

☎ 604-875-1998; Fairview, 3456 Cambie St; bus 15

Hard to believe, but this open-minded coffee shop decorated with vintage movie posters (it's located beside a cinema) becomes a sultry flamenco performance space at night; you'll find rumba, salsa and Latin jazz some nights, too

MONTMARTRE CAFÉ Map pp236-7

☎ 604-879-8111; SoMa, 4362 Main St; bus 3

Along bohemian South Main, this hipster café supports spoken word nights, as well as hip-hop, jazz and world beats.

WISE HALL Map p235

☎ 604-254-5858; www.wisehall.ca; East Vancouver, 1882 Adanac St; bus 20

WISE, which stands for 'Welsh, Irish, Scottish and English' and is a reflection of the origins of the club's original members, presents an erratic schedule and selection of music ranging from ska to blues to folk.

YALE Map pp230-3

☎ 604-681-9253; www.theyale.ca; downtown, 1300 Granville St; bus 4

Photos of Koko Taylor, Junior Wells and other stars who've played here adorn this 19th-century hotel. It's one of the best blues bars in the city, if not the country. It books big-name acts and hosts jam sessions on weekend afternoons.

CLUBBING

The hipness quotient of clubs comes and goes like Vancouver's rain. Cover charges vary from $5 to $15, although early birds and women may be lucky and get in free some nights. Hats, sportswear, ripped jeans and under-19s are usually not allowed inside. You can put yourself on the VIP list (no waiting, no cover), which is possible at individual clubs' own websites or via www.clubvibes.com and www.clubzone.com. Both of the latter have event listings as well as reviews, while www.wildvancouver.com also provides club and event information. Most clubs begin to open their doors around 9pm or 10pm (some don't really get going until quite a bit later) and most of them close at around 3am or 4am. For further information about raves and other underground happenings, ask around at music stores (p154).

Club Strips & Neighborhoods

The main club strip is corralled in the downtown area along Granville St. Yaletown has more and more dance floors that are popping up in its bars and lounges, and the West End still hosts a few, mostly gay-oriented, venues. Gastown is home to several clubs; unfortunately, recently violent incidents have tended to plague this area late at night, so patrons should stay alert and be very aware of their surroundings (for further safety information, see p215).

Top Five Clubs

- Bar None (below)
- Ginger Sixty-Two (right)
- DV8 (right)
- Sonar (opposite)
- Lotus Sound Lounge (opposite)

AUBAR Map pp230-3

☎ 604-648-2227; www.aubarnightclub.com; downtown, 674 Seymour St; ☼ closed Sun-Tue; SkyTrain Granville

Top 40, hip-hop and house blast from the speakers at this popular downtown haunt. Drop in on Wednesday for $2 drinks. Friday is ladies' night, complete with male dancers.

BAR NONE Map pp230-3

☎ 604-689-7000; www.bar-none.ca; Yaletown, 1222 Hamilton St; bus 1

Located in a converted warehouse with the original post-and-beam architecture, Bar None gives off a not-too-pretentious, young professional vibe. Soul Stream, a soul/funk/R&B band, has been packing 'em in on Monday and Tuesday for the past several years. DJs play house and hip-hop on weekends.

CAPRICE NIGHTCLUB Map pp230-3

☎ 604-685-3288; www.capricenightclub.com; downtown, 967 Granville St; ☼ closed Sun & Mon; bus 4

Caprice is a fun place to dance, dance, dance the night away to retro classics and the Top 40 hits. The next-door lounge and grill provide sustenance when your groove thing finally gives out.

DV8 Map pp230-3

☎ 604-682-4388; www.dv8lounge.com; downtown, 515 Davie St; bus 1

These folks wrote the book on covering all the bases and doing it well: the 30-plus crowd mixes with the twentysomethings; old-school funk mixes with new wave; and vegan dishes share menu space with meaty items (see p95). There's an on-site art gallery, and live comedy on Sunday.

GINGER SIXTY-TWO Map pp230-3

☎ 604-688-5494; downtown, 1219 Granville St; ☼ closed Sun & Mon; bus 4

A posh, low-attitude spot for multicolored cocktails, with DJs spinning a variety of music styles. Curl up in a pink booth and catch the occasional burlesque show in the Fellini-esque ambience.

Gay & Lesbian Nightlife

For information on Vancouver's gay-friendly neighborhoods, queer happenings and organizations, see p211. Otherwise the best source for finding out what's on is the free alternative weekly *Xtra! West* (p214). For informative notice boards on upcoming events, in addition to gifts and books, stop by Little Sister's Book & Art Emporium (p156). FlyGirl (☎ 604-684-9872, www.flygirlproductions.com) hosts popular parties for lesbians at different venues throughout the year. In August the Vancouver Pride Parade (p10) brings thousands of visitors to the West End, which is where most gay pubs and bars are located.

Club 23 West (Map p234; ☎ 604-662-3277; Gastown, 23 W Cordova St; bus 7) There's a pool table, heated patio and multiple levels hosting themed evenings, like 'Lesbians on the Loose' and 'Naughty! Fetish Nights.'

Dufferin (Map pp230-3; ☎ 604-683-4251; downtown, 900 Seymour St; bus 4) Bills itself as 'party central' and proves it with its nightly entertainment lineup like strippers, drag shows and karaoke.

Fountainhead Pub (Map pp230-3; ☎ 604-687-2222; downtown, 1025 Davie St; bus 1) It's the 'local' pub, and many people start the night off here, where the large glass windows and outdoor patio provide a good Davie St view.

Lick (Map p234; ☎ 604-685-7777; www.lickclub.com; Lotus Hotel, 455 Abbott St; ☼ closed Sun & Mon; SkyTrain Stadium) This is the city's only all-girl-operated queer nightclub, featuring upcoming and established female DJs.

Lotus Sound Lounge (opposite)

Odyssey (Map pp230-3; ☎ 604-689-5256; www.theodysseynightclub.com; 1251 Howe St; bus 4) This long-running dance space has a reputation for being the wildest gay men's nightclub. The fun includes GoGo boys, feather boa drag shows and gay bingo.

Pumpjack Pub (Map pp230-3; ☎ 604-685-3417; 1167 Davie St; bus 1) Get all pumped up at Vancouver's leather bar, with uniform nights, pool tables and the BC Bears (a group for hairy or bearded men and their admirers).

LOTUS SOUND LOUNGE Map p234

☎ 604-685-7777; Chinatown, 455 Abbott St; SkyTrain Stadium

The underground (literally) Lotus is the place where people come just to dance and get sweaty, with the cramped floor embracing everyone from straight ravers to flamboyant drag sisters. There are two other bars in this same complex, which are known primarily as queer-friendly venues.

PLAZA CLUB Map pp230-3

☎ 604-646-0064; www.plazaclub.net; downtown, 881 Granville St; ☽ closed Sun-Tue; bus 4

Inside a converted cinema, the Plaza offers a big, big dance floor where the music shuffles through R&B, urban dance, Top 40 and more. Wednesday is ladies' night, and Thursday is Brit music night.

RICHARD'S ON RICHARDS Map pp230-3

☎ 604-687-6794; www.richardsonrichards.com; downtown, 1036 Richards St; bus 20

Vancouver's longest-running dance venue is still alive and kicking, thank you very much. Occasional hard-core live rock shows are balanced by DJ-spun disco, Top 40 and R&B dance nights, populated by lithe young divas and their dates.

ROXY Map pp230-3

☎ 604-331-7999; www.roxyvan.com; downtown, 932 Granville St; bus 4

'Vancouver Idol' wannabe singers take the stage on Monday, local garage bands compete on Tuesday and cover bands dominate the dance floor the rest of the swingin' time. It's really more about mating than music here, but no one seems to mind.

SHINE Map p234

☎ 604-408-4321; www.shinenightclub.com; Gastown, 364 Water St; SkyTrain Waterfront

Some call this the sexiest club space in Vancouver, with its main room hosting a mixed crowd of elite clubbers grooving to funk, deep house and hip-hop, plus an intimate den of shimmering candles with a 40ft red sofa.

SKYBAR Map pp230-3

☎ 604-697-9199; www.skybarvancouver.com; downtown, 670 Smithe St; ☽ closed Sun-Tue; bus 4

The city's premier place to watch women wrestle silicone into submission (via bras and

Billiards

Pool is cool, and the following establishments prove it.

Automotive Billiards (Map p230-3; ☎ 604-682-0040; Yaletown, 1286 Homer St; per hr $10.25; ☽ 3pm-1am; bus 20) This pool hall – with neon auto body shop meets lounge decor – has professionally balanced tables, so there's no excuse for missed shots. You can't blame hunger or thirst either, since the attached café serves spinach pies, sandwiches, coffee and beer.

Commodore Lanes & Billiards (Map pp230-3; ☎ 604-681-1531; downtown, 838 Granville St; per hr $10-12; ☽ 11am-midnight; bus 4) Duck down under Granville St to shoot stick and pony up a loonie or two for some seriously funky bowling shoes.

Cue (Map pp236-7; ☎ 604-731-7770; Fairview, 1070 W Broadway; per hr $6-10; ☽ 11:30am-midnight; bus 9) In an empty stretch of Broadway, this Asian pool hall just keeps going and going. Where else can you cue up with a steaming bowl of ramen by your side?

other technology). The behemoth, blue-toned club sprawls over three levels: one sports a fiber-optic martini bar; two has a dance floor; and three has a rooftop patio with retractable awnings where patrons can see and be seen under the stars.

SONAR Map p234

☎ 604-683-6695; www.sonar.bc.ca; Gastown, 66 Water St; ☽ closed Sun-Tue; bus 7

Many Vancouverites don't know it, but this is actually the city's premier club for experimental DJs and live club shows from all over the globe. On any given night you're likely to find progressive house, jazz fusion, soul, hip-hop, reggae or electronica. It's definitely worth braving the atmosphere – which is thick with attitude – if you know exactly what you're looking for.

VODA Map pp230-3

☎ 604-684-3003; www.voda.ca; downtown, 783 Homer St; ☽ closed Sun-Mon; SkyTrain Granville

Designed by an LA architect, and appearing to aspire to the same exclusivity, this club, which is located inside the Westin Grand Hotel, is strictly for the beautiful people. DJs heat up the dance floor with funk, R&B and Latin-flavored music.

Inside Zulu Records (p165), Kitsilano

CINEMA

Vancouver is a gold mine for independent, second-run and art-flick movie houses. For first-run movies, two chain cineplexes downtown on Granville St are convenient: **Capitol 6** (Map pp230-3; ☎ 604-669-6000; 820 Granville St; bus 4) and **Granville 7** (Map pp230-3; ☎ 604-684-4000; 855 Granville St; bus 4). A new multiplex is set to open nearby on Smithe St in 2005. IMAX movies play at Canada Place's **CN IMAX Theatre** (Map pp230-3; ☎ 604-682-2384; adult/senior/child 3-12 $11/10/9) and Science World's **Omnimax Theatre** (p55).

An excellent ongoing event is the **Celluloid Social Club** (☎ 604-730-8090; admission $5), which meets monthly at the ANZA Club (see p128) for screenings and drinks with local independent film and video artists. The schedule varies, so call for times.

Vancouver is a haven not only for filmmakers, but also filmmakers-to-be. The **Vancouver Film School** (Map pp230-3; ☎ 604-685-5808, 800-661-4101; www.vfs.com; downtown, 198 W Hastings St) has programs in animation, game design and visual effects, among others.

Tickets

First-run movie tickets cost $9 to $12 for adults, less for students and seniors. Matinee shows (usually before 6pm weekdays, earlier on weekends) cost from around $7. Tuesday is discount movie day for most places. Admission to repertory cinemas cost $4 to $8.

ALLIANCE ATLANTIS FIFTH AVENUE CINEMAS Map pp238-9

☎ 604-734-7469; www.allianceatlantiscinemas.com; Kitsilano, 2110 Burrard St; bus 4

The popular Fifth Avenue shows mostly indie and foreign films, though a few hand-picked Hollywood releases may slip in, too. Moviegoers can belly up to the lobby cappuccino bar for above-par baked goods before the beginning of the show. A $12 annual membership card provides about 15% savings on tickets throughout the year.

CINEMARK TINSELTOWN Map p234
☎ 604-806-0799; www.cinemark.com; Chinatown, 88 W Pender St; SkyTrain Stadium; P

Tinseltown is a Vancouver favorite, combining blockbusters and art-house offerings. It is one of the city's most technically advanced cinemas, with giant screens, stadium seating and free underground validated parking. Located in the International Village shopping mall.

DENMAN CINEMA Map pp230-3
☎ 604-683-2201; www.denmancinema.com; West End, 1737 Comox St; bus 5

This theater was a first-run movie house in the 1960s. The owners closed it, whacked out half the seats and reopened as a second-run theater with lots of leg room. There's a $6 double bill daily, except Tuesday when it's $4.

HOLLYWOOD THEATRE Map pp238-9
☎ 604-738-3211; www.hollywoodtheatre.ca; Kitsilano, 3123 W Broadway; bus 9

Another second-run, double-bill theater, this one features a concessionaire selling cookies and juice. Monday is bargain day ($4).

PACIFIC CINÉMATHÈQUE Map pp230-3
☎ 604-688-3456; www.cinematheque.bc.ca; downtown, 1131 Howe St; bus 4

It's best to think of this nonprofit repertory cinema as an arty, ongoing film festival. A $3 annual membership fee is required, then you, too, can help 'foster critical media literacy and advance cinema as an art and as a vital means of communication in British Columbia and Canada.'

RIDGE THEATRE Map pp238-9
☎ 604-738-6311; www.ridgetheatre.com; Kitsilano, 3131 Arbutus St; bus 16; P

A Vancouver institution with a great mix of foreign films and Hollywood fare, plus clever offerings, like the 'Movies for Mommies' Tuesday matinee series (including stroller parking

and lowered sound to protect little ears) and the Celluloid Kids Club on Sunday afternoons. Check out the retro building's glass-enclosed 'crying room' where parents can take wee noisemakers. The ticket office also sells gourmet teas, Italian ice sodas and popcorn drizzled in real butter.

Also recommended are:

Van East Cinema (Map p235; ☎ 604-251-1313; www .vaneast.com; East Vancouver, 2290 Commercial Dr; SkyTrain Commercial) This balconied cinema shows an eclectic schedule of critically acclaimed new and classic films, with occasional late-night screenings.

Video in Studios (Map pp236-7; ☎ 604-872-8337; www. vid eoin.ca; SoMa, 1965 Main St; bus 3) ViS presents thought-provoking new works by video artists from across Canada.

Film Festivals

While the star of the city's film festival scene is the **Vancouver International Film Festival** (p11), several offbeat and independent events pop up year-round:

- **Cinemuerte** (www.cinemuerte.com; ☾ summer or fall) Horror films galore, including headless, spider and cannibal flicks.
- **Out on Screen** (www.outonscreen.com; ☾ August) Western Canada's largest film event by and for gays and lesbians; held around the same time as **Vancouver Pride** (p10).
- **Vancouver Asian Film Festival** (www.vaff.org; ☾ November) Emerging and established North American-Asian filmmakers screen works over four days.
- **Vancouver International Digital Video Festival** (www.vidfest.com; ☾ June) Digital video, animation and experimental mixed media screenings.
- **Vancouver International Mountain Film Festival** (www.vimff.org; ☾ February) Movies about mountain culture and sports.

COMEDY & SPOKEN WORD

Vancouver has only a few venues dedicated purely to comedy; most events take place on designated nights in restaurants and bars (note the majority do not admit under-19s). The *Georgia Straight* (p214) publishes weekly Comedy and Literary Events sections among its listings. **Pandora's Collective** (☎ 604-321-4039; www.pandorascollective.com) presents literary open mics, festivals and other events around town, and keeps an excellent list of goings-on at its website. The **Vancouver International Comedy Festival** (p11) happens in October. Poetry lovers can get a weekly dose by tuning the radio dial to CFRO (102.7FM) for 'Wax Poetic' at 2pm every Wednesday afternoon.

VANCOUVER PUBLIC LIBRARY

Map pp230-3

☎ 604-331-3602; www.vpl.ca; downtown, 350 W Georgia St; admission free; ☺ schedule varies; SkyTrain Stadium

A broad array of Canadian novelists, overseas poets and children's storytellers give readings at the VPL, usually on weeknights. The World Poetry Reading Series at 7:30pm on Monday features poetry from around the globe, it is presented bilingually and often accompanied by music.

VANCOUVER THEATRESPORTS LEAGUE Map pp236-7

☎ 604-738-7013; www.vtsl.com; Granville Island, New Revue Stage, 1585 Johnston St; tickets $7-16.50; ☺ 7.30pm Wed, 7.30pm & 9.15pm Thu, 8pm, 10pm & 11.45pm Fri & Sat; bus 50

This wildly popular improv group concocts shows like 'Free Willie Shakespeare' and 'Star Trick, the Musical.' The late-night weekend shows offer a more ribald hour-long jam session. If you like what you see on stage, try it yourself: Theatresports provides wit-honing lessons in a seven-week course ($107), from 6:30pm to 9:30pm on Monday, or a two-hour drop-in class ($10), from 1:30pm to 3:30pm on Saturday.

YUK YUK'S Map pp230-3

☎ 604-696-9857; www.yukyuks.com; downtown, Century Plaza Hotel, 1015 Burrard St; cover Tue-Thu $5-10, Fri & Sat $15 ; ☺ Tue-Sat; bus 2

Stand-up comics from around the city and across North America perform at Yuk Yuk's, part of a Canadian chain of comedy clubs. Famous faces usually appear on weekends. Tuesday is Improv Night and Wednesday is the Pro-Am Comedy Jam.

Restaurants and bars hosting comedy nights, with admission from $3 to $6, include the following:

DV8 (p130; ☺ 10pm Sun) This venue also puts on Dinner in the Dark ($45; ☺ 6:30pm last Tue of month), where everyone eats, drinks and listens to a comedy performance in pitch blackness.

El Cocal (p105; ☺ 9:30pm Wed)

Urban Well (p126; ☺ improv 9pm Mon, stand-up 7:30pm & 10pm Tue)

Zizanie (p116; ☺ 9pm Thu)

Restaurants and bars hosting spoken-word nights, with admission usually free or by donation, include:

Bukowski's (p104)

Café Deux Soleil (p126)

El Cocal (p105) Happenings include Bolts of Fiction (☺ 7pm last Mon of each month), a reading and chat with a featured local author; the Twisted Poets (☺ 7pm last Fri of each month), an open-mic event; and Liars of Orpheus (☺ 9pm last Fri of each month), a literary 'jam session' where writers, musicians, artists and dancers all let loose simultaneously.

Montmartre Café (p129) The site of Thundering Wordheard (☺ 9pm Sun), a spoken-word/music fusion open-mic series.

Grind (p127)

THEATER

Theater, from mainstream to fringe, thrives in Vancouver. The main season runs from fall through spring, but summer has its share of good stuff, too, like the wonderful outdoor Bard on the Beach (opposite). Festivals include the Vancouver Fringe Festival (p11) and Vancouver International Writers & Readers Festival (p11). The Greater Vancouver Professional Theatre Alliance (☎ 604-608-6799; www.theatre.ubc.ca/gvpta) publishes a useful quarterly theater guide.

Major touring shows that come through town are usually presented at one of two places. The Centre in Vancouver for the Performing Arts (Map pp230-3; ☎ 604-602-0616; www.centreinvancouver .com; downtown, 777 Homer St; SkyTrain Stadium), an 1800 plus–seat venue designed by Vancouver Public Library architect Moshe Safdie, has gone through financial ups and downs and was black for a while. It's currently back in business hosting large-scale productions. The Queen Elizabeth Theatre (Map pp230-3; ☎ 604-665-3050; www.city.vancouver.bc.ca/theatres; downtown, 600 Hamilton St; SkyTrain Stadium) is a multi-use, city-owned complex that houses a 2929-seat theater, as well as the smaller Vancouver Playhouse (opposite) and the Media Club (p128).

Tickets

Tickets for most productions can be obtained through **Ticketmaster** (p122). For half-price tickets, try **Tickets Tonight** (p122) or inquire about 'rush' tickets at theatre box offices. Discounts are normally available for students, seniors and arts workers.

ARTS CLUB THEATRE Map pp236-7
☎ 604-687-1644; www.artsclub.com; tickets $27.50-59; ☺ shows 8pm Tue-Sun, matinees 2pm Wed & Sun, 4pm Sat

This is the city's leading theater company, performing everything from comedy to musicals, to popular classics to works by favorite regional playwrights like Morris Panych. Michael J Fox and many other Canadian actors got their start here. There are two main stages: **Granville Island Stage** (Map pp236-7; Granville Island, 1585 Johnson St; bus 50) and the refurbished 1930s **Stanley Theatre** (Map pp236-7; South Granville, 2750 Granville St; bus 10).

BARD ON THE BEACH Map pp238-9
☎ 604-739-0559; www.bardonthebeach.org; Kitsilano, Vanier Park; tickets $16-27; ☺ Jun-Sep; bus 2 or 22

Seeing Shakespeare performed outdoors as the sun sets over the mountains is a Vancouver highlight. Bard is a professional repertory company that presents three of Will's plays per season at its giant tented complex in Vanier Park. Bring a sweater, as it can get chilly.

FIREHALL ARTS CENTRE Map p234
☎ 604-689-0926; www.firehallartscentre.ca; Gastown, 280 E Cordova St; tickets $10-25; bus 7

The leader of Vancouver's avant-garde scene, this intimate venue is located inside a historic fire station. It presents culturally diverse, contemporary theatre and dance, with an emphasis on showcasing emerging talent. There's an outdoor courtyard stage and licensed lounge.

PERFORMANCE WORKS Map pp236-7
☎ 604-687-3020; Granville Island, 1218 Cartwright St; tickets $12-20; bus 50

Operated by the same group – the Granville Island Cultural Society – as the Waterfront Theatre (right), this artsy, no-frills space in an old machine shop puts on a similar eclectic range of works.

THEATRE UNDER THE STARS Map p240
☎ information 604-687-0174, box office 604-257-0366; www.tuts.bc.ca; Stanley Park, Malkin Bowl; tickets adult/child 6-16/student $29/19/24; ☺ mid-Jul–mid-Aug; bus 19

The Malkin Bowl in Stanley Park was Canada's first permanent open-air theater. The venue hosts two major Broadway musicals each summer.

VANCOUVER EAST CULTURAL CENTRE Map p235
☎ 604-251-1363; www.vecc.bc.ca; East Vancouver, 1895 Venables St; tickets $22-30; bus 20

Known locally as the 'Cultch,' this beautiful early 20th–century church presents a diverse range of theater, dance and music, ranging from funky performance art to great touring shows. It can be hit and miss, but when it hits, it hits hard.

VANCOUVER PLAYHOUSE Map pp230-3
☎ 604-873-3311; www.vancouverplayhouse.com; downtown, 600 Hamilton St; tickets $38-50; ☺ Oct-May; SkyTrain Stadium

This 660-seat venue is part of the Queen Elizabeth Theatre complex. Each season its resident company presents five or six original Canadian and international works featuring top-tier regional actors and directors.

WATERFRONT THEATRE Map pp236-7
☎ 604-685-1731; Granville Island, 1412 Cartwright St; tickets $12-20; bus 50

The 240-seat Waterfront hosts all kinds of shows. Maybe you'll see a Dickens classic, a kooky musical-comedy about Pippy Longstocking or a drama by an up-and-coming BC playwright?

Many smaller theater companies do not have their own space and so mount shows at venues around town, including some of the spaces already mentioned. Keep an eye out for these venues:

Boca del Lupo (☎ 604-684-6822; www.bocadellupo .bc.ca) Dedicated to the creation of new works of physical theatre using collaborative processes and interactions between the performers and audience.

Electric Company (☎ 604-253-4222; www.electric companytheatre.com) Presents original works with lots of visual imagery and non-traditional staging (one recent production took place around a community center's pool).

Afterglow bar (p125), Yaletown

Green Thumb Company (☎ 604-254-4055; www.green thumb.bc.ca) Long-standing company presenting theater for children, mostly at the **Vancouver East Cultural Centre** (p135).

Mortal Coil (☎ 604-874-6153; www.mortalcoil.bc.ca) Brings a sense of magic and myth to its shows through the use of stilts, masks and fantastic costuming.

Radix Theatre (☎ 604-254-0707; www.radixtheatre.org) Produces experimental, socially relevant and original works of art incorporating a variety of media.

Up in the Air (☎ 604-715-7580; www.upintheairtheatre .com) Presents new, usually humorous works; also sponsors the Walking Fish Festival in late May/early June to showcase new playwrights.

CLASSICAL MUSIC

Vancouver has a flourishing classical music scene, especially when it comes to genres like baroque, chamber and new music. While performances take place in churches and other sites about town, two of the main venues are the **Chan Centre for the Performing Arts** (Map p241; ☎ 604-822-9197; www.chancentre.com; UBC, 6265 Crescent Rd; bus 4) and the **Orpheum Theatre** (Map pp230-3; ☎ 604-665-3050; www.city.vancouver.bc.ca/theatres; downtown, 884 Granville St; bus 4). The latter may not look like much from the outside, but its interior is exquisite, decorated in a Spanish baroque motif and 1000-bulb crystal chandeliers. The **Early Music Festival** (p10) and **Vancouver Chamber Music Festival** (p10) let their notes loose in summer. For ticket information, see p135.

EARLY MUSIC VANCOUVER
☎ 604-732-1610; www.earlymusic.bc.ca; locations vary; tickets $26-55
This group is devoted to the performance and study of music from the Middle Ages all the way through to the late Romantic era. Pieces are often played on replicas of the instruments of the time. Members of the group also offer vocal and historical instrument lessons to the public.

MUSIC IN THE MORNING
☎ 604-873-4612; www.musicinthemorning.org; locations vary; tickets $15-24; 🕙 10:30am Tue-Fri Sep-Apr
A cup of coffee, classical music, all before noon – what more could you want? Artists provide a lecture about the music before they perform; pieces span the old to the new. For those who can't make it during the day, there's an evening Rush Hour series at the **Vancouver Art Gallery** (p44) at 6:45pm on some Thursday evenings.

VANCOUVER BACH CHOIR

☎ 604-921-8012; www.vancouverbachchoir.com; tickets $25-90

One hundred and fifty members lend their voices to Bach and other choral works. The group performs about five major concerts annually at the **Orpheum Theatre** (opposite). Its Christmastime 'Sing Along Messiah' is a city tradition.

VANCOUVER CHAMBER CHOIR

☎ 604-738-6822; www.vancouverchamberchoir.com; locations vary; tickets $16-40

This award-winning professional choir is noted for its diverse repertoire and performing excellence. Concerts can include music from chant to folksong, traditional to avant-garde, a cappella to orchestra or jazz trio.

VANCOUVER NEW MUSIC SOCIETY

☎ 604-633-0861; www.newmusic.org; locations vary; tickets $15-30

The Society presents new music performances that could entail anything from electronic instrumentalists to piano-accompanied song cycles and compositions utilizing audiovisual media.

VANCOUVER OPERA

☎ 604-683-0222; www.vanopera.bc.ca; tickets $20-120; ☉ Oct-May

The city's well-regarded opera company stages four annual productions at the **Queen Elizabeth Theatre** (p134).

VANCOUVER RECITAL SOCIETY

☎ 604-602-0363; www.vanrecital.com; locations vary; tickets from $25; ☉ Oct-Apr

This group brings in some big names (think Yo Yo Ma or opera singer Jessye Norman) for performances at the **Orpheum** (opposite), while newer faces on the scene perform in series at the **Chan Centre for the Performing Arts** (opposite) and **Vancouver Playhouse** (p135).

VANCOUVER SYMPHONY ORCHESTRA

☎ 604-876-3434; www.vancouversymphony.ca; locations vary; tickets $22-70

Under maestro Bramwell Tovey, the VSO has grown into a popular night out for Vancouverites, fusing complex recitals with crossover shows of movie music, opera and even Shakespearean sonnets. Concerts take place at the Orpheum (opposite), Chan Centre (opposite) and other venues around town.

Top Five Quirky Nights on the Town

- Kino Café (p129)
- Commodore Lanes & Billiards (p131)
- DV8 Dinner in the Dark (p134)
- Mortal Coil (opposite)
- Kokoro Dance (p138)

DANCE

The best source for information on classes and performances around town is the **Dance Centre** (☎ 604-606-6400; www.thedancecentre.ca), housed in the **Scotiabank Dance Centre** (p138). The **Vancouver International Dance Festival** (p8) is in March, and the **Dancing on the Edge Festival** (p9) is in July.

BALLET BRITISH COLUMBIA Map pp230-3

☎ 604-732-5003; www.balletbc.com; tickets $26.50-70.50

Vancouver's top dance company presents classical full-length ballets and commissions new works by acclaimed Canadian dancemakers. The DanceAlive! series features works and companies from around the world. Performances take place at the **Queen Elizabeth Theatre** (p134).

EXPERIMENTAL DANCE AND MUSIC

Map pp236-7

EDAM; ☎ 604-876-9559; www.edamdance.org; SoMa, 303 E 8th Ave; tickets $15-18; bus 3

This contemporary troupe adopts a creative multimedia approach that may mix film, music and/or art into its athletic and graceful works, many of which are created through an improvisational process. EDAM has a studio theater on-site and also performs at other local venues.

KAREN JAMIESON DANCE COMPANY

☎ 604-893-8807

Bold, striking, contemporary choreography and cross-cultural First Nations thematics are just two hallmarks of this innovative local troupe, which was founded in 1983. The group performs at various locations.

KOKORO DANCE

☎ 604-662-7441; www.kokoro.ca; performance tickets $15-20

The name 'Kokoro' in Japanese means 'heart,' and it sure takes a lot of heart (not to mention guts) to perform Butoh stark naked on Wreck Beach. Most of the performances given by the company, which combine modern as well as traditional Japanese dance, grace the stage at the **Roundhouse Community Centre** (p210).

SCOTIABANK DANCE CENTRE

Map pp230-3

☎ 604-606-6400; www.thedancecentre.ca; downtown, 677 Davie St; tickets $18-25; bus 4

This amazing glass-enclosed building, designed by Arthur Erickson, supports more than 30 dance companies rehearsal space; performances are also held on-site. The venue – purpose-built for dance and dedicated to its use – is one of the few of its kind in North America.

Sports, Health & Fitness

Sports, Health & Fitness

Vancouverites aren't wearing all that fleece and Gortex to stay inside. People here are passionate about the active life, and we don't just mean hockey. Outdoor activities are definitely where it's at, with folks cycling, blading and running along the seawall trails, paddling kayaks through False Creek and Indian Arm, and swimming at the city's 11 beaches during summer. In winter, skiing reigns supreme, with residents dashing out after work for the 20-minute drive to the North Shore mountains (the runs are lit at night), or heading north to attack Whistler's peaks (p193) for the weekend. The city's unique proximity to the great outdoors makes it all so easy.

As active as Vancouverites are, they love to sit and watch others play as well, and the sports scene is tightly intertwined in the city's culture. The big deal in town – and some would argue the only deal in town, since Vancouver lost its NBA basketball team in 2002 – is the Canucks hockey team. Seeing blood spilled on the ice is a quintessential experience, though you might have to spill a bit of blood yourself to get a ticket.

It's no surprise that the fitness craze in Vancouver combines with the city's earthy, hippie past and the result is a mellow, 'healthy lifestyle' way of being. Yoga is all the rage, and down-to-earth spas offer laid-back pampering. Even tattoos have a healthy lifestyle twist here, often appearing on toned backs peeking out of the low-slung yoga pants everyone seems to be wearing.

Top 10 Sporty Things to Do

- Catch a **Canucks game** (opposite)
- Inhale a hot dog and a beer at **Nat Bailey Stadium** (below)
- **Kayak** the waters of False Creek or Indian Arm (p146)
- **Cycle** a portion of the Seawall (p142)
- Don your white trousers at the **Stanley Park Lawn Bowling Club** (p144)
- **Skimboard** at Spanish Banks Beach (p147)
- Take a saltwater dip and enjoy the spectacle surrounding **Kitsilano Outdoor Pool** (p147)
- Toss around the **frisbee** with the Vancouver Ultimate League (p143)
- **Ski** down Cypress, Grouse or Seymour mountains at night (p145)
- **Hike** through Lighthouse Park (p143)

WATCHING SPORTS

Tickets & Reservations

Ticketmaster (☎ 604-280-4400; www.ticketmaster.ca) sells advance tickets, but be aware of the booking fee. Box offices at GM Place and BC Place also sell tickets. Scalpers, ie independent operators who resell prime seats, congregate on the corner of Georgia and Beatty Sts for GM Place events, and at the Expo Blvd entrances for BC Place events.

BASEBALL
VANCOUVER CANADIANS

☎ 604-872-5232; www.canadiansbaseball.com; Nat Bailey Stadium, 4601 Ontario St; tickets $7.50-20; ⏱ regular season Jun-Sep; bus 3

The minor-league, single-A farm team to Major League Baseball's Oakland A's, the Canadians play at 6500-seat Nat Bailey Stadium by Queen Elizabeth Park. 'The Nat' is known as 'the prettiest ballpark in the world' thanks to its mountain backdrop. Evening and afternoon games, the latter slyly referred to as 'nooners,' are perfect for inhaling foot-long hot dogs and cups of beer.

FOOTBALL
BC LIONS

☎ 604-589-7627; www.bclions.com; BC Place Stadium, 777 Pacific Blvd; tickets $20-60; ⏱ regular season Jun-Oct; SkyTrain Stadium

The Lions is Vancouver's team in the Canadian Football League (CFL), arguably a more exciting game than its US counterpart. The Lions have had some decent showings in the last few years, winning the Grey Cup championship most recently in 2000. The team relies on its jump-out-of-your-seat offense. Tickets are easy to come by, so don't bother with the scalpers outside.

HOCKEY
VANCOUVER CANUCKS
☎ 604-899-4625; www.canucks.com; GM Place, 800 Griffiths Way; tickets from $45; ☷ regular season Oct-Apr; SkyTrain Stadium

The city's beloved National Hockey League (NHL) team toyed with fans in 1994's thrilling Stanley Cup finals before losing Game 7 to the New York Rangers and sinking to depressingly low levels in the late '90s. However, 'Go Canucks Go!' is again chanted with pride as good management and building from within have the team at the top of the standings now. Of course, with success comes popularity and the number of season tickets has risen – most home games sell out so get your tickets before you arrive, if possible.

VANCOUVER GIANTS
☎ 604-444-2687; www.vancouvergiants.com; Pacific Coliseum, 100 N Renfrew St; tickets from $13; ☷ regular season late Sep–mid-Mar; bus 16

If you can't score Canucks tickets, try to get to a Giants game – these are the future superstars. This team plays in the 20-and-under Western Hockey League (WHL) and has been able to put together a decent team in its short existence. Tickets cost a lot less, are more available and sometimes these guys play with a little more desire since they're working to get to the show.

SOCCER
VANCOUVER WHITECAPS
☎ 604-669-9283; www.whitecapsfc.com; Swanguard Stadium, cnr Boundary & Kingsway Rds in Burnaby; tickets $12-22; ☷ regular season May-Aug; SkyTrain Patterson

The city's men's and women's soccer teams share the same name and stadium, and are both very competitive within their leagues – men play in the A-League and women play in the W-League. Vancouver is arguably the soccer capital of Canada, as its history with the sport professionally goes back almost 30 years. The 5000-seat Swanguard Stadium has natural turf and covered grandstands, but it can get chilly so dress warmly.

OTHER SPORTS
VANCOUVER RAVENS
☎ 604-899-5300; www.vancouverravens.com; GM Place, 800 Griffiths Way; tickets from $15-27; ☷ regular season Dec-May; SkyTrain Stadium

Lacrosse may not be what you first think of when it comes to Canadian sports, but the National Lacrosse League has been building momentum for two decades. This lightning-fast indoor version of the game was originally played by First Nations tribes. The Ravens are one of the newer franchises.

HASTINGS PARK RACECOURSE
☎ 604-254-1631, 800-677-7702; www.hastingspark .com; Pacific National Exhibition grounds, entrance off Hastings & Renfrew Sts; ☷ Sat, Sun & holidays late Apr–Nov; bus 4; Ⓟ $6.50

Although the races at this picturesque park in East Van will never equal the Triple Crown races, there's still that feeling of freedom when the bell sounds ('Pow!'), the gates open and the thoroughbreds speed off around the dirt track. Part of the betting proceeds goes into the Hastings Park Reserve fund for nearby Hastings Park Sanctuary and Il Giardino Gardens, an oasis of birds, gargoyles and fountains where East Van's Italian community plays lawn bowl.

A runner does the Vancouver thing on the waterfront of False Creek (p55)

OUTDOOR ACTIVITIES

With Vancouver's access to forested parks, ski hills, the ocean and various sports centers, you won't have to look hard to find some activity of interest. Most summer sports are practiced between May and September. Winter sports pick up toward the end of November and last until March. Contact the Vancouver Board of Parks and Recreation (☎ 604-257-8400; www .city.vancouver.bc.ca/parks) for a seasonal activity guide, or browse its voluminous website for details on all kinds of activities listed here.

Canada's favorite outdoor mega-mart Mountain Equipment Co-op (p161) rents all sorts of gear (camping $9 to $21, climbing $22, snow sports $12 to $35), and has weekend specials where you take the goods on Thursday, bring it back Monday and only pay for Saturday and Sunday; its website is a great source of information, listing local activity clubs, trip checklists, and gear swaps. Europe Bound Outfitters (p161) nearby also rents gear. For specialist outdoor activity guides, drop by the Travel Bug (p163) or Wanderlust (p163) bookstores.

CYCLING, IN-LINE SKATING & RUNNING

Vancouver is blessed with a wealth of great places to cycling. See p205 for maps, associations and rules.

Appealing routes include the classic Seaside Route, which takes in the seawall around Stanley Park, False Creek, Kitsilano and Locarno Beach. The 9km Stanley Park portion is a Vancouver highlight, though be prepared for plenty of company along the way; see p84 if you want to give it a go. Another good portion of the route is to follow it from Granville Island through Vanier Park to Kitsilano Beach Park, then along Point Grey Rd to Jericho Beach Park and follow the shoreline to Spanish Banks Beach (it's about a 15km round-trip). From Spanish Banks you can follow Marine Dr around Point Grey to the other side of the peninsula, then take Dunbar St north back to Point Grey Rd and Kitsilano. From Granville Island this is about a 25km round-trip.

The 10km Crosstown Greenway is another alluring route that goes by several parks and heritage homes. It's accessible by SkyTrain, starting from the 22nd St Station in New Westminster and ending by the Braid Station in Burnaby.

If you are feeling really energetic, you can cycle through Stanley Park, over the Lions Gate Bridge to West Vancouver, and then along Marine Dr to Horseshoe Bay (p76). If that's not enough for one day, take the ferry over to Bowen Island (p198) and cycle round it before making the trip back. From Vancouver to Horseshoe Bay is about a 40km round-trip. Of course, you could always spend the night on Bowen Island in a B&B and return the following day.

Most cycling routes, like the Seaside Route, are also good for in-line skaters and runners. North Vancouver's Lower Seymour Conservation Reserve (p76) has trails for in-line aficionados. Mountain bikers and runners will find plenty of paths in Pacific Spirit Regional Park (p64). Developers are planning to build a mountain bike park on the north face of Black Mountain in Cypress Provincial Park (p77), set to open in July 2005.

Rentals

The epicenter of the bike- and skate-rental business is on Denman St between Georgia and Robson Sts, at the foot of Stanley Park. Prices generally include a helmet (or other assorted protective gear if you are renting in-line skates) and a lock; you'll need to give a credit card number for a deposit. Most are open from 9am to 9pm in summer, with more limited hours the rest of the year.

Bikes & Blades (Map pp230-3; ☎ 604-602-9899; West End, 718 Denman; bicycles half/full day $9/12, blades $10/12; bus 5) Brusque service but, best price on the block; accepts payment in cash only.

Our Community Bikes (Map pp236-7; ☎ 604-879-2453; www.pedalpower.org; SoMa, 3283 Main St; ◷ 11am-6pm; bus 3) A non-profit organization promoting bicycle use. It's a good source for maps and other cycling information, or if you're looking to buy a used or 'reconditioned' bicycle.

Reckless, the Bike Store (Map pp230-3; ☎ 604-648-2600; Yaletown, 110 Davie St; bus 1) and (Map pp236-7; ☎ 604-731-2420; South Granville, 1810 Fir St; bus 50) Bicycles for half/full day cost $25/32.50.

Spokes Bicycle Rentals (Map pp230-3; ☎ 604-688-5141; West End, 1798 W Georgia St; bicycles half/full day $11.25/15; bus 19) Also offers tours (p41).

FRISBEE GOLF

Frisbee golf, aka disc golf, has a rabid following in Vancouver. Conveniently located, nine-hole courses are at **Queen Elizabeth Park** (SoMa, southeast corner near 37th Ave & Ontario St; par 43) and the hillside by the **Jericho Hill Community Centre** (Kitsilano, 4196 W 4th Ave; par 27), which has fab views from the 7th tee. Contact the **BC Disc Sports Society** (☎ 604-878-7387; www.bcdss.bc.ca) for other locations, disc golf rules, tips, event information and instructions for tuning in to the disc golf radio show (yes, there really is such a thing).

There's a football-esque version of the sport, where two seven-player squads face off, pass the disc around and try to score goals. They play in the **Vancouver Ultimate League** (VUL; ☎ 604-878-6403; www.vul.bc.ca), which also sponsors free instructional clinics. Even if you decide not to play yourself, it's good fun to watch a match; contact VUL for a schedule.

GOLF

Vancouverites love to swing the sticks, and the city's mild climate allows for year-round putting. There are more than 70 golf courses within a two-hour drive of the city. Vancouver's public courses are wheelchair accessible and a 'Golf Xpress Cart' is available for players with limited mobility.

Fraserview Golf Course (Map pp228-9; ☎ automated tee times 604-280-1818, pro shop 604-257-6923; Greater Vancouver, 7800 Vivian Dr near E 54th St; green fees $26-52; par 72, 6700 yards) This city-run facility, overlooking the Fraser River, consistently wins awards as one of Canada's best public courses.

Gleneagles Golf Course (Map pp228-9; ☎ 604-921-7353; West Vancouver, 6190 Marine Dr; green fees 9/18 holes $16/32; par 35, 2800 yards) This excellent public course is nestled between the mountains and sea near Horseshoe Bay. Beware of the third hole, known as Cardiac Hill.

Langara Golf Course (Map pp228-9; ☎ automated tee times 604-280-1818, pro shop 604-713-1816; Greater Vancouver, 6706 Alberta St near W 49th Ave; green fees $26-52; par 71, 6100 yards) Another city course, with large rolling greens and narrow fairways.

Mayfair Lakes Golf Course (Map pp228-9; ☎ 604-276-0505; Richmond, 5460 No 7 Rd off Hwy 91; green fees $50-85; par 71, 6641 yards) Lakes and waterways come into play on 13 of the 18 holes at this private course close to the airport, which adds to both the aesthetics and the challenge.

University Golf Course (Map p241; ☎ 604-224-1818; UBC, 5185 University Blvd; green fees $40-70; par 72, 6157 yards) Tucked into Pacific Spirit Park on UBC Endowment Lands.

If you want the quick version of hitting the links, try one of the **pitch-and-putt courses** (green fees $9.75) at **Stanley Park** (Map p240; ☎ 604-681-8847; par 54, 1200 yards) or **Queen Elizabeth Park** (Map pp236-7; ☎ 604-874-8336; ☒ closed Dec & Jan; par 54, 1370 yards), both operated on a first-come, first-served basis. The Stanley Park course is located next to the Rhododendron Garden, making springtime play a fragrant treat.

For further information on rules, tournaments and all things golf-related, contact the **Royal Canadian Golf Association** (☎ 905-849-9700; www.rcga.org).

HIKING

Hiking opportunities abound in the many regional and provincial parks in the Lower Mainland. The **Grouse Grind** (p75) up Grouse Mountain is the most infamous huffer-and-puffer of the lot. **Lighthouse Park** (p77) and **Whytecliff Park** (p77) are scenic gems with gentle trails to tramp around. Many locals agree that **Mt Seymour Provincial Park** (p76) has the area's best hiking, though **Cypress Provincial Park** (p76) and **Pacific Spirit Regional Park** (p64) rank up there, too, each offering myriad trails to suit skill levels from easy to advanced.

For a serious hike on the North Shore, the **Baden-Powell Trail** extends 41km from Horseshoe Bay to Deep Cove, joining most of the area's major mountainous trails. The **Lions** is a 15km, seven-hour moderately difficult hike up the eponymous peaks dominating the northern skyline. The marked trail offers spectacular views of Howe Sound on one side and Vancouver on the other. The trailhead is off Mountainview Rd in Lions Bay.

In any of the North Shore parks, be prepared for continually changing mountain weather conditions – the weather can change suddenly and a warm sunny day in the city might not mean it's going to be the same, or stay the same, in the mountains. Take along a warm waterproof jacket, wear sturdy shoes and a hat, and carry a water bottle. Call for a **mountain weather forecast** (☎ 604-664-9021) before heading out for the day.

For maps and further information about regional parks, contact the **Greater Vancouver Regional District** (GVRD; ☎ general information 604-432-6350, nature program information 604-432-6359; www.gvrd.bc.ca/parks). For maps and further information about provincial parks in the Vancouver area, go to **BC Parks** (www.gov.bc.ca/bcparks) online.

ICE SKATING

If you want to practice your ice-dancing routine, or if you just want to have fun, try the city-operated **indoor skating rinks** (skate rentals $2.30, adult/child/youth $4.40/2.25/3.30) at the **West End Community Centre** (see p210; ☺ Oct-Mar) or **Britannia Community Centre** (Map p235; ☎ 604-718-5800; East Vancouver, 1661 Napier St; ☺ year-round). Public skating times vary, so call for the schedule.

Grouse Mountain (p75) has outdoor skating at its 8000-sq-ft ice skating pond. The only problem is you have to pay full Grouse admission to partake ($10 to $27), so it's most useful for people who are already up there skiing or sightseeing for the day, or who have season passes. Back in the city, **Robson Square** (p44) has an outdoor ice rink below street level. It was closed at press time, but rumored to open again in 2005.

LAWN BOWLING

Men and women in pressed whites rolling a slow ball across an emerald lawn with English Bay twinkling in the background is a Vancouver sight you're unlikely to forget. The kind folks at the **Stanley Park Lawn Bowling Club** (Map p240; ☎ 604-683-0910; www.webturf.com/lawnbowls; cnr Beach Ave & Lagoon Dr; three lessons $35; ☺ 10am Sun, 7pm Tue) will be happy to provide the equipment and initiate you in the likes of bowls, jacks, leads and skips. It's good fun, and there's something dignified and magical about the pitch that will make you feel as if you've been bowling since 1919, which is when the sport began here.

ROCK CLIMBING

There's rock climbing close to Vancouver at places such as Juniper Point in West Vancouver's **Lighthouse Park** (p77), the bluffs overlooking Indian Arm in **Deep Cove** (p76) or some of the peaks of the North Shore mountains. Serious climbers, however, head up to Squamish to scale the **Stawamus Chief** (p192) or the Smoke Bluffs, or further north to Murrin Park and Cheakamus Canyon. For regional climbing information, contact the **BC Mountaineering Club** (☎ 604-268-9502; www.bcmc.ca); for national information, contact the **Alpine Club of Canada** (☎ 403-678-3200; www.alpineclubofcanada.ca), which is in Alberta.

Climbing in Vancouver is pretty much restricted to indoor centers, which generally charge about $16 for a day pass, plus $10 for equipment. Centers to try, both of which offer a variety of climbs and programs, including some that are geared for children:

Cliffhanger Indoor Rock Climbing (Map pp236-7; ☎ 604-874-2400; www.cliffhangerclimbing.com; SoMa, 106 W 1st Ave; ☺ noon-10:30pm Mon-Thu, noon-9:30am Fri-Sun; bus 3)

Edge Climbing Centre (Map pp228-9; ☎ 604-984-9080; www.edgeclimbing.com; North Vancouver, Ste 2, 1485 Welch St; ☺ 1-11pm Mon-Fri, noon-9pm Sat & Sun; bus 240) Located just off Capilano Rd below Marine Dr.

SKATEBOARDING

Vancouver is one of world's premier skateboarding destinations. It's the site of the annual **Slam City Jam** (early May), the largest and most rippin' skateboard competition around, which attracts so many people that it has to be held in one of the city's sports arenas. Rumor has it some tourists come to Vancouver exclusively to check out the more than 30 skateparks splashed across the Lower Mainland. If you want a taste of one, check out the beauty in **Hastings Park** (Map pp228-9; Renfrew St just north of Hastings St).

The oracle of all things board-related is **PD's Hot Shop** (p164), where you can pick up a directory of the region's skateparks that includes detailed directions and facility descriptions with gracious warnings like 'beware of grumpy old Italian guys packin' Bacci balls' (Burnaby) and 'watch your back for crazed rednecks' (Abbotsford).

SKIING & SNOWBOARDING

While **Whistler** (p193) is the regional king of the snowy hill, there are excellent alpine skiing and snowboarding areas as well as cross-country skiing trails around, some of them just minutes from the city center. The season typically runs from late November to April.

Cypress Mountain Ski Area, at Cypress Provincial Park (p77; ☎ guest services 604-926-5612) in West Vancouver, accommodates several activities. There is **downhill skiing and snowboarding** (day pass adult/child 5 & under/child 6-12/senior/youth 13-18 $42/4/18/21/36, after 4pm $34/4/14/17/28), with 38 runs divided into 23% beginner, 37% intermediate and 40% advanced, plus rental, instruction and night skiing until 10pm. The mountain also features **cross-country skiing** (day pass adult/child 5 & under/child 6-12/senior/youth 13-18 $15/2/8/9/12, reduced a few dollars after 3pm), with 19km of trails total and 7km lit for night skiing; **snowshoeing** (rentals $6-8, adult & youth 13-18/child & senior $22/15); and **tubing** (2 hours $13), where participants slide down a snow chute in an inner tube and then get hauled back up via the tube tow. Many winter sport enthusiasts believe Cypress is the best of the local mountains for both downhill and cross-country skiing. The Olympic Committee must think so, too, because Cypress will be one of the venues for the 2010 Winter Olympics. A **shuttle bus service** (adult/youth & senior $15/10; ☷ Dec-Mar, call guest services for schedules) operates daily from Lonsdale Quay and Park Royal Mall.

Grouse Mountain (p75; ☎ snow information 604-986-6262), in North Vancouver, has 25 runs for **skiing and snowboarding** (day pass adult/child 5-12/youth & senior $42/18/32, after 4pm $33/15/25), with the longest being 2.4km, snowmaking facilities, rental, instruction and night skiing until 10pm. Grouse is a good place for beginners and those who are learning to ski. The Cut is

one of the mountain's most renowned runs; it's pure bliss at night, while looking down at the city. There is also the Munday Alpine Snowpark for those who would rather **show-shoe** (rentals $15, courses from $80), plus an outdoor ice-skating rink.

Mt Seymour Resorts, at Mt Seymour Provincial Park (p76; ☎ snow information 604-718-7771) in North Vancouver, has 21 runs for **skiing and snowboarding** (day pass adult/child/senior/youth $36/19/25/29, after 4pm $28/16/20/24), rental, instruction, cross-country trails and night skiing until 10pm. Seymour is the best of the local bunch for snowboarding. Visitors also can **snowshoe** (day pass $7, day pass and rentals $24), **toboggan** (day pass $6) or **tube** (2 hours $14). A **shuttle bus service** (☎ 604-986-2261; adult/senior, youth & child $9/7; ☷ Dec-Mar, call for times) operates daily from Lonsdale Quay, Phibbs Exchange and the Parkgate Mall at the foot of Mt Seymour Rd.

Cross-country skiing enthusiasts should stop by all-knowing **Sigge's Sports Villa** (p165) for rentals, lessons and trip information. On Saturday, the store offers day trips to Whistler's Lost Lake (bus transportation and equipment $60). On Sunday, it runs day trips to Manning Park (bus transportation, lesson and equipment $99), with wine and cheese to help sustain weary skiers on the ride home.

TENNIS

There is no shortage of courts in Vancouver, so you might find yourself wondering why it takes so long to get on one. Playing tennis is a popular activity and because of the Lower Mainland's relatively mild winters, it can be played outside throughout the entire year.

There are 183 free public courts in the city, most of which are located outdoors in area parks and operate on a first-come, first-served basis, with a 30-minute maximum time limit if someone is waiting to play. Contact the **Vancouver Board of Parks and Recreation** (☎ 604-257-8400; www.parks.vancouver.bc.ca) to find locations. Some of the more central courts include:

Kitsilano Beach Park Ten courts; the nearby pool and beach offer cool relief after a tough match.

Queen Elizabeth Park Twenty courts.

Stanley Park Seventeen courts by the Beach Ave entrance and four courts by Lost Lagoon at the foot of Robson St.

WATER SPORTS

Vancouver's waterways offer myriad options for exploration, be it by kayak, sailboat or skimboard. Granville Island and Jericho Beach are good places to start for many of the activities listed here.

There are some things you should know before you hit the water. If you are paddling, you should not attempt to go under the Lions Gate Bridge as the currents are extremely strong; sailboards are not allowed at the mouth of False Creek between the Burrard and Granville Bridges; and the maximum speed for boats in False Creek is five knots and sails are prohibited. Before you head out on the water for the day, call for a **marine forecast** (☎ 604-664-9010).

For information on renting motorboats and fishing gear, try **Sewell's Marina** (☎ 604-921-3474; www.sewellsmarina.com; West Vancouver, 6695 Nelson Ave; bus 250) in Horseshoe Bay.

Kayaking

The sheltering presence of Vancouver Island makes the waters of False Creek and Burrard Inlet a relatively calm area and perfect for a paddle. **Ecomarine Ocean Kayak Centre** (Map pp236-7; ☎ 604-689-7575, 888-425-2925; www.ecomarine.com; Granville Island, 1668 Duranleau St; lessons from $65, rentals $59-85 per day; ☼ 9am-6pm Sun-Wed, 9am-9pm Tue & Thu-Sat in summer, hours vary seasonally; bus 50) provides instruction and rental, as well as an excellent 2½-hour guided tour ($49) at 9:30am and 1pm of False Creek and English Bay. No experience is necessary, but call ahead to register. Ecomarine has a **seasonal outlet** (☎ 604-222-3565; ☼ May-Sep) at the Jericho Sailing Centre (see right)offers courses and educational tours of the islands in the Strait of Georgia and in Clayoquot Sound on the west coast of Vancouver Island.

The 18km Indian Arm fjord, located by the hamlet of Deep Cove, is a paddlers' paradise with calm waters and steep, forested cliffs rising up on either side. **Deep Cove Canoe & Kayak** (Map pp228-9; ☎ 604-929-2268; www.deepcovekayak.com; North Vancouver, 2156 Banbury Rd; courses from $65, rentals weekday $56-82, weekend $60-86; ☼ dawn-dusk Apr-Oct; bus 212) provides courses for all ages and skill levels, and rents equipment. There are also three-hour guided tours (adult/child 12 and under

$80/50) at 1pm daily and 5pm Monday, Wednesday, Friday from May to September, and awesome tours ($50) to watch the full moon rise over the mountains and flood the Indian Arm with silvery light.

Rafting

With all those rivers roaring down from all those mountains, you would be right to believe there are good whitewater rafting opportunities to be had near the city. The serious rivers, such as the Upper Fraser, the Thompson and the Chilliwack, offer exciting trips through canyons, the very names of which are enough to scare the life out of you, such as Hell's Gate, Jaws of Death, Devil's Cauldron and the Washing Machine.

Rafting trips are also possible in the area around Squamish and Whistler, although without offering quite the adrenalin rush you'll experience on one of the interior rivers. Leisurely float trips are also available on many of the rivers.

There are a number of companies offering trips in the region:

Canadian Outback Adventure (☎ 604-921-7250, 800-565-8735; www.canadianoutback.com; West Vancouver, Ste 100, 657 Marine Dr; 3hr trip $149; ☼ May-Sep) Runs trips in Squamish and Whistler; can arrange transfers from Vancouver to raft departure points.

Great Expeditions (☎ 604-257-2040, 800-663-3364; www.greatexpeditions.com; Fairview, 940 W King Edward Ave; trips from $2300; ☼ Jun-Sep) Six- to 12-day tours in the interior that cost a pretty penny.

Hyak Wilderness Adventures (☎ 604-734-8622, 800-663-7238; www.hyak.com; Burnaby, Ste 203, 3823 Henning Dr; day trips from $102; ☼ May-Sep) Day trips (4½ hours on the water) on the Chilliwack and Thompson rivers; two-day trips and longer on the Firth, Fraser and Nahanni rivers.

Sailing & Windsurfing

English Bay gets some good winds whipping through. For lessons and equipment rental, **Jericho Sailing Centre** (Map pp238-9; Kitsilano, 1300 Discovery St; bus 4) is a good place to start; many companies are based there, as is a fine pub (p124) and café. Hard-core windsurfers will want to head to Squamish (p191) where the winds are more fierce. The following companies are located in the Jericho Sailing Centre:

Locarno Sailing Club (☎ 604-224-6117; www.clublocarno.com; courses $15-165, membership $185; ☼ closed

Oct–mid-Apr) Not only will teach you to sail but to windsurf, kayak and row, too.

Mac Sailing (☎ 604-224-7245; www.macsailing.com; rental per hr $25-45, courses $75-245; ☺ 9am-7pm Mon-Fri, noon-6pm Sat & Sun summer, closed Oct-Apr) Will teach you to tack, gibe and skipper your own sailboat.

Windsure Windsurfing School (☎ 604-224-0615; www.windsure.com; 2hr lesson $39, full-day rental $105; ☺ 9am-8pm Apr-Sep) Promises to get even the most balance-challenged standing on a board.

Skimboarding

Skimboarding is a cross between skateboarding and surfing, where participants ride a small, surf-like board on the incoming tide, and move down the beach via shallow shoreline wash and tidal pools. Spanish Banks and Wreck Beaches are generally considered the best places to skim, and you can watch riders throw down ollies, railsides and other cool moves. **PD's Hot Shop** (p164) sells skimboards and provides free tidal charts.

Scuba Diving

Despite extremely cold temperatures, the North Shore waters have a lot to offer divers, though the general consensus is you can find more comfortable diving elsewhere in the province if your trip includes other coastal locations.

Popular local dive spots include **Lighthouse** and **Whytecliff Parks** (p77) in West Vancouver; and **Porteau Cove** on Hwy 99, 24km north of Horseshoe Bay, which is a provincial marine park and has an artificial reef made of pieces of old ships, plus a camp site with showers.

Divers will need a 6mm neoprene wetsuit as temperatures below the thermocline stay at about 10°C (50°F). A number of outfitters offer equipment, training and trips, including:

Diving Locker (Map pp238-9; ☎ 604-736-2681; www .kochersdiving.com; Kitsilano, 2745 W 4th Ave; packages from $50; ☺ 10am-6pm Mon-Fri, 9:30am-5:30pm Sat, 9:30am-4pm Sun; bus 4)

International Diving Centre (Map p77; ☎ 604-736-2541; www.diveidc.com; Kitsilano, 2572 Arbutus St; group fun dives admission free, courses from $300; ☺ 10am-7pm Mon-Thu, 10am-8pm Fri, 9:30am-6pm Sat, 10am-5pm Sun; bus 16) Group fun dives cater to divers of all experience levels, but you need to bring your own gear.

Swimming

Eleven beaches around the city are fine for swimming, and from the end of May to the beginning of September seven are patrolled by lifeguards, including **Second Beach** (p52), **Third Beach** (p52), **English Bay Beach** (p50), **Kitsilano Beach** (p62), **Jericho Beach** (p62), **Locarno Beach** (p64) and **Spanish Banks Beach** (p64).

While people do swim at Second, Third and English Bay beaches, the water is much cleaner at the West Side shores. Kits Beach is the busiest and bustiest of the lot – as many as 10,000 people may hit the sand here on a hot summer day. It gets less crowded the further you move toward Spanish Banks. Vancouver's waters are never exactly warm; they reach a high in summer of around 21°C (70°F). Sometimes the bacteria count in the water off the city beaches can get a bit too high for healthy swimming; check the newspapers for daily reports.

If swimming in the open sea doesn't appeal, try one of Vancouver's public aquatic centers. Admission to any of these facilities is adult/child/youth $4.40/2.25/3.30. The outdoor pools are generally open from mid-morning until dusk; times for public swimming in the indoor facilities vary widely throughout the year, so it's best to call first. Try the following:

Kitsilano Outdoor Pool (Map pp238-9; ☎ 604-731-0011; Kitsilano, cnr Cornwall Ave & Yew St; ☺ late May–mid-Sep; bus 2 or 22) This heated 137m saltwater pool provides the best dip in town.

Second Beach Pool (Map p240; ☎ 604-257-8371; Stanley Park, cnr N Lagoon Dr & Stanley Park Dr; ☺ late May–mid-Sep; bus 1) This pool shimmers like an aqua marine right beside the beach. It has lanes for laps as well as a children's area with waterslides.

UBC Aquatic Centre (Map p241; ☎ 604-822-4522; UBC, 6121 University Blvd; bus 4) This facility has a 50m pool, saunas and exercise areas for public use.

Vancouver Aquatic Centre (Map pp230-3; ☎ 604-665-3424; West End, 1050 Beach Ave; bus 1) At Sunset Beach beside the Burrard Bridge, this aquatic center has a 50m pool, whirlpool, diving tank, gym and sauna.

HEALTH & FITNESS

You might think Vancouver would be the perfect place to lay down the 'I can't go for a run today because it's raining' excuse. Wrong. The city hosts a wealth of gyms, yoga and Pilates studios, and offers other indoor ways to stay fit.

You can exercise at the full range of facilities here, with perks including a women-only section, yoga classes, child care and two outdoor sundecks, then blow all your hard work nearby with a milkshake at **Sophie's Cosmic Café** (p119) or chocolate bar at the **Candy Aisle** (p163).

YWCA HEALTH & WELLNESS CENTRE
Map pp230-3

☎ 604-895-5777; www.ywcavan.org/health; downtown, 535 Hornby St; ☽ 6am-10pm Mon-Fri, 8am-5:30pm Sat & Sun; SkyTrain Burrard

Despite its name, the YWCA is open to men and women. It has three studios with wood-sprung floors, and combined and women-only weight rooms, a cardio room, steam room, whirlpool, 25m pool and meditation room. There are also kickboxing, cycling, Pilates and other classes.

YOGA & PILATES

Yoga is huge in Vancouver, as you'd expect in the city that birthed **lululemon athletica** (p156) and made yoga wear into a fashion statement. Most of the city's **community centers** (p210), including those in the West End, Coal Harbour and Yaletown, offer drop-in classes. Many yoga studios also offer Pilates classes.

Single classes cost $14 to $17, but discounts are available. Sometimes your first class costs just $5, or is even completely free. A one-week introductory pass may cost just $20. Many places have a weekly 'karma class' where the fee may be reduced and all proceeds go to charity. Some places charge a nominal fee (ie $1 or $2) for mat rental. Schedules vary, but most yoga studios are open daily.

BIKRAM YOGA Map p235

☎ 604-251-9642; www.bikramyogaonthedrive.com; East Vancouver, 1109 Commercial Dr; bus 20

Dynamic yoga performed in a heated room, Bikram is a 26-asana series designed to warm and stretch muscles, ligaments and tendons. It is reputedly good at providing relief for arthritis, back problems and other chronic conditions.

YALETOWN PILATES Map pp230-3

☎ 604-646-0199; www.yaletownpilates.com; Yaletown, Ste 201, 1037 Mainland St; bus 1

The emphasis is on Pilates mat (no equipment needed), reformer (equipment needed) and pre- and post-natal classes, but the studio also offers yoga, tai chi and gyrotonic classes. The latter involves rhythmic movements that incorporate yoga, dance, gymnastics and tai chi.

Absolute Spa (opposite), at Fairmont Hotel Vancouver

GYMS & HEALTH CLUBS

Private gyms usually charge $15 to $20 for a day pass; ask about weekly or monthly membership. Vancouver's community centers charge about $5 to use their workout rooms, and the same for aerobics or other fitness classes. The **West End Community Centre** (p210) is a convenient option, with both a fitness facility and classes. Contact the **Vancouver Board of Parks and Recreation** (☎ 604-257-8400; www.city.vancouver.bc.ca/parks/cc) for other community centers that have fitness programs.

FITNESS WORLD Map pp230-3

☎ 604-662-7774; www.fitnessworld.ca; West End, 1185 W Georgia St; ☽ 24hr Mon-Fri, 8am-7pm Sat & Sun; SkyTrain Burrard

This facility's convenient hours and location near downtown attract a lot of corporate types. Get a piece of machinery by the window and work out while gazing at the North Shore mountains. The company has several additional branches around the Lower Mainland.

KITSILANO WORKOUT Map pp238-9

☎ 604-734-3481; www.kitsilanoworkout.com; Kitsilano, 1923 W 4th Ave; ☽ 24hr Sun-Fri, 7am-10pm Sat; bus 4

YALETOWN YOGA Map pp230-3

☎ 604-684-3334; www.yaletownyoga.com; Yaletown, 1232 Richards St; bus 1

This studio specializes in Moksha, another 'hot' yoga like Bikram Yoga. The room is heated, and participants go through 40 postures in 90 minutes designed to strengthen the upper body, open the hips and release tension.

WANDERING YOGI Map p235

☎ 604-251-1915; www.wanderingyogi.com; East Vancouver, 1707 Grant St; bus 20

This studio offers 90-minute Hatha classes on a lightly heated floor to encourage the release of toxins and muscular tension. There are also Kirtan classes that revolve around chanting, and a 60 minute mantra/chant class (admission free) at 6:15pm on Friday in which participants recite the Mahaa Mrityunjaya Mantra 108 times for healing and peace.

PERSONAL CARE & WELLBEING

Vancouver is a fine place to indulge in a little treat for your body, especially after a hard day cycling through the parks or skiing down the slopes. Check the alternative weekly newspapers (p214) for salon and day spa coupons, special promotions and new openings.

HAIR SALONS

Expect to pay at least $40 for a haircut and style. Try to make appointments at least a day in advance.

KNOTTY BOY Map p235

☎ 604-473-9651; www.knottyboy.com; East Vancouver, 1721 Grant St; ☽ noon-6pm Mon-Fri; bus 20

It's a 'one-stop lock shop' where you can get natural or synthetic dreadlocks done, undone, colored, extended, deep cleaned, tidied up, beaded and more. If you prefer to do it yourself, you can buy a kit that provides instructions on how to start dreads from scratch. Dread combs, all-natural dreadlock wax, itch-fighting dreadlock shampoo bars, and myriad other dread specialty products are available.

PROPAGANDA Map pp238-9

☎ 604-732-7756; Kitsilano, 2090 W 4th Ave; ☽ 10am-6pm Mon-Wed & Sat, 10am-8pm Thu & Fri, 10am-5pm Sun; bus 4

Propaganda features excellent hair washing complete with relaxing scalp massage. The staff is a mix of trendy, cool, but stylistically sensible hair professionals, and hey, dogs are welcome inside to help their owners make new-look decisions.

SUKI'S INTERNATIONAL Map pp236-7

☎ 604-738-7713; www.sukis.com; South Granville, 3157 S Granville St; ☽ 9am-5:30pm Sat-Wed, 9am-7:30pm Thu & Fri; bus 10

You know all those really great-looking, well-coifed people you see in the clubs? They get their cuts and colors at Suki's. The salons are probably the most famous for hair in Vancouver; they are particularly well known for color treatments. There are four other Suki's salons around town.

MASSAGE & DAY SPAS

Most day spas offer registered massage therapy (RMT), facials, manicures and pedicures, waxing and tanning services. Both men and women are welcome, unless otherwise stated. Appointments are always advised. Expect to pay upwards of $65 for an hour-long massage, at least $35 for a 'quickie' facial and $15 or more for any other miscellaneous services.

ABSOLUTE SPA Map pp230-3

☎ 604-648-2909; www.absolutespa.com; downtown, 900 W Georgia St; ☽ 9am-6pm Sun-Wed, 9am-9pm Thu-Sat; SkyTrain Burrard

This chain, which has outlets in several of Vancouver's upscale hotels, was set to open Canada's first male-focused spa in the Hotel Vancouver at the time of research. The new spas have an earth-toned decor, pedicure chairs boasting video games, and computers where patrons can check their stocks and sports scores, and a barber chair to sit in for hot-towel shaves. Women are still served here, too.

FLAMING JUNE Map p235

☎ 604-253-8001; www.flamingjune.com; East Vancouver, 1701 Grant St; ☽ 10am-6pm Sun-Tue, 9am-8pm Wed-Fri, 9am-6pm Sat; bus 20

Flaming June is a classic day spa with the full line of treatments available. Get a full-body wrap, aromatherapy facial, pedicure plus paraffin dip, or any of the massages on offer (deep tissue, Swedish, lymphatic drainage, reflexology or shiatsu).

Piercings & Tattoos

If you fancy emblazoning your skin with a maple leaf or piercing your navel, you've come to the right city. Hours are somewhat erratic, so call ahead for an appointment at these places:

- **Ink Bomb** (Map pp236-7; ☎ 604-874-2662; www.inkbomb.net; SoMa, 3255 Main St; bus 3) An easygoing little shop with custom tattoo designs; portfolios are available online.
- **Next! Body Piercing, Tattooing and Aftercare** (Map pp230-3; ☎ 604-684-6398; www.nextbody.com; downtown, 1068 Granville St; bus 4) Tattoos, piercings and aftercare instruction groups; heck, you can even get pierced together. Fascinating website covers the history of piercing.
- **Sacred Heart Tattoo & Piercing** (Map pp230-3; ☎ 604-647-0826; www.sacredhearttattoo.ca; downtown, 725 Nelson St; bus 4) Get pierced or tattooed by needle-wielding folks with names like 'Greta the Strong' and 'Bear', or who list their hobbies as fire spinning and Croatian folk singing.

MIRAJ HAMMAM SPA Map pp236-7

☎ 604-733-5151; www.mirajhammam.com; South Granville, 1495 W 6th Ave; ☾ 11am-7pm Tue & Wed, noon-8pm Thu & Fri, 10am-6pm Sat, 2-6pm Sun; bus 10

Canada's only hammam is based on the real Middle Eastern deal. Step into the arched and tiled interior for a steam followed by *gommage* (a full-body scrub with authentic black Moroccan soap). Men admitted only from 4pm to 8pm Saturday and 2pm to 6pm Sunday; it's women-only the rest of the time.

MODERNE Map pp236-7

☎ 604-872-8938; South Granville, 3286 Cambie St; ☾ 9:30am-6:30pm; bus 15

Located next to a cosmetology school, Moderne is staffed by students, so the prices are reasonable. They do everything here: facials, waxing, laser hair removal, lip tattooing, pore reduction, bleaching, aroma massage, and the list goes on. The hour-long, $30 pedicure is fabulous.

SKOAH Map pp230-3

☎ 604-642-0200; www.skoah.com; Yaletown, 1011 Hamilton St; ☾ 11am-8pm Mon-Fri, 10am-7pm Sat & Sun; bus 1

'No whale music and no bubbling cherubs,' as they say at this tongue-in-cheek, trying-hard-not-to-be-pretentious spa. There are deep-cleansing masques, facial massage, scalp massage, foot 'facials' and muscle stimulation treatments, all done by your 'personal skin care trainer.' Skoah also sells its own line of all-natural products.

Shopping

Shopping

Whether it's First Nations artwork, hemp lip balm, smoked salmon or the perfect snowboard, there isn't much you can't buy in Vancouver. New fashion, athletic gear and quality crafts are the city's shopping strengths. It isn't exactly a bargain-hunter's paradise, especially once taxes are figured in, but visitor refunds (p215) are possible and exchange rates happily tend to favor US and European visitors, so maybe those flashy new yoga pants aren't out of the question after all.

Remember that museum shops sell high-quality souvenirs, which may be more meaningful than another T-shirt.

Shopping Strips

Robson St in the West End is Vancouver's answer to Rodeo Dr and is the busiest shopping street in town. Tasteful fashion stores abut tacky tourist shops in a happy, frenzied scene that extends well after the usual shopping hours.

Commercial Dr is good for more offbeat stores, like those selling Che Guevara backpacks, dreadlock-care products or belly-dancing hand cymbals. Broadway in Fairview is probably the best place in Canada to swaddle yourself in fleece or Gortex, or otherwise gear up for the great outdoors.

Granville Island reigns supreme for local artisan goods. Granville St south of the island holds a collection of trendy and established galleries and fashion stores. SoMa's Main St is the less-established new kid on the block where several hip young designers have opened their doors.

True to its countercultural past, Kitsilano remains Vancouver's best neighborhood for anticommercialism, with a number of nobly minded store owners on W 4th Ave and Broadway donating a percentage of profits to charities.

Top Five Shopping Streets

- **Commercial Dr** (p158)
- **Robson St** (p156)
- **Main St** (p157)
- **W 4th Ave** (p163)
- **Granville St** (p162)

Opening Hours

Typical retail shopping hours are 10am to 6pm Monday to Saturday, noon to 5pm Sunday. But this varies depending on the season, the neighborhood and the amount of foot traffic. Prime shopping areas and malls may stay open until 9pm, especially from Thursday onward.

DOWNTOWN

Out of downtown's many shopping malls and underground arcades, **Pacific Centre** (Map pp230-3; ☎ 604-688-7235; cnr Howe & Georgia Sts; ☺ 10am-7pm Mon-Wed, 10am-9pm Thu & Fri, 9:30am-6pm Sat, 11am-6pm Sun; SkyTrain Granville) is the largest, spanning three blocks and featuring a multistory waterfall, glass skylights, and more than 200 stores, restaurants and services. Most shops are national or international chains. Several major department stores are represented, including Holt Renfrew, where you might stumble on a trunk show or famous designer making an appearance.

Other malls, like the swanky **Sinclair Centre** (Map pp230-3; ☎ 604-659-1009; 757 W Hastings St; ☺ 10am-5pm Mon-Sat; SkyTrain Waterfront), may seem half-empty except during weekday lunch and rush hours.

Shops along the Granville St pedestrian mall outfit club-savvy customers with urban street fashion and even fetish gear. On Hastings St, near its intersection with Cambie St at

Gastown's edge, a few outrageously offbeat shops sell anarchist 'zines, hemp paraphernalia, and vintage and designer clothes. The **BC Marijuana Party Bookstore** (Map pp230-3; ☎ 604-682-1172; 307 W Hastings St; ⊙ 10am-6pm Mon-Sat, 11am-5:30pm Sun; SkyTrain Waterfront) is king of the lot.

For art gallery shops, see p162.

A&B SOUND Map pp230-3 *Music*
☎ 604-687-5837; 556 Seymour St; ⊙ 9:30am-6pm Mon-Wed & Sat, 9:30am-9pm Thu & Fri, 11am-5pm Sun; SkyTrain Granville

With several other outlets around the Lower Mainland, purple-painted a&b sells all types of music and electronic equipment. Its weekend and holiday blowout sales result in long line-ups before the doors even open.

THE BAY Map pp230-3 *Department Store*
☎ 604-681-6211; 674 Granville St; ⊙ 9:30am-9pm Mon-Sat, 9:30am-7pm Sun; SkyTrain Granville

Victorian-era entrepreneur Robert Simpson's successful department store merged with the historic Hudson's Bay Company to create what is now known simply as the Bay, a megalith selling everything from armchairs to zippers.

CANADIAN MAPLE DELIGHTS
Map pp230-3 *Specialty*
☎ 604-682-6175; 769 Hornby St; ⊙ 7:30am-7pm Mon-Fri, 8am-7pm Sat & Sun; SkyTrain Granville

While this place is mainly a café specializing in all sorts of goodies using maple syrup, there is also an attached shop capitalizing on Canada's national symbol. Behold the 75 maple-inspired gifts – maple sugar, maple tea, maple leaf–shaped candy, maple tree–growing kits…you get the idea.

GRANVILLE BOOK COMPANY
Map pp230-3 *Books & Magazines*
☎ 604-687-2213; 850 Granville St; ⊙ 10am-10pm Mon-Sat, noon-10pm Sun; bus 4

Who'd expect rows of brainy books on computers, the humanities, chess, architecture and science fiction right in the midst of the Granville St club strip? This indie bookstore also overflows with magazine racks and free local newspapers.

HENRY BIRKS & SONS Map pp230-3 *Jewelry*
☎ 604-669-3333; 698 W Hastings St; ⊙ 10am-6pm Mon-Fri, 10am-5:30pm Sat, noon-5pm Sun; SkyTrain Waterfront

A Vancouver institution since 1879, Henry Birks crafts exquisite heirloom jewelry and its signature line of timepieces. It's an upscale place, similar to Tiffany's in the USA, with outlets across Canada.

Commercial Dr (p158), East Vancouver

Top Five Music Stores

- Zulu Records (p165)
- Highlife World Music (p159)
- Scratch Records (right)
- Noize Sound (below)
- Sikora's Classical Records (right)

JOHN FLUEVOG Map pp230-3 *Shoes*

☎ 604-688-2828; www.fluevog.com; 837 Granville St; ⏰ 11am-7pm Mon-Wed & Sat, 11am-8pm Thu & Fri, noon-5pm Sun; bus 4

Creating one-of-a-kind footwear with attitude, this local shoe stylist attributes '50s furniture design and anything vintage as his inspirations. The website has previews of Fluevog's latest whimsies, costing upwards of $200 per pair. Shoes come as tough-girl chunky or sex-kitten pointy as you like, with equally hip selections for men.

NOIZE SOUND Map pp230-3 *Music*

☎ 604-681-7007; 540 Seymour St; ⏰ 11:30am-6pm Mon-Fri, noon-6pm Sat, noon-5pm Sun; SkyTrain Granville

Noize is a fusty, closet-like little shop favored by vinyl aficionados, who drop by to flick through the mostly used jazz, blues, imports and classic rock collector albums. Noize also sells tickets to local shows.

SCRATCH RECORDS Map pp230-3 *Music*

☎ 604-687-6355; 726 Richards St; ⏰ 10:30am-6pm Mon-Sat, noon-5pm Sun; SkyTrain Granville

Initially a tiny specialist record store, Scratch expanded over the past 15 years to become a record label, concert promoter and international distributor. But the store remains, its bins packed with 99% independent labels, obscure releases and vinyl that the staff know intimately.

SIKORA'S CLASSICAL RECORDS

Map pp230-3 *Music*

☎ 604-685-0625; 432 W Hastings St; ⏰ 10am-6pm Mon-Sat, noon-4pm Sun; SkyTrain Waterfront

Sikora's blows away the classical inventory of mainstream music stores with its 25,000 CDs/DVDs and 50,000 LPs, both new and used. Opera, organ, choral, chamber and early music are represented, and there's a section devoted to Canadian musicians.

SOPHIA BOOKS

Map pp230-3 *Books & Magazines*

☎ 604-684-0484; 492 W Hastings St; ⏰ 9am-7pm Mon-Fri, 10am-7pm Sat, noon-6pm Sun; SkyTrain Waterfront

This foreign-language bookstore serves ESL students, homesick Francophones and Japanese manga fans. Shelves devoted to comics, *animé*, foreign magazines, language-learning tapes and Japanese origami fill the cramped aisles.

GASTOWN

With its boxes of maple sugar candy and 'Canadian Girls Kick Ass!' T-shirts, Gastown – particularly along Water St – can seem like tourist central, but its galleries display top-notch First Nations art (see opposite). Walk south to Cordova St, where the tourists dissipate and you're amid a row of antique shops and urban-fashion boutiques.

Many US citizens sneak off to RJ Clarke Tobacconist (Map p234; ☎ 604-687-4136; 3 Alexander St; ⏰ 10am-5pm Mon-Sat, noon-5pm Sun; bus 7), purveyors of fine Cuban cigars, housed in an original 19th-century Gastown building.

BIZ BOOKS Map p234 *Books & Magazines*

☎ 604-669-6431; 302 W Cordova St; ⏰ 10am-6pm Mon-Fri, 11am-5pm Sat; SkyTrain Waterfront

Biz is the city's best source for film, theater and TV industry books. Actors, writers and directors studying the craft will find plays, directories, monologue books, scene books, accent tapes and screenwriting software.

DELUXE JUNK Map p234 *Vintage Fashion*

☎ 604-685-4871; 310 W Cordova St; ⏰ 10am-6pm Mon-Sat, noon-5pm Sun; SkyTrain Waterfront

From Victorian-style lace-up boots to a jaunty beret to that rhinestone stick pin you've been coveting – it's all on the racks at this consignment clothing store, as are contemporary skirts, blouses and jeans. Prices slip the longer the items remain on the shelves.

DREAM Map p234 *Fashion*

☎ 604-683-7326; 311 W Cordova St; ⏰ 11am-6pm Mon & Tue, 10:30am-6pm Wed, Thu & Sat, 10:30am-7pm Fri, noon-6pm Sun; SkyTrain Waterfront

Dream is one of a cluster of small shops in the area near Cambie St spotlighting emerging young local fashionistas. Hip Japanese girls sift through the hats, T-shirts, thongs, purses, jewelry and other urban funk items for that must-have piece. Surprisingly, prices are not sky-high.

HILL'S NATIVE ART
Map p234   *Aboriginal Art & Crafts*
☎ 604-685-4249, 866-685-5422; www.hillsnativeart .com; 165 Water St; ☺ 9am-9pm; SkyTrain Waterfront
Begun in 1946 as a small trading post on Vancouver Island, Hill's flagship store has many carvings, prints, ceremonial masks, cozy Cowichan sweaters, traditional music and books of historical interest. Artists are often found at work in the 3rd-floor gallery.

INUIT GALLERY OF VANCOUVER
Map p234   *Aboriginal Art & Crafts*
☎ 604-688-7323, 888-615-8399; www.inuit.com; 206 Cambie St; ☺ 10am-6pm Mon-Sat, 10am-5pm Sun; SkyTrain Waterfront
Excellent collections of Inuit and northwest coast masks, carvings, prints, tapestries and jewelry are found in this government-licensed gallery. Crafts (mostly sculptures) are also sold at its sister shop, **Images for a Canadian Heritage**

(Map p234; ☎ 604-685-7046; 164 Water St; ☺ same hours; SkyTrain Waterfront).

NEW WORLD DESIGNS
Map p234   *Specialty Fashion*
☎ 604-687-3443; 306 W Cordova St; ☺ 11am-6pm Mon-Sat, noon-5pm Sun; SkyTrain Waterfront
Gothic fetishwear shares with Renaissance ball gowns and brocade corsets, all of which are a pretty tight squeeze to fit into. Less confining but still a conversation piece are the velvet capes and square-toed witch shoes. Each item of clothing is handmade by the designer/owner.

MARION SCOTT GALLERY
Map p234   *Aboriginal Art & Crafts*
☎ 604-685-1934; www.marionscottgallery.com; 308 Water St; ☺ 9:30am-5:30pm Mon-Sat, 10am-5pm Sun; SkyTrain Waterfront
Vancouver's oldest gallery has been exhibiting Inuit prints, drawings and contemporary sculpture for decades. A leading authority on art and artists from Canada's north, the gallery also produces a small but growing list of fine art publications and critical writings on the subject.

First Nations Art & Crafts

Greater Vancouver shops and galleries sell a vast range of First Nations art, everything from tourist kitsch to the very finest in contemporary and traditional designs. For help in determining quality, authenticity and fair costs, read *A Guide to Buying Contemporary Northwest Coast Indian Arts* by Karen Duffek, available at the Museum of Anthropology (p64).

Prominent symbolism used by northwest nations features ravens, killer whales and other powerful mythological animal-heroes. These animals appear on masks, ceremonial bowls and tapestries; in wood, stone and bone carvings; and in bright primary-color paintings on paper. You often can buy high-quality prints of the latter, a more affordable option than buying masks or carvings.

Chiefs' 'talking sticks' resemble small totems or are carved with a single family crest, while abstract interpretations of traditional weaving spindles appear in glass works and paintings. Masterful kerfed (or bentwood) boxes are handcrafted by steaming and bending a single wooden plank at three corners, then sealing the box with a watertight joint. Small carvings in argillite (black slate) are produced exclusively by the Haida people of the Queen Charlotte Islands from a special quarry there.

Artists whose works are worth looking out for include: Kaka Ashoona, Joe David, Beau Dick, Joy Hallauk, Judas Ooloolah, Kanaginak Pootoogook, Bill Reid, Kov Takpaungai, Lucy Tasseor Tutsweetok and Oviloo Tunnillie (see p26 for details). Keep your eyes open, too, for Inuit art, especially carvings of dancing polar bears and inukshuk, human-shaped rock sculptures used as landmarks upon Canada's arctic tundra.

Gastown is a fertile place to begin exploring. Recommended shops in Vancouver include:
- **Coastal Peoples Fine Arts Gallery** (p156)
- **Hill's Native Art** (above)
- **Inuit Gallery of Vancouver** (above)
- **Leona Lattimer Gallery** (p162)
- **Marion Scott Gallery** (above)
- **Spirit Wrestler Gallery** (p156)

SPIRIT WRESTLER GALLERY

Map p234 *Aboriginal Art & Crafts*
☎ 604-669-8813; www.spiritwrestler.com; 8 Water St; 🕙 10am-6pm Mon-Sat, noon-5pm Sun; bus 7
Spirit Wrestler specializes in sculpture, carvings and graphics that explore the themes of shamanism and transformation. It's mostly work by northwest coast and Inuit peoples, but there are also pieces by New Zealand's Maori and Canada's Plains artists.

YALETOWN

Further to the east in the warehouse-turned-yuppie-loft district of Yaletown you'll find a variety of designer furniture and homeware stores, refined boutiques, as well as a few art galleries.

BARBARA-JO'S BOOKS TO COOKS

Map pp230-3 *Books & Magazines*
☎ 604-688-6755, outside Vancouver ☎ 866-688-6744; www.bookstocooks.com; 1128 Mainland St; 🕙 10am-6pm Mon-Fri, 10:30am-5pm Sat, noon-5pm Sun; bus 1
Epicureans salivate over more than 2500 food and wine books, including out-of-print and specialty titles. The best part is the demonstration kitchen, where you can learn from new and notable chefs how to whip up the recipes they've written about.

COASTAL PEOPLES FINE ARTS

GALLERY Map pp230-3 *Aboriginal Art & Crafts*
☎ 604-685-9298; www.coastalpeoples.com; 1072 Mainland St; 🕙 10am-7pm Mon-Sat, 11am-6pm Sun; bus 1
This gallery focuses on the different carving styles of BC's coastal communities. Handcrafted jewelry is a specialty of the gallery, particularly custom wedding bands. Unique basketry, like the $12,000 Spruce Root Hat, and glasswork join the masks and sculptures lining the shelves.

WEST END

On Robson St (p50), the busiest shopping street in Vancouver, everything from couture to chocolate, Italian newspapers and fresh crab, is for sale. The trendiest section is between Burrard and Jervis Sts, while West End shops closer to Denman St are geared toward everyday needs.

BRUCE Map pp230-3 *Fashion*
☎ 604-688-8802; 1038 Alberni St; 🕙 10am-7pm Mon-Wed & Sat, 10am-9pm Thu & Fri, noon-7pm Sun; bus 5
Sleek and chic, this global design store carries ultra-mod clothing, eyewear, shoes and home objects in its bright, minimalist setting. Hard-to-find labels are a specialty, with the selection constantly changing to remain at the cutting edge of hipness.

COMOR Map pp230-3 *Outdoors Equipment*
☎ 604-899-2111; 1090 W Georgia St; 🕙 10am-6pm Mon-Wed, 10am-9pm Thu & Fri, 10am-7pm Sat, 11am-6pm Sun, to 9pm daily during ski season; SkyTrain Burrard
Spacious Comor specializes in skiing, snowboarding, surf and skateboarding gear and apparel. The shop also offers ski repairs and tune-ups by certified technicians.

LITTLE SISTER'S BOOK & ART

EMPORIUM Map pp230-3 *Books & Magazines*
☎ 604-669-1753; www.lsisters.com; 1238 Davie St; 🕙 10am-11pm; bus 1
Possibly the only queer bookshop in western Canada, Little Sister's has a vast bazaar of queer-positive books, DVDs and gifts. Proceeds of designated books support the store's long-running legal battle against Canada Customs' seizures of import items.

LULULEMON ATHLETICA

Map pp230-3 *Specialty Fashion*
☎ 604-681-3118; www.lululemon.com; 1148 Robson St; 🕙 10am-7pm Mon-Wed, 10am-9pm Thu-Sat, 11am-7pm Sun, extended in summer; bus 5
Local yoga-wear maker lululemon's trendy stores have spread like wildfire through Canada, the USA and Australia. And no wonder – the company promises its product will help you 'live a longer, healthier, more fun life.' Togs are made from moisture-wicking fabrics with flat seams, so they're comfortable for sweating and movement. They're also colorful and flattering: the Boogie Pants and Groove Pants 'give every girl a great-looking butt,' swears one devoted customer. Men's items available, too. The **flagship store** (Map pp238-9; ☎ 604-732-6111; 2113 W 4th Ave; 🕙 10am-6pm, to 7pm Thu & Fri; bus 4) is in healthy lifestyle–loving Kits.

LUSH Map pp230-3 *Personal Care*
☎ 604-687-5874, 888-733-5874; 1025 Robson St; 🕙 9:30am-8pm Sun-Thu, 9:30am-9pm Fri & Sat; bus 5

This UK-based organic body, bath and beauty store does a huge Internet business, but you can get some of its special products – Sex Bomb bath ballistics or Black Magic massage bars – for half-price if you show up in person. You'll find another **branch** (Map pp238-9; ☎ 604-733-5874; 2248 W 4th Ave; ☺ 10:30am-6:30pm Mon-Thu, 10am-7pm Fri & Sat, 11am-6pm Sun; bus 4) in Kitsilano.

ROOTS Map pp230-3   *Fashion*
☎ 604-683-4305; 1001 Robson St; ☺ 9:30am-9pm; bus 5
Basically a maple leaf–emblazoned version of the Gap, Roots designs athletic streetwear that's unmistakably Canadian. In season, look for NHL hockey souvenir merchandise here. It's a chain, so there are branches throughout town (and throughout the country, in fact).

VIRGIN MEGASTORE Map pp230-3   *Music*
☎ 604-669-2289; cnr Robson & Burrard Sts; ☺ 10am-11pm Mon-Thu, 10am-midnight Fri & Sat, 10am-10pm Sun; bus 5
This mammoth store adds to the variety of shopping outlets available on Robson St. It's the largest music store in Canada. The building was the previous home of the Vancouver Public Library.

Clothing Sizes
Measurements approximate only, try before you buy

Women's Clothing

Aus/UK	8	10	12	14	16	18
Europe	36	38	40	42	44	46
Japan	5	7	9	11	13	15
USA	6	8	10	12	14	16

Women's Shoes

Aus/USA	5	6	7	8	9	10
Europe	35	36	37	38	39	40
France only	35	36	38	39	40	42
Japan	22	23	24	25	26	27
UK	3½	4½	5½	6½	7½	8½

Men's Clothing

Aus	92	96	100	104	108	112
Europe	46	48	50	52	54	56
Japan	S		M	M		L
UK/USA	35	36	37	38	39	40

Men's Shirts (Collar Sizes)

Aus/Japan	38	39	40	41	42	43
Europe	38	39	40	41	42	43
UK/USA	15	15½	16	16½	17	17½

Men's Shoes

Aus/UK	7	8	9	10	11	12
Europe	41	42	43	44½	46	47
Japan	26	27	27½	28	29	30
USA	7½	8½	9½	10½	11½	12½

CHINATOWN
Vancouver's Chinatown sells the same things as every other Chinatown the world over: inexpensive groceries and homewares, designer knockoffs from Hong Kong, and all the Buddhist altar goods the ancestors require. Most goods are cheap, but not necessarily high quality.

The tea and herb shop **Ten Lee Hong Enterprises** (Map p234; ☎ 604-689-7598; 500 Main St; ☺ 9:45am-6pm; bus 19) is an exception. You buy good green, red, white and black teas, and the staff of women in pink pantsuits will instruct you how to brew it (and serve you samples).

If you're looking for more mainstream shopping, the ever-evolving **International Village** (Map p234; ☎ 604-647-1137; 88 W Pender St; ☺ 11am-7pm; SkyTrain Stadium) complex boasts the usual mall-wares, plus the city's most high-tech cinema (p132).

NIGHT MARKET Map p234   *Market*
☎ 604-682-8998; 100 & 200 blocks of E Keefer St; admission free; ☺ 6:30-11pm Fri-Sun Jun–mid-Sep; bus 19
This open-air night market operates on summer weekends, and captures all the fun, food, and noise and excitement of its counterparts in Asia. Vendors sell everything from faux Gucci bags and Rolex watches to dried squid and imported pottery. Plenty of electronics, hanging ducks, exotic fruit and Eastern remedies also change hands.

SOMA
Old furniture and nouveau designer threads sum up much of the SoMa shopping experience. The stores between King Edward and 29th Ave along Main St comprise what's known as **Antique Row**. Between 20th and 23rd St lies one of the city's hippest shopping districts, where up-and-coming fashion designers have huddled to sell hand-painted boxer shorts, silk-screened ascots and dresses reconstructed from vintage fabric.

While these places certainly have distinct merchandise, they are similar in that they feature locally made items (several even manufacture their own line of wares), they retail out of teeny spaces barely wide enough to turn around in, and they target fashion-forward 25- to 40-year-olds. Some of the stars include:

Barefoot Contessa (Map pp236-7; ☎ 604-879-1137; 3715 Main St; ☯ noon-6pm; bus 3) All things feminine – floaty dresses, satin slippers and French imports like lavender soap.

Eugene Choo (Map pp236-7; ☎ 604-873-8874; 3683 Main St; ☯ 11am-6pm Mon-Sat, noon-5pm Sun; bus 3) Sleek sneakers, halter tops and denim jackets.

Lazy Susan (Map pp236-7; ☎ 604-873-9722; 3647 Main St; ☯ noon-5pm Sun-Mon, 11am-6pm Wed-Sat; bus 3) Skirts made from pillowcases, jewelry from typewriter keys and other creations fashioned from 'found' objects.

Narcissist (Map pp236-7; ☎ 604-877-1555; 3659 Main St; ☯ 11am-6pm Mon-Wed & Sat, 11am-7pm Thu & Fri, noon-5pm Sun; bus 3) Best known for developing the 'Perfect T' (shirt).

Smoking Lily (Map pp236-7; ☎ 604-873-5459; 3634 Main St; ☯ 11am-6pm Mon-Sat, noon-5pm Sun; bus 3) Panties, ascots and other clothing silk-screened with blocky Asian-inspired and insect designs.

Twigg & Hottie (Map pp236-7; ☎ 604-879-8595; 3671 Main St; ☯ 11am-6pm Mon-Sat, noon-5pm Sun; bus 3) Men and women's clothing with a vintage twist.

BURCU'S ANGELS FUNKY CLOTHING

ETC Map pp236-7 *Vintage Fashion*
☎ 604-874-9773; 2535 Main St; ☯ 11am-6pm Mon, 11am-8pm Tue-Sat, noon-6pm Sun; bus 3
This outrageous place has been known to rent out its vintage stock to visiting film crews. It's best known for its collection of '70s clothing, but there's also a selection from the turn of the century to the 1950s.

LEGENDS RETRO FASHION

Map pp236-7 *Vintage Fashion*
☎ 604-875-0621; 4366 Main St; ☯ 11am-5:30pm Mon-Sat, noon-5pm Sun; bus 3
Nestled among antique shops, racks of elegant clothes from decades past are sold along with one-of-a-kind hats and rhinestone jewelry. Legends has been around for 20-plus years and has earned its reputation for having merchandise in excellent condition.

MODERN TIMES ANTIQUES

Map pp236-7 *Antiques & Collectibles*
☎ 604-875-1057; 4260 Main St; ☯ 10am-5pm Mon-Fri, 10am-6pm Sat, noon-5pm Sun; bus 3
The assortment of furniture, lamps and mirrors is as dichotomous as the name. It's got a bit of everything – old and new, local and global (particularly items from Thailand and Indonesia), Buddhas and Bugs Bunny collectibles.

PULP FICTION

Map pp236-7 *Books & Magazines*
☎ 604-876-4311; 2422 Main St; ☯ 10am-8pm Mon-Wed, 10am-9pm Thu-Sat, 11am-7pm Sun; bus 3
Pulp Fiction is practically buried under its heaps and stacks of new and used books (plus

Top Five Local Fashion Designers' Shops

- **Smoking Lily** (above)
- **John Fluevog** (p154)
- **Dream** (p154)
- **Twigg & Hottie** (above)
- **New World Designs** (p155)

a smattering of vinyl records in the back). The 'staff picks' shelf recently displayed *Satanic Verses* and *Cunnilingus & Fellatio* among its wide selection of popular, sci-fi, mystery, classic and not-so-classic volumes.

RX COMICS

Map pp236-7 *Comics & Collectibles*
☎ 604-454-5099; 2418 Main St; ☯ 11am-7pm Tue-Sat, noon-6pm Sun; bus 3
With a mission to 'give the discriminating people what they want – good comics and lots of them,' the staff at Rx eat, sleep and breathe the medium. For those who just can't wait, new comics delivery day is Wednesday.

EAST VANCOUVER

Known simply as 'The Drive,' Commercial Dr is a nonconformist version of the West End's Robson St. The 17 blocks south of Venables St are filled with mom-and-pop stores (only here 'mom and pop' likely have a mohawk) selling soy-wax candles, African drums, bondage gear, Italian shoes, poetry chapbooks and other assorted items.

DOCTOR VIGARI GALLERY

Map p235   *Art & Crafts*
☎ 604-255-9513; 1312 Commercial Dr; ☿ 11am-6pm Mon-Sat, noon-5pm Sun; bus 20

The good Doctor sells paintings, sculpture, pottery, jewelry and accessories by local artists. The pieces are unusual and not particularly cheap, but the Doctor lets you take purchases home for a 'test drive' – just bring back that leopard-print teapot if it doesn't match your wallpaper.

HIGHLIFE WORLD MUSIC

Map p235   *Music*
☎ 604-251-6964; 1317 Commercial Dr; ☿ 11am-6pm Sat-Thu, 11am-10pm Fri; bus 20

Highlife stocks CDs and vinyl from Africa plus traditional world music from around the globe. Challenge the owner to recommend obscure titles, or request special orders for anything not on the shelves. The store sponsors and sells tickets to various concerts and festivals; ask about the upcoming schedule.

KALENA'S Map p235   *Shoes*
☎ 604-255-3727; 1526 Commercial Dr; ☿ 10am-6pm Mon-Fri, 10am-5:30pm Sat, noon-5pm Sun; bus 20

True to East Van's Italian heritage, Kalena's Imports handsome leather shoes and boots from the old country. Men's and women's styles can be had for reasonable prices; there's also a big area devoted to sale items.

MAGPIE MAGAZINE GALLERY

Map p235   *Books & Magazines*
☎ 604-253-6666; 1319 Commercial Dr; ☿ 9am-6:30pm; bus 20

Magpie regularly gets voted Vancouver's best magazine shop and its 2000 titles certainly represent the city's largest selection. Prepare for a squeeze while perusing in the narrow aisles. For help in deciding what to buy, check out *The Magpie*, a quarterly journal of what's on the newsstand; the journal is published in-house.

PEOPLE'S CO-OP BOOKSTORE

Map p235   *Books & Magazines*
☎ 604-253-6442; 1391 Commercial Dr; ☿ 10am-6pm Mon-Sat, 1-5pm Sun; bus 20

Fitting in well with its bohemian surroundings, this co-op sells books on socialist politics and global history, leftist 'zines and poetry chapbooks. Established in 1945 with a membership drawn from political activists, the store is now known for supporting local writers and social justice issues.

URBAN EMPIRE

Map p235   *Toys & Collectibles*
☎ 604-254-4700; 1108 Commercial Dr; ☿ 11am-5:30pm Mon-Fri, 11am-6pm Sat, noon-6pm Sun; bus 20

This wacky, all-out kitsch shop regularly takes home the Vancouver Film Festival grand prize

Local designers' clothing at Twigg & Hottie (opposite), SoMa

for theme-window displays. Its TV-dinner fridge magnets look so real, it feels like the 1970s all over again.

VANCOUVER FLEA MARKET

Map pp228-9   *Antiques & Collectibles*
☎ 604-685-0666; 703 Terminal Ave; admission 75¢, children under 12 free; ⏰ 9am-5pm Sat & Sun & select holidays; SkyTrain Science World-Main St
The city's weekly flea market is held in the Big Red Barn, a 10-minute walk east of Pacific Central Station. You are bound to find something you need at one of the 360 tables, and it's OK to haggle politely. Get there early before the best goods are cleaned out.

VIRGIN MARY'S Map p235 *Vintage Fashion*
☎ 604-844-7848; 1035 Commercial Dr; ⏰ 11am-6pm Tue-Sat, noon-5pm Sun & Mon; bus 20

Pleasantly jumbled Virgin Mary's carries vintage clothes dating from the 1950s. New and used fashions run the gamut from burlesque-influenced items (like pasties and bloomers) to 1970s iron-on T-shirts.

WOMYNS' WARE Map p235 *Specialty*
☎ 604-254-2543, 888-996-9273; www.womynsware .com; 896 Commercial Dr; ⏰ 11am-6pm Mon-Wed & Sat, 11am-7pm Thu & Fri, 11am-5pm Sun; bus 20
The female staff at this low-key shop, carrying one of North America's largest selections of women's sex toys, are happy to explain the workings of the family jewels harness or nun's habit flogger. Womyns' Ware is the provider of all, errr, props for Showtime's lesbian-focused cable TV series *The L Word*. In homage to the 2010 Winter Olympics, the store is selling a special edition Ring-A-Ding in blue, gold, black, green or red.

GRANVILLE ISLAND

The island is awash in studios where artisans throw clay, blow glass and silversmith jewelry, and its three main streets – Duranleau, Johnston and Cartwright – are paved with the resulting high-quality craft shops. The **Net Loft building** (1666 Johnston St) even wrangles a group of them conveniently under one roof. Hard-core shoppers can part further from their money at the labyrinthine **Kids Market** (p59) and **Public Market** (p59); merchants at the latter sell fancy jams, syrups and other preserved foods that make good gifts; the fishmongers can pack fish for air shipment. Or try the **Granville Island Smokery** (Map pp236-7; ☎ 604-684-4114; 1805 Mast Tower Rd; ⏰ 9am-6pm; bus 50) for traditional smoked BC salmon.

BC WOOD CO-OP Map pp236-7 *Art & Crafts*
☎ 604-408-2553; www.thewoodco-op.com; 1592 Johnston St; ⏰ 10am-6pm; bus 50
Pacific northwest woods are transformed here into magnificent tables, chairs, toys and household accessories with a focus on contemporary design. The co-op also accepts custom orders, but it's no surprise the beautiful birch stools and laurel wood armoires don't come cheap.

CIRCLE CRAFT Map pp236-7 *Art & Crafts*
☎ 604-669-8021; www.circlecraft.net; Net Loft, 1666 Johnston St; ⏰ 10am-6pm; bus 50
This 30-plus-year-old co-operative store sells 100% BC art, including sculptures from found objects, ceramics and sleek jewelry, with hand-sewn puppets and dolls thrown in for good measure.

CRAFTHOUSE Map pp236-7 *Art & Crafts*
☎ 604-687-7270; www.cabc.net; 1386 Cartwright St; ⏰ 10:30am-5:30pm, closed Mon in Jan; bus 50
At this non-profit gallery run by the Crafts Association of British Columbia (CABC), shelves hold

everything from glass goblets to wooden boxes to silver bracelets to decorative paper – all produced by BC artists, of course. The gallery also keeps schedules of provincial craft shows.

FORGE & FORM Map pp236-7 *Jewelry*
☎ 604-684-6298; 1334 Cartwright St; ⏰ 10am-6pm; bus 50
Visiting stars like the *X-Files'* Gillian Anderson have climbed the steps of this nondescript trailer to buy exquisite works by renowned local gold and silversmiths, who are best known for their unique gemstone tension settings.

GALLERY OF BC CERAMICS

Map pp236-7   *Art & Crafts*
☎ 604-669-5645; www.bcpotters.com; 1359 Cartwright St; ⏰ 10am-6pm, closed Mon Jan-Mar; bus 50
The BC Potters Guild runs exhibitions for member artists and sells striking ceramic works, from functional bowls and cups to figurative sculpture and ritual objects of art. Artists range from Emily Carr grad newbies to potters with international reputations.

MAIWA HANDPRINTS

Map pp236-7   *Art & Crafts*

☎ 604-669-3939; www.maiwa.com; Net Loft, 1666 Johnston St; 10am-6pm; bus 50

Textiles, both local and global, are the name of the game at Maiwa. It's like stepping into a South Asian bazaar, where you're surrounded by indigo and vegetable-dyed fabric quilts, clothes and beautiful art books. Fabric and dyeing workshops are taught regularly, and Maiwa sells a complete selection of dyes, fabric paints and other tools of the trade.

MALASPINA PRINTMAKERS GALLERY

Map pp236-7   *Art & Crafts*

☎ 604-688-1724; www.malaspinaprintmakers.com; 1555 Duranleau St; 11am-5pm; bus 50

This studio gallery displays more than 1000 original lithograph, monotype, relief and intaglio prints by contemporary BC artists, whose styles range from photo-realism to abstraction. Ask about the hands-on printmaking workshops.

SILK WEAVING STUDIO

Map pp236-7   *Fashion*

☎ 604-687-7455; www.silkweavingstudio.com; 1551 Johnston St; 10am-5pm; bus 50

Weavers turn out luxurious, hand-dyed silk dresses, blouses, scarves, shawls, lingerie, belts and hats in a rainbow of colors. Visitors are welcome to wander through the small waterfront studio and watch the weaving process in action. Silk yarns and fabrics are sold, too.

WEST SIDE
FAIRVIEW

The section of Broadway just west of Main St is known as 'Fleece Row' for its preponderance of camping, hiking and expedition equipment stores

EUROPE BOUND OUTFITTERS

Map pp236-7   *Outdoors Equipment*

☎ 604-874-7456; www.europebound.com; 195 W Broadway; 10am-6pm Sat-Wed, 10am-7pm Thu, 10am-8pm Fri; bus 9

This nationally known store carries brand-name gear like Columbia and the North Face. Whether you're looking for winter jackets, hydration daypacks, cycling accessories, maps or travel guidebooks, you're bound to get outfitted here.

HOLLYWOOD COWBOYS

Map pp236-7   *Collectibles*

☎ 604-873-9322; 254 W Broadway; noon-6pm Mon-Fri, noon-5pm Sat; bus 9

Who says there isn't any truth in advertising? The aisles at Hollywood Cowboys are filled with movie posters and star memorabilia mixed with cowboy boots and Western wear. The posters are probably the main draw – there are 3000 of them, and choices include some sci-fi and horror greats.

INTERNATIONAL TRAVEL MAPS & BOOKS Map pp236-7 *Books & Maps*

☎ 604-879-3621; 530 W Broadway; 9am-6pm Mon-Fri, 10am-6pm Sat, noon-6pm Sun; bus 9

For maps, atlases, globes and guides covering nearly every region of the world, check ITMB – it publishes 200 titles of its own and distributes 23,000 titles by other manufacturers. Ask the staff any geographic question from Andorra to Zambia, and they'll be able to find the map to answer it.

MOUNTAIN EQUIPMENT CO-OP

Map pp236-7   *Outdoors Equipment*

MEC; ☎ 604-872-7858, 888-847-0770; www.mec.ca; 130 W Broadway; 10am-7pm Mon-Wed, 10am-9pm Thu & Fri, 9am-6pm Sat, 11am-5pm Sun; bus 9

You almost need overnight gear to get around the showroom floor of the largest outdoor-equipment store in Canada, which started out in a humble locker at the University of British Columbia. Ecologically sensitive MEC sells an in-house line of affordable backpacks and backcountry gear, as well as providing a program of workshops, equipment rental and gear repair services. Note that you must pay the $5 lifetime membership fee to make a purchase.

WARRIORS AND WONDERS

Map pp236-7   *Specialty*

☎ 604-875-1867; 3381 Cambie St; 11am-7pm Mon-Fri, 11am-5pm Sat & Sun; bus 15

If you're a Dungeons & Dragons or *Lord of the Rings* fantasy aficionado – or just a plain old sword collector – you'll want to stop in here to peruse the Roman daggers, double-bladed battle axes, leather scabbards and Sword of Arwen. It'll probably be easier to get home on the airplane if you purchase some of W&W's other items, like its Buddha, fairy, dragon and gargoyle figurines.

SOUTH GRANVILLE

They don't call it Gallery Row for nothing: A short walk south of Granville Island, Granville St is chock-a-block with fine art galleries (see the boxed text below), antique stores and high-end toggeries that will thin your wallet. **Mayfair News** (Map pp236-7; ☎ 604-738-8951; 1535 W Broadway; ☯ 8am-10:30pm Mon-Fri, 9am-10:30pm Sat, 9am-10pm Sun; bus 10) is the place to go for newspapers and magazines from around the world.

CHAPTERS Map pp236-7 *Books & Magazines*
☎ 604-731-7822; www.chapters.indigo.ca; 2505 Granville St; ☯ 9am-10pm Mon-Sat, 11am-10pm Sun; bus 10
Chapters, which merged not long ago with Indigo Books, is Canada's bookselling juggernaut. This outlet has two big floors, which are filled with magazines, books, CDs and DVDs catering to the masses. Some of the nice touches include the couch seating upstairs in front of the fish tank; you'll find it just north of the children's area.

LEONA LATTIMER
Map pp236-7 *Aboriginal Art & Crafts*
☎ 604-732-4556; www.lattimergallery.com; 1590 W 2nd Ave; ☯ 10am-6pm Mon-Sat, 11am-5pm Sun; bus 50
This gallery sells some of the city's more affordable northwest coast gold and silver jewelry, drums, soapstone sculptures, steam bent boxes and masks. The interior replicates a traditional longhouse, and there's no pressure from staff toward visitors who just want to come in for a look-see.

Art Galleries

A good way to see a cross-section of contemporary Canadian art in various media, even if you're not in the market to buy, is to visit some of Vancouver's private studios and galleries. You'll find excellent listings in *Preview* (www.preview-art.com), a free quarterly gallery guide available at most galleries, and the *Georgia Straight* (p214). Most galleries are clustered downtown and along South Granville's Gallery Row. All of the following host rotating exhibitions by international and Canadian artists in several media.

Downtown & West End

Buschlen Mowatt Fine Arts (Map pp230-3; ☎ 604-682-1234; 1445 W Georgia St; ☯ 10am-6pm Mon-Sat, noon-5pm Sun; bus 240) Considered the city's foremost mainstream gallery.

Exposure Gallery (Map pp230-3; ☎ 604-688-9501; 851 Beatty St; ☯ noon-5pm Thu-Sun; SkyTrain Stadium) Specializing in photography.

Rendez-Vous Gallery (Map pp230-3; ☎ 604-687-7466; 671 Howe St; ☯ 10am-5:30pm Mon-Sat, 11am-5pm Sun; SkyTrain Granville) Contemporary paintings and sculptures by Canadian artists.

South Granville

Bau-Xi Gallery (Map pp236-7; ☎ 604-733-7011; 3045 Granville St; ☯ 10am-5:30pm Mon-Sat, noon-4pm Sun; bus 10)

Diane Farris Gallery (Map pp236-7; ☎ 604-737-2629; 1590 W 7th Ave; ☯ 10am-5:30pm Tue-Fri, 10am-5pm Sat; bus 10)

Douglas Udell Gallery (☎ 604-736-8900; 1558 W 6th Ave; ☯ 10am-5pm Tue-Sat; bus 10)

Equinox Gallery (Map pp236-7; ☎ 604-736-2405; 2321 Granville St; ☯ 10am-5pm Tue-Sat; bus 10) Modern works.

Petley-Jones Gallery (Map pp236-7; ☎ 604-732-5353; 2235 Granville St; ☯ 10am-6pm Mon-Sat; bus 10) Historical European, Canadian and American works.

Uno Langmann Ltd (Map pp236-7; ☎ 604-736-8825; 2117 Granville St; ☯ 10am-5pm Tue-Sat; bus 10) Eighteenth-to-20th-century paintings plus silver, objets d'art and antique furniture.

Also keep an eye out for Salt Spring watercolorist **Jill Louise Campbell**, who at the time of research, was planning to open a gallery on Granville St at 7th Ave.

MARTHA STURDY Map pp236-7 *Art & Crafts*
☎ 604-737-0037; www.marthasturdy.com; 3039 Granville St; 🕐 10am-6pm Mon-Sat, noon-5pm Sun; bus 10

The cast-resin homewares, glass works and hand-crafted jewelry of this famed Vancouver designer have been photographed and celebrated by *Vogue* magazine and have been exhibited in museums all the way across North America. Sturdy's trademark brass dining tables, blocky chairs and steel candleholders, as well as her chili pepper–red lamps will make any home museum-worthy.

OSCAR'S Map pp236-7 *Books & Magazines*
☎ 604-731-0553; 1533 W Broadway; 🕐 9am-9pm Mon-Fri, 10am-6pm Sat & Sun; bus 10

Browsing Oscar's collection of arty coffee-table books and photographic catalogs is a treat for sore eyes. The whole city buys its calendars here each year, thanks to the great selection and reasonable prices.

ZONDA NELLIS Map pp236-7 *Fashion*
☎ 604-736-5668; www.zondanellis.com; 2203 Granville St; 🕐 10am-5pm Mon-Fri, 11am-5pm Sat; bus 10

Aretha Franklin and one of those princesses of Monaco are fans of this expensive Vancouver designer's hand-woven and hand-painted evening wear. Nellis is known for her ability to knead luxurious fabrics into simple styles. She also creates a line of accessories, including gold-embossed cushions, beaded necklaces and velvet scarves.

KITSILANO

Though Kits has been well and truly gentrified for years now, a whiff of hippie-ness still lingers like the scent of patchouli. The neighborhood is rife with Birkenstock stores, hemp shops, crystal-swinging bookstores, yoga-wear retailers (this is where the lululemon craze began; see p156) and socially conscious merchants, generously layered among the upscale clothing boutiques and homeware shops. Broadway and 4th Aves are the commercial drags.

Among the plentiful outdoor-equipment stores is the **Sports Exchange** (Map pp238-9; ☎ 604-739-8990; 2151 Burrard St; 🕐 10am-6pm Mon-Thu & Sat, 10am 8pm Fri, noon-5pm Sun; bus 4), a consignment sporting goods store excellent for picking up used mountain bikes and other gear.

For guidebooks, maps and travel accessories, visit the **Travel Bug** (Map pp238-9; ☎ 604-737-1122; 3065 W Broadway; 🕐 10am-6pm Mon-Wed & Sat, 10am-7pm Thu & Fri, noon-5:30pm Sun; bus 9) or **Wanderlust** (Map pp238-9; ☎ 604-739-2182; 1929 W 4th Ave; 🕐 10am-7pm Mon-Fri, 10am-6pm Sat, noon-5pm Sun; bus 4).

Shopping – West Side

BANYEN BOOKS & SOUND
Map pp238-9 *Books & Magazines*
☎ 604-737-8858; www.banyen.com; 3608 W 4th Ave; 🕐 10am-9pm Mon-Fri, 10am-8pm Sat, 11am-7pm Sun; bus 4

Walk into an oasis of incense and sacred music, where yoga mats are stacked against the walls. Categories that wouldn't be given much shelf space at other bookstores – Tibetan Buddhism, herbalism, organic gardening and the like – enjoy entire rows here.

BROADWAY SHOE SALON
Map pp238-9 *Shoes*
☎ 604-731-1410; 2809 W Broadway; 🕐 9:30am-6pm Mon-Thu & Sat, 9:30am-7pm Fri, noon-6pm Sun; bus 9

This modest shop sells well-priced Birkenstocks, Naot sandals from Israel, and other comfy, durable footwear from Europe and beyond. It's got lots of shoes in specialty widths, too.

Top Five Bookstores
- Duthie Books (p164)
- Women in Print (p165)
- Pulp Fiction (p158)
- Banyen Books & Sound (left)
- Sophia Books (p154)

CANDY AISLE Map pp238-9 *Sweets*
☎ 604-739-3330; 2083 W 4th Ave; 🕐 10am-6pm Sun-Wed, 10am-9pm Thu-Sat; bus 4

It's enough to make even Willy Wonka drool with envy: Candy Aisle has amassed simply hundreds of chocolate bar brands from around the world, so the homesick in Vancouver can stock up on Twirls, Flakes and other Cadbury products; Aussie Tim Tams and Violet Crumbles; also to be found are lollipops, sours, jelly beans and gum.

COMICSHOP

Map pp238-9   *Comics & Collectibles*

☎ 604-738-8122; 2089 W 4th Ave; ✪ 11am-6pm
Mon-Tue, Thu & Sat, 11am-7pm Wed, 11am-8pm Fri,
noon-5pm Sun; bus 4

This 30-year-old store carries an impressive
selection of new and used comics. Upstairs
contains back issues, rare and underground
comics, plus the $1 bin. The ground floor
houses kids' comics, mature-reader graphic
novels, pop-culture books along the lines of
Hong Kong cinema history or Barney Fife biog-
raphy, action figures, posters and T-shirts.

DOES YOUR MOTHER KNOW?

Map pp238-9   *Books & Magazines*

☎ 604-730-1110; 2139 W 4th Ave; ✪ 11am-10pm;
bus 4

Scads of mainstream and special-interest magazines, covering everything from jewelry making
to imported cars and high fashion to naughty
photos (but with well-written articles, of course),
sit beside international newspapers.

DUTHIE BOOKS

Map pp238-9   *Books & Magazines*

☎ 604-732-5344; 2239 W 4th Ave; ✪ 9am-9pm Mon-
Fri, 9am-6pm Sat, 10am-6pm Sun; bus 4

Many Vancouverites swear their allegiance to
Duthie's – Vancouver's longest-running book
retailer – despite financial troubles that have
left it with just this one outlet. It's bright and
airy, with solid chairs and stools to perch on
while thumbing through the good fiction, Canadian and international sections.

HOPE UNLIMITED Map pp238-9 *Art & Crafts*
☎ 604-732-4438; 2206 W 4th Ave; ✪ 10am-6pm
Sun-Wed, 10am-7pm Thu-Sat, extended in summer;
bus 4

Hope Unlimited selects its giftware stock –
beaded jewelry, candles, paper and more –
based not only on its appeal, but also on its
social and environmental impact. More than
75% of items are Canadian-made. The store
donates 10% of profits to charities, such as
the YWCA, Children International and AIDS
Vancouver.

KIDSBOOKS Map pp238-9 *Books & Magazines*
☎ 604-738-5335; 3083 W Broadway; ✪ 9:30am-6pm
Mon-Thu & Sat, 9:30am-9pm Fri, noon-5pm Sun; bus 9

If your children don't lose themselves in this
store, then you just might. Kidsbooks has a
fabulous collection of every kind of children's

*Clothing and other goodies at Kitsilano
Hemp Company (below)*

book imaginable, plus it stocks assorted toys
and games.

KITSILANO HEMP COMPANY

Map pp238-9   *Specialty Fashion*

☎ 604-730-1865; 2918 W 4th Ave; ✪ noon-5pm Sun-
Fri, 11am-6pm Sat; bus 4

The 'hempire' stocks clothes, jewelry, pipes
and personal care products, like lotions and
lip balm made with the eponymous herb. The
store has some famous customers: Tommy
Chong came in and bought a marijuana-leaf
bandana. Woody Harrelson partook in a chess
game and drum jam, then proclaimed the
HempCo 'the coolest' hemp store he'd ever
seen.

PD'S HOT SHOP

Map pp238-9   ***Outdoors Equipment***

☎ 604-739-7796; www.skullskates.com; 2868 W 4th
Ave; ✪ noon-6pm Mon-Sat; bus 4

PD's sells its own Skull Skates brand of skate-
boards, snowboards, skimboards, BMX bikes
and clothing. The company has been around
forever – 'skating since you were swimming
in dad's nutsack,' as the official motto goes.
It remains *the* place for the boarding scene,
and provides resources like a skatepark directory and tidal pool charts for skimboarding.
Cash only.

Shopping – West Side

Two other stores cater to boarders:

Pacific Boarder (Map pp238-9; ☎ 604-734-7245; 1793 W 4th Ave; ⏰ 10am-6pm Mon-Wed & Sat, 10am-8pm Thu & Fri, 11am-5pm Sun; bus 4) For aquatic pursuits. **Westbeach** (Map pp238-9; ☎ 604-731-6449; 1766 W 4th Ave; ⏰ 10am-6pm Mon-Wed & Sat, 10am-8pm Thu & Fri, 11am-6pm Sun; bus 4) Founded by the same marketing genius who started lululemon, and carrying surf, skateboard and snowboard gear.

SIGGE'S SPORTS VILLA

Map pp238-9   *Outdoors Equipment*
☎ 604-731-8818; 2077 W 4th Ave; ⏰ 9:30am-6pm Mon-Wed & Sat, 9:30am-9pm Thu & Fri, 11am-5pm Sun Oct-Mar, 10am-6pm Mon-Thu & Sat, 10am-8pm Fri, 11am-5pm Sun Sep & Apr, closed May-Aug; bus 4
Sigge's is dedicated to cross-country gear, providing all the skis, boots, poles, waxes and wisdom you'll ever need to glide through the region's parks. The store also rents equipment, provides lessons, and sponsors day and weekend trips; the Sunday wine-and-cheese outings to Manning Park are legendary (see p145).

TEN THOUSAND VILLAGES

Map pp238-9   *Art & Crafts*
☎ 604-730-6831; 2909 W Broadway; ⏰ 10am-6pm Mon-Sat, 11am-5pm Sun; bus 9

You'll find decorative paper from Bangladesh, baskets from Vietnam, hammocks, drums, clothing and other 'fairly traded' handicrafts from around the world. The store is part of a non-profit program that buys from 120 artisan groups in 30 countries; outlets are located throughout North America.

WOMEN IN PRINT

Map pp238-9   *Books & Magazines*
☎ 604-732-4128; www.womeninprint.ca; 3566 W 4th Ave; ⏰ 10am-6pm Mon-Sat, noon-5pm Sun; bus 4
This female-owned store focuses on books by, for and about women and carries an extensive collection of lesbian works. It's one of the leading places to come to find out about women-centered events in Vancouver, many of which happen on-site in the form of readings and workshops.

ZULU RECORDS Map pp238-9   *Music*
☎ 604-738-3232; www.zulurecords.com; 1972 W 4th Ave; ⏰ 10:30am-7pm Mon-Wed, 10:30am-9pm Thu & Fri, 9:30am-6pm Sat, noon-6pm Sun; bus 4
Zulu is Vancouver's best-vibe independent modern music store for vinyl and hard-to-find imports, plus used CDs. Check out any of the 30,000 titles at the sweet listening booths with retro chairs. Zulu also sponsors and sells tickets to most of the hip shows that come to town.

GREATER VANCOUVER

Many tourists ride the SeaBus to check out North Vancouver's **Lonsdale Quay Market** (p75). West Vancouver's **Park Royal** (Map pp228-9) has the distinction of being Canada's first shopping mall.

In Richmond, aka Vancouver's 'new' Chinatown, Asian-style malls abound near No 3 Rd, reachable from downtown via bus 98 B-Line. Traditional grocers and herbalists to cutting-edge Japanese designers have set up shop around **Aberdeen Centre** (Map pp228-9; ☎ 604-273-1234; 4151 Hazelbridge Way), **President Plaza** (Map pp228-9; ☎ 604-270-8677; 8181 Cambie Rd)

Antique Alley

If you are in the market for vintage kitsch or collectibles, or just enjoy browsing in antique stores, you'll have a field day along **Antique Alley**, near Westminster Quay (Map p228-9) in New Westminster. There are more than a dozen shops open year-round and a summer Saturday flea market. Notable are:

Armstrongs & Fitzgeralds (Map pp228-9; ☎ 604-520-1478; 701B Front St; ⏰ 11am-5pm Tue-Sat, noon-5pm Sun; SkyTrain New Westminster) Well-priced martini shakers, sports memorabilia, cocktail lounge lamps and a revolving assortment of Pez dispensers, plus coffee and homemade cinnamon rolls at the diner counter.

Collectors' Choice Antique Mall (Map pp228-9; ☎ 604-529-1999; 605 Front St; ⏰ 11am-5pm; SkyTrain New Westminster) Antique tableware, retro lunchboxes and old-fashioned bingo sets on consignment, with rapid stock turnover.

and **Yaohan Centre** (Map pp228-9; ☎ 604-231-0601; 3700 No 3 Rd). For a more typical suburban shopping mall, there's **Richmond Centre** (Map pp228-9; ☎ 604-713-7467; 6551 No 3 Rd).

The mother of suburban mega-malls is **Metrotown Centre** (Map pp228-9; ☎ 604-438-2444; off Kingsway between Willingdon and Nelson Aves; SkyTrain Metrotown), a monument to rampant consumerism. Even with 4000 free parking spaces over 11 hectares, it still can be difficult to find a space.

Dorothy Grant (☎ 604-681-0201; www.dorothygrant.com) is a renowned Haida artist who employs traditional motifs throughout her modern collections of clothing and handbags. At the time of research, Grant was in the process of moving her eponymous store; call for the new location.

Sleeping

Sleeping

Booking good-value accommodations is likely to be the thorniest issue in planning your trip to Vancouver. Reservations are absolutely necessary in summer. From Victoria Day through Labour Day – and beyond that for as long as the summer weather holds – decent places to stay are full. If you're arriving during major holidays or special events (p8), such as the Vancouver International Jazz Festival or Vancouver Folk Music Festival, rooms are booked out months in advance.

Accommodation listings in this book are arranged alphabetically, with Cheap Sleeps (budget options) listed at the end of most neighborhood sections. Add room taxes of 17% to most rates quoted here, which is 10% provincial tax and 7% federal goods and services tax (GST), although visitors may be eligible for a refund of the 7% GST (see p215). The exception may be some smaller hostels and B&Bs that don't charge the full tax. The prices quoted in this book are generally for the peak summer season; rates drop by 25% to 50% in the off-season. Typical cancellation fees range from $20 to the entire first night's charge.

At hotels, rates fluctuate wildly from day to day based on occupancy. Mid-range hotels and motels charge $75 to $200 for a double. Once you get over $200 a night, you're in the 'top end' at deluxe establishments with international reputations and very high standards. Such places commonly have swimming pools, fitness rooms, bars and fine restaurants, and valet parking, as well as concierges who can assist your every whim. Vancouver is unusual in that many moderately priced accommodations remain in the otherwise high-rent downtown area. Always ask if parking, local phone calls and high-speed Internet access are included, and inquire about discounts for students, seniors, CAA/AAA members and long-term (eg multi-night, weekly or monthly) stays. Many hotels offer discounts for Internet bookings and special package deals via their own websites. At smaller hotels, B&Bs and guesthouses, you may be able to negotiate a good deal during slow periods if you ask politely.

Cheap Sleeps in this book include hostels and guesthouses offering dormitory beds from $20 to $25 and private rooms (usually with bathroom) starting under $75. Ask about weekly discounts. All the downtown hostels offer Internet access, luggage storage, common

Booking B&Bs

B&Bs average $80 to $125 for a double with shared bathroom, and $95 to $175 with private bathroom. Be forewarned that some B&Bs require a two-night minimum stay, especially on weekends, and that cancellation policies can be harsh. A great place to start looking online is www.bbcanada.com, which has nearly 90 listings in the Vancouver area.

B&B reservation agencies check, list and book rooms in the participating members' homes. The service is free to travelers. When you indicate your preferences, all attempts will be made to find a suitable host. If you plan on staying for more than a few days, these agencies often rent out suites and apartments on a weekly or monthly basis, which is almost always better value than staying at a hotel.

For last-minute reservations, the best place to call is the **TouristInfo Centre** (☎ 604-683-2000; www.tourismvancouver.com). Other reliable booking agencies include:

Canada-West Accommodations (☎ 604-990-6730, 800-561-3223; www.b-b.com) Big registry and 17-plus years booking accommodation throughout BC and Alberta.

Old English B&B Registry (☎ 604-986-5069; www.bandbinn.com) Friendly, long-standing entity that books for Vancouver, environs and Victoria.

Town & Country B&B Service (☎ 604-731-5942; www.townandcountrybedandbreakfast.com) Books several properties in Vancouver, the Lower Mainland and Victoria.

Western Canada B&B Innkeepers Association (☎ 604-255-9199; www.wcbbia.com) Not a booking agency, but it provides a good directory with listings in Vancouver and throughout BC.

kitchens and laundry facilities. Beware some hostels may pull the rug out from under you and renege on booked rooms at busy times.

Note that many places do not have air-conditioned rooms, but that rarely is a problem since Vancouver remains temperate even in high summer. The non-smoking icon is used in listings only if a place is *entirely* non-smoking; the remainder of lodgings usually have both types of rooms available. See the inside front cover of this guidebook for definitions of other text symbols.

The **Tourist InfoCentre** (☎ 604-683-2000; www.tourismvancouver.com) offers a free accommodations reservation service that can be indispensable if you are trying to find a room at the last minute or book a room online. The **Tourism British Columbia reservation service** (☎ 800-435-5622; www.hellobc.com) can also be a great help in finding reasonably priced accommodations. With many rooms at their disposal, its operators can often get you lodging at prices lower than what the hotels may quote you.

DOWNTOWN

Downtown hosts the majority of Vancouver's hotels, both brand-new towers with luxury accommodations and elegant older buildings. Options are clustered around Canada Place and BC Place Stadium, as well as on Howe and Granville Sts. The latter streets are safe but nightlife-oriented, with clubbers coming and going into the wee hours, and panhandlers trying to make a dollar off them.

BOSMAN'S VANCOUVER HOTEL

Map pp230-3 *Motel*

☎ 604-682-3171, 888-267-6267; www.bosmanshotel .com; 1060 Howe St; s/d $119/129; bus 4; **P**

A well-maintained 1970s style motel in the heart of the city, Bosman's is everything most people will ever need in a moderately priced lodging. It's clean, hospitable and well located, with an outdoor pool and kitsch-y restaurant that's good for breakfast. The basic, salmon-pink rooms won't spoil or improve your Vancouver stay, as long as you get one off the ground floor.

BURRARD MOTOR INN Map pp230-3 *Motel*

☎ 604-681-2331, 800-663-0366; www.vancouver -bc.com/burrardmotorinn; 1100 Burrard St; s/d $89/94; bus 2; **P**

Rooms at the Burrard are a bit worn. However, the price is right, the location is convenient, and it works well for families since many of the rooms come with kitchenettes (including stove and refrigerator) for an extra $5. All rooms have TV and phone; some overlook a pretty garden courtyard. There's free parking, and the helpful staff provide fans upon request.

CENTURY PLAZA HOTEL & SPA

Map pp230-3 *Hotel*

☎ 604-687-0575, 800-663-1818; www.century-plaza .com; 1015 Burrard St; r/ste from $169/209; bus 2; **P** $9

The Century Plaza offers the usual business hotel fixings – tastefully decorated rooms, high-

speed Internet access – as well as an indoor pool and steam room, and even a spa if you feel the urge to be pampered via seaweed. Most of the rooms also have en-suite kitchens attached.

COMFORT INN DOWNTOWN

Map pp230-3 *Hotel*

☎ 604-605-4333, 888-605-5333; www.comfortinn .com; 654 Nelson St; r from $139/149 weekday/week-end; bus 4; **P** $11

In the heart of Granville St's theater and club scene, this recently renovated hotel is uncharacteristically swanky for the Comfort Inn chain. The rooms have mod, lively orange and yellow decor; 'superior' rooms (costing $20 more) have a jacuzzi. Amenities include continental breakfast, high-speed Internet access and off-site fitness facility use. Rooms on the lowest floor are cheapest, but overlook a brick wall.

Top Five Downtown Sleeps

- Best historic hotel – **Fairmont Hotel Vancouver** (p170)
- Best boutique hotel – **Wedgewood Hotel** (p172)
- Best penny-pincher – **Victorian Hotel** (p171)
- Best European-style hotel – **Georgian Court Hotel** (p170)
- Best quirky property – **Bosman's Vancouver Hotel** (left)

Fairmont Hotel Vancouver (below)

CROWNE PLAZA HOTEL GEORGIA

Map pp230-3   *Historic Hotel*

☎ 604-682-5566, 800-663-1111; www.hotelgeorgia
.bc.ca; 801 W Georgia St; r from $209; SkyTrain
Granville; Ⓟ $22

The charming Hotel Georgia has the marble, mahogany, chandeliers and brass ornamentation you'd expect from early-20th-century beaux-arts architecture. For this class of hotel, the contemporary, sapphire-blue rooms offer good value, and include high-speed Internet access and CD players, plus fitness-center use. Sinatra and the Rolling Stones stayed here, as did Elvis, who would have enjoyed the deep chocolate cookies now offered in **sen5es** (p94) bakery downstairs.

FAIRMONT HOTEL VANCOUVER

Map pp230-3   *Historic Hotel*

☎ 604-684-3131, 800-441-1414; www.fairmont
.com/hotelvancouver; 900 W Georgia St; r from $309;
SkyTrain Burrard; Ⓟ $25

Built in the 1930s by the Canadian Pacific railroad company, this hotel is one of the largest and most famous in Vancouver, if not Canada, offering all the comforts known to the modern hospitality industry, including an excellent fitness facility and indoor pool. The Grand Lady boasts 556 rooms under her green oxidized-copper roof; ask about 'getaway packages,' which reduce rates.

FOUR SEASONS HOTEL

Map pp230-3   *Luxury Hotel*

☎ 604-689-9333; www.fourseasons.com/vancouver;
791 W Georgia St; r from $320; SkyTrain Granville;
Ⓟ $25

Vancouver's highest-rated hotel juts 28 stories above the Pacific Centre shopping complex. The high-ceilinged rooms seem gigantic and come with the expected amenities. Features like the waterfall-laden garden terrace and indoor and outdoor pools add to the opulence. The hotel pays special attention to kids, offering a children's video library and bedtime milk and cookies.

GEORGIAN COURT HOTEL

Map pp230-3   *Hotel*

☎ 604-682-5555, 800-663-1155; www.georgiancourt
.com; 773 Beatty St; s/d from $165/180; SkyTrain
Stadium; Ⓟ $9

The old-world, European-style Georgian Court offers fabulous service in the center of the entertainment district (by the sports arenas and big playhouses). It's the kind of place where a grandfather clock chimes away in the lobby and bow-tied staff are attentive to your every need. The blue-and-taupe, sun-filled rooms have high-speed Internet access, and there's a fitness center with sauna.

HOLIDAY INN HOTEL & SUITES
DOWNTOWN
Map pp230-3   *Hotel*

☎ 604-684-2151, 800-663-9151; www.hivancouver
downtown.com; 1110 Howe St; r from $189; bus 4;
Ⓟ $12

Near Davie St, this place is above par for a chain hotel, though still a bit pricey. The 24-hour indoor pool and health club are nice touches. Rooms are decent sized, with high-speed Internet access, and some have kitchens; rooms in Tower 2 have little balconies. Booking 21 days in advance knocks the price down by about 25%.

HOWARD JOHNSON HOTEL

Map pp230-3   *Hotel*

☎ 604-688-8701, 800-446-4656; www.hojovancouver
.com; 1176 Granville St; weekday/weekend r from
$139/149, ste from $169/179; bus 4; Ⓟ $10

While it's not glamorous, this hotel does rank as one of HoJo's nicer properties. The suites come with a microwave, refrigerator and high speed Internet access. Use of the fitness facility across the street is complimentary for guests.

JOLLY TAXPAYER HOTEL

Map pp230-3 *Hotel*

☎ 604-681-3550; www.jollytaxpayerhotel.com; 828 W Hastings St; s/d/ste with breakfast $70/80/130; SkyTrain Waterfront

The Jolly Taxpayer is a British-style lodging, with two floors of rooms above a warm, cheerful pub. It's a lovely concept, location (two blocks from the Canada Place) and price, but the utilitarian rooms are a bit faded. Toilets and sinks are en suite, with showers down the hall.

KINGSTON HOTEL Map pp230-3 *Hotel*

☎ 604-684-9024, 888-713-3304; www.kingstonhotel vancouver.com; 757 Richards St; s without bathroom $48-58, d without bathroom $68-78, d with bathroom $98-115, tw with bathroom $98-135; SkyTrain Granville; Ⓟ $10

Conveniently located by Robson Square, the malls and sports arenas, the Kingston is a European-style pension regarded as one of the city's best bargains. Rooms are basic (all have phones; only 10 have a private bathroom and TV), but the place is clean, comfy and well run. Extras include continental breakfast, sauna, coin laundry and TV lounge. Prices may rise by $20 or so after a planned renovation.

METROPOLITAN HOTEL

Map pp230-3 *Luxury Hotel*

☎ 604-687-1122, 800-667-2300; www.metropolitan .com; 645 Howe St; r from $279; SkyTrain Granville; Ⓟ $23

This swish hotel defines elegance on modern terms. It's not avant-garde, but provides subtle reminders of luxury, like Italian linens, earth-toned decor, marble washrooms and soaker tubs. Extras include an indoor pool, health club with squash courts, and high-speed Internet access, plus a top restaurant, **Diva** (p94).

PAN PACIFIC HOTEL

Map pp230-3 *Luxury Hotel*

☎ 604-662-8111, in Canada 800-663-1515, in USA 800-937-1515; www.vancouver.panpacific.com; 999 Canada Place; r with city/harbor view from $429/479; SkyTrain Waterfront; Ⓟ $20

This is a deluxe convention hotel inside Canada Place with every facility imaginable, including three restaurants, a state-of-the-art health club and outdoor heated pool, open year-round. The rooms are huge and aren't filled with furniture, giving the impression that you're actually outdoors as you look out the floor-to-ceiling windows.

SANDMAN HOTEL – DOWNTOWN VANCOUVER Map pp230-3 *Hotel*

☎ 604-681-2211, 800-726-3626; www.sandman.ca; 180 W Georgia St; r from $159; SkyTrain Stadium; Ⓟ $8

Sandman is a Canadian chain, and the rooms here are bland in that chain kind of way, but spacious and equipped with Internet access. The hotel is usefully located at downtown's eastern edge, near BC Place, and has an indoor swimming pool and health club.

SHERATON WALL CENTRE HOTEL

Map pp230-3 *Luxury Hotel*

☎ 604-331-1000, 800-663-9255; www.sheraton wallcentre.com; 1088 Burrard St; r from $269; bus 2; Ⓟ $20

This stylish high-rise – Vancouver's tallest building – has a distinctly arty and modern atmosphere. It comprises two towers; the north one is newer, but both have fantastic ocean, mountain and city views that you'll see via the floor-to-ceiling windows. Business amenities abound, and there's an indoor pool and fitness center.

ST REGIS HOTEL Map pp230-3 *Hotel*

☎ 604-681-1135, 800-770-7929; www.stregishotel .com; 602 Dunsmuir St; r/ste from $119/129; SkyTrain Granville

A low-key landmark since 1916, the St Regis is definite value, considering its location right in downtown's core. The cheaper rooms are fairly basic and small, but ask about upgrading for $10 to the 5th floor's nicer rooms. Prices include continental breakfast and off-site fitness facility use. Loads of coffee shops, budget travel agencies and cybercafés surround the 'Reeg.' No parking is available on site; the closest lot is at Pacific Centre Mall ($12 per day).

VICTORIAN HOTEL Map pp230-3 *Hotel*

☎ 604-681-6369, 877-681-6369; www.victorianhotel .ca; 514 Homer St; s/d without bathroom from $69/79, s/d with bathroom $109/119; SkyTrain Granville; Ⓟ $10

This place should be your first stop in Vancouver. It's a beautifully renovated Victorian building that's been converted into a European-style pension. The 27 spick-and-span rooms vary in layout and color, but all have glossy hardwood floors, down duvets, sturdy wood furnishings, phone and TV; many have bay windows. Muffins, tea and coffee are served each morning.

WEDGEWOOD HOTEL

Map pp230-3   *Boutique Hotel*

☎ 604-689-7777, 800-663-0666; www.wedgewood
hotel.com; 845 Hornby St; r $295-900; bus 5; P $19
Combining European elegance with a North
American flair for good service, this 83-room
vintage boutique hotel is a favorite of visiting
dignitaries and stars, and continually ranks as
one of the world's best lodgings in travel industry surveys. Guests are pampered in a personal-
ized way, and treated to homemade cookies,
cordless phones and a health club. Stately Bac-
chus (p125) is the ground-floor bar.

CHEAP SLEEPS

HOSTELLING INTERNATIONAL
VANCOUVER CENTRAL Map pp230-3 *Hostel*

☎ 604-685-5335, 888-203-8333; www.hihostels.ca;
1025 Granville St; members/nonmembers dm
$25.50/29.50, r without bathroom $62.50/71.50, r with
bathroom $74.50/83.50 incl tax; bus 4
This is one of the nicest hostels you'll see, located
right in the middle of Granville St. The place has a
mod vibe with velvet curtains and walls painted
in Tuscan yellow and deep reds. Amenities are
top-notch – private rooms have TVs, and most
have bathrooms and air-con. Definitely splurge
the extra $12 for the en-suite bathroom as those
rooms are much nicer. Dorm rooms have four
beds. Free shuttle to Pacific Central Station and
HI's Jericho and Downtown hostels.

SAMESUN VANCOUVER
BACKPACKER LODGE Map pp230-3 *Hostel*

☎ 604-682-8226, 877-562-2783; www.samesun.com;
1018 Granville St; 4-bed dm $23.50/27 with/without
discount card, r without bathroom $53, r with bath-
room $60; bus 4
Loud music and loud conversations are the
norm at this youthful, bright-colored hostel,
but it's the kind of place where that works
just fine. Located amid the Granville St entertainment strip, the lodge's features include a
rooftop patio, nightly pub/club runs with
no–lining up access, good apartment and job
boards, bike storage, licensed lounge with
pool table and shuttles to Kelowna in winter.

YWCA HOTEL Map pp230-3 *Hostel*

☎ 604-895-5830, 800-663-1424; www.ywcahotel
.com; 733 Beatty St; s/d from $59/70, tr $99; SkyTrain
Stadium; P $8
Near BC Place Stadium, this outstanding Y has
the feel of a 'real' hotel, and it accommodates

men, women, couples or families. It's a bustling
place with a communal kitchen on every other
floor and 155 rooms in various configurations
ranging from singles to five-bed dorms. All
rooms have a refrigerator and air-con; most have
TVs. Bathrooms come in private, semi-private (ie
shared with one other room) and down-the-
hall varieties. There's laundry and Internet access
on-site, and an off-site fitness center and pool
nearby. Weekly rates and discounts for students,
seniors and YWCA members are available.

GASTOWN

Hotels abound on Hastings St, three or four
blocks on either side of Main St. These are
cheap, but shabby; many are residence
hotels with unsavory characters and high
crime rates.

CHEAP SLEEPS

CAMBIE INTERNATIONAL HOSTEL

Map p234   *Hostel*

☎ 604-684-6466, 877-395-5335; www.cambiehostels
.com; 300 Cambie St; 4/6/8-bed dm $18.50/16.50/15.50,
tw $22.50, r $45; bus 3
It shares a building with one of the most fun,
down-to-earth pubs downtown, so expect the
same from this bunkhouse – it's like staying
over after a house party. The sleeping rooms are
OK, with four to eight oversized beds, and some
en-suite bathrooms and showers. Weekly rates
are available. Continental breakfast, Internet
access, laundry, 24-hour reception, TV lounge,
and free pick-ups from Pacific Central Station or
the airport round out the package. The Cambie operates a second, somewhat more sedate
hostel (Map pp230-3; ☎ 604-684-7757; 515 Seymour St) downtown with similar amenities.

YALETOWN

Stay here, and you're in the thick of sizzling
restaurants and nightlife.

OPUS HOTEL Map pp230-3   *Boutique Hotel*
☎ 604-642-6787; 866-642-6787; www.opushotel
.com; 322 Davie St; r from $289; bus 1; Ⓟ $25
One of Vancouver's newest top-end hotels, it
has taken on the principle of 'less is more…but
more is more as well' – less clutter, more color;
fewer barriers, more windows; less forced
character, a more simple and natural style. Not
to be confused with post-modernistic non-
sense, the oddly shaped furniture is comfortable, and the gutsy colors and open spaces are
refreshing. And how about those glass-walled
bathrooms? It's where the young and fashionable (Justin Timberlake, Britney Spears etc) stay
when they come to town.

WEST END

The West End has loads of options, from
B&Bs to standard business-class hotels.
Also prevalent are former apartment buildings that been converted into suite-style
properties, with kitchens and a bit of room
to spread out. Robson St is rife with places
between Bute and Nicola Sts, which is a
glass half-full/half-empty situation: you're
steps away from all the restaurants and
shops, but it's busy and noisy 24/7.

ASTON ROSELLEN SUITES
Map pp230-3   *Serviced Apartments*
☎ 604-689-4807, 888-317-6648; www.rosellensuites
.com; 2030 Barclay St; 1/2-bedroom ste $199/249; bus
5; Ⓟ $7.50
Almost in Stanley Park, this nondescript brick
building is not unlike the other apartments
around it – except inside are spacious, tasteful, fully furnished apartments that are the
epitome of home away from home. The staff
understands you're staying at a place like this
because you appreciate a certain amount of
privacy, but they're also there for any needs,
or sights and activity advice as well. Kath-
erine Hepburn used to rent the penthouse.

Top Five West End Sleeps
- Best boutique hotel – **Pacific Palisades** (p175)
- Best views – **Blue Horizon Hotel** (right)
- Best penny-pincher – **Buchan Hotel** (p174)
- Best gay-friendly property – **Nelson House** (p174)
- Best B&B – **Barclay House** (right)

The Rosellen requires a minimum booking
of three nights; a health-club membership is
provided.

BARCLAY HOTEL Map pp230-3   *Hotel*
☎ 604-688-8850; www.barclayhotel.com; 1348
Robson St; s/d/ste from $75/95/129; bus 5; Ⓟ $5
This heritage building has wide hallways and
nice woodwork, but is now a tad faded. The
cheaper rooms are small, though clean; try to
get one off the 1st floor. All rooms have air-
con, TV and phone. There's a licensed lounge
and restaurant, where a continental breakfast
costs $5. Not a bad deal if you're just looking
for a place to lay your head at night.

BARCLAY HOUSE IN THE WEST END
Map pp230-3   *B&B*
☎ 604-605-1351, 800-971-1351; www.barclayhouse
.com; 1351 Barclay St; r $145-235; bus 5; Ⓟ
This peach-colored Victorian B&B, on a leafy
street near Barclay Heritage Square, makes an
excellent retreat. Each of the five rooms has its
own bathroom, soft beds and linens, TV, VCR
(with choices from the video library) and CD
player; four of five rooms have soaker tubs. The
gourmet breakfasts will leave you stuffed. The
front porch and parlor with fireplace beckon
to readers.

BEST WESTERN SANDS HOTEL
Map pp230-3   *Hotel*
☎ 604-682-1831, 800-663-9400; www.rpbhotels.com;
1755 Davie St; r $179-239; bus 5; Ⓟ $7
Across the street from English Bay Beach, this
hotel offers pleasant enough rooms with high-
speed Internet access and cable TV; some have
refrigerators (ask when you book). Continental
breakfasts, a coin-operated laundry, a fitness
room, two bars and a restaurant are also part
of the deal.

BLUE HORIZON HOTEL Map pp230-3   *Hotel*
☎ 604-688-1411, 800-663-1333; www.bluehorizon
hotel.com; 1225 Robson St; r without/with view from
$159/179; bus 5; Ⓟ $10
Views at affordable prices are the selling point
at the sleek, busy Blue Horizon; all rooms
have balconies and sizeable sitting areas
from which to enjoy the environs. Amenities include an indoor pool, fitness center,
Internet access, restaurants and a bar. The
9th floor is the 'Green Floor,' with energy-
efficient lighting, low-flow shower heads and
recycling bins.

BUCHAN HOTEL Map pp230-3 *Hotel*

☎ 604-685-5354, 800-668-6654; www.buchanhotel
.com; 1906 Haro St; s/d without bathroom $69/75, with
bathroom $85/95; bus 5; ℗ $10

A cheerful, tidy heritage property next door to Stanley Park, the Buchan may lack an elevator but it has bags of charm, and its ski and bike storage facilities make this an ideal stopover for sports enthusiasts. The small rooms have TVs but no phones; east-side rooms are a bit brighter. Laundry facilities are a nice touch.

COAST PLAZA HOTEL & SUITES

Map pp230-3 *Hotel*

☎ 604-688-7711, 800-663-1144; www.coasthotels
.com; 1763 Comox St; r from $239, ste from $279; bus
5; ℗ $10

Just off Denman St, this hotel has spectacular views, an indoor pool, exercise room and squash courts. Three floors are devoted to meeting, conference and banquet facilities, plus services for business travelers. Rooms are generous, with floor-to-ceiling windows and balconies; suites have kitchens. Prices drop substantially on weekends.

EMPIRE LANDMARK HOTEL

Map pp230-3 *Hotel*

☎ 604-687-0511, 800-830-6144; www.empireland
markhotel.com; 1400 Robson St; r from $210; bus 5;
℗ $10

The Landmark, affectionately known by locals as 'the eyesore,' is Vancouver's tallest hotel and has the views to prove it. The decor in some rooms is dated; amenities include Internet access and a fitness room. The hotel often has promotions where room rates drop considerably, but if you're paying top dollar (over $200), you're better off elsewhere.

ENGLISH BAY INN Map pp230-3 *B&B*

☎ 604-683-8002, 866-683-8002; www.englishbayinn
.com; 1968 Comox St; r $190-225, ste $330; bus 5; ℗

Each of the five rooms in this pretty, Tudor-style B&B has a private bathroom and nice touches like a four-poster bed. There is an elegant parlor, a formal dining room and small garden where you can relax on a sunny day. The price includes free parking, full breakfast and evening port.

GREENBRIER HOTEL Map pp230-3 *Hotel*

☎ 604-683-4558, 888-355-5888; www.greenbrier
hotel.com; 1393 Robson St; r $99-179; bus 5; ℗

Similar to the Robsonstrasse, Riviera and Barclay, the Greenbrier is a former apartment

building that has been transformed into a hotel with both basic rooms and one-bedroom suites with kitchens. It's nicer than it looks from the outside, but do try to get a room off the parking-lot level.

LISTEL VANCOUVER

Map pp230-3 *Boutique Hotel*

☎ 604-684-8461, 800-663-5491; www.listel-vancou
ver.com; 1300 Robson St; r from $199; bus 5; ℗ $19

This classy place is known as the 'art hotel.' Rooms on the 4th and 5th 'gallery floors' feature original works; rooms on the 'museum floor' display First Nations artwork (curated by UBC's Museum of Anthropology), plus native-carved cedar headboards and armoires. It's situated right in the thick of Robson St, though you wouldn't know it from the soundproof, business traveler–friendly rooms.

NELSON HOUSE Map pp230-3 *B&B*

☎ 604-684-9793, 866-684-9793; www.downtown
bedandbreakfast.com; 977 Broughton St; r $108-198;
bus 5; ℗

This three-story 1907 house has five rooms and a top-floor suite. Each room is themed, eg one looks like a rustic cabin, another is Raj inspired; two share a bathroom. Close to Robson St and Barclay Heritage Square, it offers a full breakfast, fireplaces and a lovely garden. It's gay friendly.

Murano glass chandelier, Pacific Pasilades Hotel (opposite)

O CANADA HOUSE Map pp230-3 *B&B*
☎ 604-688-0555, 877-688-1114; www.ocanadahouse
.com; 1114 Barclay St; r $185-255; bus 5; Ⓟ

The seven rooms here are dripping with Victorian furnishings and charm. And history – it's where Ewing Buchan wrote the lyrics to Canada's national anthem. The beds are comfy, and each room has a TV, VCR, refrigerator and phone. Guests are treated to a full breakfast, all-day baked goods to munch on and a sherry hour each evening.

OCEANSIDE HOTEL Map pp230-3 *Hotel*
☎ 604-682-5641, 877-506-2326; www.oceanside
-hotel.com; 1847 Pendrell St; r $150; bus 5; Ⓟ

While the decor is somewhat fusty, the Oceanside's digs near English Bay Beach and Stanley Park, coupled with its roominess (all accommodations are one-bedroom suites) and full kitchens, make it a family favorite. Parking is free; rooms have phones and cable TV.

PACIFIC PALISADES HOTEL
Map pp230-3 *Boutique Hotel*
☎ 604-688-0461, 800-663-1815; www.pacific
palisadeshotel.com; 1277 Robson St; r/ste from
$195/275; bus 5; Ⓟ $25

The hip, low-attitude Pacific Palisades has several fun and unusual features: an eye-popping, retro color scheme, mini-bar selection including Clif Bars and Cracker Jacks, complimentary wine hour in the on-site art gallery and free yoga classes. Rooms are big and sunny, with high-speed Internet access. There is also an on-site health club and indoor pool complete with a kids' play area.

RIVIERA SUITES HOTEL Map pp230-3 *Hotel*
☎ 604-685-1301, 888-699-5222; www.rivieraon
robson.com; 1431 Robson St; r $128-148; bus 5; Ⓟ

The Riv is another of Robson St's many converted apartment buildings, on par with the nearby Robsonstrasse and Greenbrier hotels. Rooms are cheaply furnished, but have full kitchens, balconies, decent views, TVs and free parking.

ROBSONSTRASSE HOTEL & SUITES
Map pp230-3 *Hotel*
☎ 604-687-1674, 888-667-8877; www.robsonstrasse
hotel.com; 1394 Robson St; r/ste from $119/149; bus
5; Ⓟ

Many travelers have recommended this place, with its large rooms, helpful staff and accessible Robson St location. The rooms are furnished in a standard, chain-hotel kind of way, and have

a kitchenette, Internet access and cable TV. There's also free parking and guest laundry.

SUNSET INN TRAVEL APARTMENTS
Map pp230-3 *Serviced Apartments*
☎ 604-688-2474, 800-786-1997; www.sunsetinn
.com; 1111 Burnaby St; studio $168-188, ste $178-218;
bus 6; Ⓟ

Yes, it's another converted apartment hotel, but what sets it apart is its quiet location off Robson St, yet is still close to the action and Sunset Beach. Each studio or one-bedroom suite is substantial, and features a balcony, fully equipped kitchen, cable TV, phone and dataport, plus free parking, an exercise room and laundry.

SYLVIA HOTEL Map pp230-3 *Hotel*
☎ 604-681-9321; www.sylviahotel.com; 1154 Gilford
St; r $90-250, ste $165-180; bus 5; Ⓟ $7

Built in 1912 and named after the owner's daughter, the beloved, ivy-covered Sylvia enjoys a prime location on English Bay close to Stanley Park. While the lobby charms with its stained glass, red carpet and granite steps, the rooms are nothing special; 23 have kitchens. Still, you won't find waterside accommodation for less money. Families love it here, and many return for visits, so book a year ahead for a bayside view in summer. Sylvia's restaurant patio and candlelit bar are neighborhood favorites.

TROPICANA SUITE HOTEL
Map pp230-3 *Hotel*
☎ 604-687-6631; www.tropicanasuites.com; 1361
Robson St; s/d $139/159; bus 5; Ⓟ

The Tropicana offers one-bedroom suites that have either a double or twin beds, plus a living room with sofa bed and full kitchenette. While it's not high class, it's definitely one of the best mid-range options among the many on Robson St, with its clean, spacious rooms, indoor pool and free parking. The upper floors have good views to boot.

WEST END GUEST HOUSE
Map pp230-3 *B&B*
☎ 604-681-2889, 888-546-3327; www.westendguest
house.com; 1362 Haro St; r $139-255; bus 5; Ⓟ

This peaceful pink guesthouse is just a block from Robson St, but it seems like another world. The seven rooms each have fluffy, inviting beds, a private bathroom, TV and modem jack. Guests share the communal parlor, which has both a fireplace and sundeck. Full breakfast and bicycle use are part of the package.

WESTIN BAYSHORE RESORT & MARINA

Map pp230-3 *Luxury Hotel*

☎ 604-682-3377, 800-937-8461; www.westin.com; 1601 Bayshore Dr; r from $229; bus 19; Ⓟ $18.50

The Westin provides high-quality amenities (in- and outdoor pools, fitness center, balconies) from its location on Coal Harbour's waterfront, close to Stanley Park and Denman St. The hotel is famous for having billionaire recluse Howard Hughes stay for three months in 1972; he meandered through the lobby in a bathrobe.

CHEAP SLEEPS

HOSTELLING INTERNATIONAL VANCOUVER DOWNTOWN

Map pp230-3 *Hostel*

☎ 604-684-4565, 888-203-4302; www.hihostels.ca; 1114 Burnaby St; members/nonmembers dm $25.50/29.50, r $62.50/71.50 incl tax; bus 6; Ⓟ

This low-key, hospitable hostel enjoys an excellent location, quiet but close to the action; it's a block from Davie St and a short walk from downtown. Dorms have four beds; all rooms – even the private ones – share a bathroom. Amenities include bike rental and storage, patio, library, Internet, 24-hour reception, on-site budget travel agency, and free shuttle to Pacific Central Station and HI's Jericho and Central hostels.

EAST VANCOUVER

Stay near Commercial Dr, and you'll never lack for food or drink (whether it's caffeinated or otherwise).

ABERDEEN MANSION

Map p235 *Guesthouse*

☎ 604-254-2229; www.aberdeenmansion.com; 1110 Victoria Dr; r $75-200; bus 20; Ⓟ

Situated a block over from Commercial Dr, Aberdeen is a rambling 1910 home, which offers six antique-laden rooms that contain kitchens and cable TV. Guests also have access to laundry facilities and an Internet terminal; the building also has wireless connectivity if you have the facilities in your pc. Breakfast is not included, but can be arranged at a nearby restaurant.

PLACE AT PENNY'S

Map p235 *Serviced Apartments*

☎ 604-254-2229; www.pennysplacevancouver.com; 810 Commercial Dr; r $75-175; bus 20; Ⓟ

Owned by the same folks as Aberdeen Mansion, Penny's is an industrial-looking, apartment-like building right on Commercial Dr. Rooms come with TV, phone, private bathroom and kitchen.

GRANVILLE ISLAND

There's just one real lodging option here, but it's a winner.

GRANVILLE ISLAND HOTEL

Map pp236-7 *Boutique Hotel*

☎ 604-683-7373, 800-663-1840; www.granville islandhotel.com; 1253 Johnston St; s/d room $220/230, s/d ste $250/$260; bus 50; Ⓟ $6

This gracious, 85-room boutique hotel is best regarded for its location, with wonderful views of False Creek, close proximity to the island's famed market, galleries and theaters, and seconds away from downtown or Kitsilano via the mini-ferries. The well-furnished, naturally lit rooms offer high-speed Internet access and cable TV. After a hard day, visitors can soak in the glass-enclosed, vista-friendly spa or knock back a beer in the **Dockside Brewing Company** (p123).

WEST SIDE
FAIRVIEW

There are excellent deals to be had in this neighborhood, and it's a central location to boot.

DOUGLAS GUEST HOUSE

Map pp236-7 *B&B*

☎ 604-872-3060, 888-872-3060; www.dougwin.com; 456 W 13th Ave; s/d without bathroom $65/75, r with bathroom $95-135; bus 15; Ⓟ

Just off Cambie St, this tangerine-colored Edwardian home has six rooms, including two suites that can sleep up to five people. The good-value rooms each have period-style mahogany furniture and cable TV. Rates include a full breakfast and off-street parking. The pleasant staff speak English, German, Dutch, French and Tagalog. It's the smaller sister property to the **Windsor** (below).

PILLOW SUITES

Map pp236-7 *Guesthouse/Extended Stay*

☎ 604-879-8977; www.pillow.net; 2859 Manitoba St; ste $115-170, house $255; bus 9; Ⓟ

Not far from City Hall, between W 12th and 13th Aves, this is a lovely place to stay if you want accommodation for a minimum of five nights. The six executive travel suites are located in a 1910 heritage corner-store building and in two converted coach houses (one of these is rented out in its entirety). All rooms include private bathroom and kitchen.

PLAZA 500 HOTEL Map pp236-7 *Hotel*

☎ 604-873-1811, 800-473-1811; www.plaza500.com; 500 W 12th Ave; r from $129; bus 15; Ⓟ

The Plaza at Cambie St, across from City Hall, has spectacular views from some of its rooms, many of which come with a private balcony, as well as cable TV and Internet access. Amenities include parking and fitness-facility use. The Plaza is tastefully furnished and darn good value.

WINDSOR GUEST HOUSE Map pp236-7 *B&B*

☎ 604-872-3060, 888-872-3060; www.dougwin.com; 325 E 11th Ave; r without bathroom $75-85, r with bathroom $95-105; bus 9; Ⓟ

This 1895 home has 10 quality rooms, six with private bathrooms. It's a sister property to the **Douglas** (above), just a couple of blocks away, and offers the same top-notch amenities (full breakfast, cable TV, parking; multilingual staff).

Cheap Sleeps
SHAUGHNESSY VILLAGE

Map pp236-7 *Serviced Apartments*

☎ 604-736-5511; www.shaughnessyvillage.com; 1125 W 12th Ave; studio $40-70, 2-room ste $70-99, additional person $10; bus 9; Ⓟ $6.50

The high-rise Shaughnessy is actually an apartment building that rents on a short-term basis. The decor is a hoot, where frumpy meets nautical. The least expensive rooms are ship-like; tight-quartered studios with a pull-out bed, cable TV and tiny kitchen. Amenities include free breakfast in the on-site restaurant, pool and fitness room use, discounted ski passes, an on-site cybercafé and shuffleboard courts. Note the location on busy 12th Ave is sometimes noisy.

KITSILANO

Sad but true: Kits' choices are lessening as many of these glorious old homes are getting sold and converted into more lucrative rental properties.

JOHNSON HERITAGE HOUSE B&B

Map pp228-9 *B&B*

☎ 604-266-4175; www.johnsons-inn-vancouver.com; 2278 W 34th Ave; r $125-185; May-Oct; bus 16; Ⓟ

Each of the three rooms has a themed bathroom, and the 10-foot antique gas pump in the Carousel room adds a certain charm. The whole place is filled with knick-knacks, and the fun-loving hosts want you to get the most out of Vancouver with guides to local restaurants and step-by-step directions to Victoria and Whistler. It's located south in moneyed Kerrisdale.

MAPLE HOUSE B&B Map pp238-9 *B&B*

☎ 604-739-5833; www.maplehouse.com; 1533 Maple St; r $85-130; bus 2; Ⓟ

The excellent location sets Maple House apart; it's just off Cornwall Ave, close to Kits Beach and Vanier Park. The blue-shingled heritage building has five rooms, of which the lower-cost ones share a bathroom. The price includes full breakfast, off-street parking and use of the owner's high-speed Internet connection. Staff also can arrange a shuttle service to Whistler.

MICKEY'S KITS BEACH CHALET

Map pp238-9 *B&B*

☎ 604-739-3342, 888-739-3342; www.mickeysbandb .com; 2142 W 1st Ave; r $105-140; bus 2; Ⓟ

Another B&B with a handy location two blocks from Kitsilano Beach, Mickey's has

Sleeping – West Side

three rooms, one with a bathroom and two that share. Each room has cable TV; the Yew room has a fireplace and balcony. There is a wonderful hedged-in garden terrace for relaxation, and a continental-style breakfast is served.

PENNY FARTHING INN Map pp238-9 *B&B*
☎ 604-739-9002; www.pennyfarthinginn.com; 2855 W 6th Ave; s/d $110/120, ste $145-180; bus 2; P
The four rooms at Penny's range from the tiny Lucinda's all the way to the ultra-elegant Bettina's, with hardwood floors, high-back chairs and a wood-burning fireplace. Sophie's is a good choice, with its four-poster bed and

Top Five West Side & Greater Vancouver Sleeps

- Best amenities – **Fairmont Vancouver Airport** (p179)
- Best affordable views – **Plaza 500 Hotel** (p177)
- Best penny-pincher – **Douglas Guest House** (p177)
- Best location by Kits beach– **Maple House B&B** (p177)
- Best B&B – **Penny Farthing Inn** (above)

small balcony overlooking the garden. Breakfast starts with pastries and jams and continues to huge portions of dishes, like smoked salmon crepes. The inn is six blocks from the beach.

Cheap Sleeps
HI VANCOUVER JERICHO BEACH

Map pp238-9 *Hostel*
☎ 604-224-3208, 888-203-4303; www.hihostels.ca; 1515 Discovery St; members/nonmembers dm $25.50/29.50, r $62.50/71.50; ☺ May-Sep; bus 4; P
For the activity minded, this is the place. It's Canada's largest hostel, with 286 beds, and is superbly located seconds from Jericho Beach, close to the restaurants on W 4th Ave and 20 minutes from downtown by bus. Bike rental and storage, volleyball courts, a licensed café, 24-hour reception and Internet access are all part of the package. There are 10 private rooms, and the rest are 14-, 18- or 34-bed dorms.

UBC

Lodging options near the University are surrounded by hiking and biking trails, and are close to sights like the Museum of Anthropology and Wreck Beach, but it's pretty far off the beaten track from everything else.

Cheap Sleeps
PACIFIC SPIRIT HOSTEL

Map p241 *Hostel/University Housing*
☎ 604-822-1000; www.ubcaccommodation.com;
Place Vanier Residence, 1935 Lower Mall; r per person
$24; ☼ May-Aug; bus 4; Ⓟ $5
This hostel, located on UBC's campus, is unique in that its rooms accommodate only one or two people (with either a single or two twin beds) instead of the usual dorm-style setup. There are TV lounges, bathrooms and payphones on each floor; an Internet kiosk is in the lobby or you can pay $9 for a high-speed connection in your room.

GREATER VANCOUVER
North and West Vancouver have some good lodging options if you want to be close to the mountains for skiing or any of the other outdoor activities on offer, but most of these places are not terribly convenient if you plan on spending your time downtown and thereabouts (particularly if you don't have a car).

BEACHSIDE B&B Map pp228-9 *B&B*
☎ 604-922-7773, 800-563-3311; www.beach.bc.ca;
West Van, 4208 Evergreen Ave; r $250; bus 250; Ⓟ
The name doesn't lie – this B&B is right on the beach with views of Point Grey and the Lions Gate Bridge. It's a pretty spectacular setting in ritzy West Van, and offers a seaside whirlpool, good breakfasts and the feeling that the city is far, far away. Each of the three units has its own bathroom, refrigerator, microwave and wireless Internet access.

CAPILANO B&B Map pp228-9 *B&B*
☎ 604-990-8889; www.capilanobb.com; North
Vancouver, 1374 Plateau Dr; r $105-199; bus 236; Ⓟ
This B&B is close to Capilano Rd and the Upper Levels Hwy (Hwy 1). The four airy rooms each have down duvets, private bathroom and cable TV; full breakfast is included.

LONSDALE QUAY HOTEL

Map pp228-9 *Hotel*
☎ 604-986-6111, 800-836-6111; www.lonsdalequay
hotel.com; North Vancouver, 123 Carrie Cates Crt; r
from $129; SeaBus; Ⓟ $7
This hotel has great views of the city, and a unique location 15 minutes from both downtown (via the SeaBus, which can be caught below the Lonsdale Quay Market) and the North Shore's sights. The rooms themselves are fine, though nothing special. Pets are allowed in certain rooms.

THISTLEDOWN HOUSE B&B

Map pp228-9 *B&B*
☎ 604-986-7173, 888-633-7173; www.thistle-down
.com; North Vancouver, 3910 Capilano Rd; r $150-275;
bus 236; Ⓟ
This 1920's house has a country inn feel and is exceptionally good value. It's close to the Capilano Suspension Bridge and Salmon Hatchery, and on the road to Grouse Mountain.

Airport Alternatives

As there are easy connections to/from downtown (p205), most travelers won't need to stay near the airport (or want to, since it's not a very dynamic area). One exception might be visitors going directly to/from Whistler. If you do need airport accommodation, try the following:

Delta Vancouver Airport Hotel & Marina (Map pp228-9; ☎ 604-278-1241, 877-814-7706; www.deltavancouverair
port.com; 3500 Cessna Dr; r from $125; Ⓟ $10) Situated on nine acres fronting the Fraser River, a few kilometers from the airport, the Delta has standard, comfortable, business-class rooms, some with high-speed Internet access (ask when you book). It provides a 24-hour airport shuttle (or free taxi during the wee hours), 24-hour health club and outdoor pool. Look online for price-lowering package deals.

Fairmont Vancouver Airport (Map pp228-9; ☎ 604-207-5200, 800-441-1414; www.fairmont.com; Vancouver International Airport; r from $209; Ⓟ $20.50) You can't stay any closer to the airport than this. Accessed by a walkway next to the US departure hall, this hotel offers sound-proofed, amenity-laden rooms that cater to the jetlagged traveler (remote control drapes, anyone?). The indoor pool, fitness center and spa rejuvenate weary bodies. The hotel offers day-use rooms for people with long layovers (from $129). There's also a floor of allergen-controlled rooms, plus a good restaurant called Globe@YVR.

The gourmet breakfast is scrumptious and, if you're around in the afternoon, there are homemade cakes, pastries and other delicious items for tea. All five rooms have en-suite bathrooms.

There's a cluster of motels with similar prices and facilities in North Vancouver, close to the Lions Gate Bridge and not far from Grouse Mountain. Look along Marine Dr and north up Capilano Rd.

Best Western Capilano Inn & Suites (Map pp228-9; ☎ 604-987-8185, 800-937-8376; www.bestwesterncapilano.com; North Vancouver, 1634 Capilano Rd; r from $119; bus 240; ℗)

Grouse Inn (Map pp228-9; ☎ 604-988-7101, 800-779-7888; www.grouseinn.com; North Vancouver, 1633 Capilano Rd; r from $99; bus 240; ℗)

Excursions

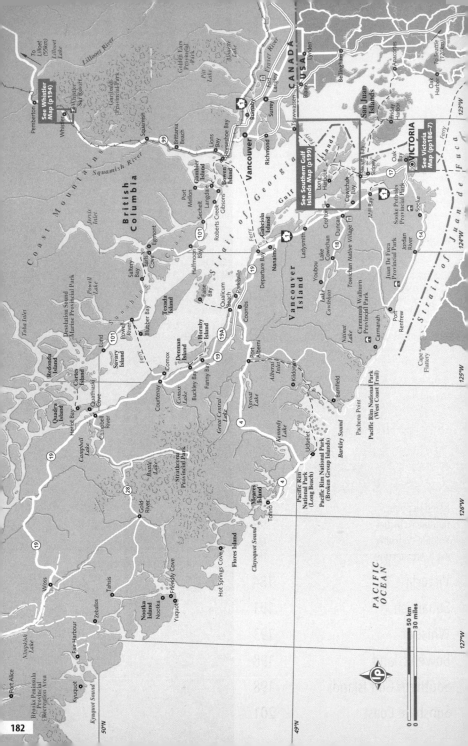

Excursions

And you thought Vancouver's brew of mountain, wilderness, sea and sky was intoxicating? Puh-leez – you've merely sipped on what's available. A couple of hours away by road or ferry (and often both), everything kicks up a notch: the peaks loom larger, the forests grow thicker, the whales are more plentiful and even that pesky rain problem dries up.

Victoria and Whistler are the region's big-ticket excursions. The former is British Columbia's provincial capital, a quiet, traditional seat of Anglophilia that Rudyard Kipling once described as 'Brighton Pavilion with the Himalayas for a backdrop.' With the mildest climate in Canada, its famous gardens and afternoon tea at the Empress Hotel, it's not surprising that two million tourists visit Victoria annually. Many travelers also use the city as a springboard into outdoor adventures, including whale watching and diving.

Whistler is best known as North America's top ski resort, and is fast becoming a year-round destination with its slew of summertime adrenaline-rush activities. Despite getting all gussied up for the 2010 Winter Olympics, the town retains a bit of a nonconformist image and draws people from all walks of life. You can see a baggy pants–wearing snowboarder, a muddied-up mountain biker and a woman in a business suit all downing coffee within 15m of each other.

En route to Whistler along the gorgeous Sea to Sky Hwy, Squamish is the place to go for rock climbing, windsurfing and eagle watching. The Southern Gulf Islands lure artists and counterculture types with bewitching bluffs, bays and teensy, secluded communities. The Sunshine Coast can be relied upon to deliver – it really enjoys more bright days than anywhere else on the mainland, making it a haven for recreation.

And for those who think they have no time for excursions when visiting Vancouver: consider little Bowen Island, just a stone's throw from the mainland.

The prices listed in this chapter are for peak season, which runs from late May to early September. Whistler is the exception, when winter is prime time. During the off-season, many places reduce their hours and some even close entirely.

ISLAND HOPPING

You won't go wrong visiting any of the region's islands, so let time be the deciding factor. If you only have a half day, sample the 'Happy Isle' – Bowen (p198) – a 20-minute ferry ride from West Vancouver and a fine place for a quick hike or nautical-style pint. Victoria (p184) on Vancouver Island can be visited in a day, but it'll be a long-ass one, so consider spending at least a night. The Southern Gulf Islands (p198) recharge the soul with aqua skies seemingly close enough to touch. The islands aren't that far away, but the infrequent ferries can make day trips difficult. BC Ferries services all of these places, and often the ride itself – as the boat slithers through a labyrinth of lighthouse-punctuated islands – is every bit as rewarding as the destination.

OUTDOOR ACTIVITIES

Sorry, but you will not be pardoned for sitting around on your duff. The array of activities on offer is mind-blowing, and you're bound to find something that suits. Victoria offers scuba diving (p184) and cycling (p184). Further out on Vancouver Island, Tofino (p188) is a hot spot for surfing and kayaking. In Squamish (p191), rock climbers can attack the 652m Stawamus Chief and windsurfers can harness 60km per hour gusts. Whistler has an activity for every season: skiing, snowboarding and dog sledding in winter (p193); mountain biking, rafting and hiking in summer (p195).

WILDLIFE WATCHING

The most popular excursions to commune with nature are whale watching (p184) in Victoria, usually a three-hour boat tour where mostly orcas are viewed; as well as eagle watching (p192) in Brackendale, near Squamish, where birds feast on the local rivers' spawning salmon. **Pacific Rim National Park Reserve** (p188), near Tofino, has rainforests of huge cedar and fir trees, bears, whales and storms to beat the band. For those who like their nature fix indoors, at Victoria's **Bug Zoo** (p189) the white-eyed assassin bug and Pinkie, the Brazilian Birdeater Tarantula, spin their webs.

ART & ARCHITECTURE

The architectural draws are Victoria's **Parliament Buildings** (p189) and the **Fairmont Empress Hotel** (p189), both built by famed and shamed celebrity architect Francis Rattenbury. The city also boasts the **Art Gallery of Greater Victoria** (p188), with substantial collections of Asian, pre-Columbian and Latin American art, plus works by local painter Emily Carr. Dig deeper into the psyche of the latter by visiting **Emily Carr House** (p189). The Southern Gulf Islands are a magnet for artists, and many have studios here. **Salt Spring** (p201) hosts the biggest scene, with its Saturday morning market and Festival of the Arts in July.

VICTORIA

Poor Victoria gets a bad rap, often referred to as a destination for the 'newly wed, nearly dead and overfed.' Sure, there's a bit of stodginess in a place that publicizes afternoon tea and flowery gardens as its main attractions. As Canada's warmest city, it does attract a lot of retirees. But let's not forget whale watching, scuba diving, microbreweries, quirky ghost tours and exceptional flavors dished up by island chefs (p191).

Victoria sits at the tip of Vancouver Island. The **Inner Harbour** is the heart of the city, watched over by the **Fairmont Empress Hotel** and **Parliament Buildings**. From there, Wharf St leads northwest to **Bastion Square**, a restaurant and retail area. At the northern edge of downtown, Victoria's small **Chinatown** is the oldest in Canada. Look for **Fan Tan Alley**, a narrow passageway between Fisgard St and Pandora Ave, which was a good spot to buy opium in the 1800s. Just south is **Market Square**, another restaurant and retail complex. **Fisherman's Wharf**, where fish and chips sizzle in the fryer, is west of the Inner Harbour, reachable by mini ferry or a brisk walk.

Government St is the main drag with all the tourist shops. **Murchie's** and **Silk Road** tea companies sell soothing wares. Sweets lovers face a challenge at **Roger's Chocolates**, deciding which hulking Victorian Cream flavor to bite into.

About 90 orcas (killer whales) lurk in waters just off the island's southern point from April to October, drawn to the local salmon migration like Homer Simpson to donuts. Check at the **Info Centre** (p188) for a tour that matches your taste; keep in mind a three-hour trip shouldn't cost more than $90 per adult. Sighting success rates should be posted, but if not, ask. **Ocean Explorations**, **Prince of Whales** and **SpringTide** are reliable companies.

Scuba diving in Victoria's clear, nutrient-rich waters is a popular activity. **Frank White's Scuba Shop** and **Odgen Point Dive Centre** offer packages. Many visitors cycle the **Galloping Goose Trail**, built on abandoned railway beds stretching from Swartz Bay to Sooke. **Cycling Victoria** (www.cyclingvictoria.com) and **Greater Victoria Cycling Coalition** (www.gvcc.bc.ca) have information. **Cycle BC Rentals** and **Sports Rent** hire out bicycles; the latter is good for other equipment (kayaking, surf etc), too.

With all the rugged natural beauty in BC, it's a bit ironic that one of the province's top tourism draws is the 20 hectares of elaborate, manicured foliage at **Butchart Gardens**, 21km north in Brentwood Bay. It takes about 1½ hours to wander through; don't miss the impressive Sunken Gardens.

Back in town, the **Royal BC Museum** is a must-see. Hushed tones prevail as visitors wander through the totem pole displays, a replica of a 19th-century Haida village and Nawalagwatsi, 'the cave of supernatural power.' In summer, you may be able to speak with First Nations artists at work in the carving shed in adjacent **Thunderbird Park**, the site of several additional totem poles

Architect Francis Rattenbury designed the multi-turreted **Parliament Buildings**. A 25-year-old unknown at the time, his construction used all native materials to stimulate the local

Transportation

Distance from Vancouver 100km
Direction Southwest
Travel time 3-3½hr, incl 90-min ferry ride
Car From Vancouver to the BC Ferries terminal in Tsawwassen, take Oak St south 8km to Hwy 99. Stay on Hwy 99 for 14km to Hwy 17, then go southwest for 11km to the terminal. After arriving at Swartz Bay on Vancouver Island, take Hwy 17 south into Victoria (32km).
Air From Vancouver, Air Canada and Pacific Coastal fly into **Victoria International Airport** (YYJ; ☎ 250-953-7500; www.cyyj.ca), which is located in Sidney, 26km north of Victoria off Hwy 17. Jetsgo and WestJet fly from other Canadian cities, and Horizon Air and WestJet fly from Seattle. West Coast Air and Harbour Air (both located on Wharf St) fly 18-seat seaplanes harbor-to-harbor from Vancouver to Victoria's seaplane terminal. See p204 for airline contact details.
Bus From Vancouver **Pacific Coach Lines** (p206) goes to/from Victoria and back several times daily, and **Vancouver Island Coach Lines** (☎ 250-385-4411, www.victoriatours.com) covers Vancouver Island with several buses to Nanaimo ($19.60, 2hr) and a few onward to Courtenay ($39.20, 2hr). **Gray Line Express Shuttle** (☎ 250-388-6539) offers the quickest way to Butchart Gardens ($8). The bus station for Pacific Coach, Vancouver Island Coach and Gray Line Express is at 700 Douglas St. To travel to Tofino catch the **Tofino Bus** (☎ 250-725-2871, 866-986-3466; www.tofinobus.com; departs from HI Hostel), with buses travelling at 8:15am year-round and at 2:45pm from May to October ($50, 5hr). Bus 70 with **BC Transit** (☎ 250-382-6161; www.busonline.ca) runs frequently from the Swartz Bay ferry terminal to downtown, veering off to the airport six times daily (adult/child $2/1.25 for Zone 1, $2.75/2 for Zone 2). Bus 5 stops by the Royal BC Museum and other downtown sights, while bus 11 goes west on Fort St by the art gallery and Craigdarroch Castle. Have exact change ready. The **Info Centre** (p188) has schedules and sells day passes (adult/child $6/4).
Ferry For ferries to Washington head to the **Belleville Ferry Terminal** (near cnr Belleville and Menzies Sts). US change is given, but Canadian money is accepted. For cars, **Black Ball Transport** (☎ 250-386-2202) has services to Port Angeles (adult/child/car US$9/4.50/33.50, 90min), about 85 miles from Seattle. Departures are at 6:10am, 10:30am, 3pm and 7:30pm. Passenger-only ferries include: **Victoria Express** (☎ 250-361-9144; www.victoriaexpress.com), a one-hour journey to Port Angele (US$10, bicycles US$5), with departures at 9:45am and 6:15pm from late May to September, and at 2pm and 6:30pm from mid-July to early September; **Clipper Navigation** (☎ 250-382-8100; www.victoriaclipper.com), operating catamarans to Seattle (adult/child US77/38.50), with departures at 11:30am, 5:30pm and 7pm from mid-May to early September (reduced services rest of year); and **Victoria-San Juan Cruises** (☎ 360-738-8099; www.whales.com) travelling to Bellingham (adult/child US$49.50/24.75), with departures at 5pm from mid-May to early October. Go to the **BC Ferries Terminal** (☎ 250-386-3431, in BC 888-223-3779; www.bcferries.com), located at Swartz Bay, for ferries to Vancouver (adult/child 5-11/car $10.25/5.25/35.75, 90mins), departing hourly in summer from 7am to 10pm (every two hours rest of year). Obtain schedules from the Info Centre or **BC Ferries information office** (☎ 250-656-0757; 1112 Fort St). See p206 for more information. The **Victoria Harbour Ferry** (☎ 250-708-0201) has cool 12-person boats that wobble between the Info Centre, Fisherman's Wharf, Spinnakers Brewpub and other stops (adult/child under 12 from $3.50/1.75, every 15min).
Train The scenic Esquimalt & Nanaimo (E&N) Railiner, aka the *Malahat*, to Nanaimo ($23, 2½hr) and Courtenay ($44, 4½hr) is operated by **VIA Rail** (☎ 888-842-7245; www.viarail.ca; 450 Pandora Ave). There is one train daily in each direction, and it's popular, so book ahead.

economy. It took five years and cost twice the original budget for a total of $1 million before the 'Marble Palace' was opened in 1898. Rattenbury went on to become BC's most popular architect, also designing the **Empress Hotel**. His success fell apart when he began an affair with a woman 30 years his junior, Alma Victoria Clark Dolling Pakenham. The scandal so outraged polite society that he and his young bride moved to Bournemouth, England, in 1929. A few years later Rattenbury was murdered by his chauffeur, George Stoner, one of Alma's many lovers. Stoner was sentenced to life in prison, but was eventually released; Alma took her own life. Find out more during free tours of Parliament, or on the fascinating **Walkabouts Historic Tour** of the Empress. The **Ghostly Walks** and **Victoria Bobby Walking Tours** (led by an enthusiastic gentleman in an English policeman's uniform) are also good fun.

A short jaunt from downtown, 61-hectare **Beacon Hill Park** is an oasis of trees, gardens, ponds, pathways and playing fields. At the park's southwest corner, the **'Mile 0' marker** represents the Pacific terminus of the nearly 8000km-long Trans-Canada Hwy. Not far away, look for a staircase down to the beach off the walking path across Dallas Rd.

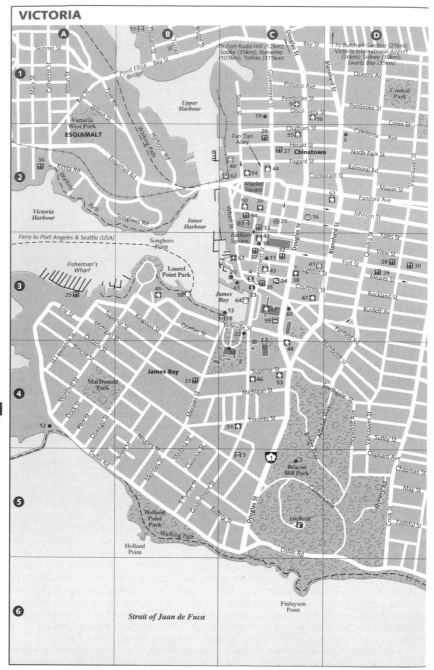

Excursions – Victoria

Excursions – Victoria

Scale
0 ——————— 500 m
0 ——————— 0.3 miles

EATING 🍴 (p190)
Barb's Place.................................25 A3
Blue Fox Café..............................26 D3
Brasserie L'ecole.........................27 C2
Café Brio....................................28 D3
Herald St Café............................29 C2
J&J Noodles................................30 D3
James Bay Tearoom.....................31 B4
Pagliacci's..................................32 C3
Re-Bar.......................................33 C2
Reef..34 C2
Sam's Deli..................................35 C3
Spinnakers.................................36 A2
Temple......................................37 C3

DRINKING 🍷 (pp190–1)
Big Bad John's.......................(see 38)
Legends......................................38 C3
Steamers Public House.................39 C2
Sticky Wicket Pub.................(see 38)

ENTERTAINMENT 🎭 (pp190–1)
Bengal Lounge.......................(see 49)
Canoe Brewpub...........................40 C3
Mocambo Coffee.........................41 C3
Swans Brewpub.....................(see 54)

SHOPPING 🛍 (p191)
Murchie's...................................42 C3
Rogers' Chocolates......................43 C3
Silk Road Aromatherapy and Tea
    Company..............................44 C2

SLEEPING 🛏 (pp189–90)
Admiral Inn................................45 B3
Birdcage Walk Guest House..........46 C4
Chateau Victoria.........................47 C3
Crystal Court Motel.....................48 C4
Fairmont Empress Hotel...............49 C3
HI Victoria Hostel........................50 C2
James Bay Inn.............................51 C4
Ocean Island Backpackers Inn.......52 D2
Shamrock Suites on the Park........53 C4
Swans Hotel................................54 C2
Traveller's Inn............................55 C2
Traveller's Inn............................56 C1

TRANSPORT (p185)
BC Ferries Information Office.........57 E3
Belleville Ferry Terminal...............58 B3
Bus Station.................................59 C3
Cycle BC Rentals (Seasonal
    Office)...................................60 C3
Cycle BC Rentals.........................61 C3
E&N Railiner Station.....................62 C3
Seaplane Terminal.......................63 C3
Victoria Harbour Ferry Ticket
    Centre...................................64 C3

INFORMATION
Royal Jubilee Hospital..................65 H1

SIGHTS & ACTIVITIES (pp188–9)
Art Gallery of Greater Victoria........1 E3
Beacon Hill Park............................2 C5
Craigdarroch Castle.......................3 F3
Custom House Currency Exchange..4 C3
Emily Carr House...........................5 C5
Frank White's Scuba Shop..............6 D2
Government House.........................7 F4
Maritime Museum..........................8 C2
Mayfair Walk-In Clinic....................9 C1
Miniature World....................(see 49)
Munro's Books.............................10 C3
Ocean Explorations......................11 C3
Ogden Point Dive Centre..............12 A4
Pacific Underseas Gardens............13 C3
Parliament Buildings.....................14 C4
Point Ellice House & Gardens........15 B1
Post Office..................................16 C2
Prince of Whales...................(see 23)
Royal British Columbia Museum....17 C3
Royal London Wax Museum.........18 C3
Sports Rent.................................19 C1
SpringTide Victoria Whale
    Watching...............................20 C3
Stain Internet Café.......................21 C2
Thunderbird Park.........................22 C3
Tourism Victoria Visitor Info
    Centre...................................23 C3
Victoria Bug Zoo..........................24 C3

Often overlooked, the substantial **Art Gallery of Greater Victoria** has excellent collections of Asian, pre-Columbian and Latin American art, and several Emily Carr works. At **Emily Carr House**, displays and videos bring to life the artistry and passion of Carr, one of BC's most renowned artists (p27).

Craigdarroch Castle is a mansion built in the mid-1880s by Robert Dunsmuir, a coal millionaire who died before it was completed. The Castle Tower offers breathtaking views across the Strait of San Juan de Fuca to the Olympic Mountains in Washington State. Nearby is **Government House**, residence of the province's lieutenant governor, which has impressive gardens open to the public.

The **Maritime Museum** explores Vancouver Island's seafaring history through displays on piracy, shipwrecks and 400 model ships. Four more peculiar museums reside downtown: the **Royal London Wax Museum** (see Napoleon, Cleopatra and the Chamber of Horrors), **Pacific Underseas Gardens** (where a diver plays with an octopus), **Victoria Bug Zoo** (scary 6-inch bush crickets) and **Miniature World** (teeny tiny everything).

Soulfully scenic, 18-hectare **Ft Rodd Hill National Historic Site** is 12km northwest off Ocean Blvd. The **Sooke Potholes**, 35km west on Sooke Rd (Hwy 14), are another out-of-town jaunt, providing a good place to swim.

Major festivals and events include the **TerrifVic Jazz Party** (www.terrifvic.com; mid-Apr), **Swiftsure International Yacht Race** (www.swiftsure.org; late May), **Jazzfest International** (www.vicjazz.bc.ca; late Jun), **Victoria Fringe Theatre Festival** (www.victoriafringe.com; late Aug) and **Great Canadian Beer Festival** (www.gcbf.com; Labour Day weekend, Sep).

Several companies in Vancouver offer guided, 13-hour tours of Victoria that take in Butchart Gardens, the Empress Hotel and more. Try **Pacific Spirit Tours** (☎ 604-683-0209; www.pacificspirittours.com; adult/child $118/68), **Gray Line** (p40; adult/child $125/79) or **Landsea Tours** (p40; adult/child $114/65). Fares include admission prices.

Information

Many downtown businesses accept US currency, but the exchange rate is poor. It's better to use an ATM; several are located along Douglas St.

Custom House Currency Exchange (☎ 250-389-6007; 815 Wharf St; 9am-9pm)

Detour: Tofino

Little Tofino has boomed as the jump-off point into the rainforests of **Pacific Rim National Park Reserve**. Hardy souls embark upon the **West Coast Trail**, a 75km backpacking route – simultaneously brilliant and backbreaking – past sandstone cliffs, waterfalls, caves and sea arches. Tofino's **Visitor Info Centre** (☎ 250-725-3414; www.tofinobc.org; 1426 Pacific Rim Hwy; 10am-6pm May-Sep) can help with activities: Clayoquot Sound is famed for kayaking; the mondo waves rolling in, unstopped by any land mass from there to Japan, make for good surfing; and spectacular storms that break over the area have sparked an industry of storm-watching tours. **Tofino Bus** (p185) will get you here from Victoria or Nanaimo. **Regency Express** (☎ 604-278-1608, 800-228-6608) flies to/from Vancouver ($135). **Moose Travel** (☎ 604-777-9905, 888-244-6673; www.moosenetwork.com) offers a four-day trip ($229) taking in Victoria, Tofino and Pacific Rim park.

Cycling Victoria (www.cyclingvictoria.com)

Greater Victoria Cycling Coalition (www.gvcc.bc.ca)

Mayfair Walk-In Clinic (☎ 250-383-9898; 3147 Douglas St; 9am-5pm Mon-Fri, 9am-2pm Sat)

Munro's Books (☎ 250-382-2464, 888-243-2464; 1108 Government St; 9am-6pm Mon-Thu, 9am-9pm Fri & Sat, 9:30am-6pm Sun)

Post Office (250-953-1352; 706 Yates St; 8am-5pm Mon-Fri)

Royal Jubilee Hospital (☎ 250-370-8000; 1900 Fort St)

Stain Internet Café (☎ 250-382-3352; 609 Yates St; per hr $3; 10am-2am)

Tourism Victoria Visitor Info Centre (☎ 250-953-2033, 800-663-3883; www.tourismvictoria.com; 812 Wharf St; 8:30am-6:30pm mid-Jun–Sep, 9am-5pm Oct–mid-Jun) Activity and accommodation booking services.

Sights & Activities

Art Gallery of Greater Victoria (☎ 250-384-4101; www.aggv.bc.ca; 1040 Moss St; adult/senior & student $6/4; 10am-5pm, to 9pm Thu)

Beacon Hill Park (admission free; 24hr)

Butchart Gardens (☎ 250-652-5256, 866-652-4422; www.butchartgardens.com; 800 Benvenuto Ave; adult/child 5-12/youth $21/2/10.50 mid-Jun–Sep, reduced rest of year; 9am-10:30pm mid-June–Aug, dusk rest of year)

Craigdarroch Castle (☎ 250-592-5323; 1050 Joan Cres; adult/child 6-12/student $10/3.50/6.50; ☻ 9am-7pm mid-Jun–early Sep, 10am-4:30pm rest of year)

Cycle BC Rentals (☎ 250-380-2453; main office 747 Douglas St, seasonal office 950 Wharf St; bicycle rental per day $19; ☻ 9am-5pm)

Emily Carr House (☎ 250-383-5843; 207 Government St; admission by donation; ☻ 11am-4pm mid-May–early Sep, 11am-4pm Tue-Sat early Sep–mid-Oct)

Fort Rodd Hill National Historic Site (☎ 250-478-5849; 603 Fort Rodd Hill Rd; adult/child/senior $4/2/3; ☻ 9am-4:30pm Nov-Feb, 10am-5:30pm rest of year)

Frank White's Scuba Shop (☎ 250-385-4713; 1855 Blanshard St; dive packages from $45; ☻ 9am-6pm)

Ghostly Walks (☎ 250-384-6698; www.discoverthe past.com; adult/child 6-12/senior/student/family $12/8/10/10/30; ☻ departs Info Centre 7:30pm Jul & Aug, Fri or Sat only rest of year)

Government House (☎ 250-387-2080; 1401 Rockland Ave; admission free; ☻ dawn-dusk)

Maritime Museum (☎ 250-385-4222; 28 Bastion Sq; adult/child 6-11/senior/student $8/3/5/5; ☻ 9:30am-4:30pm)

Miniature World (☎ 250-385-9731; www.miniature world.com; Fairmont Empress Hotel, 649 Humboldt St; adult/child 5-11/student $9/7/8; ☻ 9am-5pm, extended hours mid-May–mid-Sep)

Ocean Explorations (☎ 250-383-6722; www.ocean explorations.com; 602 Broughton St; tours adult/child $79/59; ☻ hourly 9am-3pm & 5pm)

Ogden Point Dive Centre (☎ 250-380-9119; www .divevictoria.com; 199 Dallas Rd; packages from $59; ☻ 9am-6pm)

Pacific Underseas Gardens (☎ 250-382-5717; 490 Belleville St; adult/child/senior $8.50/4.50/7.50; ☻ 10am-7pm Jul-Aug, 10am-5pm Sep-Jun)

Parliament Buildings (☎ 250-387-3046; 501 Belleville St; 35min tours free; ☻ 8:30am-5pm daily Jun–early Sep, Sat & Sun rest of year)

Point Ellice House & Gardens (☎ 250-380-6506; 2616 Pleasant St; admission adult/child $5/3, afternoon tea & tour $17; ☻ 10am-4pm May-Sep)

Prince of Whales (☎ 250-383-4884, 888-383-4884; www.princeofwhales.com; 812 Wharf St; tours adult/child $79/59; ☻ 9am-5pm)

Royal British Columbia Museum (☎ 250-356-7226, 888-447-7977; www.royalbcmuseum.bc.ca; 675 Belleville St; adult/child 6-18 $11/7.70; ☻ 9am-5pm, extended in summer)

Royal London Wax Museum (☎ 250-388-4461; 470 Belleville St; adult/child/student $9/4.50/7; ☻ 9:30am-5pm, extended in summer)

SpringTide Whale Watching Tours (☎ 250-386-6016; www.springtidecharters.com; 950 Wharf St; tours adult/child $89/59; ☻ 9am-6pm)

Sports Rent (☎ 250-385-7368; www.sportsrentbc.com; 1950 Government St; bicycle per day $20, canoe/kayak per day $40; ☻ 9am-5:30pm Mon-Thu, 9am-6pm Fri, 9am-5pm Sat, 10am-5pm Sun, extended in summer)

Victoria Bobby Walking Tours (☎ 250-995-0233; www .walkvictoria.com; tours $15; ☻ departs Info Centre 11am May-Sep)

Victoria Bug Zoo (☎ 250-384-2847; 631 Courtney St; adult/child 3-16/senior $7/4.50/5; ☻ 9:30am-5:30pm Mon-Sat, 11am-5:30pm Sun, extended in summer)

WalkAbouts Historical Tours' Empress Tour (☎ 250-592-9255; www.walkabouts.ca; Empress Hotel; tours $9; ☻ 10am May-Oct) Purchase tickets at the hotel's Dining Reservations Desk.

Sleeping

Prices indicated are for the May to September peak season (sans taxes), when it is difficult to find something for less than $100 nightly; rooms are reduced by up to 50% off peak. B&Bs are big business here; many agencies in Vancouver (p168) also book for Victoria. The Info Centre's **room reservation service** (☎ 800-663-3883; www.tour ismvictoria.com) books B&Bs, hotels and everything else.

Birdcage Walk Guest House (☎ 250-389-0804, 877-389-0804; 505 Government St; r $100-150) Convenient to the Inner Harbour, this historic home hosts five solid guest rooms with private bathrooms and cooking facilities. Breakfast is delivered to your door.

Chateau Victoria (☎ 250-382-4221, 800-663-5891; www.chateauvictoria.com; 740 Burdett Ave; r/ste from $122/162) The hotel's 177 rooms are not particularly remarkable, but they offer excellent value given all of their business-traveler amenities. The Vista 18 (18th floor) lounge unfurls the city's best views.

Crystal Court Motel (☎ 250-384-0551; 701 Belleville St; r $89) Fusty, somewhat noisy motel-style rooms, but a good option given its heart-of-town location near the Empress. About half of its rooms have kitchens.

Fairmont Empress Hotel (☎ 250-384-8111, 866-540-4229; www.fairmont.com/empress/; 721 Government St; r standard/deluxe/harbor view $199/239/299; P $22) Victoria's 1908 grand dame is absolutely mammoth, and her regal, bygone-era opulence knows no bounds. It's mostly filled with honeymooners and bus-tour groups.

HI Victoria Hostel (☎ 250-385-4511, 888-883-0099; www.hihostels.ca; 516 Yates St; dm members/non-members $18/22) Great location just up from the Inner Harbour and close to the sights. Although it has room for more than 100 people in barrack-style dorms, it's wildly popular with travelers of all ages, so reserve ahead.

James Bay Inn (☎ 250-384-7151, 800-836-2649; www .jamesbayinn.com; 270 Government St; r $126-193, ste $203-237) This old-time, dark-wood inn offers well-kept rooms with bay windows; some have kitchens. Quiet location, yet not far from the action.

Ocean Island Backpackers Inn (☎ 250-385-1788, 888-888-4180; www.oceanisland.com; 791 Pandora Ave; 4- to-6-bed dm $20-25, r from $27; **P** $5) Catering more to a younger crowd, this fun, colorful hostel has a licensed lounge, and quality staff plan cheap day trips and nightly group outings.

Shamrock Suites on the Park (☎ 250-385-8768, 800-294-5544; www.shamrocksuites.com; 675 Superior St; r/ste $145/175; **P** $5) A great location across from Beacon Hill Park, and big windows from which to see it; full kitchen and parkside patio for lounging.

Swans Hotel (☎ 250-361-3310, 800-668-7926; www .swanshotel.com; 506 Pandora Ave; r $159, 1-bed/2-bed ste $189/259; **P** $8) Billed as the 'art hotel,' this is one of the nicest refurbished heritage hotels in Old Town, right on the waterfront. All rooms have kitchens.

Traveller's Inn (☎ 250-953-1000, 888-877-9444; www .travellersinn.com; 1961 Douglas St; r weekday/weekend $120/130) Has 10 locations around Victoria, including one just a block away (☎ 250-381-1000, 888-254-6476; 1850 Douglas St). It's good value, especially if using the discount coupons available at the ferry terminals and Info Centre. Kids stay free.

Eating

See opposite for additional restaurants.

Barb's Place (☎ 250-384-6515; 310 St Lawrence St, Fisherman's Wharf; items $7-9; 10am-dusk Mar-Oct) It's mighty popular just as a fish-and-chips shack on a dock.

Blue Fox Café (☎ 250-380-1683; 101/919 Fort St; meals from $8; 7:30am-4pm Mon-Fri, 9am-3pm Sat & Sun) A breakfast-lovers' delight, with pancakes, omelettes and 'Toadstool Berry Very Fat French Toast.'

Café Brio (☎ 250-383-0009; 944 Fort St; mains $16-27; from 5:30pm) Another Island Chefs member, whipping up everything from pumpkin and squash soup to confit of Cowichan Bay Farm chicken.

Herald St Café (☎ 250-381-1441; 546 Herald St; lunch $11-15, dinner mains $17-27; lunch 11:30am-3pm Wed-Sat, 11am-3pm Sun, dinner 5:30-10pm Mon-Sun) Devilled crab sandwiches, cashew-crusted chicken, and herb and mushroom stuffed crepes, complemented with pasta and bread from the on-site bakery, satisfy at this west coast fusion bistro.

J&J Noodles (☎ 250-383-0680; 1012 Fort St; dishes $8-15; 11am-2pm & 4:30-8:30pm Tue-Sat) Utilitarian, cafeteria-esque booths and tables, but locals of all ages pile in for the firebranded Chinese hot pot concoctions.

Pagliacci's (☎ 250-386-1662; 1011 Broad St; lunch $7-10, dinner $11-21; 11:30am-3pm & 5:30-10pm, to 11pm Fri & Sat) Unlimited baskets of fresh focaccia bread and marble-topped tables. Generous pasta servings from the cinema-themed menu almost defy devouring; try the Hemingway Short Story (beef-stuffed tortellini).

Re-Bar (☎ 250-360-2401; 50 Bastion Sq; dishes $9-13; 8:30am-9pm Mon-Thu, 8:30am-10pm Fri & Sat, 8:30am-3:30pm Sun) A happening, primarily vegetarian spot with an eclectic, international menu.

Reef (☎ 250-388-5375; 533 Yates St; mains $8-13; 11am-midnight Sun-Wed, 11-1am Thu-Sat) Same delectable Caribbean dishes as in Vancouver (p103).

Sam's Deli (☎ 250-382-8424; 805 Government St; sandwiches $6-11; 7:30am-7pm) Opposite the Info Centre, Sam's is the perfect spot for a coffee or bottle of beer and a sandwich big enough to feed two.

Entertainment

Check the free weekly *Monday Magazine* for listings.

Bengal Lounge (☎ 250-384-8111; Fairmont Empress, 721 Government St) A whiff of the Raj, including puka fans and a tiger skin over the fireplace.

Tea Time

Yes it's touristy, but it's also tasty. Go ahead – treat yourself to the British extravagance of afternoon tea with crustless finger sandwiches, clotted cream, berries, scones, lemon tarts and cakes.

Butchart Gardens (☎ 250-652-8222; 800 Benvenuto Ave; tea $22; noon-5pm, reduced in winter) Tea is served either in the glassed-in conservatory, or inside the dining room among beautiful floral arrangements.

Fairmont Empress Hotel (☎ 250-389-2727; 721 Government St; tea $50, less in winter; 12:30-5pm, reduced in winter) Shameless sumptuousness, fit for a queen. The Empress even has its own house blend made from Darjeeling, China and Ceylon leaves. Reservations required, and there's a dress code.

James Bay Tearoom (☎ 250-382-8282; 332 Menzies St; tea $10.25; 7am-5pm Mon-Sat, 8am-5pm Sun) Bargain-priced tea served all day, plus equally reasonable Yorkshire pudding, steak-and-kidney pie and other Brit dishes.

Point Ellice House & Gardens (☎ 250-380-6506; tea $17; 11am-3pm May-Sep) Tea in a charming Victorian setting, and you can play croquet afterward. The tab includes a tour of the historic site.

Radical Island Chefs Cook up a Scene *John Lee*

With its double decker–filled streets and quaint candy stores, Victoria will always be an empire outpost fond of dainty afternoon tea. But a radical band of young city chefs has recently begun serving up a culinary scene that goes way beyond Earl Grey and crumpets. And they're doing it with an unusual collective approach that showcases Vancouver Island's luscious smorgasbord of indigenous ingredients.

The **Island Chef's Collaborative** (ICC; www.victoriafestivalofwine.com/icc) brings together some of Victoria's leading culinary auteurs, each dedicated to sourcing and serving high-quality, mostly organic foods from local farmers, fishers and foragers. Mostly in their 30s, these chefs work closely with regional purveyors, enjoying in return a wealth of uniquely flavorful ingredients, including Cowichan Valley duck, earthy foraged mushrooms and luscious fresh fruit, such as salmonberries, tayberries and marionberries.

While the chefs work together to share resources, produce and suppliers, they remain highly competitive when it comes to chefing up the goods. Sean Brennan's approach at **Brasserie L'Ecole** (☎ 250-475-6260; www.lecole.ca; 1715 Government St; meals $20-30; ⏰ dinner Thu-Sat), for example, is pure, country-style French cooking served in a casual atmosphere. His classic peasant dishes include creamed chanterelles on toast with shallots and a little bacon, while heartier fare includes lamb shank served with mustard-creamed root vegetables and braised chard.

A short drive from Victoria in the waterfront town of Sidney, at **Dock 503** (☎ 250-656-0828; www.dock503 .vanislemarina.com; 2320 Harbour Rd, Sidney; meals $18-30; ⏰ dinner daily, brunch Sun), chef Simon Manvell is reinventing west coast cuisine for his marina-side customers. Preparation-intensive dishes, like slow-roasted duck served with wild mushroom risotto, grilled vegetables and truffle demi-glace, are popular with many diners. Summer desserts, such as bowls of fresh local figs and small, sweet strawberries, tend to be simple and to the point.

It's an approach that also works over at **Spinnakers** (☎ 250-386-2739; www.spinnakers.com; 308 Catherine St; dinner mains $9-19; meals $10-20; ⏰ breakfast, lunch & dinner) – a gourmet brewpub legend that produces its own craft beers and piquant vinegars – where chef Ken Hueston highlights the region's unique flavors with a strong emphasis on comfort food. Among his popular dishes is a seasonal paysan-style platter: a BC seafood celebration of Salt Spring Island clams, Tofino swimming scallops and Queen Charlotte Islands salmon. Asking for a recommended house-brewed beer as an accompaniment is always a good idea here.

For those with less time who want to sample as widely as possible, the small plates at loungy, late-night **Temple** (☎ 250-383-2313; www.thetemple.ca; 525 Fort St; plates $6-18; ⏰ dinner Tue-Sat) are ideal. Chef Sam Benedetto fuses international influences with local ingredients to produce contemporary taste-tripping dishes, like maple-glazed salmon with yam tempura and miso sauce. True culinary adventurers will head straight for his seaweed salad – available from May to October – which features four seasonal varieties served raw, blanched, dressed or lightly pickled.

Canoe Brewpub (☎ 250-361-1940; 450 Swift St) Sip a River Rock Bitter on the waterside patio.

Mocambo Coffee (☎ 250-384-4468; 1028 Blanshard St; ⏰ 7am-6pm Mon-Thu, 7am-11pm Fri, 8:30am-5pm Sat) Serves the island's best coffee and has Friday night poetry readings.

Steamers Public House (☎ 250-381-4340; 570 Yates St) Live rock, jazz or blues bands nightly.

Strathcona Hotel (☎ 250-383-7137; 919 Douglas St) Multi-venue complex that includes the rooftop volleyball courts of **Sticky Wicket Pub**; hillbilly, peanut-shell-on-the-ground haven of **Big Bad John's**; and touring musical acts at **Legends**.

Swans Brewpub (☎ 250-361-3310, 800-668-7926; 506 Pandora Ave) Mmm, Oatmeal Stout.

Shopping

Murchie's (☎ 250-383-3112; 1110 Government St; ⏰ 9am-6pm Sat-Wed, 9am-9pm Thu & Fri) Long-standing tea merchant.

Rogers' Chocolates (☎ 250- 384-7021; 913 Government St; ⏰ 9am-9pm Mon-Sat, 9am-7pm Sun) Jumbo-sized Victorian Creams.

Silk Road Aromatherapy & Tea Company (☎ 250-704-2688; 1624 Government St; ⏰ 10am-6pm Mon-Sat, 11am-5pm Sun) Tea blended by monastic principles.

SQUAMISH

Halfway between Vancouver and Whistler (p193), small Squamish enjoys an incredible natural setting at the fingertip of Howe Sound. Avid rock climbers and windsurfers, plus ice climbers and eagle watchers, all find reasons to spend time here.

The big chief in town is the **Stawamus Chief**, a 652m behemoth whose dark bulk is nearly as great as Gibraltar. The Chief takes its name from an image on the rock that looks like a sleeping First Nations chief facing the sky. It's widely considered the province's top destination for rock climbing, with about 200 different routes to the top. For climbing information, guides or instruction, call **Vertical Reality**. A 3km hiking trail connects the Chief with **Shannon Falls** (335m), which ranks among Canada's highest and most beautiful waterfalls. In winter, when the falls freeze, climbers pick and pull their way to the top. Both attractions are signposted from the highway a few kilometers south of town.

Western Canada's best windsurfing is at Squamish Harbour, where winds from the mouth of the Squamish River push sailboards to speeds as high as 60km per hour (Squamish is a Coast Salish word meaning 'Mother of the Winds'). **Sea to Sky Ocean Sports** provides gear and instruction. Mountain biking also draws lots of enthusiasts to more than 60 trails in the Squamish vicinity. **Tantalus** rents bikes and has information on the best routes.

A pathway through the flower beds in Butchart Gardens (p188), Victoria

And then there are the eagles. One of the world's largest concentrations of these birds congregates from early November to mid-February at Brackendale, 7km north of Squamish. As many as 3700 bald eagles feed along a 15km stretch of the Squamish River on dead salmon that float downstream after spawning. The main viewing site is at Eagle Run, beside Government Rd north of Garibaldi Way and south of Depot Rd. Eagle 'floats' in rafts by outfitters like **Sunwolf Outdoor Centre** are popular, too.

Information

Visitor Info Centre (☎ 604-892-9244; 37950 Cleveland Ave; ☯ 9am-5pm Mon-Fri, 10am-2pm Sat & Sun)

Sights & Activities

Sea to Sky Ocean Sports (☎ 604-892-3366; 37819 Second Ave; 4hr windsurfing class $50)

Tantalus (☎ 604-898-2588; 40446 Government Rd; bicycle rental per day $39; ☯ 9:30am-5:30pm)

Vertical Reality (☎ 604-892-8248; 37835 2nd Ave; ☯ 9:30am-6pm Mon-Sat, 10am-5pm Sun)

Sleeping & Eating

HI Squamish Hostel (☎ 604-892-9240; www.hihostels .ca; 38220 Hwy 99; 6-bed dm member/non-member $19.50/23.50) BC's newest hostel is a beauty, and its patio has killer views of the Chief.

Howe Sound Inn & Brewing Company (☎ 604-892-2603, 800-919-2537; www.howesound.com; 37801

Cleveland Ave; r $95-105, mains $12-19; ☯ 7am-9pm, to 10pm Fri & Sat) The inn's welcoming rooms have thick duvets. Lip-smacking refreshment is served at the inn's well-known brewpub and its slightly more upscale cousin, the Red Heather Grill. Bread made daily on the premises accompanies cedar plank grilled fish or pasta.

Transportation

Distance from Vancouver 67km
Direction North
Travel time 1-1½hr
Car See Whistler driving directions (opposite) for instructions on how to reach Hwy 99 from Vancouver. From the highway, turn left on to Cleveland Ave to reach downtown Squamish.
Bus The **bus station** (☎ 604-898-3914) is at 40446 Government Rd. **Greyhound Canada** (p206) stops at Squamish ($8, 1½hr) en route to Whistler. Local bus services are provided by **Squamish Transit** (☎ 604-892-5559), including one to Brackendale ($1.75).

Sunflower Bakery (☎ 604-892-2231; 38086 Cleveland Ave; items $2-5; ⊗ 8am-5:30pm Mon-Sat) A cheerful café, where the vegetarian pastries and soups are outdone only by the homemade berry pies.

Sunwolf Outdoor Centre (☎ 604-898-1537, 877-806-8046; www.sunwolf.net; 70002 Squamish Valley Rd; cabins $90, with kitchenette $100) Riverside cabins, plus guided eagle viewing and rafting trips.

WHISTLER

'Whistler' – the name applied to the area lorded over by both Whistler and Blackcomb mountains – appears after a heart-leaping, humbling drive through peaks that shadow the Sea to Sky Hwy. Whistler has been called the best ski destination in North America many times over, and its summertime popularity has begun to climb, too, as adventure enthusiasts flock in to get their rushes from mountain biking, 'ziptrekking' and glacier skiing.

The 'town' is made up of four neighborhoods: **Whistler Creekside**, **Whistler Village**, **Village North** and **Upper Village**. Approaching from the south, you'll enter at Whistler Creekside, the original base. While it has undergone major redevelopment recently, it's still sleepier than its counterparts. If you're looking for action, head north to the other three areas. They reside 4km north past Alta Lake, and tend to blur into one large village. From Hwy 99, turn right (east) on to Village Gate Blvd, which divides Whistler Village (at the base of Whistler Mountain) from Village North. The road ends at Blackcomb Way, which divides the two aforementioned areas from Upper Village; there are also parking lots on the east side of Blackcomb Way. Whistler Village is the center of most commercial activity, but it's all connected by cobblestone pedestrian malls.

To get your bearings regarding the activities on offer, visit the **Whistler Chamber Visitor Information Centre**. To book activities or accommodations, stop by the **Tourism Whistler Activity & Information Centre**. The best deals are often obtained directly from the outfitters, though.

Showing off its Olympic mettle (about half of the events will take place here during the 2010 Winter Olympics), Whistler-Blackcomb offers over 8100 acres of skiable terrain, 200 longer-than-average trails, 12 alpine bowls and three glaciers. The usually reliable snowfall, mile-high vertical drops and mild Pacific air combine to provide some of the most pleasant skiing to be found anywhere. What's more, the season runs into June, with glacier skiing and snowboarding (on Blackcomb's Horstman Glacier) available well into August.

It does get crowded, but the five major bases (Whistler Creekside, Whistler Village, Excalibur Village, Excalibur Base II and Upper Village Blackcomb) and all the available terrain allow skiers to spread out. High-speed lifts make exceptionally long lines move fairly quickly, but prepare for half-hour waits on weekends. **Intrawest** is the resort corporation that owns, manages and maintains the whole of Whistler Blackcomb. Call Intrawest direct for information on lessons, ski schools and women-only programs. For gear rental, look into its **Mountain Adventure Centres** sprinkled around town.

Transportation

Distance from Vancouver 125km
Direction North
Travel time 2-2½hr

Car Take Georgia St through Stanley Park and over the Lions Gate Bridge. Exit the bridge on the Marine Dr West turnoff. Take the first right on to Taylor Way. Travel up the hill and turn left on to Hwy 1. Follow the signs and take Exit 2 (just before the Horseshoe Bay ferry terminal) to Hwy 99 – aka the Sea to Sky Hwy – which takes you all the way to Whistler Village. The highway is undergoing massive reconstruction to prepare for Olympic traffic flow. Check the **hotline** (☎ 877-472-3399; www.seatoskyimprovements.ca) to avoid brutal delays. There are four free gravel parking lots east of Blackcomb Way. Lots 1, 2 and 3 are for day skiers; lot 4 is for overnight visitors.

Bus Six to seven buses travel daily to/from Vancouver ($18, 2½hr) with **Greyhound Canada** (p206). The bus loop is by the Visitor Info Centre. There is no indoor 'station,' just benches under a shelter. Buy tickets from the driver. **Perimeter** (p207) is the best option for shuttle buses if you're coming directly from Vancouver's airport; **Bigfoot Adventure Tours** (p207) caters more to the backpacker crowd. The **Whistler and Valley Express** (WAVE; ☎ 604-932-4020; www.busonline.ca) is the local bus service (cash-only adult fare $1.50). Buses are equipped with ski and bicycle racks.

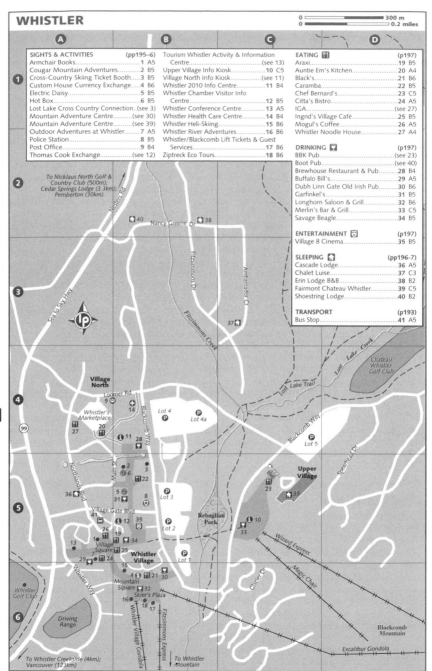

0 _____ 300 m
0 _____ 0.2 miles

SIGHTS & ACTIVITIES (pp195–6)
Armchair Books................................1 A5
Cougar Mountain Adventures..........2 B5
Cross-Country Skiing Ticket Booth....3 B5
Custom House Currency Exchange....4 B6
Electric Daisy..................................5 B5
Hot Box...6 B5
Lost Lake Cross Country Connection..(see 3)
Mountain Adventure Centre........(see 30)
Mountain Adventure Centre........(see 39)
Outdoor Adventures at Whistler........7 A5
Police Station.................................8 B5
Post Office......................................9 B4
Thomas Cook Exchange................(see 12)

Tourism Whistler Activity & Information
    Centre....................................(see 13)
Upper Village Info Kiosk.................10 C5
Village North Info Kiosk...............(see 11)
Whistler 2010 Info Centre..............11 B4
Whistler Chamber Visitor Info
    Centre..................................12 B5
Whistler Conference Centre............13 A5
Whistler Health Care Centre...........14 B4
Whistler Heli-Skiing.......................15 B6
Whistler River Adventures..............16 B6
Whistler/Blackcomb Lift Tickets & Guest
    Services...............................17 B6
Ziptrek Eco Tours...........................18 B6

EATING (p197)
Araxi...19 B5
Auntie Em's Kitchen.......................20 A4
Black's...21 B6
Caramba.......................................22 B5
Chef Bernard's...............................23 C5
Citta's Bistro.................................24 A5
IGA...(see 27)
Ingrid's Village Café.......................25 B5
Mogul's Coffee..............................26 B5
Whistler Noodle House...................27 A4

DRINKING (p197)
BBK Pub.....................................(see 23)
Boot Pub.....................................(see 40)
Brewhouse Restaurant & Pub..........28 B4
Buffalo Bill's................................29 A5
Dubh Linn Gate Old Irish Pub..........30 B6
Garfinkel's...................................31 B5
Longhorn Saloon & Grill.................32 B6
Merlin's Bar & Grill........................33 C5
Savage Beagle...............................34 B5

ENTERTAINMENT (p197)
Village 8 Cinema...........................35 B5

SLEEPING (pp196-7)
Cascade Lodge..............................36 A5
Chalet Luise..................................37 C3
Erin Lodge B&B.............................38 B2
Fairmont Chateau Whistler..............39 C5
Shoestring Lodge...........................40 B2

TRANSPORT (p193)
Bus Stop.......................................41 A5

To Nicklaus North Golf &
Country Club (500m);
Cedar Springs Lodge (3.3km);
Pemberton (30km)

Nancy Greene Dr

Nelson Rd

Fitzsimmons Dr

Ambassador Cr

Fitzsimmons Creek

Sea to Sky Hwy

Chateau Whistler Golf Club

Lost Lake Creek

Lost Lake Trail

Village North

Lorimer Rd

Whistler's Marketplace

Blackcomb Way

Main St

Northlands Blvd

99

Lot 4
Lot 4a

Lot 5

Chateau Blvd

Upper Village

Spearhead Dr

Lot 3

Village Gate Blvd

Rebagliati Park

Lot 2

Wizard Express

Village Square

Whistler Village

Lot 1

Whistler Way

Mountain Square

Skier's Plaza

Whistler Golf Club

Driving Range

Fitzsimmons Express

Whistler Village Gondola

To Whistler Creekside (4km);
Vancouver (123km)

To Whistler Mountain

Chicar Dr

Magic Chair

Blackcomb Mountain

Excalibur Gondola

Visitors can play in the snow in other ways, too. Whistler Municipality grooms more than 30km of cross-country ski trails through serene Lost Lake Park. **Lost Lake Cross-Country Connection**, beside the cross-country ticket booth, rents equipment and runs tours. **Cougar Mountain Adventures** also leads tours, as well as more adventurous snowmobiling and dog sledding jaunts. For showshoeing equipment and tours, contact **Outdoor Adventures at Whistler**. And for those who need still more thrills, **Whistler Heli-Skiing** offers day trips to access the untouched powder of backcountry peaks.

While less busy, summer isn't exactly a slack season. In addition to summer skiing and snowboarding, Whistler's **Mountain Bike Park** will get you vertical. Ride the Whistler Village or Fitzsimmons gondola to mid-mountain, then enjoy a gravity-fed adrenaline rush down. Opportunities range from easy trails for recreational riders to hard-core mountain descents for experienced cyclists. Call **Intrawest** for learn-to-ride clinics and guided rides. **Spokeswomen** runs weekend skills camps for women.

Summer hiking happens along the same principle: take the Whistler Village Gondola to the top, and then let your jaw drop as the alpine panoramas unfurl around you. Detailed hiking maps are free, as are the twice-daily guided nature walks from the gondola station. Don't miss the last gondola down (usually around 5:30pm), otherwise it's a tricky three-hour, 10km descent on foot.

Nearby white-water rafting includes family-friendly paddles along the Green and Cheakamus Rivers and continuous white water on the Birkenhead River; contact **Whistler River Adventures**. This outfitter also rustles up horses for two-hour tours up Cougar Mountain.

Whistler's golf courses are open from May through October. Beside Green Lake, prestigious **Nicklaus North Golf & Country Club** was designed by Jack himself, while classic **Whistler Golf Club** is Arnold Palmer's work. At Blackcomb's base, **Chateau Whistler Golf Club** affords mountain views and power carts with GPS positioning systems.

One of the new entries into the adventure market, year-round **Ziptrek Eco Tours** snuggles visitors into a full-body harness attached to a cable, then sends said visitor – suspended by the harness – flying over Fitzsimmons Creek and through the forest valley.

You'd expect Canada's top ski resort to be a partying place, and it is. The concept of 'après' – post-skiing time to swap tales and injuries over a couple of drinks – lives on in the slew of bars and restaurants. Festivals and events include **Altitude**, a gay and lesbian ski week (early February), **Whistler Jazz & Blues Weekend** (mid-June) and the **Summit Concert Series** (weekends in August) with on-mountain performances. Food and wine festivities in the fall include **Oktoberfest** (mid-October) and **Cornucopia** (early November).

Day trips from Vancouver are available with **Pacific Spirit Tours** (☎ 604-683-0209; www .pacificspirittours.com; adult/child $71/39) and **Gray Line** (p40; adult/child $85/55).

Information

Armchair Books (☎ 604-932-5557; 4205 Village Sq; 🕙 9am-8pm)

Custom House Currency Exchange (☎ 604-938-6658; 4227 Village Stroll; 🕙 9am-7pm)

Electric Daisy (☎ 604-938-9961; 4308 Main St; per hr $10; 🕙 10am-10pm) Offers Internet access.

Hot Box (☎ 604-905-5644; 109-4369 Main St; per 15min $4; 🕙 8am-10pm) Offers Internet access.

Post Office (☎ 604-932-5012; 106-4360 Lorimer Rd; 🕙 8am-5pm Mon-Fri, 8am-noon Sat)

Thomas Cook Exchange (☎ 604-938-0101; 4230 Gateway Dr; 🕙 9am-5pm Mon-Sat)

Tourism Whistler Activity & Information Centre (☎ information 604-938-2769, 877-991-9988, reservations 604-664-5625, 800-944-7853; www.tourismwhistler.com; Whistler, Conference Centre, 4010 Whistler Way; 🕙 9am-

5pm) Books activities or accommodations, but note an $8 to $20 'processing fee' is added to orders totaling $150 or more.

Whistler 2010 Info Centre (☎ 604-932-2010, 866-932-2010; www.winter2010.com; 4365 Blackcomb Way; 🕙 11am-5pm Thu-Mon) Provides Olympics information.

Whistler Chamber Visitor Information Centre (☎ 604-932-5922, ext 17; www.whistlerchamber.com; 4230 Gateway Dr; 🕙 9am-6pm) Also operates kiosks in Village North (🕙 11am-6pm summer) and Upper Village (🕙 10am-6pm summer). Provides information on all things local.

Whistler Health Care Centre (☎ 604-932-4911; 4380 Lorimer Rd; 🕙 8am-10pm)

Sights & Activities

Hours vary seasonally. Ski equipment rentals cost from $32 per day.

Chateau Whistler Golf Club (☎ 604-938-2092, 877-938-2092; 4612 Blackcomb Way; green fees $225; ⏱ May-Oct)

Cougar Mountain Adventures (☎ 888-297-2222; www.cougarmountain.ca; 4314 Main St; tours from $49; ⏱ 10:30am-3pm)

Intrawest (☎ 604-932-3434, 800-766-0449; www.whistlerblackcomb.com) This corporation operates the two mountains' winter skiing (lift adult/child 7-12/child 13-18 per day $69/35/59; ⏱ 8:30am-3pm Nov–late Jan, 8:30am-3:30pm late Jan–Mar, 8:30am-4pm Mar–season end), with the season ending late April on Blackcomb and early June on Whistler; summer glacier skiing (lift adult/child 7-12/child 13-18 per day $45/22/36; ⏱ noon-3pm early Jun–early Aug); mountain biking park (adult/child 10-12/child 13-17 $39/19/35, bike rental per half day adult/child $70/50; ⏱ 10am-5pm mid-May–early Oct); and hiking (lift adult/child 7-12/child 13-18 per day $25/7/20; ⏱ 10am-5pm late Jun–early Oct). Buy tickets by the Whistler Village Gondola base. Winter discount passes are available at 7-11 and other grocery and convenience stores around Greater Vancouver.

Lost Lake Cross Country Connection (☎ 604-905-0071; www.crosscountryconnection.bc.ca; rentals adult/child $24/16, tours from $28; ⏱ 9am-8pm Mon-Sat, 9am-5pm Sun) Located by the cross-country ticket booth.

Mountain Adventure Centre (☎ Whistler 604-905-2295; 4320 Sundial Cres, by Dubh Linn pub; ⏱ 10am-6pm; ☎ Blackcomb 604-938-2017; FairmontChateau Whistler, 4599 Chateau Blvd; ski rentals adult/child per day from $32/21; ⏱ 10am-6pm)

Nicklaus North Golf & Country Club (☎ 604-938-9898, 800-386-9898; 8080 Nicklaus North Blvd; green fees $210; ⏱ early May–early Oct)

Outdoor Adventures at Whistler (☎ 604-932-0647; www.adventureswhistler.com; 4205 Village Sq; snowshoeing tours from $55; ⏱ 8:30am-5pm)

Spokeswomen (☎ 604-932-3434, 800-766-0449; www.spokeswomen.com; weekend biking camps from $249)

Whistler Golf Club (☎ 604-932-4544, 800-376-1777; 4001 Whistler Way; green fees $159; ⏱ May–mid-Oct)

Whistler Heli-Skiing (☎ 604-932-4105, 888-435-4754; www.heliskiwhistler.com; 3-4241 Village Stroll; tours from $640; ⏱ 10am-6pm)

Whistler Municipality Cross-Country Skiing Ticket Booth (Lot 4A off Lorimer Rd; ticket adult/child $10/5; ⏱ 8am-9pm Nov-Mar)

Whistler Outdoor Experience (☎ 604-932-3389, 877-386-1888; www.whistleroutdoor.com; call for directions; horseback tours from $45; ⏱ 10am-4pm)

Whistler River Adventures (☎ 604-932-3532, 888-932-3532; www.whistlerriver.com; near Whistler Village Gondola; horseback tours $60, rafting tours from $69)

Ziptrek Eco Tours (☎ 604-935-0001; www.ziptrek.com; Carleton Lodge, 4290 Mountain Lane; adult/child 14 & under $98/78; ⏱ 8am-6pm)

Sleeping

During winter you'll be hard-pressed to find a room for less than $150 per night; book well in advance and note many places have minimum stay requirements. Summer and shoulder seasons bring discounts, with prices practically halved. If you book through the **Central Reservation Service** (☎ 604-664-5625, 800-944-7853; www.tourismwhistler.com), beware the 'processing fee.'

Cascade Lodge (☎ 604-905-4875, 866-580-6643; www.whistler-cascadelodge.com; 4315 Northlands Blvd; r/ste $89/109 summer, $251/350 winter) What sets the Cascade apart is its quiet location, though it's still near the heart of the action.

Cedar Springs Lodge (☎ 604-938-8007, 800-727-7547; www.whistlerbb.com; 8106 Cedar Springs Rd; r $75-159 summer, $119-255 winter) A comfy, eight-room B&B (two rooms share a bathroom), with a shared hot tub, roaring fireplace and freshly baked cookies.

Chalet Luise (☎ 604-932-4187; www.chaletluise.com; 7461 Ambassador Cres; r $125-160) An eight-room B&B within walking distance of Whistler Village and the lifts: jacuzzi, sauna, private bathroom and a cooked breakfast are part of the deal.

Erin Lodge B&B (☎ 604-932-3641, 800-665-2003; www.erinlodgewhistler.com; 7162 Nancy Greene Dr; r $95-125 summer, $125-275 winter) Eight charming and bright rooms with private bathrooms. A mighty breakfast and afternoon whisky round out the Irish hospitality.

Fairmont Chateau Whistler (☎ 604-938-8000, 800-441-1414; www.fairmont.com; 4599 Chateau Blvd;

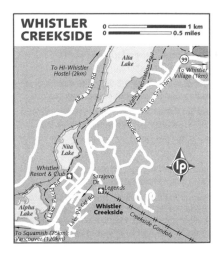

Excursions – Whistler

r from $459/759 summer/winter) An enormous castle with ski-in/ski-out proximity to the lifts.

HI Whistler Hostel (☎ 604-932-5492; www.hihostels .ca; 5678 Alta Lake Rd; dm members/non-members $20/24 summer, $24/28 winter) It's remote, but enjoys a beautiful setting on Alta Lake, with a dead-on view of Blackcomb. Perks include canoes and bike rentals. It's a 4km (45-min) walk to Whistler Village.

Legends (☎ 604-938-9999; 2036 London Lane, Creekside; ste $139-229) Ski-in/ski-out access to the Whistler Creekside Gondola gives you more time in the hot tub and in your modern-rustic suite.

Shoestring Lodge (☎ 604-932-3338; www.shoestring lodge.com; 7124 Nancy Greene Dr; dm/r $19/75 summer, $29/109 winter) The motel-style rooms and 4-bed dorms are cleaner than you'd expect. It can get rowdy here, with the Boot Pub on the premises, so ask for a room down the hall if you want quiet.

Whistler Resort & Club (☎ 604-932-2343; www.rain bowretreats.com; 2129 Lake Placid Rd, Creekside; r/ste $70/85 summer, $99/130 winter) Harkens back to the 1970s, with red brick fireplaces, wood paneling and some pull-down Murphy beds. Free use of canoes, tennis courts and bicycles in summer.

Eating

Stock up at the IGA grocery store in Village North.

Araxi (☎ 604-932-4540; 4222 Village Sq; tapas $8-13, mains $18-23; ⏰ 11am-11pm, from 5pm in winter) The crisp menu is divided between 'Aqua' and 'Terra' selections, with BC cheese platters for dessert.

Auntie Em's (☎ 604-932-1163; Whistler's Marketplace; items $5-8; ⏰ 6:30am-6pm) A simple café selling fresh baked goods and sandwiches.

Black's (☎ 604-932-6408; 4270 Mountain Sq; mains $8-15; ⏰ 7am-11pm) Black's is best known for its pizza, selection of 99 beers and upstairs patio for a hot toddy while you watch skiers schuss down the slopes.

Caramba (☎ 604-938-1879; 12-4314 Main St; mains $12-19; ⏰ 5-10pm, from 11:30am Fri-Sun) Caramba's Mediterranean fare is highly recommended.

Chef Bernard's (☎ 604-932-7051; 4573 Chateau Blvd; dishes $5-10; ⏰ 8am-4pm) The Fairmont's former chef works with local producers to bring griddle cakes, smoked wild sockeye bagels and other scrumptious dishes to your table. Dinner is served in **BBK Pub** (right).

Citta's Bistro (☎ 604-932-4177; 4217 Village Stroll; mains $9-13; ⏰ 9am-11pm) This relaxed modern bistro has a short menu of creative food; try the Guinness chicken fajita or BC salmon with fruit salsa and ravioli.

Ingrid's Village Café (☎ 604-932-7000; 4305 Skiers Approach; items $5-8; ⏰ 7:30am-6pm) Just off Village

Sq, this makes a perfect stop for breakfast or lunch, with several varieties of egg sandwiches and vegetarian burgers on wholegrain bread.

Mogul's Coffee (☎ 604-932-4845; Village Sq; sandwiches under $6; ⏰ 6:30am-9pm) Fulfill your caffeine needs and watch the bustle of the square.

Whistler Noodle House (☎ 604-932-2228; 9-4330 Northlands Blvd; mains $9-13; ⏰ lunch & dinner) Nothing delivers comfort like a bowl of warm, slurpy noodles.

Entertainment

Check the free *Pique Newsmagazine* and *Whistler Question* for listings.

BBK Pub (☎ 604-932-7051; 4573 Chateau Rd) It's BC's smallest pub, so they say, with 24 snug seats.

Boot Pub (☎ 604-932-3338; 7124 Nancy Greene Dr) Live bands play, but the exotic dancers of 'Das Boot Ballet' are the draw.

BrewHouse Restaurant & Pub (☎ 604-905-2739; 4355 Blackcomb Way) Operated by Vancouver's **Yaletown Brewing Company** (p124), it produces its own hoppy suds – try the Lifty Lager or Big Wolf Bitter.

Buffalo Bill's (☎ 604-932-6613; 4122 Village Green) Where the over-30s' crowd hoists pints.

Dubh Linn Gate Old Irish Pub (☎ 604-905-4047; 4320 Sundial Cres) Hand-built in the old country, with a traditional menu of country cooking and often live music.

Garfinkel's (☎ 604-932-2323; 1-4308 Main St; ⏰ Thu-Sat) People cram in to dance to hip-hop and rock on nights not dominated by touring musical acts.

Longhorn Saloon & Grill (☎ 604-932-5999; 4290 Mountain Sq) Attracts crowds off the slopes right at Whistler base.

Merlin's Bar & Grill (☎ 604-938-7700; Upper Village, base of Blackcomb) Sit on the patio and watch your buddies ski down Blackcomb.

Savage Beagle (☎ 604-938-3337; 4222 Village Sq) Top 40 music and younger crowds.

Detour: Pemberton

A 30km drive north of Whistler on Hwy 99 takes you into the cowboy territory of Pemberton. Horseback riders amble along pokey trails, skiers whoosh through powdery backcountry, snowmobilers tear across the Pemberton Ice Cap and weary adventure seekers soak in **Meager Creek Hot Springs**. Pemberton's **Visitor Info Centre** (☎ 604-894-6175; www.pemberton .net; cnr Hwy 99 & Pemberton Rd; ⏰ 9am-5pm May-Sep) provides information on sights and tour companies, while www.pembertonbandb.com lists specifics on the 10 or so lodging options in town.

Excursions – Whistler

197

BOWEN ISLAND

So you want to visit the Gulf Islands, but don't think you have time? You do. Just allow 20 minutes for the ferry ride to Bowen, West Vancouver's laid-back island suburb.

Known as the 'Happy Isle,' Bowen hit its stride as a picnickers' paradise in the 1920s when the Union Steamship Company arrived, providing regular service from the mainland. Today you can stroll the waterfront boardwalks near Snug Cove, the small village where the ferry docks. Most of the town, with its early-20th-century heritage buildings housing restaurants, pubs, galleries and shops, straddles Government Rd, which runs straight up from the ferry terminal. The **Visitor Info Centre** and **Chamber of Commerce** provide a useful visitor guide with maps.

Good swimming beaches are found at **Mannion Bay**, next to Snug Cove, and **Bowen Bay**, at the west end of the island. There are numerous walking trails, which range from a five-minute stroll toward the picnic tables at Snug Cove to a 45-minute trek from the ferry dock to **Crippen Regional Park**. Inside the park an easy 4km loop around Killarney Lake is favored by bird watchers; the more difficult 10km Mt Gardner Trail reaches the island's highest point (719m). Many other trails are accessible to cyclists and horseback riders. If you have something more adventurous in mind, **Bowen Island Sea Kayaking** offers rentals and short kayaking tours, including a sunset paddle.

Information

Visitor Info Centre (☎ 604-947-9024; www.bowen island.org/visitors; near Snug Cove, at the crossroads; ☺ 10am-3:30pm Wed-Thu, 10am-4pm Fri-Sun in summer) Visit the **Chamber of Commerce** (432 Cardena Rd) next door at other times.

Sights & Activities

Bowen Island Sea Kayaking (☎ 604-947-9266, 800-605-2925; www.bowenislandkayaking.com; 3hr tour $50) Located by the ferry dock.

Sleeping & Eating

Lodge at the Old Dorm (☎ 604-947-0947; www.lodgeat theolddorm.com; 460 Melmore Rd; r $75-125) A five-minute stroll from the ferry dock, this heritage building has six rooms with art deco accents; continental breakfast included.

Doc Morgan's Inn (☎ 604-947-0808; pub fare $6-12, dinner mains $15-22; ☺ 11am-11pm) This pub and restaurant is reminiscent of a seafarer's inn. Entertainment ranges from comedians to bagpipers. Cozy up to the river-rock fireplace inside, or eat fish and chips on the outdoor deck.

Snug (☎ 604-947-0402; meals around $5; ☺ 5am-4pm Mon-Fri, 7am-5pm Sat & Sun) This cozy little coffeehouse serves breakfast, and sandwiches, chili and shepherd's pie at lunch.

Transportation

Distance from Vancouver 19km
Direction Northwest
Travel time 1hr, incl ferry ride from Horseshoe Bay (p77)
Ferry There is a 20-minute crossing with BC Ferries (☎ 250-386-3431, in BC 888-223-3779; www.bc ferries.com) from Horseshoe Bay to Snug Cove (round-trip adult/child 5-11/bicycle $6.25/3.25/1.50m, 15 sailings from 6am to 9:30pm). See p206 for directions to Horseshoe Bay terminal.
Bus Island-spanning public transportation is available via the **Bowen Island Community Shuttle** (☎ 604-947-0229) for $2. Service is provided from 5.35am to 9:35am and 3:35pm to 6:35pm Monday to Friday, and weekends in summer.

SOUTHERN GULF ISLANDS

When Canadians refer to BC as 'lotus land,' the Gulf Islands are what they have in mind. The mild climate, relative isolation and natural beauty combine to make these 200 small and mostly uninhabited islands an escapist's dream destination. Traditionally, they've attracted folks who shun the nine-to-five grind of mainland life.

Salt Spring Island is the largest and most populous of the southern islands, with nearly 12,000 permanent residents. The island is renowned as an artists' colony, a hideaway for music and movie stars, and an organic farmers' haven. The principal village of **Ganges** is close to the Long Harbour ferry landing. The **Visitor Info Centre** here keeps listings of special events, and maps of galleries and artists' studios open to the public. A vibrant **Saturday morning market**

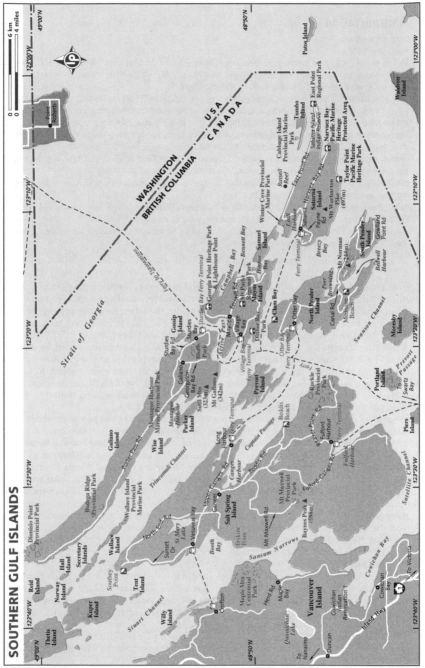

SOUTHERN GULF ISLANDS

Transportation

Direction Southwest

Travel time 1-3hr

Air Two companies fly from Vancouver to the various islands: **Harbour Air Seaplanes** (☎ 604-274-1277, 800-665-0212; www.harbour-air.com) and **Seair** (☎ 604-273-8900, 800-447-3247; www.seairseaplanes.com); call for schedules. A typical one-way fare is $80 for a 30- to 75-minute flight.

Ferry From Tsawwassen on the mainland ferries go to Saturna, Mayne, Galiano, Pender and Salt Spring Islands, and cost $10.25/38 per passenger/car; the return trip costs $4.75/19.75. Ferries also depart from Swartz Bay on Vancouver Island and head to the islands, costing $6.50/21 per passenger/car. Once on the islands, inter-island ferries cost $3.50/7.50. Reservations for cars are strongly advised during summer. Pick up a ferry schedule at any Visitor Info Centre or check out **BC Ferries** (☎ 250-386-3431, in BC 888-223-3779; www.bcferries.com). Be aware that many routes involve stops, transfers and other potentially confusing arrangements. **Gulf Islands Water Taxi** (☎ 250-537-2510; www.gulfislands.com/watertaxi) provides private speedboat service ($15) among the islands; call for schedule.

Bus On Galiano use the **Go Galiano Island Shuttle** (☎ 250-539-0202; www.gogaliano.com). Rates to just about anywhere on the island are listed on its website.

Public Transportation There isn't any on the islands, so many people hitchhike.

Cycling Bicycle rental (about $30 per day) is usually available near the ferry terminals. Cycling the quiet island roads is a popular pastime, but check a topographic map first. On Salt Spring, for instance, the roads are narrow, winding and almost impossibly steep. Mayne offers the friendliest terrain.

(☯ 8am-4pm Apr-Oct) for artists, craftspeople and farmers is probably the best of its kind on the islands. If you want to get out and about, **Mt Maxwell Provincial Park** offers sweeping views and horseback riding; **Salt Spring Guided Rides** can help with the latter. Ranking among the Gulf Islands' best parks, **Ruckle Provincial Park**, 10km east of the Fulford Harbour ferry terminal, offers easy forest and shore hikes. The island's **Festival of the Arts** takes place in July.

Recreation trumps the arts on the **Pender Islands** – actually two islands joined by a short bridge. The 2000-plus residents prefer to spend their time playing in the glorious natural surroundings, where the sea, sky and neighboring islands all seem close enough to touch. Wherever you go, watch for the tame deer wandering about. Near Medicine Beach at Bedwell Harbour, North Pender's **Prior Centennial Provincial Park** has several walking trails. On South Pender good views reward the hour-long hike up **Mt Norman** (255m).

Despite its proximity to Tsawwassen, long and narrow **Galiano Island** has fewer than 1000 residents, most living on the southeast side near **Sturdies Bay**. About 75% of the island is forest and bush. The island has excellent beaches, especially at **Montague Harbour Provincial Marine Park**. You can hike nearly the entire length of the east coast and climb either **Sutil Mountain** (323m) or **Mt Galiano** (342m) for panoramic views. There's good scuba diving at Alcala Point, home to friendly wolf eels; contact **Galiano Diving** for equipment and charters. The **Visitor Info Centre** is on the right-hand side as you leave the Sturdies ferry terminal. Call **Go Galiano Island Shuttle** for pickups or trips around the island.

Mayne Island springs from a colorful past as a stopover point for gold-rush miners. **Village Bay**, on the island's southwestern side, harbors the ferry terminal. **Miner's Bay**, on Active Pass a few kilometers east, is the commercial area. Mayne's back roads offer some of the best cycling in the Gulf Islands. Its protected waters make it a good place to learn to kayak; try **Mayne Island Canoe & Kayak Rentals**.

The most lightly populated island, **Saturna** (population 350) is harder to reach than the other islands, making it all the more attractive as a tranquil escape. At the top of 497m **Mt Warburton Pike** is a wildlife reserve with feral goats and fine views (though you'll also have to look at telecommunications equipment). **Saturna Island Vineyards** offers free tours and tastings. The ferry terminal in **Lyall Harbour** has eating options nearby.

The **Gulf Island National Park Reserve** (☎ 250-654-4000; www.pc.gc.ca/gulf) was formed in 2003 to protect the region's fragile coastal eco-system. It spans portions of Mayne, Saturna and the Penders, as well as 12 other islands.

Lodging is tight throughout the islands, so reservations are mandatory, especially in the peak summer season. Many places close between November and April. **Canadian Gulf Islands**

Reservations (☎ 250-539-3089, 866-539-3089; www.gulfislandsreservations.com) handles bookings for 200 B&Bs and inns. Most restaurants on the islands are associated with accommodations, so they're not cheap. Many of the islands don't have ATMs. Check out the links at www.gulfislands.com for a sneak preview of life on the islands.

Salt Spring Island

Visitor Info Centre (☎ 250-537-5252; www.saltspringtoday.com; 121 Lower Ganges Rd; ⊙ 11am-3pm)

Ferry Terminals Long Harbour on Salt Spring Island serves Vancouver, Swartz Bay and other Southern Gulf Islands; Fulford Harbour serves Swartz Bay; and Vesuvius Bay is for ferries headed to Crofton, roughly midway between Nanaimo and Victoria.

Salt Spring Guided Rides (☎ 250-537-5761; 121 Wright Rd) Offers horseback riding.

Old Farmhouse B&B (☎ 250-537-4113; www.oldfarmhouse.ca; 1077 North End Rd; r $155-185) Near St Mary Lake, this century-old restored farmhouse has four rooms with private bathrooms and balconies.

Seabreeze Inne (☎ 250-537-4145; www.seabreezeinns.com; 101 Bittancourt Rd; r from $90) Provides rooms overlooking Ganges Harbour; a few have kitchenettes (add $10).

Moby's Marine Pub (☎ 250-537-5559; Ganges, 124 Upper Ganges Rd; meals from $12) Moby's offers a winning combination of excellent food, entertainment and views of Ganges Harbour.

Treehouse Café (☎ 250-537-5379; 106 Purvis Lane, Ganges; dishes $3-8; ⊙ from 8am) Close to the Ganges waterfront, this hip spot has outdoor tables for breakfast and lunch, plus dinner in summer.

North & South Pender Islands

Inn on Pender Island (☎ 250-629-3353, 800-550-0172; www.innonpender.com; 4709 Canal Rd; s/d from $79/89, cabins $139) Located by Prior Centennial Park, this small inn in the woods is popular with cyclists. There's a hot tub and an excellent licensed restaurant.

Galiano Island

Visitor Info Centre (☎ 250-539-2233; www.galianoisland.com; 2590 Sturdies Bay Rd Galiano Island)

Galiano Diving (☎ 250-539-3109; www.galianodiving.ca; single dive from $30)

Bodega Resort (☎ 250-539-2677; www.bodegaresort.com; 120 Cook Rd; cottages $120) A favorite family resort providing seven fully furnished log cabins, each with three bedrooms, kitchen and sundeck.

Hummingbird Pub (☎ 250-539-5472; Sturdies Bay, 47 Sturdies Bay Rd) There's live entertainment on summer weekends, and an outdoor picnic and barbecue area.

Max & Moritz Spicy Island Food House (☎ 250-539-5888; Sturdies Bay, Sturdies Bay Rd; dishes under $11) Arrive early at the ferry so you can sample the delicious Indonesian and German food.

Mayne Island

Chamber of Commerce (www.mayneislandchamber.ca)

Mayne Island Canoe & Kayak Rentals (☎ 250-539-2667; www.maynekayak.com; Miners Bay, 411 Fernhill Rd)

Tinkerers B&B (☎ 250-539-2280; www.bbcanada.com/133.html; Miners Bay, 417 Sunset Pl; r $95-115) Five rooms, some with shared bathroom, and hammocks to laze in and enjoy the sea views.

Springwater Lodge (☎ 250-539-5521; www.springwaterlodge.com; Fernhill Rd, near Miners Bay dock; dinner mains $15-20; ⊙ breakfast, lunch & dinner) This pub and restaurant is attached to BC's oldest continuously operating hotel and serves loggers' portions.

Saturna Island

Saturna Island Tourism Association (www.saturnatourism.com)

Saturna Island Vineyards (☎ 250-539-5139; www.saturnavineyards.com; ⊙ 11:30am-4:30pm May-Oct)

Breezy Bay B&B (☎ 250-539-3339; www.saturnacan.net/breezy; 131 Payne Rd; s/d $60/85; ⊙ May-Oct only) This 1890s' farmhouse is about 2km from the ferry terminal, with a long veranda overlooking orchards and a pond. Only shared bathrooms available.

SUNSHINE COAST

The Sunshine Coast is a geographical orphan, separated from the rest of the Lower Mainland by the Coast Mountains. Yes, the entire maritime region really does enjoy more sunshine annually than anywhere else on the mainland, and it's popular for kayaking, boating and other watery pursuits. Awesome ferry rides take over in spots where the highway runs out of land.

Gibsons Landing is the gateway to the Coast and a good destination if you want to sample the area for a day. This small yet well-trafficked fishing village sits 5km from **Langdale ferry terminal**.

Transportation

Distance from Vancouver Gibsons Landing 39km
Direction Northwest
Travel time 1½hr, incl ferry ride from Horseshoe Bay (p77)
Car Hwy 101 winds nearly the entire length of the coast, starting from Gibsons. It is interrupted by water between Earls Cove and Saltery Bay, where BC Ferries bridges the gap. Allow at least 1½ hours for the winding 84km drive from Gibsons to Earls Cove. It's possible to drive from Gibsons to Powell River in three hours (including ferry ride), but it's best to allow more time.
Ferry Services are run by **BC Ferries** (☎ 250-386-3431, in BC 888-223-3779; www.bcferries.com). It sails eight times daily between Horseshoe Bay and Langdale, near Gibsons (adult/child/car $8.50/4.25/30, 40min). This fare covers either the return trip to Horseshoe Bay or the ferry ride you'll need down the road from Earls Cove to Saltery Bay (50min). At Powell River, four ferries depart daily for Comox on Vancouver Island (adult/child/car $8/4/27, 75min). See p206 for Horseshoe Bay directions and Circlepac discount pass information.
Bus From Van to Powell River, **Malaspina Coach Lines** (p206) runs services. The **Sunshine Coast Transit System** (☎ 604-885-3234; www.busonline.ca) has public buses that ply the route between Langdale and Sechelt ($1.75).

Most visitors are charmed by the quaint shopping area along **Gower Point Rd**. You can buy fresh seafood right off the dock or visit the wharfside establishments for a bite. You probably will notice the many references to *The Beachcombers*, a popular CBC TV series that was filmed here in the '70s. There's a **seasonal information center** at the landing and a year-round **Visitor Info Centre** in Upper Gibsons, the commercial strip further up the hill along Hwy 101.

About 10km northwest of Gibsons, but light years away in spirit, counter-cultural **Roberts Creek** was settled during the Vietnam War era by US draft dodgers. Roberts Creek Rd, off Hwy 101, leads to the anti-commercial, rural center of town. Check the placards around town or www.robertscreek.com to see what's happening at the community hall.

About 31km north of the **Saltery Bay ferry terminal**, **Powell River** is an industrial town anchoring the top of the Coast. The **Visitor Info Centre** has a good map of the 180km **Sunshine Coast Trail** and its 27 shorter trails; it can also recommend kayaking, mountain-biking and scuba-diving outfitters, and tour operators to **Desolation Sound**. The sound is accessible only by boat, as is tropical **Savary Island**, sometimes called 'the Hawaii of the North,' with its sandy beaches.

Gibsons Landing

Visitor Info Centre (☎ 604-886-2325; www.gibsons chamber.com; Sunnycrest Mall, 900 Gibsons Way; ☺ 9am-5pm Tue-Sat)

Seasonal Information Center (☺ 9am-6pm summer; at the landing)

Gibsons Fish Market (☎ 604-886-8363; 292 Gower Point Rd) Enjoy the tasty fish and chips.

Gramma's Pub (☎ 604-886-8215; 412 Marine Dr; mains $7-15; ☺ lunch & dinner) Gramma's has a great view of the harbor and is where Gibsons' seafolk unwind.

Molly's Reach (☎ 604-886-9710; cnr Marine Dr & Gower Point Rd; breakfast & lunch dishes $6-11, dinner mains $13-21) This greasy spoon boasts harbor views, *Beachcombers* memorabilia and well-prepared seafood.

Roberts Creek

Gumboot Garden Café (☎ 604-885-4216; 1057 Roberts Creek Rd; mains $7-14; ☺ breakfast, lunch & dinner) An earthy, wood-filled café serving homemade granola, veggie sandwiches, burritos and more.

Powell River

Visitor Info Centre (☎ 604-485-4701, 877-817-8669; www.discoverpowellriver.com; 4690 Marine Ave; ☺ 9am-5pm)

Old Courthouse Inn & Hostel (☎ 604-483-4000; 6243 Walnut St; r $20-75) In the Townsite section, this beautifully restored courthouse and police station has antique-furnished rooms and a great little café; ask about low-cost pickups from the bus or ferry.

Directory

Directory

TRANSPORTATION
AIR
Airlines

Airlines serving Vancouver's international airport include:

Aeromexico (☎ 800-237-6639; www.aeromexico.com)

Air Canada (☎ 888-247-2262; www.aircanada.ca)

Air China (☎ 604-685-0921; www.airchina.com.cn)

Air New Zealand (☎ 800-663-5494; www.airnewzealand.com)

Air North (☎ 800-661-0407, in the USA ☎ 800-764-0407; www.flyairnorth.com)

Air Pacific (☎ 800-227-4446; www.airpacific.com)

Air Transat (☎ 866-847-1112; www.airtransat.com)

Alaska Airlines (☎ 800-252-7522; www.alaskaair.com)

Aloha Airlines (☎ 800-367-5250; www.alohaairlines.com)

America West Airlines (☎ 800-363-2597; www.americawest.com)

American Airlines (☎ 800-433-7300; www.aa.com)

British Airways (☎ 800-247-9297; www.britishairways.com)

Cathay Pacific (☎ 604-606-8888, 888-338-1668; www.cathaypacific.com)

China Airlines (☎ 604-682-6777; www.china-airlines.com)

Continental Airlines (☎ 800-523-3273; www.continental.com)

Delta Air Lines (☎ 800-221-1212; www.delta.com)

EVA Air (☎ 800-695-1188; www.evaair.com)

Horizon Air (☎ 800-547-9308; www.horizonair.com)

Japan Airlines (☎ 800-525-3663; www.jal.co.jp/en/)

Jetsgo (☎ 866-440-0441; www.jetsgo.net)

Korean Air (☎ 800-438-5000; www.koreanair.com)

Lufthansa (☎ 800-563-5954; www.lufthansa.com)

Mexicana Airlines (☎ 800-531-7921; www.mexicana.com)

Northwest Airlines/KLM (☎ 800-447-4747; www.nwa.com)

Pacific Coastal Airlines Ltd (☎ 604-273-8666; www.pacific-coastal.com)

Qantas Airways (☎ 800-227-4500; www.qantas.com.au)

Scandinavian Airlines (☎ 800-221-2350; www.scandinavian.net)

Singapore Airlines (☎ 604-689-1223; www.singaporeair.com)

SkyWest Airlines (☎ 800-701-9448; www.skywest.com)

Thai Airways International (☎ 800-426-5204; www.thaiair.com)

Thomas Cook Airlines (☎ 877-894-4333; www.thomascook.ca)

United Airlines (☎ 800-241-6522; www.united.ca)

WestJet (☎ 800-538-5696; www.westjet.com)

ZOOM Airlines (☎ 866-359-9666; www.flyzoom.com)

Brilliant views and downtown harbor-to-harbor convenience make seaplanes a top mode of travel. A typical one-way fare to Vancouver Island is $99 to Victoria, $54 to Nanaimo. Airlines operating seaplane services from Vancouver include:

Baxter Aviation (☎ 604-683-6525, 800-661-5599; www.baxterair.com) To Nanaimo.

Harbour Air Seaplanes (☎ 604-274-1277, 800-665-0212; www.harbour-air.com) To Victoria, Nanaimo and Gulf Islands.

West Coast Air (☎ 800-347-2222; www.westcoastair.com) To Victoria.

If you prefer helicopters, **Helijet Airways** (☎ 800-665-4354) flies from Vancouver to Victoria in 12-passenger S-76 Sikorsky helicopters (one way $119).

TICKETING WEBSITES/AGENCIES

In addition to airline companies' own websites, which often offer Internet-only deals, a number of third-party websites can be helpful in finding flight discounts. Try the following:

www.cheaptickets.ca

www.expedia.ca

www.lowestfare.com

www.orbitz.com

www.priceline.ca

www.sta.com

www.travelocity.ca

Recommended agencies that offer bargain flight deals include **Travel CUTS** (☎ 866-246-9762; www.travelcuts.com), Canada's national student travel agency, and **Flight Centre** (☎ 866-967-5351; www.flightcentres.com), both with multiple offices in Vancouver, including:

Flight Centre (☎ 604-684-7951; Ste 203, Vancouver Public Library, 345 Robson St; ⏰ 10am-6pm Mon-Fri, 10am-4pm Sat; SkyTrain Stadium)

Travel CUTS (☎ 604-659-2845; HI-Downtown Hostel, 1114 Burnaby St; ⏰ 10am-2pm & 3-6pm Mon-Fri; bus 6)

Note that high season in Vancouver is June to September and around Christmas. The best rates are available November through March. It may be cheaper to fly into US west coast cities like Seattle rather than directly into Vancouver.

Airports

Tickets for flights departing Canada, whether purchased in Canada or abroad, usually include departure taxes.

Canada's second-busiest airport, **Vancouver International Airport** (YVR; Map pp228-9; ☎ 604-207-7077; www.yvr.ca) is about 13km south of the city on Sea Island in Richmond. There are two main terminals – international (including flights to the USA) and domestic – as well as a south terminal for seaplanes and smaller aircraft. Each of the main terminals has food courts, convenience shops, a spa, baggage storage facilities, ATMs, currency exchange booths and tourist information desks. The domestic terminal also has a medical clinic, dental clinic and pharmacy, while the international terminal has the goods and services tax (GST) refund office (see p215). Baggage carts are free throughout the airport. A free, twice-hourly shuttle bus links the main terminals to the South Terminal (which is too far to walk).

In downtown Vancouver there is a **seaplane terminal** (Map pp230-3) in Coal Harbour just west of Canada Place and a **helicopter terminal** (Map pp230-3) near Waterfront Station.

GETTING TO/FROM THE AIRPORT

The mint-green **Vancouver Airporter** (☎ 604-946-8866, 800-668-3141; www.yvrairporter.com; adult/child 5-12 one way $12/5, return $18/10) plies the route between Vancouver International Airport and the major downtown hotels from approximately 6:30am to 11pm. Buses depart every 20 to 30 minutes; the one-way trip takes about 35 minutes, depending on

traffic. Tickets can be purchased from the airporter ticket office on level 2 of the airport (outside the main terminal and adjacent to the bus departure zone), from the driver or from the hotels.

If you're not carrying heavy luggage and don't mind switching buses, the cheapest way between the airport and city is via **TransLink** (p208). From the airport, catch bus 424 to Airport Station, then go to Bay No 1 and transfer to bus 98-B-Line to Burrard SkyTrain station (located in downtown's core). The total trip takes 45 to 60 minutes and costs $3 (after 6:30pm or on weekends $2); the service operates 5:30am to 12:30am. Eventually TransLink is planning to build a light rail line from the airport to downtown; stay tuned for details.

A metered taxi to central Vancouver takes about 25 minutes, depending on traffic, and costs $25 to $35. If you're driving, proceed east after leaving the airport on Grant McConachie Way, and follow the Vancouver signs over the Arthur Laing Bridge. Take the Granville St exit and travel north along Granville St, continuing over the eponymous bridge into downtown. Parking at the airport garage costs $2.25 to $2.75 per half-hour. Long-term parking at an off-site lot costs $9 per day or $56 per week (including taxes), and free terminal shuttles are available.

BICYCLE

Vancouver has 16 cycling routes covering almost 130km. Two maps are available at various bicycle shops and bookstores: the *Regional Vancouver Cycling Map* ($3.95) by **TransLink** (p208) and *Cycling in Vancouver* (free) by the city transportation department's **Bicycle Hotline** (☎ 604-871-6070; www.city.vancouver.bc.ca /engsvcs/transport/cycling). The **Vancouver Area Cycling Coalition** (☎ 604-878-8222; www.vacc .bc.ca) and **Cycling BC** (☎ 604-737-3034; www .cycling.bc.ca) are also good resources. For further information, including equipment rentals, see p142.

Cyclists must wear helmets and stay off sidewalks. TransLink permits bicycles on most buses, SkyTrain and SeaBus, except during weekday morning (6:30am to 9:30am) and afternoon (3pm to 6:30pm) rush hours. Bicycles are allowed on **BC Ferries** (p206) and **Aquabus** (p206) ferries.

BOAT

Vessels large and small sail Vancouver's waterways. Cruise ships are big business from

May to September, generating $500 million from 330 sailings annually. Ships dock at **Canada Place** (Map pp230-3) downtown or **Ballantyne Pier** (Map pp228-9) to the east; a free shuttle runs between the two.

Ferries

BC Ferries (☎ 250-386-3431, in British Columbia 888-223-3779; www.bcferries.com) travel to Vancouver Island, the Gulf Islands, Sunshine Coast and beyond. Vancouver's two ferry terminals are at Tsawwassen and Horseshoe Bay. Most ferries from Tsawwassen (38km south of downtown Vancouver) go to Swartz Bay (32km north of Victoria on Vancouver Island) and the Southern Gulf Islands. Ferries from Horseshoe Bay (21km northwest of downtown Vancouver) mostly depart for the Sunshine Coast and Nanaimo (97km northwest of Victoria).

You can buy passenger-only tickets at the ferry terminals (no reservations accepted). You can also make vehicle reservations for a $15 fee – definitely recommended if you're traveling on weekends or anytime in July or August. BC Ferries' Circlepac is a four-route pass that saves 15% as you loop from the mainland to Vancouver Island to the Sunshine Coast (or in the opposite direction).

To reach Tsawwassen terminal by **TransLink** (p208), catch southbound bus 601 (South Delta) at Burrard SkyTrain station in downtown Vancouver and take it to the Ladner Exchange. From Ladner take bus 620 (Tsawwassen Ferry). To reach Horseshoe Bay, take northbound bus 257 (Horseshoe Bay Express) or 250 (Horseshoe Bay) from Georgia St near Granville St in downtown Vancouver. Either trip takes about 1¼ hours and costs $2 to $4. **Pacific Coach** (right) provides a more costly option that's less of a hassle. See the boxed text on p185 for directions to/from Victoria's terminals.

HarbourLynx (Map pp230-3; ☎ 604-688-5465, 866-206-5969; www.harbourlynx.com; tickets & boarding at Waterfront Station) operates 80-minute, high-speed ferry trips to downtown Nanaimo from Vancouver thrice daily (one way adult/child 2-11 $25/15).

Ferries do not run between Vancouver and Washington state, though many do operate between Victoria, on Vancouver Island, and Washington (see p185).

Mini Ferries

Back in Vancouver, **Aquabus** (☎ 604-689-5858; www.aquabus.bc.ca) and **False Creek Ferries** (FCF;

☎ 604-684-7781; www.granvilleislandferries .bc.ca) operate nifty mini-ferries that resemble bath-tub boats around False Creek from about 7am to 10pm (reduced schedule in winter). Both sail similar routes from Granville Island to Stamp's Landing to Yaletown ($3) or to Science World ($5). Aquabus also plies the route between Granville Island and the south foot of Hornby St ($2; this is the only route that also allows bicycles, which cost 50¢ extra); adult/child day passes cost $10/8. FCF goes from Sunset Beach's Aquatic Centre to Vanier Park's museums or Granville Island ($2); day passes cost $12/8.

BUS

Buses to Canadian and US destinations originate at **Pacific Central Station** (Map p234; ☎ 604-661-0325; 1150 Station St; ☼ 5am-midnight), as do trains (p208). The magnificent terminal has currency exchange booths, left-luggage lockers and an information desk. When making reservations, always ask for the direct or express bus. Purchasing round-trip versus one-way tickets often provides a small discount. Advance tickets do not guarantee a seat.

Greyhound Canada (☎ 604-482-8747, 800-661-8747; www.greyhound.ca) goes to points east and north in Canada, as well as Seattle. For further travel throughout the USA, contact **Greyhound Lines** (☎ 214-849-8100, 800-229-9424; www.greyhound.com). Note Greyhound does not go to Victoria. Discounts on standard one-way adult fares are given to ISIC cardholders, seniors, children and pairs traveling together. Purchase tickets at least a week in advance for the best prices. Routes and average fares from Vancouver include:

Calgary	$134	15-17½hr
Jasper	$116	12hr
Nanaimo	$22	3hr
Seattle	$34	3½-4½hr
Whistler	$18	2½hr
Whitehorse	$160	44½hr

Other useful bus companies:

Bigfoot Adventure Tours (☎ 604-777-9905, 888-244-6673; www.bigfoottours.com) Shuttle buses to Seattle year-round ($34, 3hr), Whistler ($35, 2½hr) and Banff in winter ($107 excluding overnight accommodation in Squilax, 12hr). Also offers guided hop-on, hop-off backpacker tours through Western Canada in summer.

Malaspina Coach Lines (☎ 877-227-8287) Two buses daily (one in winter) from Pacific Central Station to the

Sunshine Coast, including Gibsons Landing ($15, 1¾hr) and Powell River ($37, 5¼hr).

Pacific Coach Lines (☎ 604-662-8074, 800-661-1725; www.pacificcoach.com) Buses to Victoria ($32.50 including ferry, 3½hr) depart almost hourly (fewer in winter) from Pacific Central Station; will also pick up at the airport and Canada Place downtown.

Perimeter (☎ 604-266-5386, 877-317-7788; www .perimeterbus.com) Eight to 11 buses daily between Vancouver and Whistler (one way adult/child 5-11 $65/45); departures from most downtown hotels and the airport.

Quick Coach Lines (☎ 604-940-4428, 800-665-2122; www.quickcoach.com) Several shuttle buses daily to downtown Seattle (US$33, 4hr) and Sea-Tac airport (US$41, 4½hr); departures from Vancouver airport and various downtown hotels.

CAR & MOTORCYCLE

For sightseeing around town, you'll be fine without a car. However, for visits that incorporate Greater Vancouver's mountains and suburbs, a car makes life much simpler.

Driving

Odd but true: Vancouver doesn't have any expressways going through its core. While this gives the city a laid-back feel, it also creates congestion, which reaches epic proportions along the city's bridges (best avoided at rush hour, roughly 8am to 9:30am and 4:30pm to 6:30pm).

Petrol (gasoline) in Vancouver averages 90¢ per liter, which equals nearly US$3.65 per US gallon. The use of seat belts is compulsory throughout Canada, and motorcyclists must wear helmets. Drivers can turn right on a red light after first having made a full stop; drivers must stop for pedestrians at crosswalks.

With few exceptions, you can legally drive in Canada as long as you have a valid driver's license issued by your home country. You may be required to show an international driving permit if your license isn't written in English (or French). Short-term US visitors can bring in their own vehicles without special permits, provided they have insurance. If you've rented a car in the USA and you are driving it into Canada, bring a copy of the rental agreement to save any possible hassle by border officials.

On weekends and holidays, especially during summer, major land border crossings with the USA quickly become jammed. You can check border wait times online before leaving at www.cbsa-asfc.gc.ca/general/times/menu -e.html. Smaller, secondary US–Canada border crossings are usually not busy, but sometimes are so quiet that the customs officers have nothing better to do than tear your luggage apart – it's a crapshoot.

Parking

Finding street parking downtown is a challenge. Meters can cost up to $2 per hour and be limited to just one or two hours. Unmetered parking on side streets may look inviting, but often is available only to those with neighborhood residency permits; check the signs. Tow trucks show no mercy, and getting your vehicle back will cost a bundle in cash and aggravation.

Easier to use, though more expensive, are public parkades; check the Transportation boxes throughout the Neighborhoods chapter for costs and locations. In this book, the parking icon **P** is used for venues that have free parking; if on-site parking is available for a fee, the amount follows the icon.

Rental

Rates go up and down like the stock market, so it's worth phoning around or surfing the web to see what's available. Booking ahead usually ensures the best rates, with the airport often being cheaper than downtown. Typically, a small car might cost $25 to $40 per day, or $175 to $300 per week. But after adding insurance, taxes, excess kilometers and any other fees, you could be handed a pretty surprising bill. Heavily discounted weekend rates (less than $100) may include 'extra days,' say from noon Thursday until noon Monday.

Major car-rental agencies that have reservation desks at Vancouver's airport, as well as city-wide offices, include:

Budget (☎ 604-668-7000, 800-268-8900; www.budget .com)

Enterprise (☎ 604-688-5500, 800-736-8222; www .enterprise.com)

Hertz (☎ 604-606-4711, in Canada 800-263-0600; www .hertz.com)

Thrifty (☎ 604-681-4869, 800-847-4389; www.thrifty .com)

Smaller independent agencies offer lower rates, but may have fewer (and perhaps older) cars available. Try:

Lo-Cost Rent-A-Car (Map pp230-3; ☎ 604-689-9664, 888-556-2678; 1105 Granville St; 🕑 8am-6pm)

Rent-A-Wreck (Map pp230-3; ☎ 604-688-0001, 800-327-0116; www.rentawreckvancouver.com; 1349 Hornby St; ☽ 8am-7pm Mon-Fri, 9am-6pm Sat, 9am-5pm Sun)

TAXI

Metered fares start at $2.55; add $1.35 for each additional kilometer, depending on traffic. Drivers usually will take you where you want to go without hassle or overcharging. Note it's not easy to hail a taxi on the street, unless you are near a hotel; it's best to call. Reliable companies include:

Black Top & Checker Cabs (☎ 604-731-1111)

Vancouver Taxi (☎ 604-871-1111) Has a fleet of wheelchair-accessible vehicles.

Yellow Cab (☎ 604-681-1111)

TRAIN

Canadians feel a special attachment to the 'ribbons of steel' from coast to coast, although they don't take the train often. Trains chug into **Pacific Central Station** (p206), which has currency exchange booths and luggage lockers, among other amenities.

VIA Rail (☎ 888-842-7245; www.viarail.ca) runs only one service to/from Vancouver. It's called the *Canadian*, and it runs east through Kamloops, Jasper, Edmonton and Winnipeg en route to Toronto. Spectacular scenery and excellent facilities make this North America's greatest train ride, hands down. Trains leave Vancouver on Tuesday, Friday and Sunday at 5:30pm. Stopovers are permitted, but you must re-reserve a seat for your onward journey. Fares vary wildly, but are cheaper if tickets are purchased at least one week in advance. Average one-way economy-class fares include:

Jasper	$215	16½hr
Edmonton	$290	23hr
Toronto	$710	72hr

Amtrak (☎ 800-872-7245; www.amtrak.com) runs the *Cascades* line between Vancouver and Seattle, departing daily at 6pm. In addition, Amtrak runs three buses a day from Vancouver to Seattle, where passengers can connect with Los Angeles- and Chicago-bound trains. The one-way fare is the same for the train or bus – US$23 to US$31 – and it takes four hours. International passengers are responsible for securing all necessary documentation (ie passports and visas) prior to on-board customs and immigration procedures. Reservations are required.

TRANSLINK

TransLink (☎ 604-953-3333; www.translink.bc .ca) runs the SkyTrain, SeaBus and street bus system throughout Vancouver. Sample fares include adult 1/2/3 zones $2/3/4; students and seniors 1/2/3 zones $1.50/2/3; day pass $8; and tickets after 6:30pm on weekends and holidays $2. The *Transportation Map & Guide for Greater Vancouver* ($1.95) provides route, fare and schedule information. It's available at convenience stores and bookstores, and also is posted at busy bus stops and SkyTrain stations.

The transport system is divided into three zones, and fares depend on how many zones you'll be traveling in. Zone 1 covers central Vancouver; Zone 2 includes the suburbs of Richmond, Burnaby, New Westminster, North Vancouver, West Vancouver and Sea Island; and Zone 3 is everything beyond.

Buy bus tickets from the driver (exact change required). You can buy SkyTrain and SeaBus tickets from dispensers near the station entry (these machines provide change). Be sure to obtain a paper transfer from bus drivers (ticket machines bestow them automatically), as this enables you to transfer to any other bus, SkyTrain or SeaBus at no extra charge during the next 90 minutes.

Day passes are valid for unlimited rides; purchase them at SeaBus/SkyTrain stations or shops displaying the 'FareDealer' sign. A book of 10 FareSaver tickets for one/two/three zones costs $18/27/36.

Buses

City buses (both electric trolley buses connected to overhead cables and standard diesel-powered buses) fill in the myriad gaps left by SkyTrain and SeaBus. Most buses run from early morning to late evening and come by every 10 minutes during rush hour peak times, but service can dwindle to every 30 to 60 minutes otherwise. Big, blue 'B-Line' buses provide quicker action, as they make limited stops only along major routes. Useful ones include the 98 B-Line from Richmond Centre to Burrard SkyTrain Station by way of the airport, and 99 B-Line from UBC to Broadway Station/Commercial Dr. Buses display their route number and final destination on the vehicle's front. A reduced Night Bus schedule goes into effect during the wee hours. Buses will let you off between designated stops if the driver deems it safe to do so traffic-wise; just ask.

SeaBus

Passenger ferries glide between Waterfront Station downtown and Lonsdale Quay in North Vancouver (a nifty 12-minute ride). SeaBus operates from approximately 6am to 12:30am, every 15 to 30 minutes.

SkyTrain

The elevated light-rail system has two lines. The Expo Line runs from Waterfront Station downtown to King George Station in Surrey. The Millennium Line parallels it to Columbia Station in New Westminster, then circles back northeast through Burnaby and connects to Expo again at Broadway Station/Commercial Dr. SkyTrain operates from about 5:30am to 1am, running every five to 10 minutes.

PRACTICALITIES

ACCOMMODATIONS

Peak summer season runs from Victoria Day until Labour Day. Rooms are scarcest and rates highest during this time, and the situation is compounded during major special events (p8), like the Vancouver International Jazz Festival. See p168 for price ranges, special deals, advice on making reservations and a list of B&B booking services. Accommodations listings in this book are arranged alphabetically, with 'Cheap Sleeps' (budget options) listed at the end of most neighborhood sections. Count on adding room taxes of 17% to rates quoted in this book (although visitors may be eligible for a refund of the 7% federal GST – see p215). Places that offer valet or self-parking are marked with a **P** icon; if it's not free, the typical overnight charge follows the icon.

BUSINESS HOURS

Normal business hours are 9am to 5pm weekdays. Some postal outlets may stay open later and on weekends. Banks usually keep shorter hours; certain branches are open Saturday morning. Typical retail shopping hours are 10am to 6pm Monday to Saturday, noon to 5pm on Sunday (although some shops are closed on Sunday). Shopping malls often stay open later. Restaurants are usually open for lunch on weekdays from 11:30am until 2:30pm and serve dinner from 5pm until 9pm daily, later on weekends. If they take a day off, it's Monday or Tuesday. A few serve breakfast, and many serve weekend brunch.

Bars usually open late afternoon, but some unlock their doors before noon. Clubs may open in the evening around 9pm, but most don't get busy before 11pm. Bars and clubs can serve liquor until 3am. It's not a problem finding 24-hour supermarkets, pharmacies or convenience stores.

Tourist attractions often keep longer hours during summer and reduced hours in winter (frequently closing on Monday or Tuesday).

CHILDREN

Children are welcome almost everywhere in Vancouver. Good, free resources on entertaining wee ones include the *Kids' Guide to Vancouver*, a brochure/map available at **Tourist Info Centres** (p216); **Kid Friendly! British Columbia** (☎ 604-541-6192; www.kidfriendly.org), which publishes a directory of – yes – kid-friendly businesses and services; and www.kidsvancouver .com, with information on parks, playgrounds and other places to keep kids amused. See p57 for a list of top children's attractions.

Children can usually stay with their parents at motels and hotels for no extra charge. B&Bs may refuse to accept pint-sized patrons, while others charge full price for tots. The **Four Seasons Hotel** (p170) provides a children's video library and bedtime milk and cookies among its excellent kiddy amenities.

Make sure children coming to Canada from other countries (including the USA) have a passport or birth certificate with them. Divorced parents with a child should carry a copy of their custody agreement. Children traveling with a non-parent should have a letter of permission from the parent or legal guardian.

Car-rental companies rent car seats, which are legally required for young children, for a few dollars per day, but you'll need to reserve them in advance.

For more information on enjoying travel with young ones, read Lonely Planet's *Travel with Children* by Cathy Lanigan.

Childcare equipment can be rented at the following:

Cribs and Carriages (☎ 604-988-2742) Rents cribs, playpens and other accessories.

Baby-sitting

Always ask for a licensed and bonded baby-sitting service, which hotel concierges can direct you to. An option includes:

KidScenes (☎ 800-665-9296) A reputable agency charging $60 minimum for four hours.

CLIMATE

Vancouver's climate is the mildest in Canada, averaging 20°C in summer and 2°C in winter. But you don't hear much about that accolade. Instead you hear about the rain. Yes, bucket loads of it fall, especially in winter (January, February and March). In the mountains, a mere 20 minutes away, this translates into snow for excellent skiing. The official wet stuff number is 116cm (46in) annually. July through October are the best bets for sunshine. Call ☎ 604-664-9010 for weather information. See also p5 and p8 for further details.

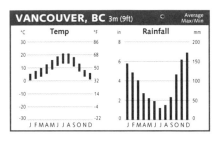

COURSES
Art & Crafts

Vancouver's community centers offer inexpensive classes in everything from drawing to flower arranging to knitting:

Coal Harbour Community Centre (Map pp230-3; ☎ 604-718-8222; www.coalharbourcc.vancouver.bc.ca; West End, 480 Broughton St)

Roundhouse Community Centre (Map pp230-3; ☎ 604-713-1800; www.roundhouse.ca; Yaletown, 181 Roundhouse Mews)

West End Community Centre (Map pp230-3; ☎ 604-257-8333; www.westendcc.vancouver.bc.ca; West End, 870 Denman St)

Cooking

The city's top chefs often teach classes at **Barbara-Jo's Books to Cooks** (p156), which has a **Cookshop&Cookschool** (Map pp236-7; ☎ 604-873-5683; www.cookshop.ca; Fairview, 555 W 12th Ave)

Language

ESL schools are rampant and popular with students from Asia. For other languages, try:

Berlitz (Map pp230-3; ☎ 604-685-9331; www.berlitz.ca; downtown, 808 W Hastings St)

Chinese Cultural Centre (p54)

Italian Cultural Centre (Map pp228-9; ☎ 604-430-3337; www.italianculturalcentre.ca; East Vancouver, 3075 Slocan St)

Le Centre Culturel Francophone de Vancouver (Map pp236-7; ☎ 604-736-9806; www.lecentreculturel.com; South Granville, 1551 W 7th Ave)

CUSTOMS

Adults aged 19 and older can bring in 1.5L of wine or 1.14L of liquor (or a case of beer), 200 cigarettes, 50 cigars and 200g of tobacco. You can also bring in gifts valued up to $60 plus a 'reasonable amount' of personal effects, including cars, computers and outdoors equipment. Dispose of any perishable items, such as fruit, vegetables or plants, before crossing the border. Mace, pepper spray and many firearms are also prohibited. For the latest regulations, contact the **Canada Customs and Revenue Agency** (☎ 204-983-3500, 800-461-9999; www.ccra-adrc.gc.ca).

DISABLED TRAVELERS

Guide dogs may legally be brought into restaurants, hotels and other businesses. Many public service phone numbers and some payphones are adapted for the hearing mpaired. About 90% of downtown's sidewalks have sloping ramps, and most public buildings are wheelchair accessible.

A directory of accessible hotels, museums etc, called *Accessible Vancouver*, is published by the **Canadian Paraplegic Association of BC** (☎ 604-324-3611; www.canparaplegic.org/bc). **Freedom Rentals** (☎ 604-952-4499; www.wheelchairvanrentals.com) provides lift-equipped vans. The government lists accessible transport throughout Canada at www.accesstotravel.gc.ca online.

TransLink (p208) runs lift-equipped buses on more than half its routes; all buses should be accessible by 2007. All SkyTrain stations, except Granville, are wheelchair accessible; Granville should be accessible by 2006. TransLink's **HandyDART** (☎ 604-453-4634) vans offer custom door-to-door service; users need a HandyPass, which usually takes three days to process.

VIA Rail (p208) and long-distance bus companies (p206) can accommodate wheelchairs if given sufficient advance notice. For accessible taxis, see p208. Apply for disabled parking permits ($15) via **SPARC BC** (☎ 604-718-7744; www.sparc.bc.ca).

Other helpful resources include:

BC Coalition of People with Disabilities (☎ 604-875-0188, TDD 604-875-8835; www.bccpd.bc.ca)

Canadian National Institute for the Blind (☎ 604-431-2121; www.cnib.ca)

Mobility International USA (☎ 541-343-1284; www.miusa.org)

Society for Accessible Travel & Hospitality (☎ 212-447-7284; www.sath.org)

DISCOUNT CARDS

The **Vancouver City Passport** (☎ 604-694-2489, 877-694-2489; www.vancouvercitypassport.com) is a coupon book providing 50% off or 2-for-1 discounts at 35 of the city's museums, theaters, tour companies and restaurants. It costs $25 and must be purchased in advance by phone or online. Check the website for other city and regional discount passes.

ELECTRICITY

Canada, like the USA, operates on 110V, 60-cycle electric power. Gadgets built for higher voltage, and cycles (such as 220/240V, 50-cycle appliances from Europe) will function poorly. North American electrical goods have plugs with two (flat) or three (two flat, one round) pins. Overseas visitors should bring an adapter, or buy one, if they wish to use their own razors, hair dryers or other appliances.

EMBASSIES & CONSULATES

Most countries maintain embassies in Ottawa in the province of Ontario. Vancouver consulates are generally open only on weekday mornings, although a few are also open after lunch until 4pm.

Australia (Map pp230-3; ☎ 604-684-1177; downtown, Ste 1225, 888 Dunsmuir St)

China (Map pp236-7; ☎ 604-734-0704; Fairview, Ste 288, 1338 W Broadway)

Denmark (Map pp228-9; ☎ 604-982-8892; North Vancouver, Ste 101, 245 Fell Ave)

France (Map pp230-3; ☎ 604-681-4345; West End, Ste 1100, 1130 W Pender St)

Germany (Map pp230-3; ☎ 604-684-8377; downtown, Ste 704, 999 Canada Place)

India (Map pp230-3; ☎ 604-662-8811; downtown, 325 Howe St)

Ireland (Map pp236-7; ☎ 604-683-9233; Fairview, Ste 401, 1385 W 8th Ave)

Italy (Map pp230-3; ☎ 604-684-7288; downtown, Ste 1100, 510 W Hastings St)

Japan (Map pp230-3; ☎ 604-684-5868; West End, Ste 800, 1177 W Hastings St)

Korea (Map pp230-3; ☎ 604-681-9581; West End, Ste 1600, 1090 W Georgia St)

Mexico (Map pp230-3; ☎ 604-684-3547; West End, Ste 710, 1177 W Hastings St)

Netherlands (Map pp230-3; ☎ 604-684-6448; downtown, Ste 821, 475 Howe St)

New Zealand (Map pp230-3; ☎ 604-684-7388; downtown, Ste 1200, 888 Dunsmuir St)

UK (Map pp230-3; ☎ 604-683-4421; West End, Ste 800, 1111 Melville St)

USA (Map pp230-3; ☎ 604-685-4311; West End, 1095 W Pender St)

EMERGENCY

Crisis Centre	☎ 604-872-3311
Police, Fire & Ambulance	☎ 911
Police (non-emergency)	☎ 604-717-3321
Rape Crisis Centre	☎ 604-255-6344

The 24/7 **Crisis Centre** provides counselors who can help with all types of emotional crises. The **Rape Crisis Centre** is open 9am to 5pm Monday to Friday only, but its answering service can often hook you up with a counselor during nonoperational hours. See p213 for hospital emergency rooms and clinics.

GAY & LESBIAN TRAVELERS

Vancouver's gay and lesbian scene is part of Vancouver's culture, rather than a subsection of it. The legalization of same-sex marriages in BC has resulted in a huge number of couples using Vancouver as a kind of gay Vegas. For more information, visit www.vs.gov.bc.ca/marriage/howto.html.

The West End (p49) is the heart and soul of the city's gay community, while the lesbian contingent is centered on Commercial Dr (p49). For entertainment options, see p130. Vancouver's annual Pride Parade (p10) and film fest (p133) take place in August. Whistler hosts a gay and lesbian ski week (www.ou tontheslopes.com) from late January to early February.

Helpful local resources include:

Gay & Lesbian Business Association (☎ 604-739-4522; www.glba.org)

Gay & Lesbian Centre (Map pp230-3; ☎ 604-684-5307, help line ☎ 604-684-6869; www.lgtbcentrevancouver .com; West End, 1170 Bute St; bus 1) Library, health clinic and legal services.

Also check out **Little Sister's Bookstore** (p156) and the newspaper *Xtra!* (p214). For current happenings, see www.gayvan.com and www .superdyke.com.

HOLIDAYS

During national public holidays, all banks, schools and government offices (including post offices) are closed, and transportation, museums and other services are on a Sunday schedule. Holidays falling on a weekend are usually observed the following Monday.

Major public holidays in Vancouver:

New Year's Day	January 1
Good Friday & Easter Monday	late March to mid-April
Victoria Day	third Monday in May
Canada Day	July 1
BC Day	first Monday in August
Labour Day	first Monday in September
Thanksgiving	second Monday in October
Remembrance Day	November 11
Christmas Day	December 25
Boxing Day	December 26

See p8 for special events and peak travel seasons.

INTERNET ACCESS

Major Internet Service Providers (ISPs) have dozens of dial-up numbers across Canada for those traveling with laptops. Contact details for some of these include:

AOL (☎ 888-265-4357; www.aol.ca)

CompuServe (☎ 800-848-8990; www.compuserve.com)

Earthlink (☎ 800-327-8454; www.earthlink.net)

Many motel, B&B and hotel rooms have phones equipped with data ports, and some offer high-speed Internet access. Deluxe hotels often have fully equipped business centers, with computers, photocopiers, fax and In-

ternet services. Some coffee shops also offer high-speed connections for laptop users. Check www.wififreespot.com for free wi-fi locations around town.

Cheap cybercafés are clustered all along Robson St near Denman St and Davie St near Thurlow St in the West End, and on Pender and Seymour Sts near Simon Fraser University's downtown campus. Rates start at $2 per hour at the following cybercafés:

Internet Coffee (Map pp230-3; ☎ 604-682-6668; West End, 1104 Davie St; ⌚ 9-2:30am; bus 1)

Mail Room (Map pp230-3; ☎ 604-681-6562; West End, 1755 Robson St; ⌚ 9am-6pm Mon-Fri, 11am-3pm Sat; bus 5)

Kinko's (www.kinkos.com) offers Internet access for $7.50 per hour. Many branches are open 24 hourly, including the one **downtown** (Map pp230-3; ☎ 604-685-3338; 789 W Pender St; SkyTrain Granville).

LEGAL MATTERS

The Canadian federal government permits the use of marijuana for medicinal purposes, but official prescription cannabis is strictly regulated. It's illegal to consume alcohol anywhere other than a residence or licensed premises, which puts parks, beaches and other public spaces off limits.

You can incur stiff fines, jail time and penalties if caught driving under the influence of alcohol or any illegal substance (eg marijuana). The blood-alcohol limit over which you are considered legally drunk is 0.08%, which is reached after just two beers. Penalties include throwing you in jail overnight, followed by a court appearance, heavy fine and/or further incarceration.

If you are arrested, you have the right to remain silent. However, never walk away from law enforcement personnel without permission. After being arrested you have the right to an interpreter and one phone call. For free or low-cost legal advice, try contacting the **Legal Services Society** (Map p235; information

How Old Is Old Enough?	
Driving a car	16
Voting in an election	18
Drinking alcoholic beverages	19
Age of homosexual consent (for males)	18
Age of consent for other sexual activity	14

☎ 604-408-2172, appointments ☎ 604-601-6206; www.lss.bc.ca; East Vancouver, Ste 820, 1140 W Pender St).

MAPS

The detailed maps in this guide will be enough for all but in-depth explorations. Lonely Planet's full-color, fold-out *Vancouver City Map* has a handy street index and laminated write-on, wipe-off surface. **Tourism BC** (p216) provides free provincial maps. **MapArt** (www.mapart.com) publishes an excellent series of affordable maps covering central Vancouver, Greater Vancouver and beyond; they're sold at bookstores and newsstands. For specialist activity maps, drop by **Mountain Equipment Co-op** (p161) or **Europe Bound Outfitters** (p161).

MEDICAL SERVICES

There are no reciprocal healthcare arrangements between Canada and other countries. Non-Canadians usually pay cash up front for treatment, so taking out travel insurance with a medical cover component is strongly advised. Medical treatment in Canada is expensive, too; the standard rate for a bed is around $500 and up to $2500 a day for nonresidents.

Clinics

Care Point Medical Centre operates 10 city walk-in clinics open 9am to 9pm. Convenient offices are in the **West End** (Map pp230-3; ☎ 604-681-5338; 1175 Denman St; bus 5) and **East Vancouver** (Map p235; ☎ 604-254-5554; 1623 Commercial Dr; bus 20). The **Travel Medicine & Vaccination Centre** (Map pp230-3; ☎ 604-681-5656; downtown, Ste 314, 1030 W Georgia St, ☿ by appointment; Skytrain Burrard) provides shots for onward travel.

For dental services, try the **Vancouver Airport Dental Centre** (☎ 604-276-2121; Level 1, Domestic Terminal; ☿ 8am-6pm Mon-Fri, 9am-2pm Sat) or call the **College of Dental Surgeons** (☎ 604-736-3621) for a referral.

Emergency Rooms

Vancouver's emergency rooms include:

BC Children's Hospital (Map pp236-7; ☎ 604-875-2134; West Side, 4480 Oak St)

St Paul's Hospital (Map pp230-3; ☎ 604-806-8686; West End, 1081 Burrard St)

Vancouver General Hospital (Map pp236-7; ☎ 604-875-4995; West Side, 855 W 12th Ave)

METRIC SYSTEM

Canada officially changed over from imperial measurement to the metric system in the mid-1970s, but the systems co-exist in everyday life. For example, all speed-limit signs are in kilometers per hour and gasoline is sold by the liter, but produce is often sold by the pound. For help in converting between the two systems, use the chart found on the inside front cover of this guidebook.

MONEY

All prices quoted in this book are all provided in Canadian dollars ($) and do not include taxes, unless it's otherwise noted. See also Economy & Costs (p16). Most Canadians do not carry large amounts of cash for everyday use, they rely instead on electronic transactions: credit cards, ATMs and direct debit cards. Personal checks are rarely accepted, unlike in the USA. See the inside front cover of this guidebook for exchange rates.

ATMs

Interbank ATM exchange rates usually beat the rates offered for traveler's checks or exchanging foreign currency. Canadian ATM fees are low (usually $1 to $1.50 per transaction), but your home bank may charge another fee on top of that.

Changing Money

It's best to change your money at a recognized bank or other financial institution. Some hotels, souvenir shops and tourist offices exchange money, but rates aren't likely to be good. After regular banking hours (p209), try the following:

American Express (Map pp230-3; ☎ 604-669-2813; downtown, 666 Burrard St; ☿ 8:30am-5:30pm Mon-Fri, 10am-4pm Sat & Sun; SkyTrain Burrard)

Gastown Currency Exchange (Map p234; ☎ 604-683-9666; Gastown, 375 Water St; ☿ 10am-6pm; SkyTrain Waterfront)

Money Mart (Map pp230-3; ☎ 604-606-9555; www.moneymart.ca; downtown, 1195 Davie St; ☿ 24hr; bus 6)

QuickEx (☎ 604-683-6789; www.quickex.ca; ☿ 24hr) Currency exchange machines located throughout the city.

Travelex (Map pp230-3; ☎ 604-641-1229; www.travelex.com; downtown, Pan Pacific Hotel, 999 Canada Pl; ☿ 9am-5pm Mon-Sat, 10am-3pm Sun; SkyTrain Waterfront)

Credit Cards

Visa, MasterCard, American Express and JCB cards are widely accepted in Canada. Credit cards can get you cash advances at bank ATMs, generally for a 3% surcharge. Beware many US-based credit cards now convert foreign charges using highly unfavorable exchange rates and fees.

Currency

Paper bills most often come in $5 (blue), $10 (purple), $20 (green) and $50 (red) denominations. Coins include the penny (1¢), nickel (5¢), dime (10¢), quarter (25¢), 'loonie' ($1) and 'toonie' ($2). The 11-sided, gold-colored 'loonie' coins feature the common loon, a North American waterbird. The two-toned 'toonie' was introduced in 1996.

Traveler's Cheques

American Express, Thomas Cook and Visa traveler's checks in Canadian dollars are usually accepted as cash at many hotels, restaurants and stores. However, the savings you might make on exchange rates by carrying traveler's checks in a foreign currency (even US$) really don't make up for the hassle of having to exchange them at banks or other financial institutions.

NEWSPAPERS & MAGAZINES

Most 'daily' newspapers are not published on Sunday; the hefty weekend edition appears on Saturday instead.

City Food (www.cityfood.com) A free primer on the regional culinary scene; available at restaurants and bookstores.

Financial Post (www.nationalpost.com/financialpost) Canada's answer to the USA's *Wall Street Journal*.

Georgia Straight (www.straight.com) Alternative weekly providing Vancouver's best entertainment scoop, free every Thursday.

Globe & Mail (www.theglobeandmail.com) Canada's premier national daily, published in Toronto but available countrywide.

Province (www.vancouverprovince.com) Vancouver's 'tabloid' daily newspaper.

Vancouver Magazine (www.vancouvermagazine.com) Upscale lifestyle, dining and entertainment monthly magazine.

Vancouver Sun (www.vancouversun.com) Vancouver's straight-laced daily newspaper.

Terminal City (www.terminalcity.ca) Freebie scene guide that's light on pages but heavy with attitude.

WestEnder (www.westender.com) Weekly freebie covering restaurants and entertainment for moneyed urbanites.

Where Vancouver (www.where.ca/vancouver) Free glossy tourist magazine.

Xtra! West (www.xtra.ca) Free gay-oriented alternative paper, distributed biweekly on Wednesday.

PASSPORTS

Visitors from almost all countries need a passport. For US citizens, a passport or birth certificate plus photo ID is required. You may get by with just a driver's license when crossing a land border, but don't count on it. US citizens entering Canada from a third country must have a valid passport. Permanent residents of the US who aren't citizens should carry their green card.

PHARMACIES

One popular chain is **Shoppers Drug Mart**, which has 24-hour stores in the **West End** (Map pp230-3; ☎ 604-685-6445; 1125 Davie St; bus 1) and **Kitsilano** (Map pp238-9; ☎ 604-738-3138; 2302 W 4th Ave; bus 4). If you're downtown, try **Pharmasave** (Map pp230-3; ☎ 604-801-6991; 499 Granville St; ☼ 7:30am-7:30pm Mon-Fri, 9am-5:30pm Sat; SkyTrain Granville).

POST

Canada Post/Postes Canada (☎ 416-979-8822, in Canada 800-267-1177; www.canadapost.ca) may not be remarkably quick, but it is reliable. Standard postcards or 1st-class air-mail letters (up to 30g) cost 49¢ to destinations within Canada, more to the USA (80¢) or any other destination ($1.40).

Poste-restante mail should be addressed as follows:

FAMILY NAME, First Name
c/o General Delivery
349 W Georgia St
Vancouver, BC V6B 3P7

Poste restante will be held for 15 days before being returned. Pick up mail at the **Main Post Office** (Map pp230-3; ☎ 416-979-8822, in Canada 800-267-1177; 349 W Georgia St; ☼ 8am-5:30pm Mon-Fri; SkyTrain Granville). Any packages sent to you in Canada will be ruthlessly inspected by customs officials, who then assess duties.

Stamps and postal services are also available at many pharmacies and convenience stores; look for the Canada Post sign in the front window. **Georgia Post Plus** (Map pp230-3; ☎ 604-632-4226; 1358 W Georgia St; ☒ 9:30am-6pm Mon-Fri, 10am-4pm Sat; bus 240) is a handy shipping outlet.

RADIO

Around Vancouver, flip the dial to:

CBC Radio One (690AM) Canadian Broadcasting Corporation's commercial-free news and talk by day, classical by night.

CFOX (99.3FM) Hard rock.

CFRO (102.7FM) Community co-op station where anything goes: storytelling, poetry, Armenian variety shows and First Nations fusion.

CITR (101.9FM) UBC's station of indie music, news, spoken word and arts.

CJSF (90.1FM) Simon Fraser University's alt.rock twangings.

CKWX (1130AM) News 24/7.

JACK-FM (96.9FM) Groovy rock mix.

The Team (1040AM) Sports and talk 24/7.

The Z (95.3FM) Pop.

SAFETY

Violent crime is unusual in Vancouver (statistically you're a lot more likely to be held up and robbed in the Vatican City); however, property theft is common, especially car break-ins and bicycle theft. Many of these crimes are committed by drug addicts who are looking for quick cash. Use common sense and park in high-traffic areas, remove valuables from sight and lock up.

The 'poorest postal code in Canada' is centered around Main and Hastings Sts in East Vancouver. Specifically, on Hastings St running east from Abbott St is where you'll see lots of injecting drug users and other people down on their luck. While it is generally harmless enough to walk around here by day, it is definitely not an area to dawdle at night. Many residents spread out and panhandle in the abutting Gastown and Chinatown areas, on Granville St (especially between Pender and Davie Sts) and along Commercial Dr. The area around Pacific Central Station (Map pp228-9) is dodgy late at night, as is Stanley Park in the wee hours.

SENIOR TRAVELERS

People over the age of 65 (sometimes 50) typically qualify for the same discounts as students. Any photo ID is usually sufficient proof of age. Seniors who are BC residents travel free on **BC Ferries** (p206) from Monday to Thursday, except on public holidays. Useful organizations include:

Canadian Association of Retired Persons (☎ 416-363-8748, in Canada 800-363-9736; www.fifty-plus.net; 1yr membership $20) Has excellent, free cyber resources.

Elderhostel (☎ 877-426-8056; www.elderhostel.org) Specializes in inexpensive, educational packages for people 55 years or older; accommodation ranges from university dorms to mid-range hotels.

Seniors One-Stop Information Line (☎ 604-983-3303) A good resource for local and provincial services.

TAX & REFUNDS

The federal goods and services tax (GST), variously known as the 'Gouge and Screw' or 'Grab and Steal' tax, adds 7% to nearly every product, service or transaction, on top of which is usually a 7.5% BC provincial sales tax (PST). Accommodation and alcohol have additional taxes; see p168 and p92.

Visitors are eligible for refunds on GST paid for short-term accommodation and goods that are non-consumable, although the refund process is inconvenient. To wit: your purchase amounts (before taxes) must total at least $200, and each individual receipt must show a minimum amount of $50 before taxes. You must have original receipts (credit-card slips and photocopies are not accepted), and the receipts are not returned. Receipts for goods (not accommodation) must be stamped by Canadian customs to be refund-eligible (at the airport go to the Refund Office; at land borders go to the customs office or a refund-designated duty-free shop). Visitors departing Canada by commercial carrier (including air, rail, non-charter bus or ferry) must also include their original boarding pass or carrier ticket with the refund claim.

Once you've met all the criteria above, it's time to fill out and mail in the rebate form, widely available at 'tourist' shops, hotels and tourist offices. You also can contact the **Canada Customs and Revenue Agency's Visitor Rebate Program** (☎ 800-668-4748 in Canada, 902-432-5608 outside Canada; www.ccra.gc.ca/visitors; Ste 104, 275 Pope Rd, Summerside, PE C1N 6C6). Expect to wait four to six weeks for your check, which is paid in Canadian dollars, unless issued to a US address, in which case it will be in US dollars. Note you also can get on-the-spot refunds of amounts under $500 at land borders that have specially designated duty-free shops.

TELEPHONE

Local calls cost 25¢ from public pay phones. Public pay phones are either coin or card operated; a few accept credit cards or have data ports for laptop Internet connections.

Most downtown and Greater Vancouver phone numbers, as well as Whistler and the Sunshine Coast, take the ☎604 area code, although ☎778 is being used for new numbers. Dial all 10 digits of a given phone number, including the three-digit area code and seven-digit number, even for local calls. In some instances (ie between Vancouver and Whistler), numbers will have the same area code but be long distance; at such times, you need to dial '1' before the area code, and an operator will come on the line to inform you of this.

Always dial '1' before other domestic long-distance and toll-free (☎800, 888, 877, etc) numbers. Some toll-free numbers are good anywhere in North America, others within Canada only. International rates apply for calls to the USA, even though the dialing code (+1) is the same as for Canadian long-distance calls. Dial ☎011 followed by the country code for all other overseas direct-dial calls.

Faxes

To send faxes, visit **Kinko's** (p212) or **Georgia Post Plus** (p214). Expect to pay $1 or $2 per page for local faxes and around $5 for international ones.

Mobile Phones

North America uses a variety of mobile phone systems, most of which are incompatible with the GSM 900/1800 standard used throughout Europe, Asia and Africa. Check with your cellular service provider about using your phone in Canada. Calls may be routed internationally, and US travelers should beware of roaming surcharges (it can become very expensive for a 'local' call).

Phonecards

Sold at many convenience stores, private pre-paid phonecards often give rates that are su-

perior to the country's Bell networks. Beware those phonecards that advertise the cheapest per-minute rates, as they may also charge hefty connection fees for each call, especially for using the toll-free access number from payphones. You can avoid the surcharges for the latter by depositing 25¢ and dialing the local access number instead. **Telus** (☎888-969-9699) is a well-known company that has a range of phonecards available in post offices and at retail outlets.

TIME

Vancouver is in the Pacific time zone (PST/PDT), the same as the US West Coast. At noon in Vancouver it's:

11am Anchorage
3pm Toronto
2pm Chicago
8pm London
9pm Paris
6am (the next day) Sydney
8am (the next day) Auckland

During Daylight Saving Time (from the first Sunday in April to the last Sunday in October), the clock moves ahead one hour.

TIPPING

Tip restaurant servers 15% of the pre-tax bill for good service, and up to 20% for excellent service. Bartenders get at least $1 per drink, 15% when buying a round. Tip taxi drivers about 10% of the fare, rounding up to the nearest dollar. Skycaps, bellhops and cloakroom attendants get around $2 per item; housekeepers are tipped $2 to $5 per night you stay.

TOURIST INFORMATION

The mother lode of resources is provided by **Tourism Vancouver TouristInfo Centre** (Map pp230-3; ☎604-683-2000, 800-435-5622; www.tourism vancouver.com; downtown, Plaza Level, 200 Burrard St; ⏰8:30am-5pm Mon-Fri, 9am-5pm Sat Oct–mid-May, 8am-6pm Mon-Sun mid-May–Sep; SkyTrain Waterfront): free map, visitor guide, half-price theater tickets, automated currency exchange and accommodation/tour bookings. Sub-branches are found at the following locations:

Airport (Map pp228-9; Domestic & International Terminals; ☉ 8am-11pm)

Ballantyne Pier and Canada Place cruise ship terminals (Map pp228-9 & Map pp230-3, respectively; ☉ 8am-4pm on days when ships arrive)

Peach Arch Border Crossing (Hwy 99, just north of the US–Canada border; ☉ 8am-6pm)

Call **Tourism British Columbia** (☎ 604-435-5622, 800-435-5622; www.hellobc.com) for province-wide information or accommodation booking; its brochures and maps are available at the TouristInfo Centre.

VISAS

Short-term visitors from most Western countries, except parts of Eastern Europe, normally don't require visas. As visa requirements change frequently, it's a good idea to check with the **Canadian Immigration Centre** (☎ 416-973-4444; www.cic.gc.ca) or the Canadian embassy or consulate in your home country to see if you're exempt.

A passport and/or visa does not guarantee entry. Proof of sufficient funds or possibly a return ticket out of the country may be required. Visitors with medical conditions may only be refused if they 'might reasonably be expected to cause excessive demand on health and social services' (ie they admit to needing treatment during their stay in Canada).

If you're refused entry but have a visa, you have the right of appeal at the port of entry. If you're arriving by land, the best course is simply to try again later (after a shift change) or at a different border crossing.

To/From the USA

Visitors to Canada who also plan to spend time in the USA should know that admission requirements are subject to rapid change. Check with **US Citizenship and Immigration Services** (☎ 800-375-5283; www.uscis.gov) for the latest information. Under the US visa waiver program, visas currently are not required for citizens of the EU, Australia and New Zealand for visits up to 90 days. However, visitors may be fingerprinted and photographed upon entry, and are subject to a US$6 entry fee at land border crossings. Be sure your entry permit to Canada includes multiple entries.

WOMEN TRAVELERS

Vancouver is generally quite safe for women travelers. On the main streets, busy foot traffic continues past 11pm, though there are certainly areas to avoid — see p215. Note it is illegal to carry pepper spray or mace in Canada. The **Vancouver Women's Health Collective information line** (☎ 604-736-5262; www.womenshealthcollective.ca) provides advice and referrals for health issues. See Emergencies (p211) for other helpful resources, including sexual assault crisis lines. The **Women in Print bookstore** (p165) has bulletin boards and flyers advertising woman-centered activities, classes and happenings.

WORK

It is difficult to get a work permit because employment opportunities go to Canadians first. In most cases, you'll need to take a validated job offer from a specific employer to a Canadian consulate or embassy abroad.

Each year a limited number of one-year working holiday visas are available to New Zealanders (NZ$195) and Australians (A$165) between the ages of 18 and 30. Competition is stiff, so apply as early as possible. Applications are available through Sydney's **Canadian Consulate General** (☎ 02-9364-3082; www.whpcanada.org.au) or Wellington's **Canadian High Commission** (☎ 04-473-9577; www.dfait-maeci.gc.ca/newzealand).

The **Student Work Abroad Program (SWAP)** facilitates additional working holidays for students and people under 30 (sometimes 35). Participants come from nearly 20 countries, including Australia, France, Germany, New Zealand, the UK and the USA. **SWAP Canada** (www.swap.ca) or **Travel CUTS** (p205) can tell you which travel agency to contact in your own country for further details.

Doing Business

Vancouver does brisk business in conventions and trade shows, with the city's **Convention & Exhibition Centre** (Map pp230-3; ☎ 604-689-8232; www.vanconex.com; Canada Pl) hosting more than 350 events annually. The facility will be tripling its massive space by 2008. **Tourism Vancouver** (p216) also assists business travelers and provides a list of suppliers (copying, printing etc) on its website. **Kinko's** (p212) offers a full range of services, from on-site computer rental to high-quality color printing, and accepts FedEx drop-offs.

Behind the Scenes

THE LONELY PLANET STORY

The story begins with a classic travel adventure: Tony and Maureen Wheeler's 1972 journey across Europe and Asia to Australia. There was no useful information about the overland trail then, so Tony and Maureen published the first Lonely Planet guidebook to meet a growing need.

From a kitchen table, Lonely Planet has grown to become the largest independent travel publisher in the world, with offices in Melbourne (Australia), Oakland (USA) and London (UK). Today Lonely Planet guidebooks cover the globe. There is an ever-growing list of books and information in a variety of media. Some things haven't changed. The main aim is still to make it possible for adventurous travelers to get out there – to explore and better understand the world.

At Lonely Planet we believe travelers can make a positive contribution to the countries they visit – if they respect their host communities and spend their money wisely. Every year 5% of company profit is donated to charities around the world.

THIS BOOK

This 3rd edition of *Vancouver* was researched and written by Karla Zimmerman. The second edition was written by Sara 'Sam' Benson with Chris Wyness, and Chris also wrote the 1st edition. This book was commissioned and developed in Lonely Planet's Oakland office and produced in Melbourne. The project team included:

Commissioning Editor Sara Benson
Coordinating Editor Lucy Monie
Coordinating Cartographer Jack Gavran
Coordinating Layout Designer Wibowo Rusli
Assisting Editors & Proofreaders Kate McLeod, Kristin Odijk, Vicki Beale
Assisting Cartographers Csanad Csutoros, Jacqui Saunders, Andrew Smith, Natasha Velleley
Cover Designer Brendan Dempsey
Managing Cartographers Alison Lyall, Anthony Phelan
Managing Editor Melanie Dankel
Layout Managers Adriana Mammarella, Sally Darmody
Project Manager Glenn van der Knijff
Regional Publishing Manager David Zingarelli

Cover photographs by Lonely Planet Images: View past silhouetted pine trees to misty blue mountains, Chris Barton (top); Vancouver from Stanley Park, John Elk III (bottom); Beluga whales in the Vancouver Aquarium Marine Science Centre at Stanley Park, Lawrence Worcester (back).

Internal photographs by Lonely Planet Images and Lawrence Worcester except for the following: p192 Frank Carter; p114 (#2) Richard Cummins; p114 (#1) Sally Dillon; p114 (#3) Glenn van der Knijff. All images are the copyright of the photographers unless otherwise indicated. Many of the images in this guide are available for licensing from Lonely Planet Images: www.lonelyplanetimages.com.

ACKNOWLEDGEMENTS

Many thanks to TransLink for the use of the Vancouver Transit Map ©TransLink 2004.

THANKS
KARLA ZIMMERMAN

So many kind people helped me with this project. I pledge undying gratitude, my first born and even a kidney if need be to Vancouverites Janessa Laskin, John Lee, Sheryl Robinson, Andrew Hussey, Robin Steen and the entire Phillet-Martin-Steen household, Simon Goland, Vicki Tyndall, Tom Stow, Tori, Gwyn, Darren, Linda, Eve, Stefan, Hagen, Edwardo, Matt P, Emily Armstrong, Wendy Underwood and the helpful folks at Tourism Vancouver. Huge mega-thanks to Sam Benson, Lucy, Glenn and the LP production team who worked with me throughout a challenging situation. Finally, deep gratefulness goes out to my parents, in-laws, siblings, friends and partner-for-life Eric, who is everything to me.

OUR READERS

Many thanks to the travelers who used the last edition and wrote to us with helpful hints, useful advice and interesting anecdotes. Your names follow:

Peter Anderson, Gill Ankers, S Arnold, John Atkin, Michelle Bishop, Harvey Black, Dwight Burditt, Colleen Carroll, Janet Carruthers, Julian Chen, Felix Cheng, Chungwah Chow, Florence Ciavatta, Victoria Conlin, Leanne Cormack, Krystyna Cynar, Chuck Davis, Marisa Drago, Chris Enting, Emily Evans, Amanda Ferris, Christina Gamouras, Richard Gavey, Lana Gee-Gott, Ferdinando Emilio Giammichele, Eddie Glennon, Curtis Goldsberry, Dayna Gorman, Ronalie Green, Ken Guappone, Lisa Guiton, Gill Hamson, Deborah Hardoon, Patrick

Heagney, Mario Heinzig, Martin Helmantel, Saskia Helmantel, Kate Hill, James Holgate, Simon Huang, Winona Hubbard, Graham Hunt, Martin Hunt, Catriona Johnson, Sally Johnston, Marina Kelly, Tom Korecki, Andreas Krueger, Daniel Kruse, Mario La Blanche, Stuart Lamble, Andy Macintosh, Mary Jane Mahony, Andy McClurg, Tony McCurdy, Dudley McFadden, Paul McFarlane, Bronwyn McNaughton, Simon Miller, Karen Mistilis, Stephanie Monaghan, Renate Moser, Peter Murray, Luca Nonato, Kate Norris, Cathal O'Donnell, Phyllis Oster, Neil Pattemore, Vanessa Pocock, Eduardo L Quetulio, Alex Rooke, Marco Roos, Petra Rossback, Gwyn Sarkar, Robin Sarkar, Jeanne Schmidt, Richard Semple, David Simmonds, Elaine Sipos, Karen Skerrit, Peter Smith, Jill Speizer, Kaz Stafford, Joe Stead, Calvin Tam, John Turecek, Dennis Urbonas, Madelon van Luijk, Isabelle Vassot, Angele Vautour, Vincent Verdult, Veronica Villa, Robert Walter, Carl Weaver, Susan Winter, A Wright, James Yeo, Coran York, Andrew Young, Natacha Zana

SEND US YOUR FEEDBACK

We love to hear from travelers – your comments keep us on our toes and help make our books better. Our well-traveled team reads every word on what you loved or loathed about this book. Although we cannot reply individually to postal submissions, we always guarantee that your feedback goes straight to the appropriate authors, in time for the next edition. Each person who sends us information is thanked in the next edition – and the most useful submissions are rewarded with a free book.

To send us your updates – and find out about Lonely Planet events, newsletters and travel news – visit our award-winning website: www.lonelyplanet.com/feedback

Note: We may edit, reproduce and incorporate your comments in Lonely Planet products such as guidebooks, websites and digital products, so let us know if you don't want your comments reproduced or your name acknowledged. For a copy of our privacy policy visit www.lonelyplanet.com/privacy.

Notes

Index

000 map pages
000 photographs

Index

Index

223

Index

225

Index

000 map pages
000 photographs

MAP LEGEND

ROUTES

Tollway	One-Way Street
Freeway	Mall/Steps
Primary Road	Tunnel
Secondary Road	Walking Tour
Tertiary Road	Walking Tour Detour
Lane	Walking Trail
Under Construction	Walking Path
Track	Pedestrian Overpass
Unsealed Road	

TRANSPORT

Ferry	Bus Route
Metro/SkyTrain	Rail

HYDROGRAPHY

River, Creek	Canal
Intermittent River	Water
Swamp	Lake (Dry)
Mangrove	Lake (Salt)
Reef	Mudflats
Glacier	

BOUNDARIES

International	Regional, Suburb
State, Provincial	Ancient Wall
Disputed	Cliff
Marine Park	

AREA FEATURES

Airport	Forest
Area of Interest	Land
Beach, Desert	Mall
Building, Featured	Park
Building, Information	Reservation
Building, Other	Rocks
Building, Transport	Sports
Cemetery, Christian	Urban
Cemetery, Other	

POPULATION

◉ CAPITAL (NATIONAL)	◉ CAPITAL (STATE)
● **Large City**	● Medium City
● Small City	● Town, Village

SYMBOLS

Sights/Activities	Entertainment	Information
Beach	Entertainment	Bank, ATM
Buddhist	**Shopping**	Embassy/Consulate
Christian	Shopping	Hospital, Medical
Monument	**Sleeping**	Information
Museum, Gallery	Sleeping	Internet Facilities
Sikh	**Transport**	Police Station
Skiing	Airport, Airfield	Post Office, GPO
Swimming Pool	Bus Station	**Geographic**
Zoo, Bird Sanctuary	Cycling, Bicycle Path	Lighthouse
Eating	**Other**	Lookout
Eating	● Other Site	▲ Mountain, Volcano
Drinking	Parking Area	National Park
Drinking		
Café		

Map Section

GREATER VANCOUVER

Stanley Park

Lost Lagoon Dr

Lost Lagoon

Royal Vancouver
Yacht Club

Coal Harbour

A **B** **C** **D**

1 Second Beach

Stanley Park
Pitch & Putt

Devonian
Harbour
Park

99

1A

Baydore Dr

Lagoon Dr

Park La

144

Haro St

Barclay St

70

3

21

187

76

Coal
Harbour
Quay

150

Chilco St

224

66

58

212

135

61

W Georgia St

W Pender St

201

Coal
Harbour
Park

158

Gilford St

39

121

230

206

133

Alberni St

Robson St

176

See Stanley Park Map (p240)

2

Pendrell St

Beach Ave

173

35

Denman St

46

96

157

162

49

Broughton St

Jervis St

7

183

200

154

Haro St

Barclay
Heritage
Square

177

145

80

43

174

31

Bidwell St

6

63

62

147

English
Bay Beach

17

169

186

148

Cardero St

171

146

44

West End

34

Nicola St

41

129

71

3

English Bay

65

Davie St

Nelson St

Barclay St

172

Alexandra
Park

Comox St

215

Burnaby St

Pendrell St

143

Sunset
Beach
Park

Harwood St

83

128

205

153

See Kitsilano Map (pp238–9)

53

214

107

181

Jervis St

Bute St

Thurlow St

218

208

4

Pacific St

182

56

217

60

Kitsilano
Point

Hadden
Park

164

81

Burrard St

77

151

32

Ogden Ave

Vanier Park

Seawall Promenade

Beach Ave

104

14

193

See SoMa, Granville Island & Around Map (pp236–7)

False Creek

Davie St

165

102

98

194

Drake St

59

Howe St

85

112

23

24

50

116

Granville St

16

191

Burrard Bridge

Whyte Ave

Seymour St

48

5

Creelman Ave

57

40

Richards St

229

2

Cornwall Ave

Seabreeze
Walk

189

37

Pacific Blvd

Laburnum St

Walnut St

Chestnut St

Burrard St

Granville Bridge

*Broker's
Bay*

Durandeau St

Johnston St

*Granville
Island*

York Ave

Arbutus St

Maple St

Cypress St

6 **Kitsilano**

W 1st Ave

W 2nd Ave

Old Bridge St

Cartwright St

W 3rd Ave

99

0 _____ 400 m
0 _____ 0.2 miles

SIGHTS & ACTIVITIES (pp46 & 53)
Architectural Institute of BC........1 B4
Byrnes Block.............................(see 6)
Chinese Cultural Centre Museum &
  Archives.................................2 C4
Chinese Cultural Centre of
  Vancouver...............................3 C4
Dr Sun Yat-Sen Classical Chinese
  Garden & Park..........................4 B4
Gaolers Mews...........................(see 6)
Gassy Jack Statue......................(see 6)
Gastown Steam Clock...................5 B3
Maple Tree Square.......................6 B3
Sam Kee Building........................7 B4
Science World............................8 C6
Storyeum..................................9 B3
Vancouver Police Centennial
  Museum.................................10 D4

EATING 🍴 (pp96 & 101)
Alibi Room................................11 C3
Borgo Antico Al Porto.................12 B3
Brickhouse Late Night Bar &
  Bistro....................................13 C5
Buddhist Vegetarian Restaurant....14 C4
Cook Studio Café........................15 D3
Foo's Ho Ho Restaurant...............16 C4
Hon's Wun-Tun House.................17 D4
Incendio..................................18 C3
Only Seafood Restaurant.............19 C4
Phnom Penh.............................20 D5
Thai Palace...............................21 B3
Water Street Café.......................22 B3
Wild Rice.................................23 B4

DRINKING 🍷🍸 (pp123–7)
Café Luna................................24 B3
Cambie....................................(see 43)
Irish Heather.............................25 B3
Steamworks Brewing Company..26 A3

ENTERTAINMENT 🎭 (pp128–38)
Cinemark Tinseltown..................(see 38)
Club 23 West.............................27 B3
Cobalt.....................................28 C5
Firehall Arts Centre.....................29 D4
Lick...(see 30)
Lotus Sound Lounge...................30 B4
OMNIMAX Theatre....................(see 8)
Shine......................................31 A3
Sonar......................................32 B3

SHOPPING 🛍 (pp154 & 157)
Biz Books.................................33 B3
Deluxe Junk.............................34 A3
Dream.....................................35 A3
Hill's Native Art.........................36 B3
Images for a Canadian Heritage...37 B3
International Village....................38 B4
Inuit Gallery of Vancouver..........(see 37)
Marion Scott Gallery...................39 B3
New World Designs....................40 A3
RJ Clarke Tobacconist.................41 C3
Spirit Wrestler Gallery................(see 6)
Ten Lee Hong Enterprises............42 C4

SLEEPING 🛏 (p172)
Cambie International Hostel......43 B3

TRANSPORT (pp46 & 53)
Ferry Dock...............................44 C6
Helijet Airways Terminal..............45 B2
Pacific Central Station.................46 D6

INFORMATION
Gastown Currency Exchange.....47 A3
Post Office...............................48 C4

OTHER
Carnegie Community Centre.....49 C4
Millennium Gate........................50 B4
Parking....................................51 B3
Parking....................................52 C4
Parking....................................53 C5
Parking....................................54 C6

EAST VANCOUVER

0 — 400 m
0 — 0.2 miles

SIGHTS & ACTIVITIES (pp56–7)
Bikram Yoga 1 C3
Flaming June 2 C4
Knotty Boy 3 C4
Wandering Yogi 4 C4

EATING 🍴 (pp104–6)
Belgian Fries 5 C5
Bukowski's 6 C4
Clove Café & Record Bar 7 C5
Deserts 8 C3
Drive Organics ....(see 9)
El Cocal 9 C3
Havana 10 C3
Juicy Lucy's Good Eats 11 C4
La Casa Gelato 12 A2
Latin Quarter 13 C3
Marcello's 14 C4
Pink Pearl 15 A1
Sweet Cherubim 16 C3
Thai Away Home 17 C4
Tony's Neighbourhood Deli &
    Café 18 C4
WaaZuBee Café 19 C4
Yogi's 20 C4

DRINKING 🍺 (pp126–7)
Café Deux Soleil 21 C5
Caffé Calabria 22 C4
Continental Coffee 23 C5
JJ Bean 24 C6
Joe's 25 C3
Roma Café 26 C4

ENTERTAINMENT 🎭 (pp127–38)
Van East Cinema 27 C6
Vancouver East Cultural Centre ...28 C2
WISE Hall 29 C2

SHOPPING 🛍 (pp158–60)
Dr Vigari Gallery 30 C4
Highlife World Music 31 C4
Kalena's 32 C4
Magpie Magazine Gallery ...(see 31)
People's Co-op Bookstore ....(see 31)
Urban Empire 33 C3
Virgin Mary's 34 C3
Womyns' Ware 35 C2

SLEEPING 🏠 (p176)
Aberdeen Mansion 36 C3
Place at Penny's 37 C2

INFORMATION
Care Point Medical Centre 38 C4
Legal Services Society 39 A2

235

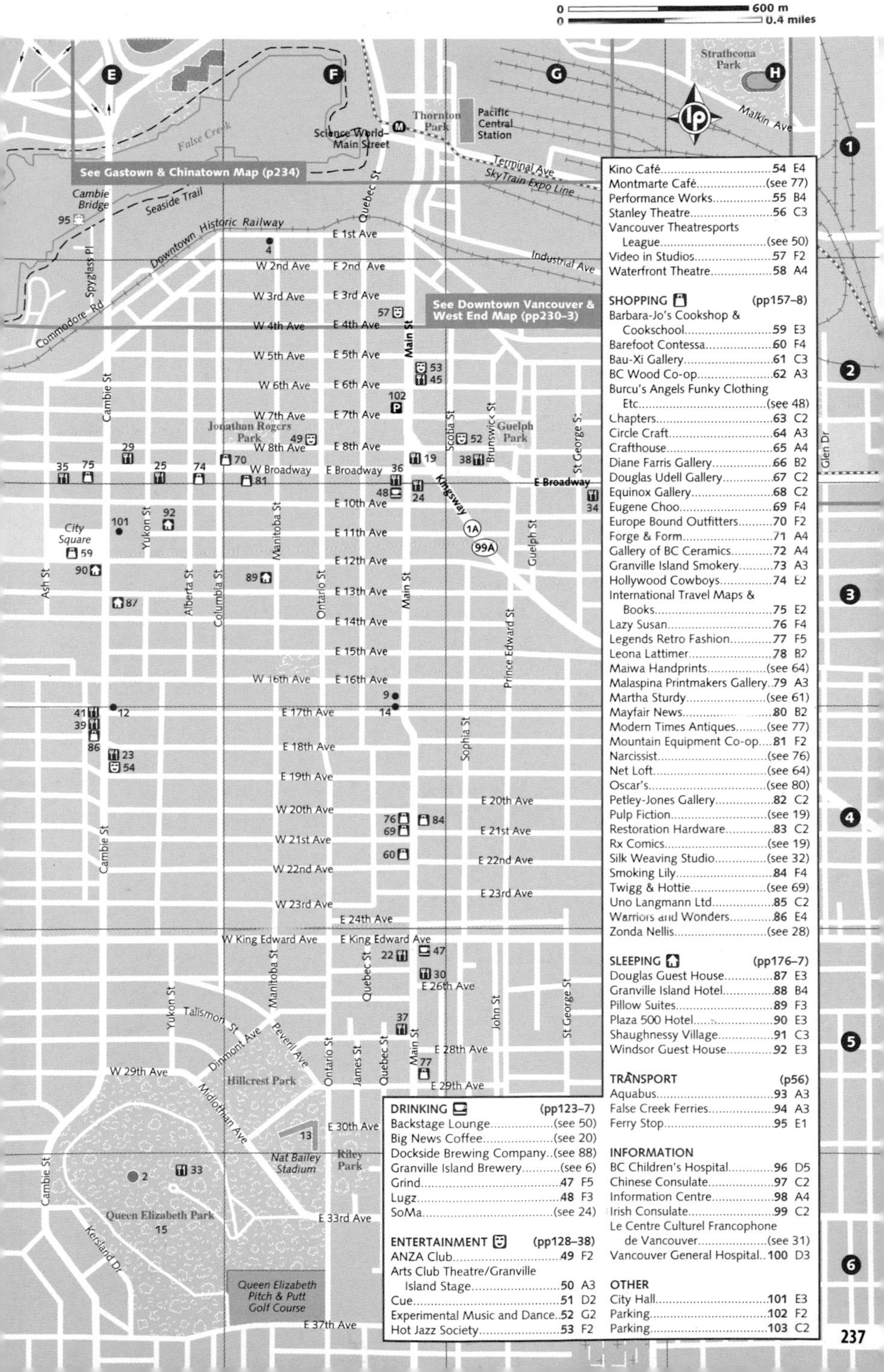

0 600 m
0 0.4 miles
E
F
G
H
Strathcona Park
Malkin Ave
Thornton Park
Pacific Central Station
Science World-Main Street
False Creek
See Gastown & Chinatown Map (p234)
Terminal Ave
SkyTrain Expo Line
Cambie Bridge
Seaside Trail
Downtown Historic Railway
Quebec St
E 1st Ave
Industrial Ave
W 2nd Ave
E 2nd Ave
W 3rd Ave
E 3rd Ave
See Downtown Vancouver & West End Map (pp230–3)
Spyglass Pl
Commodore Rd
W 4th Ave
E 4th Ave
Main St
W 5th Ave
E 5th Ave
W 6th Ave
E 6th Ave
W 7th Ave
E 7th Ave
Cambie St
Jonathan Rogers Park
W 8th Ave
E 8th Ave
Scotia St
Brunswick St
Guelph Park
St George St
Glen Dr
W Broadway
E Broadway
Kingsway
E 10th Ave
City Square
Yukon St
E 11th Ave
1A
99A
Guelph St
Manitoba St
E 12th Ave
Ash St
Alberta St
Columbia St
Ontario St
E 13th Ave
E 14th Ave
Prince Edward St
E 15th Ave
W 16th Ave
E 16th Ave
E 17th Ave
E 18th Ave
Sophia St
E 19th Ave
W 20th Ave
E 20th Ave
W 21st Ave
E 21st Ave
W 22nd Ave
E 22nd Ave
W 23rd Ave
E 23rd Ave
E 24th Ave
W King Edward Ave
E King Edward Ave
E 26th Ave
Talismon St
Dinmont Ave
Peveril Ave
John St
James St
E 28th Ave
W 29th Ave
Hillcrest Park
E 29th Ave
Midlothian Ave
E 30th Ave
Nat Bailey Stadium
Riley Park
Queen Elizabeth Park
E 33rd Ave
Kersland Dr
Queen Elizabeth Pitch & Putt Golf Course
E 37th Ave

DRINKING (pp123–7)

Backstage Lounge.....(see 50)
Big News Coffee.....(see 20)
Dockside Brewing Company..(see 88)
Granville Island Brewery.....(see 6)
Grind.....47 F5
Lugz.....48 F3
SoMa.....(see 24)

ENTERTAINMENT (pp128–38)

ANZA Club.....49 F2
Arts Club Theatre/Granville Island Stage.....50 A3
Cue.....51 D2
Experimental Music and Dance..52 G2
Hot Jazz Society.....53 F2
Kino Café.....54 E4
Montmarte Café.....(see 77)
Performance Works.....55 B4
Stanley Theatre.....56 C3
Vancouver Theatresports League.....(see 50)
Video in Studios.....57 F2
Waterfront Theatre.....58 A4

SHOPPING (pp157–8)

Barbara-Jo's Cookshop & Cookschool.....59 E3
Barefoot Contessa.....60 F4
Bau-Xi Gallery.....61 C3
BC Wood Co-op.....62 A3
Burcu's Angels Funky Clothing Etc.....(see 48)
Chapters.....63 C2
Circle Craft.....64 A3
Crafthouse.....65 A4
Diane Farris Gallery.....66 B2
Douglas Udell Gallery.....67 C2
Equinox Gallery.....68 C2
Eugene Choo.....69 F4
Europe Bound Outfitters.....70 F2
Forge & Form.....71 A4
Gallery of BC Ceramics.....72 A4
Granville Island Smokery.....73 A3
Hollywood Cowboys.....74 E2
International Travel Maps & Books.....75 E2
Lazy Susan.....76 F4
Legends Retro Fashion.....77 F5
Leona Lattimer.....78 B2
Maiwa Handprints.....(see 64)
Malaspina Printmakers Gallery..79 A3
Martha Sturdy.....(see 61)
Mayfair News.....80 B2
Modern Times Antiques.....(see 77)
Mountain Equipment Co-op.....81 F2
Narcissist.....(see 76)
Net Loft.....(see 64)
Oscar's.....(see 80)
Petley-Jones Gallery.....82 C2
Pulp Fiction.....(see 19)
Restoration Hardware.....83 C2
Rx Comics.....(see 19)
Silk Weaving Studio.....(see 32)
Smoking Lily.....84 F4
Twigg & Hottie.....(see 69)
Uno Langmann Ltd.....85 C2
Warriors and Wonders.....86 E4
Zonda Nellis.....(see 28)

SLEEPING (pp176–7)

Douglas Guest House.....87 E3
Granville Island Hotel.....88 B4
Pillow Suites.....89 F3
Plaza 500 Hotel.....90 E3
Shaughnessy Village.....91 C3
Windsor Guest House.....92 E3

TRANSPORT (p56)

Aquabus.....93 A3
False Creek Ferries.....94 A3
Ferry Stop.....95 E1

INFORMATION

BC Children's Hospital.....96 D5
Chinese Consulate.....97 C2
Information Centre.....98 A4
Irish Consulate.....99 C2
Le Centre Culturel Francophone de Vancouver.....(see 31)
Vancouver General Hospital..100 D3

OTHER

City Hall.....101 E3
Parking.....102 F2
Parking.....103 C2

KITSILANO

Burrard Inlet

Locarno
Beach

Discovery St

Belmont Ave

67

NW Marine Dr

Jericho
Beach

5

Jericho Beach Park

Hastings
Mill Park

3

Point Grey Rd

W 1st Ave

W 1st Ave

W 2nd Ave

Highbury St

Alma St

W 2nd Ave

W 3rd Ave

W 3rd Ave

W 4th Ave

W 4th Ave

45 65

McBride
Park

W 5th Ave

W 5th Ave

Department of
National Defence

W 6th Ave

W 6th Ave

Collingwood St

Waterloo St

Blenheim St

Trutch St

West
Point Grey
Park

W 7th Ave

W 7th Ave

W 8th Ave

W 8th Ave

W 9th Ave

Crown Cr

Wallace Cr

24

42

19

W Broadway

30

W 10th Ave

16

W 10th Ave

Trimble St

Discovery St

Courtenay St

Camosun St

Crown St

Wallace St

Highbury St

Alma St

Dunbar St

W 11th Ave

W 11th Ave

W 12th Ave

W 13th Ave

Almond
Park

W 13th Ave

W 14th Ave

Point Grey

W 14th Ave

W 15th Ave

W 15th Ave

W 16th Ave

Quesnel Dr

W 17th Ave

W 18th Ave

W 19th Ave

W 20th Ave

W 21st Ave

Dunbar St

W 22nd Ave

Highbury St

Collingwood St

Blenheim St

Wallace St

W 23rd Ave

W 24th Ave

W King Edward Ave

Chaldecott
Park

See University of British Columbia Map (p241)

Map labels (geographic):

English Bay

See Downtown Vancouver & West End Map (pp230-3)

Kitsilano Point

Hadden Park

Ogden Ave

McNicoll Ave

Whyte Ave

Creelman Ave

Vanier Park

Kitsilano Beach

Kitsilano Beach Park

Cornwall Ave

York Ave

W 1st Ave

W 2nd Ave

See SoMa, Granville Island & Around Map (pp236-7)

Point Grey Rd

Kitsilano

W 3rd Ave

W 4th Ave

W 5th Ave

W 6th Ave

W 7th Ave

W 8th Ave

W Broadway

W 9th Ave

W 10th Ave

Connaught Park

W 11th Ave

W 12th Ave

W 13th Ave

W 14th Ave

W 15th Ave

W 16th Ave

Granville Park

Carnarvon Park

W 18th Ave

Valley Drive

W 19th Ave

W 20th Ave

W 21st Ave

W 22nd Ave

W 23rd Ave

W King Edward Ave

Burrard Bridge

Street names: Balaclava St, Bayswater St, Macdonald St, Stephens St, Trafalgar St, Larch St, Balsam St, Vine St, Yew St, Arbutus St, Maple St, Cypress St, Burrard St, Pine St, Carnarvon St, MacKenzie St, Puget Dr, Laburnum St, Walnut St, Chestnut St

DRINKING (pp123-7)
Bean Around the World	(see 21)
Bimini's Tap House	**36** G3
Elwood's Joint	**37** E4
Fringe Café	**38** E4
Jericho Sailing Centre	(see 2)
Malone's Sports Bar	**39** G2
Urban Well	**40** G2

ENTERTAINMENT (pp128-38)
Alliance Atlantis Fifth Avenue Cinemas	**41** H3
Cellar Jazz Café	**42** D4
Hollywood Theatre	**43** E4
Ridge Theatre	**44** G5

SHOPPING (pp163-5)
Banyen Books & Sound	**45** D3
Broadway Shoe Salon	**46** E4
Candy Aisle	**47** G3
Comicshop	(see 47)
Does Your Mother Know?	**48** G3
Duthie Books	**49** G3
Hope Unlimited	**50** G3
Kidsbooks	**51** E4
Kitsilano Hemp Company	**52** E3
lululemon	**53** G3
Lush	**54** G3
Pacific Boarder	**55** H3
PD's Hot Shop	**56** E3
Safeway	**57** F4
Safeway	**58** G3
Sigge's Sports Villa	**59** G3
Sports Exchange	**60** H3
Ten Thousand Villages	**61** E4
Travel Bug	**62** E4
Wanderlust	**63** H3
Westbeach	**64** H3
Women in Print	**65** D3
Zulu Records	**66** H3

SLEEPING (pp177-8)
HI Vancouver Jericho Beach	**67** A2
Maple House B&B	**68** G2
Mickey's Kits Beach Chalet	**69** G2
Penny Farthing Inn	**70** E3

TRANSPORT (p62)
Ferry Stop	**71** H1

INFORMATION
Shoppers Drug Mart	**72** G3

0 — 600 m
0 — 0.4 miles

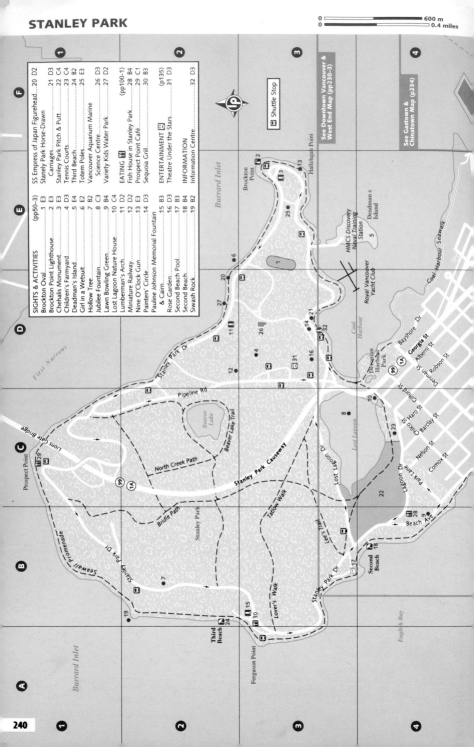

UNIVERSITY OF BRITISH COLUMBIA

0 _____ 800 m
0 _____ 0.5 miles

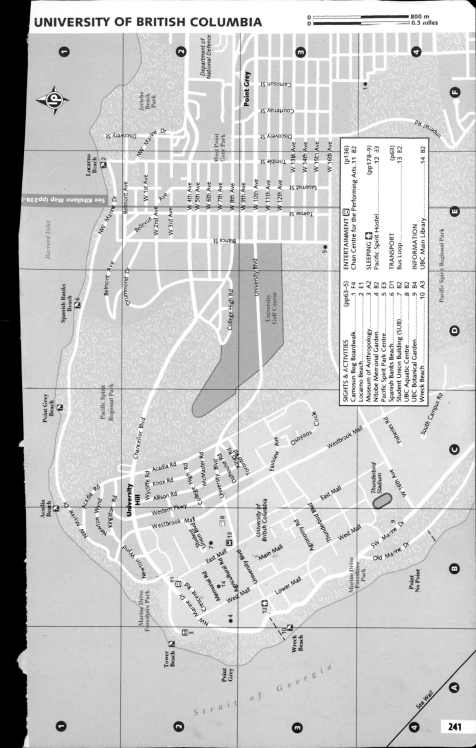

SIGHTS & ACTIVITIES   (pp63–5)
Camosun Bog Boardwalk........................1 F4
Locarno Beach..2 E1
Museum of Anthropology......................3 A2
Nitobe Memorial Garden........................4 B2
Pacific Spirit Park Centre.......................5 E3
Spanish Banks Beach..............................6 D1
Student Union Building (SUB)................7 B2
UBC Aquatic Centre................................8 B2
UBC Botanical Garden............................9 B4
Wreck Beach..10 A3

ENTERTAINMENT 🎭   (p136)
Chan Centre for the Performing Arts...11 B2

SLEEPING 🛏   (pp178–9)
Pacific Spirit Hostel.........................12 33

TRANSPORT   (p63)
Bus Loop..13 E2

INFORMATION
UBC Main Library.............................14 B2

241

VANCOUVER TRANSLINK MAP

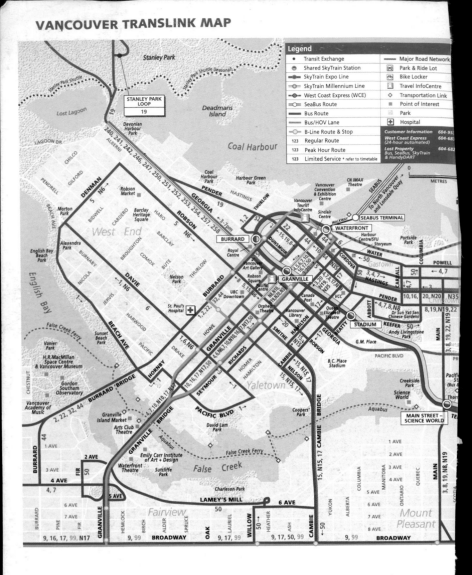